fiction | non-fiction

second edition

fiction | non-fiction

a reader and rhetoric

Garry Engkent   Lucia Engkent

THOMSON

NELSON

Australia   Canada   Mexico   Singapore   Spain   United Kingdom   United States

THOMSON
NELSON

Fiction/Non-Fiction: A Reader
and Rhetoric, Second Edition

by Garry Engkent and
Lucia Engkent

**Associate Vice-President,
Editorial Director:**
Evelyn Veitch

Executive Editors:
Anne Williams and
Rod Banister

Senior Developmental Editor:
Mike Thompson

Permissions Coordinator:
Patricia Buckley

Senior Production Editor:
Bob Kohlmeier

Copy-Editor:
Madeline Koch

Proofreader:
Sarah Robertson

Indexer:
Dennis A. Mills

Production Coordinator:
Ferial Suleman

Creative Director:
Angela Cluer

Interior Design:
Roxanna Bennett

Cover Design:
Gillian Tsintziras—The
Brookview Group Inc.

Cover Image:
Stephen Simpson/Solus/First
Light

Compositor:
Nelson Gonzalez

Printer:
Transcontinental

**Library and Archives Canada
Cataloguing in Publication**

Engkent, Garry, 1948–
Fiction/non-fiction : a reader
and rhetoric / Garry Engkent
and Lucia Engkent. — 2nd ed.

Includes index.
ISBN 0-17-641415-0

1. College readers. 2. English
language—Rhetoric.
I. Engkent, Lucia Pietrusiak,
1955– II. Title.

PE1417.E53 2005   808'.0427
C2004-905625-5

Preface

The second edition of *Fiction/Non-Fiction: A Reader and Rhetoric* is designed to meet the needs of students in college-level reading and writing courses.

The text is divided into three parts: the first is a selection of short stories, the second has essays and articles, and the third is a brief overview of essay writing, with discussions of structure and language use. The two reading sections are introduced with an explanation of reading skills. Each reading is accompanied by helpful notes, comprehension and discussion questions, a review of literary techniques, and suggestions for writing assignments.

Including both fiction and non-fiction has many advantages. It expands students' reading diet, opening up the world of imagination, ideas, and thought. It addresses the need of college students to explore themes in literature. It offers variety and flexibility to the instructor in theme, subject matter, and context for class discussions. For instance, the same topic can be explored in both fiction and non-fiction.

The selection of stories offers variety in length, theme, and complexity. Some stories are simple and amusing; others are thought-provoking and symbolic. Most of the selections are Canadian. Some are classic short stories that instructors will be familiar with, and some introduce relatively unknown writers. Instructors can choose stories to suit the needs, interests, and level of the class.

The essays also offer variety. Many are taken from magazines and newspapers; these include columns, op-ed (opinion-editorial) pieces, and personal essays. A few are excerpts from books. Different writing strategies, such as argumentation, process, definition, and compare/contrast, are presented. In addition, the readings explore current topics of interest, such as technology and society.

Keeping in mind that some students may have English as a second language, we have included notes to explain aspects of language and culture. For example, we explain the names of characters and what they signify. We also explain references and put articles and stories in context. However, we do not give vocabulary notes for words that are easily found in a dictionary.

Comprehension and discussion questions are grouped together in one section. They begin with content questions and move toward broader discussion questions and topics. In the content questions, we generally follow the sequence and logic of the article or the short story. The later questions open up the discussion to students' interpretations and opinions. Some of these questions can also be used as essay topics.

In the literary techniques section, we focus on the strategies used by the writers. These range from the use of symbolism to the organization of an essay.

The assignment questions are broad and open-ended so that instructors can further define what they expect students to do, tailoring the work to course requirements. For example, a question posed in the assignment section could be written up as a short paragraph or as an essay. We have focused on academic writing, since that is what most courses require. However, instructors can easily take the suggested topics and require students to write a letter or a dialogue. A suggestion to seek further information could be followed up by a written or oral report. Instructors can also determine the length and detail of the work to be submitted. In addition, we have made links to other stories and articles so that comparisons can be made. Because some instructors like to show videos and films of stories, we have mentioned whether a film version exists. We have included only minimal biographical information about the writers; however, students could be assigned the task of researching the authors.

The writing section is a short review and reminder; it is not a comprehensive treatment of essay writing and grammar. We assume that students have learned the basics of writing essays and of doing research. The book has a short review of some common writing problems but does not offer grammar exercises. The students are expected to work on their writing skills as they write essays.

Because the rhetoric section is meant to be dipped into as needed, there is some overlap and repetition of points. We do not expect students to proceed through the chapters in order. Instructors can direct students to whatever sections they need.

For the second edition, we have changed many of the readings, mostly in the non-fiction section. The essays on technology have all been replaced with more up-to-date articles. In the third part, we have included more model essays and expanded the documentation chapter.

INSTRUCTOR'S MANUAL

An instructor's manual is available for use with this book. It has additional notes on the readings, teaching suggestions, summaries of readings, grammar and vocabulary exercises, sample answers for reading comprehension questions, and additional model paragraphs and essays. In addition, ESL help is provided in reading notes and grammar exercises on such problem areas as countable and uncountable nouns. Some of the pages are set up so that they can be photocopied or made into transparencies easily.

ACKNOWLEDGMENTS

We would like to thank the staff and students at Seneca College, especially Rhett Andrew, Maggie Bricker, and Joyce Hall.

The following people reviewed the manuscript and gave helpful comments and suggestions: Lesley Checkland, John Abbott College; Gail Clenman, Seneca College; Arlene Davies-Fuhr, Grant MacEwan College; Stefanie Ketley, Fanshawe College; Nancie Line, Durham College; Peter C. Miller, Seneca College; Shawn Pentecost, Algonquin College; and Melanie A. Rubens, Seneca College.

Thanks also to the hard-working and talented staff at Thomson Nelson, especially Anne Williams and Mike Thompson, who got this project going.

And finally, a thank-you to our children, David, Susan, and Emily, who read stories and gave their opinions.

A NOTE FROM THE PUBLISHER

Thank you for selecting *Fiction/Non-Fiction: A Reader and Rhetoric* by Garry Engkent and Lucia Engkent. The authors and publisher have devoted considerable time and care to the development of this book. We appreciate your recognition of this effort and accomplishment.

Contents

Thematic Contents

MEDIA

RELIGION

SPORTS

TECHNOLOGY

part one | reading fiction

READING FICTION

INTRODUCTION

"Fiction" means a made-up story. Synonyms for fiction include "not true," "not real," and "not existing." The characters and the action exist only in the writer's imagination. The story may be based on real events, but it is, on the whole, a fabrication. Fiction includes novels and short stories. "Literature" is a word we use to describe the best of fiction, works that display the beauty of language, that show artistry, and that engage readers' feelings. One of the main activities of English courses is reading and analyzing literature.

Some people question the value of reading fiction. Why read made-up stories? It's better to read about things that are "real." However, fiction can take us to places that we will never see and even to places that do not exist. We can visit other times and meet people who will never physically cross our paths. While the laws of physics bind reality, no such rules govern the imagination.

Reading fiction is an important intellectual activity. On one level, it is exercise for the brain. It requires readers to understand what is going on, to follow a story line, to understand what is done and why it is done, to imagine people and places, and to sympathize with characters. It draws on experience and knowledge. It makes us think.

Furthermore, reading fiction is good therapy. It can help us understand how other people feel and why they act the way they do. It can show us that we are not alone in our fears and our problems. Conversely, it brings us joy, wonder, and compassion. Made-up lives can affect us profoundly, making us cry, laugh, or sigh. Reading fiction makes us feel for the characters. Some of these fictitious beings stay in our memory for years, long after the story line has been forgotten. We know them as we would a neighbour, a friend, or a family member.

The value of literature is far-reaching. A society without its stories lacks spirit, soul, and hope, because stories tell of a people: who they are, what they believe in, how they solve problems, how they live, what their dreams are. Literature, then, is sharing individual and collective realities, sorrows and aspirations, fears and philosophies. It binds heart and mind, emotion and intellect. Literature broadens readers' horizons.

Sometimes the dividing line between fiction and non-fiction is not so distinct. Some non-fiction articles step into the domain of imagination; and some fictional stories enter the realm of reality. For instance, a journalist may create a composite character to cover identities in a piece on prostitution. Docudramas on television re-create events based on what could have happened. Novels can be based on real events and can speculate on the lives of real people. However, the line between fiction and non-fiction is still valid. Just as libraries categorize their books into fiction and non-fiction, we have used this distinction in this text. More on the difference between fiction and non-fiction can be found in the introduction to non-fiction.

SHORT STORIES

A short story is a piece of literature that ranges from 100 to 10,000 words. It has all the elements of the novel, such as plot, character, and conflict. It tells a story. For the writer, it is a difficult art form to master. For the reader, it is a quick read, a dip into another world. However, such a general definition may do short fiction an injustice.

All short stories are imaginary. When we read a story, we enter the world created by the writer. For example, in Charles de Lint's "Mr. Truepenny's Book Emporium and Gallery" Sophie Etoile makes up a whole world in her daydreams; so does a story writer. The setting may have some familiar basis in reality, such as the city of Winnipeg, or the same culture as the real world. However, the events and characters never existed. They have no foundation in reality. Yet we as readers are often caught up in the fictional world, and in the characters' plights and lives.

All stories tell a truth or two. They reveal something about the human condition, the human soul, the human being. As individuals, we want to know more about other people and ourselves. We want to know what makes someone tick. In Alice Munro's "An Ounce of Cure," we see how infatuation can lead a teenaged girl to commit irrational deeds. Seeing what happens to fictional people, we understand what makes us do, say, or feel certain things. We need to know we share in the well of human experience: the emotions, the passions, the thoughts, and the actions. A good story often gives us a glimpse of reality, truth, a fact of life.

All stories aim to entertain. As social beings, we need to be amused. A good story can let us live a life vicariously through the characters. For instance, we can identify with the family that tries to give the mother the best Mother's Day in Stephen Leacock's "How We Kept Mother's Day." A good story lets us escape from the drudgery of everyday routine, for when we start reading a story we willingly suspend our disbelief that the world we enter is only a fabrication of the writer's creative mind. At times, we yearn to escape our own real problems and lose ourselves in the story. And what a world we enter: a time traveller can change history; a princess decides whether to give up her beloved to another woman or have him devoured by a tiger; a young girl defends herself admirably from oafish, bullying adults on a plane ride and acquits herself well. Sometimes we are so engaged in that world we feel reluctant to leave it.

A story can also teach us about other cultures, other races, other ways of living, other ways of thinking and believing, other times. We learn about the commonality of being human or about the differences that divide us. For example, in "The Man I Killed," Tim O'Brien not only gives life to the dead but also shows how people — cultures and distances apart — share the same goals. Often fiction can do all this better than a text on sociology, politics, history, or anthropology. We may not know as many facts and statistics from fiction, but we comprehend facets of the human soul. And for those of us who prefer a pragmatic purpose to reading fiction, we can use both understanding and knowledge in our dealings with relatives, friends, neighbours, co-workers, and strangers.

Such is the role of fiction. Short stories entertain us, educate us, and expand our horizons and our imagination. They are, indeed, worth reading.

ELEMENTS OF FICTION

Once you have read, and hopefully enjoyed, the story, it's time to talk about it. To do this you need to know some literary terminology, the tools of the trade. If you want to discuss computers, you have to learn words such as bytes, interface, RAM, ROM, and motherboard. If you are going into nursing, you need to know terms such as IV, CPR, and Code Blue. Similarly, in the study of literature, you should know the common terms used in texts and by instructors.

The elements we have defined below are not meant to be a complete listing, just commonly used terms of reference. Moreover, we lean toward giving basic meanings rather than engaging in literary theories and criticisms.

PLOT

It has been said that there are only three categories of plot: the struggle against nature, against other persons, and against oneself. And then there are stories without a plot. Dramatic situations are classified as part of plot: boy meets girl, a character makes an unpleasant choice, or a protagonist braves a storm.

Plot is conflict. Without conflict, there is no suspense. Without suspense, the reader loses interest. For example, the protagonist may struggle within herself and with her parents about her need to be an individual and to conform to parental wishes. In addition to conflict, a story has a crisis or a turning point in which the character makes a choice. The working out of the decision comes to a climax. From there, the story comes to a resolution, a logical or satisfactory ending.

Plot is cause and effect. Cause is anything that makes a character act or think in a certain way. In short, cause is the reason certain things happen. Effect is the result of an action. Often an effect can turn into a cause, similar to domino tiles tumbling one after another. In a story, a character's actions may result in something entirely different from what was anticipated by the character himself or by the reader.

Plot is the organized series of events. It must have a logical sequence that makes sense when we finish the story. Plot creates suspense when the anticipated outcome does not happen or is delayed. In such cases, the writer may set up new complications that the character must overcome before the resolution. Or, in other cases, the writer uses a plot twist, offering up an ending that the reader does not expect but is logically prepared for.

Traditionally, plot has a beginning, a middle, and an end — but not necessarily in that order. All stories begin in the middle of things. The opening scene of a story is usually closest to the main conflict or action, but it is not really the beginning. To have a "real beginning" the writer should start with the birth of the character or even the birth of the parents or grandparents. Since such details are not always relevant to the plot, the writer chooses an incident that engages the reader's curiosity. When and if necessary, the writer will use a flashback — that is, a scene or event in the past — to explain the current situation. In addition, the writer may hint at a possible outcome of the situation by foreshadowing. Finally, a story may have a distorted chronology. The ending may not be the real ending at all.

CHARACTER

A character is a recognizable person of either gender. There can be several characters in a short story. A protagonist is the main character in the plot. He or she moves the story to its conclusion; the protagonist has conflicts and struggles to resolve them. The protagonist is the hero or heroine, who usually has admirable traits and is the good person. An antagonist goes against the desires of the protagonist. In common parlance, the antagonist is the villain who attempts to thwart the hero. Sometimes the villain is not a wicked person but merely one who opposes the protagonist.

Characters make the story, for, without them, the plot does not move and becomes merely a series of events. Characters can be real human beings, animals, or abstractions. But they all must have recognizable human traits. For example, Winnie-the-Pooh looks like a stuffed teddy bear, but he acts like a small child. Human traits can be abstract qualities such as desiring love, feeling compassion, longing for recognition, struggling toward a goal, doing the wrong thing, and being sad or happy.

Many characters reveal their traits almost in the same way we judge real people — actions speak louder than words. A person who steals is seen as untrustworthy or wicked. Or, conversely, a judge dispensing justice in the courtroom suggests a person of honour and wisdom. What the characters say and how they say it reveal personality. What is said about them by other characters is equally significant.

Characters can be flat, two-dimensional, or stereotyped. In a short story, flat characters are usually supporting ones. They are not fully fleshed out. They play a specific role. For example, the sidekick helps the hero and has no other purpose in the plot. Similarly, the antagonist is often two-dimensional in that the role of the villain calls for stopping the hero from completing the task.

Often writers take shortcuts by using archetypal characters. An "archetype" is a recognizable, generic figure found in literature. Writers tap into a ready-made emotional response created by the familiar character. For example, the biblical Delilah is seen as the temptress who seduces men. In modern stories, she becomes the woman in red, the siren who leads men to their doom.

At other times, writers use stereotypes. With minimal differences, these characters are duplicates, readily identifiable, interchangeable from one story to another. They are static quick fixes. They could be identified by physical characteristics: a small, scrawny child, for example. Names are also used as shortcuts. For example, a character named "Moose" suggests not only size but also mentality. "Kiowa" or "Mrs. Hong" identifies nationality and suggests racial or cultural traits in the character. Sometimes revealing the occupation of the character is enough—she could be a lawyer or he a bus driver. These characters do not develop.

The main characters, however, are developed; that is, they are changed by the end of the story. Rarely does the protagonist remain as ignorant or unmoved as he was at the moment we first met up with him. The transformation is usually gradual: the protagonist must earn this change in character. Often the change comes in learning a lesson, in doing the right thing, and in understanding.

Characters are us. As ungrammatical as this statement is, it holds true: we want to identify with the protagonist or with the characters in the story. Characters provide us, the readers, with vicarious experiences. They become our surrogate selves. They do things we would like to do but dare not. They are the people we want to be or not to be. They stir our emotions and challenge our intellect. And they make us want to believe that they are not fictional but real.

Such is the power of characters in the story. We can like them, hate them, or fear them, just as real people. They remain with us long after we have finished reading the story.

SETTING

Setting is topography or place. A mere word like Toronto or Vancouver opens up the reader's imagination to a specific locale. Additional information, such as the corner of Yonge and Dundas Streets, or Pender Street, gives a clearer picture. For imaginary places, the writer may create worlds beyond our experience — a frozen planet, for example — or build on places we are already comfortable with. For example, in Charles de Lint's "Mr. Truepenny's Book Emporium and Gallery," the shop and the neighbourhood are ones we can easily imagine because we have seen such city locations.

Setting includes time. Knowing when the story takes place is important. For example, a story set in 1929 brings to mind the stock market crash and the coming of the Great Depression. The month of May suggests spring and rebirth or renewal after the dead of winter. The hour of 3 a.m. or twelve noon conjures up certain associations. Therefore, temporal information can do much to create mood, define context, and fix purpose.

Setting gives readers a grounding. While it is true that a picture is worth a thousand words, often in a short story the writer is limited in what can be detailed. He or she describes enough for us to fill in other pieces of information. In "The Lottery," Shirley Jackson gives this descriptive setting:

> The morning of June 27th was clear and sunny, with the fresh warmth of a full-summer day; the flowers were blossoming profusely and the grass was richly green. The people of the village began to gather in the square, between the post office and the bank, around ten o'clock. (p. 107)

We can visualize the day, the town, and the people with these words, but we also fill in our own details. Moreover, the writer's selection of details conveys more than location or time. It helps us understand character and environment.

Setting helps to achieve focus for the plot. Satisfying the questions "where" and "when" does much to allay confusion and irritation in the reader.

THEME

Theme is the main subject matter. Around this central idea, the writer arranges the sequence of events (plot) for the characters to play out. Theme does not always moralize; rather, it dramatizes. It follows the axiom "show rather than tell." For example, in the folktale "The Cowherd," the theme is "Don't abuse your mother." However, merely stating this subject lacks punch. Having read the entire tale, we come to understand the message.

Theme is like a thesis statement. It can be the controlling device to keep the story on track. However, unlike a thesis, which is directly stated, the theme is a concept to be discovered by the reader. At times, the subject matter does not have a moral lesson at all. Theme can be as simple as what the story is about.

POINT OF VIEW

Point of view is the approach the writer takes in telling the story. Sometimes this term is synonymous with narration. As with all aspects of writing, the manner in which the story is told is important. Not all stories can be narrated from the first-person point of view; not all stories are suited to the third-person point of view. Some authors rewrite their stories using different points of view until they decide on the one that tells the tale the best.

There are three "persons" in grammatical terms: first-person singular "I" and plural "we"; second-person "you"; and third-person singular "he" or "she" and plural "they." In storytelling, the writer has the choice of all these "persons" to tell the story. The second person ("you") and the plural forms are unconventional but have been used effectively. Generally speaking, the two most popular persons used in storytelling are the first-person singular and the third-person singular.

First Person

When discussing the use of the first-person point of view, we must make a distinction between narrator and author. A woman can choose to write in a male voice, for example, as Barbara Scott does in "Lifeguard." Some readers may see the "I" not as a character but rather as the author. This mistake often comes about when the "I" has no identifying name in the story. Do not assume that the "I" character is the author.

There are three basic variants in the use of the first-person singular as the narrator of the story. First, the speaker is the main character. Second, the speaker is a secondary character who talks about the protagonist. And third, the narrator is the writer who slips into the story with creative asides.

The most common of the three variants is the narrator as the protagonist. We readers tend to identify with the narrator as the plot unfolds. Like the narrator, we know only what the narrator knows and what he or she tells us. Because of this restriction, the scope of the story may be limited to what the narrator hears, sees, does, and reports. On the other hand, the writer may solve this limiting problem by having two or more "I" narrators; this device is more often found in novels than in short stories.

Second, the narrator may be a secondary character who accompanies the protagonist (who is spoken of in the third person). For example, in Sir Arthur Conan Doyle's famous Sherlock Holmes series, the narrator is Dr. John Watson, rather than the main character Sherlock Holmes. The secondary character reports the words and actions of the hero but cannot read his mind. Moreover, the speaker can make comments on the protagonist's actions or speculate on future doings.

The third variant is the writer as narrator. In humorous pieces, such as Stephen Leacock's Mariposa stories, the writer's intrusion is obvious. Leacock makes fun of his characters with his asides and comments.

Similarly, in David Arnason's "A Girl's Story," the writer necessarily has to appear because he tells us how a story is written. This method tends to break the illusion of fiction and mixes fact with fiction.

On rare occasions, some writers use the first-person plural. The collective "we" does not distinguish individuals but sees from the point of view of the group. For example, Leacock's "How We Kept Mother's Day" has the "we," including father and children. By doing so, Leacock makes a distinction between them and the mother.

Second Person

The second-person point of view is infrequent in fiction. It forces the reader to become the narrator. Properly done, the technique draws the reader into the story with a certain detachment that is not found in the "I" narration. In addition, the "you" is still a distinct character. Because of the forced identification with the reader, the "you" generally has no name.

Third Person

The most common point of view in fiction is the third-person singular. It, too, has three branches: totally omniscient, partially omniscient, and objective.

In total omniscience, the writer tells not only the actions and words of all the characters but also their thoughts. However, total omniscience is often selective. That is, the writer chooses when to reveal the innermost thoughts of his or her characters.

In partial omniscience, only one character reveals his or her thoughts. By this device, the writer can sustain suspense and arouse curiosity. The character does not necessarily have to be the protagonist, but usually is.

In third-person objective, the writer tells the story only from the actions and words of the characters. The writer does not reveal the thoughts of any character. The reader then must anticipate future action from the information given and nothing more.

Point of view as part of narrative technique is important. It creates not only reader identification with the protagonist but also suspense and curiosity.

STYLE

The way the writer chooses words and puts them down on paper is called style. Ernest Hemingway and James Joyce have distinctive, recognizable styles. Hemingway's sentences depend on nouns and strong verbs to move the action, rather than adjectives and adverbs; his description is minimal. Joyce's sentences are generally long and detailed with plenty of description. These are identifiable elements in their writing.

However, style is not only individual. Certain genres of stories are said to have a kind of style. For example, in the parable of "The Prodigal Son," the oral tradition is imitated with the repetition of words to begin each new thought. In addition, the time period when the story was written influences style. For instance, in "The Lady or the Tiger?," written in the late 19th century, Frank Stockton reveals a flowery, old-fashioned style of expressing ideas:

> In the very olden time, there lived a semi-barbaric king, whose ideas, though somewhat polished and sharpened by the progressiveness of distant Latin neighbors, were still large, florid, and untrammeled, as became the half of him which was barbaric. He was a man of exuberant fancy, and, withal, of an authority so irresistible that, at his will, he turned his varied fancies into facts. (p. 202)

Style is difficult to define but easily recognizable if the reader has read a lot of a particular writer's works or a certain genre of story.

TONE

How the writer says something is as important as what he or she says. Tone can be serious and sombre, or humorous and light. It provides a clue as to how the writer deals with the subject matter. For example, in "The Cask of Amontillado," Edgar Allan Poe begins his tale with a serious, sinister tone: "The thousand injuries of Fortunato I had borne as I best could, but when he ventured upon insult I vowed revenge" (p. 181). Tone often helps define the story.

MOOD

Closely related to tone is mood. At times, these two concepts in literature are indistinguishable, and the differences are subtle and minute. In general, mood is emotion whereas tone is intellect. For example, in "Greasy Lake" (p. 33), the tone is ironic when the boys escape their attacker's wrath after their practical joke goes awry. However, the mood is sombre when the narrator compares the destruction of his car with the corpse in the lake: "My car was wrecked; he was dead" (paragraph 31).

LITERARY TECHNIQUES

Here are some of the common techniques used by writers. This list is a quick reference to commonly used literary terminology. Although some of these terms fit drama and poetry, we have selected ones particularly relevant to short stories. Some of these techniques are discussed further in the notes that follow the individual stories.

Allusion A reference to a person, event, or thing. Often writers draw relationships by making reference to something else. The reader must catch such oblique references.

Climax The maximum disturbance, or the greatest tension in the story. It is often confused with crisis. Usually, the climax occurs before the conclusion or resolution.

Crisis The turning point in the story. The protagonist must make a decision that will affect the outcome. Usually, the crisis comes at the midpoint of the story.

Denouement/Conclusion/Resolution The outcome of the story.

Dramatic licence Liberties taken with accepted facts and reality to heighten the story. For example, the writer may have altered the historical sequence of events, or placed a real person in an imaginary setting.

Exposition Essential information the reader needs to know to understand the story. Usually, it is found at the beginning of the story, along with the setting.

Flashback Recalls an earlier scene to explain a dramatic point or to show cause. A flashback not only gives dramatic pause to the action but also fills in information needed to understand the action or incident. Flashbacks can be lengthy or brief.

Foreshadowing Clues given early in the story. The method creates antic-ipation and some suspense. Also, the writer prepares the reader for the outcome.

Imagery Involves all five senses — hearing, feeling, tasting, seeing, smell-ing. Most often, imagery consists of pictures that the reader can visualize from the words.

In medias res In the middle of things. In this technique, the story starts at the most crucial incident or scene, then uses flashbacks to fill in back-ground information.

Irony (a) Verbal irony: what is said and done are diametrically opposed, or what is said and meant are in direct opposition; (b) Dramatic irony: the reader and a character know more than the other characters in the story and can distinguish the double meaning in the dialogue.

Juxtapositioning Putting two scenes side by side for effect. Often this shortcut brings dramatic moments together; at other times, it contrasts one scene with the next.

Metaphor A figure of speech used to make comparisons between unlike objects. For example, in the metaphor "He is a tiger in the boardroom," the person is not literally a tiger; rather, he has certain qualities of a tiger. A metaphor does not use "as" or "like."

Simile A figure of speech used to draw similarities. A simile uses "like" or "as." For example, "Like a mother hen, the residence counsellor protects her charges."

Surprise ending A conclusion that the reader is not prepared for. The sur-prise ending is quite popular in short stories, where the punch line comes in the last paragraph or sentence.

Symbol Something concrete representing something abstract. For example, the concept of love may be represented by a gold ring; the belief in Christianity, by a cross. A symbol has a distinct meaning beyond the thing itself. For example, a rock can be just a rock. However, the writer may choose to add extra meaning to that rock; then it becomes a symbol. In literature, there are many symbols. Some have been standardized and

are recognizable by their constant use. Other symbols are story-specific —
that is, developed for a particular story.

ANALYZING LITERATURE

When you analyze a short story, you take it apart and examine the various
elements separately. Why do you do this?

Analyzing literature reinforces skills you already possess. The first
skill is thinking. You engage not only your personal experience, but also
what you have learned in school. You draw connections that may not
always be obvious.

The second skill is vicarious learning. By reading, you can understand
actions and emotions you may never have experienced. From fiction to real
life, you begin to comprehend why people act in certain ways. Conversely,
from your sharpened awareness, you observe how reality validates stories.

The third skill is appreciation of artistry. By taking the story apart, you
come to understand how each separate item, such as plot, must be logical
and compatible with the setting or the character. Or you may marvel at how
the writer has manipulated your feelings with mere words. Part of artistry
is making complex things seem simple.

Throughout all this analysis of a story, or a number of stories, you want
to know the answers to the following questions.

"Do writers deliberately put all those details in the story?" Yes, they
do. A writer makes decisions about everything that goes into a story.
Whether the character is right-handed or left-handed, or has blue eyes, will
be integral to the plot. If something is not important or relevant, the writer
does not waste time putting it in the story. David Arnason illustrates this
process in "A Girl's Story" (p. 20).

"How do you see all these things in the story that I can't?" Part of the
answer is that as you read more and more literature, you develop experience. Because many writers use traditional materials and time-honoured
concepts and themes, you eventually discover and recognize common elements in fiction. For example, a character with a cleft foot or a limp in the
left leg has been associated with the devil. Or a character with the name of
Mr. Graves suggests death, cemeteries, and ominous qualities.

In addition, the cultivation of knowledge of other disciplines will help
you to better understand literature. History gives you a grounding in different periods in setting and events. For example, a writer who mentions the

War Measures Act has set the time as 1970 and alluded to the FLQ (Front de Libération du Québec) crisis, a historic event. Psychology helps us understand human behaviour. For example, in Tim O'Brien's "The Man I Killed" (p. 174), the narrator projects his feelings and desires onto the dead man. The term is called projection. Writers draw from religious texts, especially the Bible. When a character comments, "Let's kill the fatted calf," the allusion is to the parable of "The Prodigal Son" (p. 147). Thus, a knowledge of other subjects contributes to the understanding of the short story.

"Doesn't analyzing the story kill the enjoyment in reading?" If reading is merely for entertainment, the answer would be yes. But taking a story apart and examining its separate parts gives greater appreciation of the story. There is joy in such discoveries.

In addition, analysis gives you more practice in examining objectively the society or world you live in. If you can pick a story apart, you can use the same skill to solve or attack problems. Practice makes things easier as you go on. In short, analyzing a story has practical as well as academic applications.

Several popular methods of analyzing fiction exist, including checklist, context, and interpretation.

THE CHECKLIST

Using Poe's "The Cask of Amontillado" (p. 181), we can draw up a series of questions and answers to examine each of the elements of fiction described above and see how they work in context with the theme:

What is the title of the story?	"The Cask of Amontillado"
Why is it so titled?	Bait to lure Fortunato, the victim; Amontillado is an expensive wine
Who wrote it?	Edgar Allan Poe, a 19th-century American writer
What kind of story is this (genre)?	Horror
What is the point of the story (theme)?	Getting away with murder
Who are the main characters?	Montresor and Fortunato
Who is the "hero" (protagonist)?	None
Describe him or her briefly.	—

Who is the "villain" (antagonist)?	Montresor, the narrator
Describe him or her briefly.	Vengeful, careful, intelligent, knows human nature
Who are the secondary characters, if any?	Fortunato, the victim
Name them and give a sketch.	A gullible drunkard
How is the story told?	First-person narration by Montresor
What happens in the story (plot summary)?	Montresor avenges Fortunato's insult by walling him alive in the catacombs
What is the conflict?	The conflict between Montresor's guile and Fortunato's pride
How does the story end?	With a surprise; Montresor gets away with murder for fifty years; he confesses to a priest
What is (are) the setting(s)?	Italy, during carnival time with people in masquerade; could be 19th century or Renaissance
How do the other elements support the plot, characterization, and theme?	The descent into the catacombs and the trowel support Montresor's sinister plan; Fortunato's clown-like clothes and drunken state reinforce his gullibility
How does the author create mood and atmosphere?	Description of the dampness, evening, isolation
Is there irony?	Fortunato doesn't realize his situation until the end, and there is no cask of Amontillado
Is there humour?	Macabre humour (e.g., a wine is called "de Grave")

Are there any obvious symbols?	Montresor's trowel, the catacombs (graves), going downward as to hell or the grave
Is this story effectively written?	Yes
How?	We are at once shocked by the nature of the crime and fascinated by Montresor's ingenuity in planning Fortunato's demise and in escaping detection.
Why?	He gets away with murder and wants to do so in heaven. That's why he confesses to a priest.
Is there something more to the story?	The nature of evil is deceptive; beware of treachery

Of course, we can keep on asking more detailed questions. This method certainly covers all aspects of the story, but it can be tedious to go through such detail.

CONTEXT

In this type of analysis, the story is seen in relation to social, historical, auto-biographical factors. This method requires not only a good understanding of the story but also information not included in the telling. You may need to research a number of peripheral areas, including the following:

Author's other works Writers tend to return to favourite themes, concepts, or symbols. For example, James Joyce wrote mainly about Dublin, Ireland, and his basic theme is spiritual dryness.

Biography Knowing something about the author's life may help you understand and appreciate the story. What were the writer's inspirations and influences? Whose work did he or she read?

History An author living in one century can certainly write convincingly about other epochs, but that writer is still influenced by his or her own period.

Setting Where did the author write? A Canadian author would certainly see patriotism quite differently than an American writer.

Social context What were some of the main preoccupations of the people in that place and at that time? For example, in the mid-1930s in Canada, what did people think about immigration or homosexuality?

Time When did the author write? That is, was the author writing in the 20th century? 18th century? Each period has certain recognizable, collective patterns in theme and technique.

INTERPRETATION

You can try to understand the story or the characters according to what teachers, scholars, and literary critics say on this subject, or you can delve into your own experience.

First, let others explain what they see in the story. Their insights may help you appreciate the subtext or the significance of symbols.

Second, draw from your own experience and test the validity of feelings and actions of the characters. You may want to discuss the story's ending with other students in the class or with the instructor.

MIXED TECHNIQUES

Most of the time you will analyze the story using a bit of all the techniques discussed here. First, read the story entirely and ask yourself, "Do I like this story or not?" If your answer is "yes," a second and more important question is "Why?" What you have done is to engage both emotion and intellect. You move from feeling to thinking; you shift from subjectivity to objectivity in your analysis of the piece.

If your answer is "no," then you must find reasons for not liking the story. Is it due to the writing? The characters? The theme?

There are other ways to analyze a literary piece. Your instructor may want to share one or two techniques with you. Or he or she may dictate a certain methodology to follow. If you are left to your own devices, we suggest you try one of the procedures described above.

A Girl's Story

David Arnason

1   You've wondered what it would be like to be a character in a story, to sort of slip out of your ordinary self and into some other character. Well, I'm offering you the opportunity. I've been trying to think of a heroine for this story, and frankly, it hasn't been going too well. A writer's life isn't easy, especially if, like me, he's got a tendency sometimes to drink a little bit too much. Yesterday, I went for a beer with Dennis and Ken (they're real-life friends of mine) and we stayed a little longer than we should have. Then I came home and quickly mixed a drink and started drinking it so my wife would think the liquor on my breath came from the drink I was drinking and not from the drinks I had had earlier. I wasn't going to tell her about those drinks. Anyway, Wayne dropped over in the evening and I had some more drinks, and this morning my head isn't working very well.

2   To be absolutely frank about it, I always have trouble getting characters, even when I'm stone cold sober. I can think of plots; plots are really easy. If you can't think of one, you just pick up a book, and sure enough, there's a plot. You just move a few things around and nobody knows you stole the idea. Characters are the problem. It doesn't matter how good the plot is if your characters are dull. You can steal characters too, and put them into different plots. I've done that. I stole Eustacia Vye from Hardy and gave her another name. The problem was that she turned out a lot sulkier than I remembered and the plot I put her in was a light comedy. Now nobody wants to publish the story. I'm still sending it out, though. If you send a story to enough publishers, no matter how bad it is, somebody will ultimately publish it.

3   For this story I need a beautiful girl. You probably don't think you're beautiful enough, but I can fix that. I can do all kinds of retouching once I've got the basic material, and if I miss anything, Karl (he's my editor) will find it. So I'm going to make you fairly tall, about five-foot-eight and a quarter in your stocking feet. I'm going to give you long blonde hair because long blonde hair is sexy and virtuous. Black hair can be sexy too, but it doesn't go with virtue. I've got to deal with a whole literary tradition where black-haired women are basically evil. If I were feeling better I might be able to do it in an ironic way, then black hair would be OK, but I don't think I'm up to it this morning. If you're going to use irony, then you've got to be really careful about tone. I could make you a redhead, but redheads have a way of turning out pixie-ish, and that would wreck my plot.

So you've got long blonde hair and you're this tall slender girl with   4
amazingly blue eyes. Your face is narrow and your nose is straight and thin.
I could have turned up the nose a little, but that would have made you cute,
and I really need a beautiful girl. I'm going to put a tiny black mole on your
cheek. It's traditional. If you want your character to be really beautiful
there has to be some minor defect.

Now, I'm going to sit you on the bank of a river. I'm not much for set-   5
ting. I've read so many things where you get great long descriptions of the
setting, and mostly it's just boring. When my last book came out, one of
the reviewers suggested that the reason I don't do settings is that I'm not
very good at them. That's just silly. I'm writing a different kind of story,
not that old realist stuff. If you think I can't do setting, just watch.

There's a curl in the river just below the old dam where the water   6
seems to make a broad sweep. That flatness is deceptive, though. Under the
innocent sheen of the mirroring surface, the current is treacherous. The
water swirls, stabs, takes sharp angles and dangerous vectors. The trees
that lean from the bank shimmer with the multi-hued greenness of elm,
oak, maple and aspen. The leaves turn in the gentle breeze, showing their
paler green undersides. The undergrowth, too, is thick and green, hiding
the poison ivy, the poison sumac and the thorns. On a patch of grass that
slopes gently to the water, the only clear part of the bank on that side of the
river, a girl sits, a girl with long blonde hair. She has slipped a ring from
her finger and seems to be holding it toward the light.

You see? I could do a lot more of that, but you wouldn't like it. I   7
slipped a lot of details in there and provided all those hints about strange
and dangerous things under the surface. That's called foreshadowing. I put
in the ring at the end there so that you'd wonder what was going to
happen. That's to create suspense. You're supposed to ask yourself what
the ring means. Obviously it has something to do with love, rings always
do, and since she's taken it off, obviously something has gone wrong in
the love relationship. Now I just have to hold off answering that question
for as long as I can, and I've got my story. I've got a friend who's also a
writer who says never tell the buggers anything until they absolutely have
to know.

I'm going to have trouble with the feminists about this story. I can see   8
that already. I've got that river that's calm on the surface and boiling underneath, and I've got those trees that are gentle and beautiful with poisonous
and dangerous undergrowth. Obviously, the girl is going to be like that,
calm on the surface but passionate underneath. The feminists are going to
say that I'm perpetuating stereotypes, that by giving the impression the girl

is full of hidden passion I'm encouraging rapists. That's crazy. I'm just using a literary convention. Most of the world's great books are about the conflict between reason and passion. If you take that away, what's left to write about?

9   So I've got you sitting on the riverbank, twirling your ring. I forgot the birds. The trees are full of singing birds. There are meadowlarks and vireos and even Blackburnian warblers. I know a lot about birds but I'm not going to put in too many. You've got to be careful not to overdo things. In a minute I'm going to enter your mind and reveal what you're thinking. I'm going to do this in the third person. Using the first person is sometimes more effective, but I'm always afraid to do a female character in the first person. It seems wrong to me, like putting on a woman's dress.

10   Your name is Linda. I had to be careful not to give you a biblical name like Judith or Rachel. I don't want any symbolism in this story. Symbolism makes me sick, especially biblical symbolism. You always end up with some crazy moral argument that you don't believe and none of the readers believe. Then you lose control of your characters, because they've got to be like the biblical characters. You've got this terrific episode you'd like to use, but you can't because Rachel or Judith or whoever wouldn't do it. I think of stories with a lot of symbolism in them as sticky.

11   Here goes.

12   Linda held the ring up toward the light. The diamond flashed rainbow colours. It was a small diamond, and Linda reflected that it was probably a perfect symbol of her relationship with Gregg. Everything Gregg did was on a small scale. He was careful with his money and just as careful with his emotions. In one week they would have a small wedding and then move into a small apartment. She supposed that she ought to be happy. Gregg was very handsome, and she did love him. Why did it seem that she was walking into a trap?

13   That sounds kind of distant, but it's supposed to be distant. I'm using indirect quotation because the reader has just met Linda, and we don't want to get too intimate right away. Besides, I've got to get a lot of explaining done quickly, and if you can do it with the character's thoughts, then that's best.

14   Linda twirled the ring again, then with a suddenness that surprised her, she stood up and threw it into the river. She was immediately struck by a feeling of panic. For a moment she almost decided to dive into the river to try to recover it. Then, suddenly, she felt free. It was now impossible to marry Gregg. He would not forgive her for throwing the ring away. Gregg would say he'd had enough of her theatrics for one lifetime. He always

accused her of being a romantic. She'd never had the courage to admit that he was correct, and that she intended to continue being a romantic. She was sitting alone by the river in a long blue dress because it was a romantic pose. Anyway, she thought a little wryly, you're only likely to find romance if you look for it in romantic places and dress for the occasion.

Suddenly, she heard a rustling in the bush, the sound of someone   15 coming down the narrow path from the road above.

I had to do that, you see. I'd used up all the potential in the relation-   16 ship with Gregg, and the plot would have started to flag if I hadn't intro-duced a new character. The man who is coming down the path is tall and athletic with wavy brown hair. He has dark brown eyes that crinkle when he smiles, and he looks kind. His skin is tanned, as if he spends a lot of time outdoors, and he moves gracefully. He is smoking a pipe. I don't want to give too many details. I'm not absolutely sure what features women find attractive in men these days, but what I've described seems safe enough. I got all of it from stories written by women, and I assume they must know. I could give him a chiselled jaw, but that's about as far as I'll go.

The man stepped into the clearing. He carried an old-fashioned wicker   17 fishing creel and a telescoped fishing rod. Linda remained sitting on the grass, her blue dress spread out around her. The man noticed her and apologized.

"I'm sorry, I always come here to fish on Saturday afternoons and I've   18 never encountered anyone here before." His voice was low with something of an amused tone in it.

"Don't worry," Linda replied. "I'll only be here for a little while. Go   19 ahead and fish. I won't make any noise." In some way she couldn't under-stand, the man looked familiar to her. She felt she knew him. She thought she might have seen him on television or in a movie, but of course she knew that movie and television stars do not spend every Saturday after-noon fishing on the banks of small, muddy rivers.

"You can make all the noise you want," he told her. "The fish in this   20 river are almost entirely deaf. Besides, I don't care if I catch any. I only like the act of fishing. If I catch them, then I have to take them home and clean them. Then I've got to cook them and eat them. I don't even like fish that much, and the fish you catch here all taste of mud."

"Why do you bother fishing then?" Linda asked him. "Why don't you   21 just come and sit on the riverbank?"

"It's not that easy," he told her. "A beautiful girl in a blue dress may go   22 and sit on a riverbank any time she wants. But a man can only sit on a river-bank if he has a very good reason. Because I fish, I am a man with a hobby.

After a hard week of work, I deserve some relaxation. But if I just came and sat on the riverbank, I would be a romantic fool. People would make fun of me. They would think I was irresponsible, and before long I would be a failure." As he spoke, he attached a lure to his line, untelescoped his fishing pole and cast his line into the water.

23   You may object that this would not have happened in real life, that the conversation would have been awkward, that Linda would have been a bit frightened by the man. Well, why don't you just run out to the grocery store and buy a bottle of milk and a loaf of bread? The grocer will give you your change without even looking at you. That's what happens in real life, and if that's what you're after, why are you reading a book?

24   I'm sorry. I shouldn't have got upset. But it's not easy you know. Dialogue is about the hardest stuff to write. You've got all those "he saids" and "she saids" and "he replieds." And you've got to remember the quotation marks and whether the comma is inside or outside the quotation marks. Sometimes you can leave out the "he saids" and the "she saids" but then the reader gets confused and can't figure out who's talking. Hemingway is bad for that. Sometimes you can read an entire chapter without figuring out who is on what side.

25   Anyway, something must have been in the air that afternoon. Linda felt free and open.

26   Did I mention that it was warm and the sun was shining?

27   She chattered away, telling the stranger all about her life, what she had done when she was a little girl, the time her dad had taken the whole family to Hawaii and she got such a bad sunburn that she was peeling in February, how she was a better water skier than Gregg and how mad he got when she beat him at tennis. The man, whose name was Michael (you can use biblical names for men as long as you avoid Joshua or Isaac), told her he was a doctor, but had always wanted to be a cowboy. He told her about the time he skinned his knee when he fell off his bicycle and had to spend two weeks in the hospital because of infection. In short, they did what people who are falling in love always do. They unfolded their brightest and happiest memories and gave them to each other as gifts.

28   Then Michael took a bottle of wine and a Klik sandwich out of his wicker creel and invited Linda to join him in a picnic. He had forgotten his corkscrew and he had to push the cork down into the bottle with his filletting knife. They drank wine and laughed and spat out little pieces of cork. Michael reeled in his line, and to his amazement discovered a diamond ring on his hook. Linda didn't dare tell him where the ring had come from. Then

Michael took Linda's hand, and slipped the ring onto her finger. In a comic-solemn voice, he asked her to marry him. With the same kind of comic solemnity, she agreed. Then they kissed, a first gentle kiss with their lips barely brushing and without touching each other.

Now I've got to bring this to some kind of ending. You think writers know how stories end before they write them, but that's not true. We're wracked with confusion and guilt about how things are going to end. And just as you're playing the role of Linda in this story, Michael is my alter ego. He even looks a little like me and he smokes the same kind of pipe. We all want this to end happily. If I were going to be realistic about this, I suppose I'd have to let them make love. Then, shaken with guilt and horror, Linda would go back and marry Gregg, and the doctor would go back to his practice. But I'm not going to do that. In the story from which I stole the plot, Michael turned out not to be a doctor at all, but a returned soldier who had always been in love with Linda. She recognized him as they kissed, because they had kissed as children, and even though they had grown up and changed, she recognized the flavour of wintergreen on his breath. That's no good. It brings in too many unexplained facts at the last minute.

I'm going to end it right here at the moment of the kiss. You can do what you want with the rest of it, except you can't make him a returned soldier, and you can't have them make love then separate forever. I've eliminated those options. In fact, I think I'll eliminate all options. This is where the story ends, at the moment of the kiss. It goes on and on forever while cities burn, nations rise and fall, galaxies are born and die, and the universe snuffs out the stars one by one. It goes on, the story, the brush of a kiss.

1989

NOTES

David Arnason is an English professor at the University of Manitoba as well as a renowned short-story writer. Arnason makes fun of the stereotype of an alcoholic writer who works with a hangover in the morning. Since he refers to himself, he is self-mocking.

Eustacia Vye A character in Thomas Hardy's *The Return of the Native* (1878). She is a beautiful but tragic figure who uses her feminine wiles to escape her environment. Note the irony in Arnason's makeover of the character.

Arnason alludes to a famous poem in *The Rubáiyát of Omar Khayyám* (via Edward FitzGerald, 1859) when he has Michael taking out a sandwich and a bottle of wine:

> Here with a Loaf of Bread beneath the Bough,
> A Flask of Wine, a Book of Verse — and Thou
> Beside me singing in the Wilderness —
> And Wilderness is Paradise enow.

This verse is generally simplified to "a loaf of bread, a jug of wine, and thou," a romantic expression of a person's basic needs.

Klik A canned sandwich meat, like Spam.

COMPREHENSION AND DISCUSSION

1. What is the main story? What kind of story is it?
2. How does Arnason draw you into his story?
3. Does it matter that Arnason assumes the reader to be female? Why does he make the heroine a beautiful, blond, blue-eyed girl named Linda, with a minor defect?
4. How does Arnason differentiate between the story and the process of creating and commenting on the story?
5. Does Arnason's story follow his observation about the "conflict between reason and passion"? Is it true that "most of the world's great books" are about this conflict (paragraph 8)?
6. To what literary traditions and stereotypes does Arnason refer? Do you think they are valid? For example, are black-haired women "basically evil" (paragraph 3)?
7. Why is this a fun story to read? What makes it so?
8. What point does Arnason make when he ends the story with the two people kissing?
9. Is this story romantic? Does Arnason explain love well when he says, "In short, they did what people who are falling in love always do. They unfolded their brightest and happiest memories and gave them to each other as gifts" (paragraph 27)?

LITERARY TECHNIQUES

Arnason is doing two things simultaneously: telling a story and showing the steps involved in creating a story. This technique is called metafiction. Note how he invites the female reader to become a character in his story. Then he explains all the ingredients necessary in writing a tale: plot, character, names. As Arnason contrives the episode between Linda and Michael, he intrudes on the action to explain the techniques he is using. Finally, he tells the reader that out of the many possible endings he chooses the one he wants. In short, as creative writer, Arnason determines what goes in and what does not.

This story answers the common question, "Does the writer deliberately put all those details in the story?" Part of writing, especially in fiction, is decision making. Every detail in the story must be relevant to the whole. Arnason shows how much control he has over the basic elements of storytelling.

"A Girl's Story" also responds to the next question, "How much does the writer put himself into his story?" All writing has an element of autobiography. In this story, Arnason makes the point that the character Michael is similar to himself.

Reader participation is more than just passive reading here. Arnason engages you, the reader, by inviting you to become a character in his story. The technique is the direct address to the reader. Arnason creates the illusion that you have a part to play and that he is speaking only to you, and not just anybody.

ASSIGNMENTS

1. Look up the meanings of the names of characters that the writer mentions, such as Joshua, Isaac, Michael, Gregg, and Linda. You can find this information in a baby-name book or on the Internet.
2. Arnason has given you the process analysis of short-story writing. Write a set of instructions on how to write a story.
3. Arnason mentions brunettes, blondes, and redheads and discusses colour imagery. List the primary colours and explain what they represent. Do other cultures have the same meanings for colours?
4. If you wish to read more stories with elements of metafiction, see Tim O'Brien's "The Man I Killed" (p. 174) and Charles de Lint's "Mr. Truepenny's Book Emporium and Gallery" (p. 52). How are they the same? How do they differ?

The Fun They Had

Isaac Asimov

1   Margie even wrote about it that night in her diary. On the page headed May 17, 2157, she wrote, "Today Tommy found a real book!"

2   It was a very old book. Margie's grandfather once said that when he was a little boy *his* grandfather told him that there was a time when all stories were printed on paper.

3   They turned the pages, which were yellow and crinkly, and it was awfully funny to read words that stood still instead of moving the way they were supposed to—on a screen, you know. And then, when they turned back to the page before, it had the same words on it that it had had when they read it the first time.

4   "Gee," said Tommy, "what a waste. When you're through with the book, you just throw it away, I guess. Our television screen must have had a million books on it and it's good for plenty more. I wouldn't throw it away."

5   "Same with mine," said Margie. She was eleven and hadn't seen as many telebooks as Tommy had. He was thirteen.

6   She said, "Where did you find it?"

7   "In my house." He pointed without looking, because he was busy reading. "In the attic."

8   "What's it about?"

9   "School."

10   Margie was scornful. "School? What's there to write about school? I hate school."

11   Margie always hated school, but now she hated it more than ever. The mechanical teacher had been giving her test after test in geography and she had been doing worse and worse until her mother had shaken her head sorrowfully and sent for the County Inspector.

12   He was a round little man with a red face and a whole box of tools with dials and wires. He smiled at Margie and gave her an apple, then took the teacher apart. Margie had hoped he wouldn't know how to put it together again, but he knew how all right, and, after an hour or so, there it was again, large and black and ugly, with a big screen on which all the lessons were shown and the questions were asked. That wasn't so bad. The part Margie hated most was the slot where she had to put homework and test papers. She always had to write them out in a punch code they made her learn when she was six years old, and the mechanical teacher calculated the mark in no time.

The Inspector had smiled after he was finished and patted Margie's 13
head. He said to her mother, "It's not the little girl's fault, Mrs. Jones. I
think the geography sector was geared a little too quick. Those things
happen sometimes. I've slowed it up to an average ten-year level. Actually,
the over-all pattern of her progress is quite satisfactory." And he patted
Margie's head again.

Margie was disappointed. She had been hoping they would take the 14
teacher away altogether. They had once taken Tommy's teacher away for
nearly a month because the history sector had blanked out completely.

So she said to Tommy, "Why would anyone write about school?" 15

Tommy looked at her with very superior eyes. "Because it's not our 16
kind of school, stupid. This is the old kind of school that they had hundreds
and hundreds of years ago." He added loftily, pronouncing the word carefully, "*Centuries* ago."

Margie was hurt. "Well, I don't know what kind of school they had all 17
that time ago." She read the book over his shoulder for a while, then said,
"Anyway, they had a teacher."

"Sure they had a teacher, but it wasn't a *regular* teacher. It was a man." 18

"A man? How could a man be a teacher?" 19

"Well, he just told the boys and girls things and gave them homework 20
and asked them questions."

"A man isn't smart enough." 21

"Sure he is. My father knows as much as my teacher." 22

"He can't. A man can't know as much as a teacher." 23

"He knows almost as much, I betcha." 24

Margie wasn't prepared to dispute that. She said, "I wouldn't want a 25
strange man in my house to teach me."

Tommy screamed with laughter. "You don't know much, Margie. The 26
teachers didn't live in the house. They had a special building and all the
kids went there."

"And all the kids learned the same thing?" 27

"Sure, if they were the same age." 28

"But my mother says a teacher has to be adjusted to fit the mind of 29
each boy and girl it teaches and that each kid has to be taught differently."

"Just the same they didn't do it that way then. If you don't like it, you 30
don't have to read the book."

"I didn't say I didn't like it," Margie said quickly. She wanted to read 31
about those funny schools.

They weren't even half-finished when Margie's mother called, 32
"Margie! School!"

33   Margie looked up. "Not yet, Mamma."

34   "Now!" said Mrs. Jones. "And it's probably time for Tommy, too."

35   Margie said to Tommy, "Can I read the book some more with you after school?"

36   "Maybe," he said nonchalantly. He walked away whistling, the dusty old book tucked beneath his arm.

37   Margie went into the schoolroom. It was right next to her bedroom, and the mechanical teacher was on and waiting for her. It was always on at the same time every day except Saturday and Sunday, because her mother said little girls learned better if they learned at regular hours.

38   The screen was lit up, and it said: "Today's arithmetic lesson is on the addition of proper fractions. Please insert yesterday's homework in the proper slot."

39   Margie did so with a sigh. She was thinking about the old schools they had when her grandfather's grandfather was a little boy. All the kids from the whole neighbourhood came, laughing and shouting in the schoolyard, sitting together in the schoolroom, going home together at the end of the day. They learned the same things, so they could help one another on the homework and talk about it.

40   And the teachers were people....

41   The mechanical teacher was flashing on the screen: "When we add the fractions $1/2$ and $1/4$ — "

42   Margie was thinking about how the kids must have loved it in the old days. She was thinking about the fun they had.

1957

NOTES

Isaac Asimov (1920 – 1992) is one of the most famous and prolific science fiction writers ever, completing about 500 books in his lifetime. He was a scientist, with a doctorate in biochemistry. Some of his famous books are *I, Robot* and the *Foundation* series.

In the 1950s, when this story was written, computers were huge, room-sized machines that weighed several tons, ran on vacuum tubes, and read punch cards. Although Asimov's description of the technology is dated, the issues are the same as the ones we deal with today.

When this story was written, the term "computer," meaning an electronic machine, was not common parlance. Note how Asimov calls it a "mechanical teacher."

Punch code A method of storing information that consisted of punching holes into cards and feeding them into a computer for processing. From this action, the words "input" and "output" have entered our everyday vocabulary.

COMPREHENSION AND DISCUSSION

1. What image do Margie and Tommy have about books?
2. Describe Margie's schooling in your own words.
3. Why does Margie yearn for the school days of her great-great-grandparents? Why isn't Margie's schooling as fun as in the olden days?
4. Besides information, what else do you acquire as you go to school with other students?
5. Would you learn faster or better if you learned at home using the computer and the Internet? Explain your answer.
6. How do you know that this story is dated? What clues do you have to support your view?

LITERARY TECHNIQUES

The names of characters are an important part of the story. "Margie" and "Tommy" are both children's names. Often names that end in an "ee" sound are children's nicknames. As adults, the characters would more likely be "Marge" or "Margaret," "Tom" or "Thomas." These names were also more common in the 1950s and 1960s than today.

Science fiction is a literary genre that places science and technology in the forefront with humanity and speculates what may happen in some near or distant future. While highly imaginative, it still adheres to a sense of logic and reasonableness in speculating on things to come.

Asimov depends on the reader's experience with traditional schooling in which the pupil goes to school and reads from a printed book. In order to heighten the irony, he also speculates that the reader may not have enjoyed traditional education and may not consider school to be much fun. (In this story, irony is the contrast or contradiction between what is perceived and what is actual.)

ASSIGNMENTS

1. Discuss the advantages or disadvantages of distance education through the Internet. Would you prefer home schooling to regular schooling?
2. Write a paragraph comparing classroom learning and individual learning.
3. Will the book and the printed page be obsolete within the next hundred years? Use research on the electronic book to support your arguments.
4. Speculate on the educational system twenty years from now.
5. A major problem with books printed in the 20th century is the use of acid paper. Because acid paper deteriorates quickly, many of the books from this time are ruined, whereas older books remain in relatively good condition. Write a report on the current use of acid-free paper.
6. What is the most significant development in the evolution of computer technology? Research the history of computers to supplement what you already know.
7. Some predictions of future technological advancements have proved to be spectacularly inaccurate. For example, in 1943, Thomas Watson, the chairman of IBM, said, "I think there is a world market for maybe five computers." It was also predicted that with advances in technology, we would have trouble looking for ways to fill our ample leisure time; instead, we are working more hours than ever. Choose a prediction for the future, either in fiction or non-fiction, that was proved wrong and explain why it did not come to fruition.
8. Isaac Asimov is a character in the story "One Rejection Too Many" (p. 169). What image do you get of him from these two readings?

Greasy Lake
T. Coraghessan Boyle

It's about a mile down on the dark side of Route 88.
—*Bruce Springsteen*

There was a time when courtesy and winning ways went out of style, when it was good to be bad, when you cultivated decadence like a taste. We were all dangerous characters then. We wore torn-up leather jackets, slouched around with toothpicks in our mouths, sniffed glue and ether and what somebody claimed was cocaine. When we wheeled our parents' whining station wagons out onto the street we left a patch of rubber half a block long. We drank gin and grape juice, Tango, Thunderbird, and Bali Hai. We were nineteen. We were bad. We read André Gide and struck elaborate poses to show that we didn't give a shit about anything. At night, we went up to Greasy Lake.

Through the centre of town, up the strip, past the housing developments and shopping malls, street lights giving way to the thin streaming illumination of the headlights, trees crowding the asphalt in a black unbroken wall: that was the way out to Greasy Lake. The Indians had called it Wakan, a reference to the clarity of its waters. Now it was fetid and murky, the mud banks glittering with broken glass and strewn with beer cans and the charred remains of bonfires. There was a single ravaged island a hundred yards from shore, so stripped of vegetation it looked as if the air force had strafed it. We went up to the lake because everyone went there, because we wanted to snuff the rich scent of possibility on the breeze, watch a girl take off her clothes and plunge into the festering murk, drink beer, smoke pot, howl at the stars, savour the incongruous full-throated roar of rock and roll against the primeval susurrus of frogs and crickets. This was nature.

I was there one night, late, in the company of two dangerous characters. Digby wore a gold star in his right ear and allowed his father to pay his tuition at Cornell; Jeff was thinking of quitting school to become a painter/musician/headshop proprietor. They were both expert in the social graces, quick with a sneer, able to manage a Ford with lousy shocks over a rutted and gutted blacktop road at eighty-five while rolling a joint as compact as a Tootsie Roll Pop stick. They could lounge against a bank of booming speakers and trade "man"s with the best of them or roll out across the dance floor as if their joints worked on bearings. They were slick and quick and they wore their mirror shades at breakfast and dinner, in the shower, in closets and caves. In short, they were bad.

4   I drove. Digby pounded the dashboard and shouted along with Toots & the Maytals while Jeff hung his head out the window and streaked the side of my mother's Bel Air with vomit. It was early June, the air soft as a hand on your cheek, the third night of summer vacation. The first two nights we'd been out till dawn, looking for something we never found. On this, the third night, we'd cruised the strip sixty-seven times, been in and out of every bar and club we could think of in a twenty-mile radius, stopped twice for bucket chicken and forty-cent hamburgers, debated going to a party at the house of a girl Jeff's sister knew, and chucked two dozen raw eggs at mailboxes and hitchhikers. It was 2:00 a.m.; the bars were closing. There was nothing to do but take a bottle of lemon-flavoured gin up to Greasy Lake.

5   The taillights of a single car winked at us as we swung into the dirt lot with its tufts of weed and washboard corrugations; '57 Chevy, mint, metallic blue. On the far side of the lot, like the exoskeleton of some gaunt chrome insect, a chopper leaned against its kickstand. And that was it for excitement: some junkie halfwit biker and a car freak pumping his girl-friend. Whatever it was we were looking for, we weren't about to find it at Greasy Lake. Not that night.

6   But then all of a sudden Digby was fighting for the wheel. "Hey, that's Tony Lovett's car! Hey!" he shouted, while I stabbed at the brake pedal and the Bel Air nosed up to the gleaming bumper of the parked Chevy. Digby leaned on the horn, laughing, and instructed me to put my brights on. I flicked on the brights. This was hilarious. A joke. Tony would experience premature withdrawal and expect to be confronted by grim-looking state troopers with flashlights. We hit the horn, strobed the lights, and then jumped out of the car to press our witty faces to Tony's windows; for all we knew we might even catch a glimpse of some little fox's tit, and then we could slap backs with red-faced Tony, roughhouse a little, and go on to new heights of adventure and daring.

7   The first mistake, the one that opened the whole floodgate, was losing my grip on the keys. In the excitement, leaping from the car with the gin in one hand and a roach clip in the other, I spilled them in the grass — in the dark, rank, mysterious nighttime grass of Greasy Lake. This was a tac-tical error, as damaging and irreversible in its way as Westmoreland's deci-sion to dig in at Khe Sanh. I felt it like a jab of intuition, and I stopped there by the open door, peering vaguely into the night that puddled up round my feet.

The second mistake — and this was inextricably bound up with the   8
first — was identifying the car as Tony Lovett's. Even before the very bad
character in greasy jeans and engineer boots ripped out of the driver's door,
I began to realize that this chrome blue was much lighter than the robin's-
egg of Tony's car, and that Tony's car didn't have rear-mounted speakers.
Judging from their expressions, Digby and Jeff were privately groping
toward the same inevitable and unsettling conclusion as I was.

In any case, there was no reasoning with this bad greasy character —   9
clearly he was a man of action. The first lusty Rockette kick of his steel-
toed boot caught me under the chin, chipped my favourite tooth, and left
me sprawled in the dirt. Like a fool, I'd gone down on one knee to comb
the stiff hacked grass for the keys, my mind making connections in the
most dragged-out, testudineous way, knowing that things had gone wrong,
that I was in a lot of trouble, and that the lost ignition key was my grail and
my salvation. The three or four succeeding blows were mainly absorbed by
my right buttock and the tough piece of bone at the base of my spine.

Meanwhile, Digby vaulted the kissing bumpers and delivered a savage   10
kung-fu blow to the greasy character's collarbone. Digby had just finished
a course in martial arts for phys-ed credit and had spend the better part of
the past two nights telling us apocryphal tales of Bruce Lee types and
of the raw power invested in lightning blows shot from coiled wrists,
ankles, and elbows. The greasy character was unimpressed. He merely
backed off a step, his face like a Toltec mask, and laid Digby out with a
single whistling roundhouse blow ... but by now Jeff had got into the act,
and I was beginning to extricate myself from the dirt, a tinny compound of
shock, rage, and impotence wadded in my throat.

Jeff was on the guy's back, biting at his ear. Digby was on the ground,   11
cursing. I went for the tire iron I kept under the driver's seat. I kept it there
because bad characters always keep tire irons under the driver's seat, for
just such an occasion as this. Never mind that I hadn't been involved in a
fight since sixth grade, when a kid with a sleepy eye and two streams of
mucus depending from his nostrils hit me in the knee with a Louisville
Slugger, never mind that I'd touched the tire iron exactly twice before, to
change tires: it was there. And I went for it.

I was terrified. Blood was beating in my ears, my hands were shaking,   12
my heart turning over like a dirtbike in the wrong gear. My antagonist was
shirtless, and a single cord of muscle flashed across his chest as he bent forward to peel Jeff from his back like a wet overcoat. "Motherfucker," he spat,
over and over, and I was aware in that instant that all four of us — Digby,
Jeff, and myself included — were chanting "motherfucker, motherfucker," as

if it were a battle cry. (What happened next? the detective asks the murderer from beneath the turned-down brim of his porkpie hat. I don't know, the murderer says, something came over me. Exactly.)

13   Digby poked the flat of his hand in the bad character's face and I came at him like a kamikaze, mindless, raging, stung with humiliation — the whole thing, from the initial boot in the chin to this murderous primal instinct involving no more than sixty hyperventilating, gland-flooding seconds — I came at him and brought the tire iron down across his ear. The effect was instantaneous, astonishing. He was a stunt man and this was Hollywood, he was a big grimacing toothy balloon and I was a man with a straight pin. He collapsed. Wet his pants. Went loose in his boots.

14   A single second, big as a zeppelin, floated by. We were standing over him in a circle, gritting our teeth, jerking our necks, our limbs and hands and feet twitching with glandular discharges. No one said anything. We just stared down at the guy, the car freak, the lover, the bad greasy character laid low. Digby looked at me; so did Jeff. I was still holding the tire iron, a tuft of hair clinging to the crook like dandelion fluff, like down. Rattled, I dropped it in the dirt, already envisioning the headlines, the pitted faces of the police inquisitors, the gleam of handcuffs, clank of bars, the big black shadows rising from the back of the cell . . . when suddenly a raw torn shriek cut through me like all the juice in all the electric chairs in the country.

15   It was the fox. She was short, barefoot, dressed in panties and a man's shirt. "Animals!" she screamed, running at us with her fists clenched and wisps of blow-dried hair in her face. There was a silver chain round her ankle, and her toenails flashed in the glare of the headlights. I think it was the toenails that did it. Sure, the gin and cannibis and even the Kentucky Fried may have had a hand in it, but it was the sight of those flaming toes that set us off — the toad emerging from the loaf in *Virgin Spring*, lipstick smeared on a child; she was already tainted. We were on her like Bergman's deranged brothers — see no evil, hear none, speak none — panting, wheezing, tearing at her clothes, grabbing for flesh. We were bad characters, and we were scared and hot and three steps over the line — anything could have happened.

16   It didn't.

17   Before we could pin her to the hood of the car, our eyes masked with lust and greed and the purest primal badness, a pair of headlights swung into the lot. There we were, dirty, bloody, guilty, dissociated from humanity and civilization, the first of the Ur-crimes behind us, the second in progress, shreds of nylon panty and spandex brassiere dangling from our fingers, our flies open, lips licked — there we were, caught in the spotlight. Nailed.

We bolted. First for the car, and then, realizing we had no way of   18
starting it, for the woods. I thought nothing. I thought escape. The headlights came at me like accusing fingers. I was gone.

Ram-bam-bam, across the parking lot, past the chopper and into the   19
feculent undergrowth at the lake's edge, insects flying up in my face,
weeds whipping, frogs and snakes and red-eyed turtles splashing off into
the night: I was already ankle-deep in muck and tepid water and still going
strong. Behind me, the girl's screams rose in intensity, disconsolate,
incriminating, the screams of the Sabine women, the Christian martyrs,
Anne Frank dragged from the garret. I kept going, pursued by those cries,
imagining cops and bloodhounds. The water was up to my knees when I
realized what I was doing: I was going to swim for it. Swim the breadth of
Greasy Lake and hide myself in the thick clot of woods on the far side.
They'd never find me there.

I was breathing in sobs, in gasps. The water lapped at my waist as I   20
looked out over the moon-burnished ripples, the mats of algae that clung
to the surface like scabs. Digby and Jeff had vanished. I paused. Listened.
The girl was quieter now, screams tapering to sobs, but there were male
voices, angry, excited, and the high-pitched ticking of the second car's
engine. I waded deeper, stealthy, hunted, the ooze sucking at my sneakers.
As I was about to take the plunge — at the very instant I dropped my
shoulder for the first slashing stroke — I blundered into something.
Something unspeakable, obscene, something soft, wet, moss-grown. A
patch of weed? A log? When I reached out to touch it, it gave like a rubber
duck, it gave like flesh.

In one of those nasty little epiphanies for which we are prepared by   21
films and TV and childhood visits to the funeral home to ponder the
shrunken painted forms of dead grandparents, I understood what it was that
bobbed there so inadmissibly in the dark. Understood, and stumbled back
in horror and revulsion, my mind yanked in six different directions (I was
nineteen, a mere child, an infant, and here in the space of five minutes I'd
struck down one greasy character and blundered into the waterlogged carcass of a second), thinking, The keys, the keys, why did I have to go and
lose the keys? I stumbled back, but the muck took hold of my feet — a
sneaker snagged, balance lost — and suddenly I was pitching face forward
into the buoyant black mass, throwing out my hands in desperation while
simultaneously conjuring the image of reeking frogs and muskrats
revolving in slicks of their own deliquescing juices. AAAAArrrgh! I shot
from the water like a torpedo, the dead man rotating to expose a mossy

beard and eyes cold as the moon. I must have shouted out, thrashing around in the weeds, because the voices behind me suddenly became animated.

22   "What was that?"

23   "It's them, it's them: they tried to, tried to . . . *rape* me!" Sobs.

24   A man's voice, flat Midwestern accent. "You sons a bitches, we'll kill you!"

25   Frogs, crickets.

26   Then another voice, harsh, *r*-less, Lower East Side: "Motherfucker!" I recognized the verbal virtuosity of the bad greasy character in the engineer boots. Tooth chipped, sneakers gone, coated in mud and slime and worse, crouching breathless in the weeds waiting to have my ass thoroughly and definitively kicked and fresh from the hideous stinking embrace of a three-days-dead corpse, I suddenly felt a rush of joy and vindication: the son of a bitch was alive! Just as quickly, my bowels turned to ice. "Come on out of there, you pansy mothers!" the bad greasy character was screaming. He shouted curses till he was out of breath.

27   The crickets started up again, then the frogs. I held my breath. All at once was a sound in the reeds, a swishing, a splash: thunk-a-thunk. They were throwing rocks. The frogs fell silent. I cradled my head. Swish, swish, thunk-a-thunk. A wedge of feldspar the size of a cue ball glanced off my knee. I bit my finger.

28   It was then that they turned to the car. I heard a door slam, a curse, and then the sound of the headlights shattering — almost a good-natured sound, celebratory, like corks popping from the necks of bottles. This was succeeded by the dull booming of fenders, metal on metal, and then the icy crash of the windshield. I inched forward, elbows and knees, my belly pressed to the muck, thinking of guerrillas and commandos and *The Naked and the Dead*. I parted the weeds and squinted the length of the parking lot.

29   The second car — it was a Trans-Am — was still running, its high beams washing the scene in a lurid stagy light. Tire iron flailing, the greasy bad character was laying into the side of my mother's Bel Air like an avenging demon, his shadow riding up the trunks of the trees. Whomp. Whomp. Whomp-whomp. The other two guys — blond types, in fraternity jackets — were helping out with tree branches and skull-sized boulders. One of them was gathering up bottles, rocks, muck, candy wrappers, used condoms, poptops, and other refuse and pitching it through the window on the driver's side. I could see the fox, a white bulb behind the windshield of the '57 Chevy. "Bobbie," she whined over the thumping, "come on." The greasy character paused a moment, took one good swipe at the left taillight,

and then heaved the tire iron halfway across the lake. Then he fired up the '57 and was gone.

Blond head nodded at blond head. One said something to the other, too 30 low for me to catch. They were no doubt thinking that in helping to annihilate my mother's car they'd committed a fairly rash act, and thinking too that there were three bad characters connected with that very car watching them from the woods. Perhaps other possibilities occurred to them as well — police, jail cells, justices of the peace, reparations, lawyers, irate parents, fraternal censure. Whatever they were thinking, they suddenly dropped branches, bottles, and rocks and sprang for their car in unison, as if they'd choreographed it. Five seconds. That's all it took. The engine shrieked, the tires squealed, a cloud of dust rose from the rutted lot and then settled back on darkness.

I don't know how long I lay there, the bad breath of decay all around 31 me, my jacket heavy as a bear, the primordial ooze subtly reconstituting itself to accommodate my upper thighs and testicles. My jaws ached, my knee throbbed, my coccyx was on fire. I contemplated suicide, wondered if I'd need bridgework, scraped the recesses of my brain for some sort of excuse to give my parents — a tree had fallen on the car, I was blinded by a bread truck, hit and run, vandals had got to it while we were playing chess at Digby's. Then I thought of the dead man. He was probably the only person on the planet worse off than I was. I thought about him, fog on the lake, insects chirring eerily, and felt the tug of fear, felt the darkness opening up inside me like a set of jaws. Who was he, I wondered, this victim of time and circumstance bobbing sorrowfully in the lake at my back. The owner of the chopper, no doubt, a bad older character come to this. Shot during a murky drug deal, drowned while drunkenly frolicking in the lake. Another headline. My car was wrecked; he was dead.

When the eastern half of the sky went from black to cobalt and the 32 trees began to separate themselves from the shadows, I pushed myself up from the mud and stepped out into the open. By now the birds had begun to take over for the crickets, and dew lay slick on the leaves. There was a smell in the air, raw and sweet at the same time, the smell of the sun firing buds and opening blossoms. I contemplated the car. It lay there like a wreck along the highway, like a steel sculpture left over from a vanished civilization. Everything was still. This was nature.

I was circling the car, as dazed and bedraggled as the sole survivor of 33 an air blitz, when Digby and Jeff emerged from the trees behind me. Digby's face was crosshatched with smears of dirt; Jeff's jacket was gone and his shirt was torn across the shoulder. They slouched across the lot, looking sheepish, and silently came up beside me to gape at the ravaged automobile. No one said a word. After a while Jeff swung open the driver's door and began to scoop the broken glass and garbage off the seat. I looked at Digby. He shrugged. "At least they didn't slash the tires," he said.

34   It was true: the tires were intact. There was no windshield, the head-lights were staved in, and the body looked as if it had been sledge-hammered for a quarter a shot at the county fair, but the tires were inflated to regulation pressure. The car was drivable. In silence, all three of us bent to scrape the mud and shattered glass from the interior. I said nothing about the biker. When we were finished, I reached in my pocket for the keys, experienced a nasty stab of recollection, cursed myself, and turned to search the grass. I spotted them almost immediately, no more than five feet from the open door, glinting like jewels in the first tapering shaft of sun-light. There was no reason to get philosophical about it: I eased into the seat and turned the engine over.

35   It was at that precise moment that the silver Mustang with the flame decals rumbled into the lot. All three of us froze; then Digby and Jeff slid into the car and slammed the door. We watched as the Mustang rocked and bobbed across the ruts and finally jerked to a halt beside the forlorn chopper at the far end of the lot. "Let's go," Digby said. I hesitated, the Bel Air wheezing beneath me.

36   Two girls emerged from the Mustang. Tight jeans, stiletto heels, hair like frozen fur. They bent over the motorcycle, paced back and forth aim-lessly, glanced once or twice at us, and then ambled over to where the reeds sprang up in a green fence round the perimeter of the lake. One of them cupped her hands to her mouth. "Al," she called. "Hey, Al!"

37   "Come on," Digby hissed. "Let's get out of here."

38   But it was too late. The second girl was picking her way across the lot, unsteady on her heels, looking up at us and then away. She was older — twenty-five or -six — and as she came closer we could see there was something wrong with her: she was stoned or drunk, lurching now and waving her arms for balance. I gripped the steering wheel as if it were the ejection lever of a flaming jet, and Digby spat out my name, twice, terse and impatient.

39   "Hi," the girl said.

40   We looked at her like zombies, like war veterans, like deaf-and-dumb pencil peddlars.

41   She smiled, her lips cracked and dry. "Listen," she said, bending from the waist to look in the window, "you guys seen Al?" Her pupils were pin-

points, her eyes glass. She jerked her neck. "That's his bike over there — Al's. You seen him?"

Al. I didn't know what to say. I wanted to get out of the car and retch, 42 I wanted to go home to my parents' house and crawl into bed. Digby poked me in the ribs. "We haven't seen anybody," I said.

The girl seemed to consider this, reaching out a slim veiny arm to brace 43 herself against the car. "No matter," she said, slurring the *t*'s, "he'll turn up." And then, as if she'd just taken stock of the whole scene — the ravaged car and our battered faces, the desolation of the place — she said: "Hey, you guys look like some pretty bad characters — been fightin', huh?" We stared straight ahead, rigid as catatonics. She was fumbling in her pocket and muttering something. Finally she held out a handful of tablets in glassine wrappers: "Hey, you want to party, you want to do some of these with me and Sarah?"

I just looked at her. I thought I was going to cry. Digby broke the 44 silence. "No thanks," he said, leaning over me. "Some other time."

I put the car in gear and it inched forward with a groan, shaking off pel- 45 lets of glass like an old dog shedding water after a bath, heaving over the ruts on its worn springs, creeping toward the highway. There was a sheen of sun on the lake. I looked back. The girl was still standing there, watching us, her shoulders slumped, hand outstretched.

1979

NOTES

T. Coraghessan Boyle is an award-winning author of novels and short stories. He teaches at the University of Southern California.

The quotation at the beginning of the story is from Bruce Springsteen's song "Spirit in the Night," which talks about Greasy Lake.

Gin and grape juice, Tango, Thunderbird, and Bali Hai Names of popular alcoholic beverages.

André Gide (1869–1951) A French writer who won a Nobel Prize for Literature (1947). In his works, he expressed ideas on liberating feelings and hedonistic living. His writings influenced a generation of young rebels.

Toots & the Maytals A ska and reggae music band that lasted from 1962 to 1981 and re-formed in the 1990s.

Khe Sanh During the Vietnam War, the American soldiers were attacked by the Viet Cong and North Vietnamese soldiers at Khe Sanh (1967). In the beginning, this site had little strategic value. In short, what started as a minor incident suddenly became a major issue. General Westmoreland was the commander-in-chief of the American armed forces.

Rockettes A famous troupe of dancing girls at New York's Radio City Music Hall. They are renowned for their precision high kicks.

Testudineous resembling the shell of a tortoise

Bruce Lee (1940–1973) A Chinese-American actor and legendary kung-fu master who died in the prime of his life. His most famous movie is *Enter the Dragon*; his renowned TV role is Kato in the series *The Green Hornet*. He still has a cult following.

Toltec mask Mask made by people who lived in Mexico before the Aztecs, characteristically rigid.

Louisville Slugger A brand of baseball bat.

Fox Slang term meaning a good-looking, sexy girl.

Ingmar Bergman A Swedish filmmaker. His movies have a strong philosophical bent. His work *Virgin Spring* (1960) won an Oscar for Best Foreign Film.

Ur-crimes Archetypal or primal wrongdoings dating back to the early civilization of Ur, in Mesopotamia. The narrator refers to violent crimes, like murder, and sexual acts, like rape.

Sabine women Women who inhabited villages near Rome, and who were kidnapped by early Romans and taken as wives. This mythological story has been adapted into a musical, *Seven Brides for Seven Brothers*, and depicted in *The Rape of the Sabine Women*, a painting by Nicolas Poussin.

Anne Frank (1929–1945) A Jewish adolescent who wrote about her wartime experiences hiding from the Nazis during World War II. She was later captured and taken to a concentration camp, where she died. Her diary is now a famous book.

The Naked and the Dead (1948) Written by Norman Mailer, one of the definitive WWII novels about American soldiers in the Pacific theatre.

COMPREHENSION AND DISCUSSION

1. Describe the three main characters.
2. Explain the boys' actions in the story.
3. How do these boys define "bad"? What do you think of the values they hold?
4. Should the "greasy" character have beaten up on the three boys?
5. Who is Al? Why is he important to the rehabilitation of the narrator?
6. At what point do the boys learn from their mistakes? Or, do they learn anything at all?
7. Why is the setting of Greasy Lake important? Why do teenagers go there?
8. What is ironic about the statement, "This was nature" (paragraphs 2 and 32)?
9. When do you think this story took place?
10. How is this story about youth culture? Has anything really changed for teenagers?
11. What makes this story funny rather than tragic? Can you identify the elements used to lighten the story?
12. Why is the following statement humorous and truthful: "Understood, and stumbled back in horror and revulsion, my mind yanked in six different directions (I was nineteen, a mere child, an infant, and here in the space of five minutes I'd struck down one greasy character and blundered into the waterlogged carcass of a second), thinking, The keys, the keys, why did I have to go and lose the keys?" (paragraph 21).

LITERARY TECHNIQUES

Boyle's narrator remains nameless or anonymous throughout. The merit of this technique is that the "I" represents all young adults who must perform certain immature deeds before they learn restraint and wisdom. Do not conclude that the "I" narrator is the writer, Boyle. The "I" is a character in the story.

Boyle makes a number of allusions in this story. Allusion is a figure of speech that draws a quick reference to persons (historical or living), events, literature, and such. It taps into common knowledge, experience, or memory mutual to both reader and writer. Its purpose is to elicit recognition, comparison, and response. See the Notes section for the explanation of some allusions and references.

Note the repetition of the phrase "bad, greasy character" and its variations. The context of the word "bad" changes meaning. When the narrator refers to himself and his friends, the word has positive connotations; when he says it about others, it has negative meanings.

Humour is defined as something that causes laughter. Often in literature, humour helps lighten certain serious situations. For example, Digby's use of kung-fu is ineffectual against the "greasy" opponent. The fighting is serious, but the way it is described is funny: Upon being struck by Digby, "[t]he greasy character was unimpressed. He merely backed off a step, his face like a Toltec mask, and laid Digby out with a single whistling round-house blow ... " (paragraph 10).

ASSIGNMENTS

1. Write a short dialogue in which the narrator explains to his mother how her Bel Air car was damaged.
2. What would have happened had the boys taken up the two girls' offer at the end? Would this action confirm that they were "bad" — that they found available women and that the night was not entirely wasted? In short, imagine an alternate ending.
3. There is a short film of "Greasy Lake," but it may be hard to find. Compare it with the story.
4. Listen to the Bruce Springsteen song "Spirit in the Night" in which the lake is mentioned. Compare Springsteen's idea of Greasy Lake with Boyle's.
5. Watch George Lucas's 1973 film *American Graffiti* and compare the shenanigans of the main characters in the movie to those in Boyle's short story.
6. Read Alice Munro's "An Ounce of Cure" (p. 156). Both stories deal with teenagers getting into trouble. Explain the differences.
7. Write an essay on teenage drinking. Discuss the causes and effects.
8. Read Deborah Banks's essay "Where Do the Children Play?" (p. 228). Would the boys in "Greasy Lake" have the benefits of nature as Banks describes them?

All the Years of Her Life

Morley Callaghan

They were closing the drugstore, and Alfred Higgins, who had just taken   1
off his white jacket, was putting on his coat and getting ready to go home.
The little grey-haired man, Sam Carr, who owned the drugstore, was
bending down behind the cash register, and when Alfred Higgins passed
him, he looked up and said softly, "Just a moment, Alfred. One moment
before you go."

The soft, confident, quiet way in which Sam Carr spoke made Alfred   2
start to button his coat nervously. He felt sure his face was white. Sam Carr
usually said, "Good night," brusquely, without looking up. In the six
months he had been working in the drugstore Alfred had never heard his
employer speak softly like that. His heart began to beat so loud it was hard
for him to get his breath. "What is it, Mr. Carr?" he asked.

"Maybe you'd be good enough to take a few things out of your pocket   3
and leave them here before you go," Sam Carr said.

"What things? What are you talking about?"   4

"You've got a compact and a lipstick and at least two tubes of tooth-   5
paste in your pockets, Alfred."

"What do you mean? Do you think I'm crazy?" Alfred blustered. His   6
face got red and he knew he looked fierce with indignation. But Sam Carr,
standing by the door with his blue eyes shining brightly behind his glasses
and his lips moving underneath his grey mustache, only nodded his head a
few times, and then Alfred grew very frightened and he didn't know what to
say. Slowly he raised his hand and dipped it into his pocket, and with his eyes
never meeting Sam Carr's eyes, he took out a blue compact and two tubes of
toothpaste and a lipstick, and he laid them one by one on the counter.

"Petty thieving, eh, Alfred?" Sam Carr said. "And maybe you'd be   7
good enough to tell me how long this has been going on."

"This is the first time I ever took anything."   8

"So now you think you'll tell me a lie, eh? What kind of a sap do I look   9
like, huh? I don't know what goes on in my own store, eh? I tell you you've
been doing this pretty steady," Sam Carr said as he went over and stood
behind the cash register.

Ever since Alfred had left school he had been getting into trouble   10
wherever he worked. He lived at home with his mother and his father, who
was a printer. His two older brothers were married and his sister had got
married last year, and it would have been all right for his parents now if
Alfred had only been able to keep a job.

11   While Sam Carr smiled and stroked the side of his face very delicately with the tips of his fingers, Alfred began to feel that familiar terror growing in him that had been in him every time he had got into such trouble.

12   "I liked you," Sam Carr was saying. "I liked you and would have trusted you, and now look what I got to do." While Alfred watched with his alert, frightened blue eyes, Sam Carr drummed with his fingers on the counter. "I don't like to call a cop in point-blank," he was saying as he looked very worried. "You're a fool, and maybe I should call your father and tell him you're a fool. Maybe I should let them know I'm going to have you locked up."

13   "My father's not at home. He's a printer. He works nights," Alfred said.

14   "Who's at home?"

15   "My mother, I guess."

16   "Then we'll see what she says." Sam Carr went to the phone and dialled the number. Alfred was not so much ashamed, but there was that deep fright growing in him, and he blurted out arrogantly, like a strong, full-grown man, "Just a minute. You don't need to draw anybody else in. You don't need to tell her." He wanted to sound like a swaggering, big guy who could look after himself, yet the old, childish hope was in him, the longing that someone at home would come and help him. "Yeah, that's right, he's in trouble," Mr. Carr was saying. "Yeah, your boy works for me. You'd better come down in a hurry." And when he was finished Mr. Carr went over to the door and looked out at the street and watched the people passing in the late summer night. "I'll keep my eye out for a cop," was all he said.

17   Alfred knew how his mother would come rushing in; she would rush in with her eyes blazing, or maybe she would be crying, and she would push him away when he tried to talk to her, and make him feel her dreadful contempt; yet he longed that she might come before Mr. Carr saw the cop on the beat passing the door.

18   While they waited — and it seemed a long time — they did not speak, and when at last they heard someone tapping on the closed door, Mr. Carr, turning the latch, said crisply, "Come in, Mrs. Higgins." He looked hard-faced and stern.

19   Mrs. Higgins must have been going to bed when he telephoned, for her hair was tucked in loosely under her hat, and her hand at her throat held her light coat tight across her chest so her dress would not show. She came in, large and plump, with a little smile on her friendly face. Most of the store

lights had been turned out and at first she did not see Alfred, who was standing in the shadow at the end of the counter. Yet as soon as she saw him she did not look as Alfred thought she would look: she smiled, her blue eyes never wavered, and with a calmness and dignity that made them forget that her clothes seemed to have been thrown on her, she put out her hand to Mr. Carr and said politely, "I'm Mrs. Higgins. I'm Alfred's mother."

Mr. Carr was a bit embarrassed by her lack of terror and her simplicity, and he hardly knew what to say to her, so she asked, "Is Alfred in trouble?" 20

"He is. He's been taking things from the store. I caught him red-handed. Little things like compacts and toothpaste and lipsticks. Stuff he can sell easily," the proprietor said. 21

As she listened Mrs. Higgins looked at Alfred sometimes and nodded her head sadly, and when Sam Carr had finished she said gravely, "Is it so, Alfred?" 22

"Yes." 23

"Why have you been doing it?" 24

"I been spending money, I guess." 25

"On what?" 26

"Going around with the guys, I guess," Alfred said. 27

Mrs. Higgins put out her hand and touched Sam Carr's arms with an understanding gentleness, and speaking as though afraid of disturbing him, she said, "If you would only listen to me before doing anything." Her simple earnestness made her shy; her humility made her falter and look away, but in a moment she was smiling gravely again, and she said with a kind of patient dignity, "What did you intend to do, Mr. Carr?" 28

"I was going to get a cop. That's what I ought to do." 29

"Yes, I suppose so. It's not for me to say, because he's my son. Yet I sometimes think a little good advice is the best thing for a boy when he's at a certain period in his life," she said. 30

Alfred couldn't understand his mother's quiet composure, for if they had been at home and someone had suggested that he was going to be arrested, he knew she would be in a rage and would cry out against him. Yet now she was standing there with that gentle, pleading smile on her face, saying, "I wonder if you don't think it would be better just to let him come home with me. He looks a big fellow, doesn't he? It takes some of them a long time to get any sense," and they both stared at Alfred, who shifted away with a bit of light shining for a moment on his thin face and the tiny pimples over his cheekbone. 31

32   But even while he was turning away uneasily Alfred was realizing that Mr. Carr had become aware that his mother was really a fine woman; he knew that Sam Carr was puzzled by his mother, as if he had expected her to come in and plead with him tearfully, and instead he was being made to feel a bit ashamed by her vast tolerance. While there was only the sound of the mother's soft, assured voice in the store, Mr. Carr began to nod his head encouragingly at her. Without being alarmed, while being just large and still and simple and hopeful, she was becoming dominant there in the dimly lit store. "Of course, I don't want to be harsh," Mr. Carr was saying, "I'll tell you what I'll do. I'll just fire him and let it go at that. How's that?" and he got up and shook hands with Mrs. Higgins, bowing low to her in deep respect.

33   There was such warmth and gratitude in the way she said, "I'll never forget your kindness," that Mr. Carr began to feel warm and genial himself.

34   "Sorry we had to meet this way," he said. "But I'm glad I got in touch with you. Just wanted to do the right thing, that's all," he said.

35   "It's better to meet like this than never, isn't it?" she said. Suddenly they clasped hands as if they liked each other, as if they had known each other a long time. "Good night, sir," she said.

36   "Good night, Mrs. Higgins. I'm truly sorry," he said.

37   The mother and son walked along the street together, and the mother was taking a long, firm stride as she looked ahead with her stern face full of worry. Alfred was afraid to speak to her, he was afraid of the silence that was between them, so he only looked ahead too, for the excitement and relief was still pretty strong in him; but in a little while, going along like that in silence made him terribly aware of the strength and the sternness in her; he began to wonder what she was thinking of as she stared ahead so grimly; she seemed to have forgotten that he walked beside her; so when they were passing under the Sixth Avenue elevated and the rumble of the train seemed to break the silence, he said in his old, blustering way, "Thank God it turned out like that. I certainly won't get in a jam like that again."

38   "Be quiet. Don't speak to me. You've disgraced me again and again," she said bitterly.

39   "That's the last time. That's all I'm saying."

40   "Have the decency to be quiet," she snapped. They kept on their way, looking straight ahead.

41   When they were at home and his mother took off her coat, Alfred saw that she was really only half-dressed, and she made him feel afraid again when she said, without even looking at him, "You're a bad lot. God forgive you. It's one thing after another and always has been. Why do you stand

there stupidly? Go to bed, why don't you?" When he was going, she said, "I'm going to make myself a cup of tea. Mind, now, not a word about tonight to your father."

While Alfred was undressing in his bedroom, he heard his mother moving around in the kitchen. She filled the kettle and put it on the stove. She moved a chair. And as he listened there was no shame in him, just wonder and a kind of admiration of her strength and repose. He could still see Sam Carr nodding his head encouragingly at her; he could hear her talking simply and earnestly, and as he sat on his bed he felt a pride in her strength. "She certainly was smooth," he thought. "Gee, I'd like to tell her she sounded swell." — 42

And at last he got up and went along to the kitchen, and when he was at the door he saw his mother pouring herself a cup of tea. He watched and he didn't move. Her face, as she sat there, was a frightened, broken face utterly unlike the face of the woman who had been so assured a little while ago in the drugstore. When she reached out and lifted the kettle to pour hot water in her cup, her hand trembled and the water splashed on the stove. Leaning back in the chair, she sighed and lifted the cup to her lips, and her lips were groping loosely as if they would never reach the cup. She swallowed the hot tea eagerly, and then she straightened up in relief, though her hand holding the cup still trembled. She looked very old. — 43

It seemed to Alfred that this was the way it had been every time he had been in trouble before, that his trembling had really been in her as she hurried out half-dressed to the drugstore. He understood why she had sat alone in the kitchen the night his young sister had kept repeating doggedly that she was getting married. Now he felt all that his mother had been thinking of as they walked along the street together a little while ago. He watched his mother, and he never spoke, but at that moment his youth seemed to be over; he knew all the years of her life by the way her hand trembled as she raised the cup to her lips. — 44

1959

NOTES

Morley Callaghan (1903 – 1990) is a well-known Canadian writer. His novel *More Joy in Heaven* is one of his best-known works.

Sap A slang term meaning a stupid person or one easily fooled.

COMPREHENSION AND DISCUSSION

1. What kind of person is Alfred Higgins? Why does he steal? How old do you think he is?
2. Should Sam Carr have insisted on having Alfred arrested for shoplifting? What would that have solved?
3. Why didn't Alfred's father come instead? What does this suggest about the Higgins household?
4. Why is Alfred surprised at his mother's behaviour? How is Sam Carr affected by Mrs. Higgins?
5. How does Callaghan gain your interest in the first few paragraphs?
6. What does Alfred Higgins learn upon observing his mother in the kitchen? Do you think he will become a better person for having had this insight?

LITERARY TECHNIQUES

Callaghan uses the third-person limited point of view. We learn the thoughts of only Alfred Higgins, and of no other character. This particular restriction is important to show how the young man comes to understand what he has observed but missed in his previous scraps in which his mother bailed him out. Notice how the story follows Alfred, not his mother, and we see everything from his point of view.

Epiphany A sudden insight. James Joyce (1882–1941) coined this literary term for his collection of short stories, *The Dubliners*. Borrowed from a religious context, the literary meaning of epiphany is the sudden enlightenment of a character about himself or his surroundings. In the last paragraph, Alfred Higgins has an epiphany. Whether he becomes a better person for it is left to the reader's speculation.

ASSIGNMENTS

1. Compare this story with Boyle's "Greasy Lake" (p. 33) or Munro's "An Ounce of Cure" (p. 156). What lessons are learned, and are they the same lessons?
2. What is the difference between shoplifting and stealing? Is there a difference? Write a short piece on employee pilferage, or on the cost of shoplifting to the economy.

3. Watch the video adaptation of Callaghan's story. (It may be available at your public library.) Note the changes from print to screen. Which do you prefer, the story or the video? Explain in an essay.

4. Can a person learn the right way without first making mistakes? Is experience the best teacher?

5. Recount a moment in your experience when you have had a sudden insight into your life or your soul.

6. Compare Alfred to Chris in Barbara Scott's "Lifeguard" (p. 190).

Mr. Truepenny's Book Emporium and Gallery

Charles de Lint

The constellations were consulted for advice, but no one understood them.
— attributed to Elias Canetti

1   My name's Sophie and my friend Jilly says I have faerie blood. Maybe she's right.

2   Faeries are supposed to have problems dealing with modern technology and I certainly have trouble with anything technological. The simplest appliances develop horrendous problems when I'm around. I can't wear a watch because they start to run backwards, unless they're digital; then they just flash random numbers as though the watch's inner workings have taken to measuring fractals instead of time. If I take a subway or bus, it's sure to be late. Or it'll have a new driver who takes a wrong turn and we all get lost.

3   This actually happened to me once. I got on the number 3 at the Kelly Street Bridge and somehow, instead of going downtown on Lee, we ended up heading north into Foxville.

4   I also have strange dreams.

5   I used to think they were the place that my art came from, that my subconscious was playing around with images, tossing them up in my sleep before I put them down on canvas or paper. But then a few months ago I had this serial dream that ran on for a half dozen nights in a row, a kind of fairy tale that was either me stepping into faerie, and therefore real within its own parameters — which is what Jilly would like me to believe — or it was just my subconscious making another attempt to deal with the way my mother abandoned my father and me when I was a kid. I don't really know which I believe anymore, because I still find myself going back to that dream world from time to time and meeting the people I first met there.

6   I even have a boyfriend in that place, which probably tells you more about my usual ongoing social status than it does my state of mind.

7   Rationally, I know it's just a continuation of that serial dream. And I'd let it go at that, except it feels so damn real. Every morning when I wake up from the latest installment, my head's filled with memories of what I've done that seem as real as anything I do during the day — sometimes more so.

But I'm getting off on a tangent. I started off meaning just to introduce   8
myself, and here I am, giving you my life story. What I really wanted to tell
you about was Mr. Truepenny.

The thing you have to understand is that I made him up. He was like   9
one of those invisible childhood friends, except I deliberately created him.

We weren't exactly well-off when I was growing up. When my mother   10
left us, I ended up being one of those latchkey kids. We didn't live in the
best part of town; Upper Foxville is a rough part of the city and it could be
a scary place for a little girl who loved art and books and got teased for that
love by the other neighbourhood kids, who couldn't even be bothered to
learn how to read. When I got home from school, I went straight in and
locked the door.

I'd get supper ready for my dad, but there were always a couple of   11
hours to kill in between my arriving home and when he finished work —
longer if he had to work late. We didn't have a TV, so I read a lot, but we
couldn't afford to buy books. On Saturday mornings, we'd go to the library
and I'd take out my limit — five books — which I'd finish by Tuesday,
even if I tried to stretch them out.

To fill the rest of the time, I'd draw on shopping bags or the pads of   12
paper that dad brought me home from work, but that never seemed to
occupy enough hours. So one day I made up Mr. Truepenny.

I'd daydream about going to his shop. It was the most perfect place that   13
I could imagine: all dark wood and leaded glass, thick carpets and club
chairs with carved wooden-based reading lamps strategically placed
throughout. The shelves were filled with leather-bound books and folios,
and there was a small art gallery in the back.

The special thing about Mr. Truepenny's shop was that all of its con-   14
tents existed only within its walls. Shakespeare's *The Storm of Winter. The
Chapman's Tale* by Chaucer. *The Blissful Stream* by William Morris.
Steinbeck's companion collection to *The Long Valley*, *Salinas*. *North
Country Stoic* by Emily Brontë.

None of these books existed, of course, but being the dreamy sort of   15
kid that I was, not only could I daydream of visiting Mr. Truepenny's shop,
but I could actually read these unwritten stories. The gallery in the back of
the shop was much the same. There hung works by the masters that saw the
light of day only in my imagination. Van Goghs and Monets and da Vincis.
Rossettis and Homers and Cézannes.

Mr. Truepenny himself was a wonderfully eccentric individual who   16
never once chased me out for being unable to make a purchase. He had a
Don Quixote air about him, a sense that he was forever tilting at windmills.

He was tall and thin with a thatch of mouse-brown hair and round spectacles, a rumpled tweed suit and a huge briar pipe that he continually fussed with but never actually lit. He always greeted me with genuine affection and seemed disappointed when it was time for me to go.

17   My imagination was so vivid that my daydream visits to his shop were as real to me as when my dad took me to the library or the Newford Gallery of Fine Art. But it didn't last. I grew up, went to Butler University on student loans and the money from far too many menial jobs — "got a life," as the old saying goes. I made friends, I was so busy, there was no time, no *need* to visit the shop anymore. Eventually I simply forgot all about it.

18   Until I met Janice Petrie.

19   Wendy and I were in the Market after a late night at her place the previous evening. I was on my way home, but we'd decided to shop for groceries together before I left. Trying to make up my mind between green beans and a head of broccoli, my gaze lifted above the vegetable stand and met that of a little girl standing nearby with her parents. Her eyes widened with recognition though I'd never seen her before.

20   "You're the woman!" she cried. "You're the woman who's evicting Mr. Truepenny. I think it's a horrible thing to do. You're a horrible woman!"

21   And then she started to cry. Her mother shushed her and apologized to me for the outburst before bustling the little girl away.

22   "What was all *that* about, Sophie?" Wendy asked me.

23   "I have no idea," I said.

24   But of course I did. I was just so astonished by the encounter that I didn't know what to say. I changed the subject and that was the end of it until I got home. I dug out an old cardboard box from the back of my hall closet and rooted about in it until I came up with a folder of drawings I'd done when I still lived with my dad. Near the back I found the ones I was looking for.

25   They were studies of Mr. Truepenny and his amazing shop.

26   God, I thought, looking at these awkward drawings, pencil on brown grocery-bag paper, ballpoint on foolscap. The things we forget.

27   I took the drawings out onto my balcony and lay down on the old sofa I kept out there, studying them, one by one. There was Mr. Truepenny, writing something in his big leather-bound ledger. Here was another of him, holding his cat, Dodger, the two of them looking out the leaded glass windows of the shop. There was a view of the main aisle of the shop, leading down to the gallery, the perspective slightly askew, but not half bad considering I was no older when I did them than was the little girl in the Market today.

How could she have *known*? I found myself thinking. Mr. Truepenny   28
and his shop were something I'd made up. I couldn't remember ever telling
anyone else about them — not even Jilly. And what did she mean about my
evicting him from the shop?

I could think of no rational response. After a while, I just set the draw-   29
ings aside and tried to forget about it. Exhaustion from the late night before
soon had me nodding off, and I fell asleep only to find myself, not in my
boyfriend's faerie dream world, but on the streets of Mabon, the made-up
city in which I'd put Mr. Truepenny's Book Emporium and Gallery.

I'm half a block from the shop. The area's changed. The once-neat cobble-   30
stones are thick with grime. Refuse lies everywhere. Most of the store-
fronts are boarded up, their walls festooned with graffiti. When I reach Mr.
Truepenny's shop, I see a sign in the window that reads, CLOSING SOON DUE
TO LEASE EXPIRATION.

Half-dreading what I'll find, I open the door and hear the familiar little   31
bell tinkle as I step inside. The shop's dusty and dim, and much smaller
than I remember it. The shelves are almost bare. The door leading to the
gallery is shut and has a CLOSED sign tacked onto it.

"Ah, Miss Etoile. It's been so very long."   32

I turn to find Mr. Truepenny at his usual station behind the front   33
counter. He's smaller than I remember as well, and looks a little shabby
now. Hair thinning, tweed suit threadbare and more shapeless than ever.

"What . . . what's happened to the shop?" I ask.   34

I've forgotten that I'm asleep on the sofa out on my balcony. All I   35
know is this awful feeling I have inside as I look at what's become of my
old childhood haunt.

"Well, times change," he says. "The world moves on."   36

"This — is this my doing?"   37

His eyebrows rise quizzically.   38

"I met this little girl and she said I was evicting you."   39

"I don't blame you," Mr. Truepenny says, and I can see in his sad eyes   40
that it's true. "You've no more need for me or my wares, so it's only fair
that you let us fade."

"But you . . . that is . . . well, you're not real."   41

I feel weird saying this, because while I remember now that I'm   42
dreaming, this place is like one of my faerie dreams that feel as real as the
waking world.

43 "That's not strictly true," he tells me. "You did conceive of the city and this shop, but we were drawn to fit the blueprint of your plan from... elsewhere."

44 "What elsewhere?"

45 He frowns, brow furrowing as he thinks.

46 "I'm not really sure myself," he tells me.

47 "You're saying I didn't make you up, I just drew you here from somewhere else?"

48 He nods.

49 "And now you have to go back?"

50 "So it would seem."

51 "And this little girl — how can she know about you?"

52 "Once a reputable establishment is open for business, it really can't deny any customer access, regardless of their age or station in life."

53 "She's visiting my daydream?" I ask. This is too much to accept, even for a dream.

54 Mr. Truepenny shakes his head. "You brought this world into being through your single-minded desire, but now it has a life of its own."

55 "Until I forgot about it."

56 "You had a very strong will," he says. "You made us so real that we've been able to hang on for decades. But now we really have to go."

57 There's a very twisty sort of logic involved here, I can see. It doesn't make sense by way of the waking world's logic, but I think there are different rules in a dreamscape. After all, my faerie boyfriend can turn into a crow.

58 "Do you have more customers, other than that little girl?" I ask.

59 "Oh yes. Or at least, we did." He waves a hand to encompass the shop. "Not much stock left, I'm afraid. That was the first to go."

60 "Why doesn't *their* desire keep things running?"

61 "Well, they don't have faerie blood, now do they? They can visit, but they haven't the magic to bring us across or keep us here."

62 It figures. I think. We're back to that faerie-blood thing again. Jilly would love this.

63 I'm about to ask him to explain it all a little more clearly when I get this odd jangling sound in my ears and wake up back on the sofa. My doorbell's ringing. I go inside the apartment to accept what turns out to be a FedEx package.

64 "Can dreams be real?" I ask the courier. "Can we invent something in a dream and have it turn out to be a real place?"

65 "Beats me, lady," he replies, never blinking an eye. "Just sign here."

66 I guess he gets all kinds.

***

So now I visit Mr. Truepenny's shop on a regular basis again. The area's 67 vastly improved. There's a café nearby where Jeck — that's my boyfriend that I've been telling you about — and I go for tea after we've browsed through Mr. Truepenny's latest wares. Jeck likes this part of Mabon so much that he's now got an apartment on the same street as the shop. I think I might set up a studio nearby.

I've even run into Janice — the little girl who brought me back here in 68 the first place. She's forgiven me, of course, now that she knows it was all a misunderstanding, and lets me buy her an ice cream from the soda fountain sometimes before she goes home.

I'm very accepting of it all — you get that way after a while. The thing 69 that worries me now is, what happens to Mabon when I die? Will the city get run down again and eventually disappear? And what about its residents? There's all these people here; they've got family, friends, lives. I get the feeling it wouldn't be the same for them if they have to go back to that elsewhere place Mr. Truepenny was so vague about.

So that's the reason I've written all this down and had it printed up into 70 a little folio by one of Mr. Truepenny's friends in the waking world. I'm hoping somebody out there's like me. Someone's got enough faerie blood not only to visit, but to keep the place going. Naturally, not just anyone will do. It has to be the right sort of person, a book lover, a lover of old places and tradition, as well as the new.

If you think you're the person for the position, please send a résumé to 71 me care of Mr. Truepenny's Book Emporium and Gallery, Mabon. I'll get back to you as soon as I can.

1995

NOTES

Charles de Lint is known for his fantasy books. He lives in Ottawa.

Latchkey kid A young child with a key to the house. This term refers to children who go home to an empty house after school.

Geoffrey Chaucer (1343 – 1400) A 14th-century English poet who is best known for *The Canterbury Tales*.

William Morris (1834 – 1896) A 19th-century English poet who lived during Queen Victoria's reign.

John Steinbeck (1902 – 1968) A 20th-century American writer. His best-known work is *The Grapes of Wrath*.

Emily Brontë (1818 – 1848) A 19th-century English novelist. Her only novel is *Wuthering Heights*, a Gothic romance. Her two sisters, Charlotte and Anne, also wrote and published.

Vincent Van Gogh (1853 – 1890) A Dutch Post-Impressionist painter.

Claude Monet (1840 – 1926) A French Impressionist painter.

Leonardo da Vinci (1452 – 1519) An Italian Renaissance painter, sculptor, and architect.

Dante Gabriel Rossetti (1828 – 1882) A Victorian painter and poet who, along with his sister Christina, was one of the founders of the Pre-Raphaelite movement.

Winslow Homer (1836 – 1910) A 19th-century American painter well known for his interpretative watercolours and oils.

Paul Cézanne (1839 – 1906) A French Impressionist painter who influenced the Cubist movement in art.

Don Quixote The title character in the Spanish epic by Miguel de Cervantes (1547 – 1616). Don Quixote thought that he was a knight in armour, and attacked windmills that he believed were giants. The phrase "tilting at windmills" is used to express the idea of fighting imaginary enemies.

Sophie Etoile The character's name is significant. In Greek, *sophia* means wisdom; in French, *étoile* means star.

COMPREHENSION AND DISCUSSION

1. What relevance does faerie blood have to this story?
2. What has Sophie the narrator created in her imagination?
3. Who is Janice Petrie?
4. What has happened to Mr. Truepenny and the neighbourhood since Sophie stopped visiting?
5. Why does Sophie, as an adult, rebuild her imagined world?
6. When you are immersed in a novel, short story, or movie, are you not like Janice, who enters Sophie's created world? Has this story succeeded in transporting you into Charles de Lint's depiction of a faerie girl who creates a world that others may enter? Discuss the similarity between a writer's work and what Sophie does when she daydreams.

7. Do you create worlds in your daydreams? Do you revisit daydreams you enjoy?
8. What is reality? What is imagination? Can the distinction be blurred?

LITERARY TECHNIQUES

De Lint uses an epigraph, a quotation from Elias Canetti, a Bulgarian writer who won the Nobel Prize for Literature in 1981. An epigraph is a short quotation from another source that is relevant to the story that follows it.

Note how this story is similar to David Arnason's "A Girl's Story" (p. 20) and Tim O'Brien's "The Man I Killed" (p. 174); as the plot unfolds, the writer is also telling you how the story is created. This technique is called metafiction.

Fantasy is an offshoot of fiction. Readers know beforehand that the element of unreality and imagination is in effect. They participate by willingly suspending their disbelief and letting the story progress without objecting to the lack of logic in the plot or characters.

Mentioning historical and renowned writers and artists brings about an authentication. It makes the story sound more realistic. In this case, de Lint shows Sophie's taste in literature and art. Note that some of the titles of works by these famous artists are the product of Sophie's imagination.

ASSIGNMENTS

1. Imagination plays an important part in reading, but less so in videos and computer games. Explain why we need imagination in our lives.
2. When we read a novel, we enter the world the author created. Sometimes when we finish the book, we don't want it to be over. We want to read more about the characters' lives, or see more of the place. Choose a book you've read that had this effect on you and explain why the work was so effective.
3. Compare this story with David Arnason's "A Girl's Story" (p. 20). How are they similar on the topics of imagination and creative writing?
4. "When I was a child, I spake as a child, I understood as a child, I thought as a child, but when I became a man, I put away childish things" (1 Corinthians 13:11). Explain how this quotation is relevant to the story. Consider what "childish things" people should put away as they age.

5. Listen to the popular 1960s song "Puff the Magic Dragon" by Peter, Paul and Mary. Explain similarities in themes to de Lint's story.

6. Writers often toy with the idea that imaginary characters can interact with real people. Woody Allen has used this situation in his movie *The Purple Rose of Cairo* (1985). Watch the film and then compare it with de Lint's story.

Chickens for Christmas

Garry Engkent

My father wanted us to adapt to the new country, and one of his many schemes was to embrace the Christmas spirit. My mother thought this idea was too *fan gwei*. She was Buddhist and had some success in not celebrating the holiday in *gum san*, Canada. My father, however, had recently been made a member of two service clubs in Thibeault Falls, and admittance had fired his zeal to be Canadian. 1

"What do you know about this white devil commotion?" my mother questioned. "What is Christmas?" 2

My father was taken aback. He had been in Canada much longer than my mother and I, but when asked so straightforwardly he couldn't come up with anything more than I could. I was in grade 4, and I knew about the Nativity, the baby in the manger, the shepherds and the three wise men, Santa Claus and presents, and a lot of carols. Even though he didn't know all the words, my father liked humming *Good King Wenceslaus* off-key. 3

"Christmas is a good time for business," he said. "Make a lot of money." 4

My father owned a half-interest in the Panama Cafe, a share he'd bought from Great Uncle Liu who had founded the establishment in the early 1920s. We all toiled in the restaurant, and we slept upstairs in a cramped two-bedroom apartment. My father had liked the closeness to his work until recently. The fervour for the Canadian way got hold of him, and without my mother's consent he bought a two-storey house some distance from the restaurant, but not too far that he couldn't walk should the car not turn over in winter. 5

"In a new house, we start a new tradition," he announced. "We honour the Christmas season!" 6

"How?" my mother asked. "Chop down an evergreen and decorate it? Hang coloured lights around the veranda? We are Chinese, not *fan gwei*." 7

My mother believed she had won the argument. There would be no Christmas tradition in the Ko family. Then my father brightened. "We make Christmas, Chinese-style!" 8

My father's vision involved me. Two Saturdays before the big event he and I drove past Powassan and down snowy country roads. The farmer who supplied the restaurant with fresh eggs had some year-old chickens for sale. My father made a deal with him, and before noon we had five sacks of clucking Rhode Island Reds, three in a sack. 9

"Why didn't we buy the big white Leghorns?" I asked. 10

11   "Red is the colour of good luck."

12   Well, good luck wasn't quite with us. A sudden snow squall hit, and we returned home, eight hours later, to a worried wife and mother at midnight.

13   "So where are you going to put the hens?" my mother asked. "You can't leave them in the sacks. They'll suffocate. You can't release them in our basement, husband!"

14   My father thought of leaving them in one of the storage rooms in the Panama Cafe, but he quickly turned the idea down. The unsacked hens would make a mess, and someone might inform the health department. These live chickens were meant to be a surprise Christmas gift for the Chinese cooks, waiters, and relatives with families.

15   Fortunately, our back porch had an enclosed storage area under the floor where we kept the storm windows. Now this space became a temporary roost. At two in the morning, we went to bed, thinking the problem solved.

16   Until the chickens started crowing at first light.

17   "Aiyee, that damn farmer!" my father cursed. "Sold me a rooster! Two! No, three! They'll wake up the whole neighbourhood."

18   My poor father saw his Christmas Chinese-style crashing with each distinct cock-a-doodle-doo. If we could hear the sound inside the house, how much louder would it be outside? Canadians keep dogs and cats as domestic pets, and, yes, dogs bark and cats meow — but fifteen chickens, flapping about and crowing underneath the back porch?

19   "Find those noisy birds," my mother advised, "and — " She made a swift downward motion with her open hand. "Fresh steamed chicken for supper."

20   "You are small enough, Hardy," my father said. "You go inside and grab those damn roosters."

21   "Which ones are roosters?"

22   "The ones that crow!" he shouted, exasperated.

23   "Roosters won't crow, they'll just cluck loudly if they're frightened," my mother pointed out. "Look for a flappy red cockscomb."

24   Catching three roosters in a confined space wasn't easy. My father blocked the opening, in case the hens got out. The compartment was dark, and the only light came from the tiny door. I held a flashlight in one hand and with the other I snatched at cockscombs. All the birds began squawking and flapping their wings as they evaded capture. I started coughing, and got mouthfuls of dust and feathers. I grabbed a rooster and it pecked at me. Finally, after what seemed a long time (because my father

kept telling me to hurry up every five seconds), I handed him two roosters. As he was passing them to my mother in an unguarded moment, two birds slipped out. One was a hen; the other — the third rooster!

"Get those chickens!" my father cried. He ran after them. I stumbled 25 out of the compartment, and my mother slammed the door shut.

I would never have imagined how quickly scared fowl could dash over 26 knee-deep snow. My legs sank into it, slowing me down. As the rooster paused momentarily on top of a snowdrift, I threw myself in a desperate lunge, arms outstretched and hands poised to snatch. But I got only a handful of tail feathers. The bird squawked and escaped down the road to an uncertain freedom.

I spent the next few hours shivering in the December cold, walking 27 around the neighbourhood searching for chicken tracks. When some neighbours asked what I was doing, I didn't dare tell them the embarrassing truth. I returned home, defeated. For the next few mornings, I swore I could hear the faint cock-a-doodle-doo of a Rhode Island rooster mocking me.

The only consolation was that my mother caught the hen. The silly bird 28 backtracked right (well, almost) into her waiting hands.

"We can't give these hens as gifts," my mother said. She lifted one and 29 weighed it by bouncing it up and down. "So scrawny! That farmer didn't fatten them. By Christmas, these birds won't be worth eating."

For once my father had to agree. But he wasn't stymied. We spent the 30 afternoon scouring Thibeault Falls for poultry-fattening mash. My father sent me into the stores, figuring it was less embarrassing for a kid to ask for chicken feed than an adult. I would get amused smirks from clerks. ("A hundred-pound bag! Starting your own poultry farm, eh?") Finally, we trekked to a feed store in Powassan and loaded the trunk of my father's Oldsmobile with four fifty-pound bags of chicken feed.

When we returned home, a curious neighbour asked my father, "What 31 have you got in there, Joe? There's city ordinances against keeping farm animals, you know. Chickens, eh? I thought I heard a cock crowing this morning." He chuckled and went away, shaking his head.

My father's demeanour soured. His shoulders slumped and he let out a 32 resigned sigh. This Christmas Chinese-style thing was getting out of hand. The birds were making a ruckus. And just tossing in handfuls of chicken feed wasn't going to work. You can't keep twelve hens in the dark, in a confined area, in the cold, for two weeks. As we unloaded the chicken feed, my father could see the problems multiplying. But he brightened by the time we lugged the bags down to the basement.

33   We went to the local lumber mill and loaded up with top-quality materials. Normally, my father never rushed into such projects. My mother had been after him to fix some ill-fitting bedroom doors and that task was yet to be done. But for the chicken coop he had in mind, he took the day off work.

34   When my mother came home from the Panama Cafe, the chicken coop was almost done. It was eight feet by four by five. It had a feeding trough and watering cans, and a hinged, slatted lid, with a smaller built-in drop-latched door. It was raised six inches above the ground. "We can slip in cardboard to catch the droppings," he said.

35   My father had even used screws instead of nails. Before he went to bed that night, he put a coat of varnish on. He would apply three more coats before he deemed it worthy of housing the hens. His chicken coop was a labour of love, and he'd built it to last. It would remain in the basement, under the stairwell nook, until the house was finally sold decades later.

36   We rounded up the hens and put them in their new home. My job was to keep the troughs well supplied with fattening mash and the tin cans filled with fresh water. Every alternate day, I would replace the flattened cardboard sheets splattered with chicken droppings. One of the fringe benefits of having the hens was that some were still laying eggs, and we ended up with a generous supply, which we turned over to the restaurant. We got used to the fowl smell in the basement.

37   The hens started plumping up satisfactorily. My father would grab one or two, weigh them and nod approvingly. He would say, more to himself than to me, "Next year, we'll fatten the chickens earlier." My mother showed her disapproval with silence.

38   My father wanted to wait until Christmas Eve before distributing the live hens. He had this idea, probably from the Santa Claus stories, that gifts had to be delivered that evening. I could have told him that the three wise men didn't give the baby Jesus gold, frankincense and myrrh until twelve days after the Nativity.

39   He made a list and checked it more than twice. There weren't that many Chinese families in Thibeault Falls, maybe ten in all. My father did not include the bachelor employees. "Where would they keep a live hen? Under their beds?"

40   The Christmas Chinese-style package included a Christmas card in a red envelope with a token silver dollar, a bottle of Johnny Walker Black Label, and of course a live chicken in a cardboard box tied with red ribbon. He wrote in Chinese the name of the head of the household on the enve-

lope, and taped the envelope to the box. Then we loaded the fussing hens, liquor, and all into the Oldsmobile, both back seat and trunk. My father planned the route carefully.

"You are Santa's helper," my father said. He gave me a fluorescent-red 41 elongated toque with a white pompom. I looked in the mirror and made a face. I didn't want to be Santa's elf. Anyway, Santa's elves wore green tights, but I didn't tell my father that.

"I drive up, you take the presents to the door. If I do it, they might 42 make a fuss because they won't have a return present. But you so young, you can be excused for lack of good Chinese manners. Just hand over the stuff, say Merry Christmas, and leave. Understand?"

I didn't, but nodded anyway. I knew enough to understand that recip- 43 rocal gifts were deemed necessary. I could see that my father was becoming *fan gwei* in that 'tis better to give than to receive. My mother would surely disapprove, because this white devil concept made the other person lose face.

Our first stop was the Hong family residence on the third floor of a 44 five-storey apartment house. Mr. Hong worked as a cook for another restaurant, but he was on the list because he was my father's clan-cousin. I had to climb all those stairs with Johnny Walker tucked under one arm and both hands holding the boxed hen. I knocked on the door, and someone yelled out in broken English: "Who there?"

"Santa Claus!" I just couldn't resist. 45

"What you say?" 46

"Santa Claus. Ho-ho-ho!" 47

"Go away. I call police now!" 48

I mustered up some halting Chinese, and it came out something like: 49 "My father says to give you this." The Chinese words did the trick, and a woman opened the door a crack. Satisfied that I was too young to do her harm, she stepped out. I quickly handed her the Johnny Walker and the hen. Bewildered, she held onto the box with the agitated chicken. I dashed down the stairs, shouting loudly: "*Gong hai sing dan!*" — Merry Christmas to you.

My father looked at me expectantly as I panted. "Well? Did you give 50 it to Hong?"

"I don't think he was in. An old woman came to the door." 51

"Old woman? Apartment 306, yes?" 52

"No. 303." 53

"Aiyyeee! That's the wrong one. Can't you read what I wrote?" My 54 father slammed his hand on the steering wheel and the car horn blasted.

I broke out in a sob. "I can't read Chinese!" 55

56   We couldn't just go to apartment 303 and ask for the presents back. That would mean a loss of face for the old woman and for us. My father hoped that she couldn't make out his Chinese scrawls. Fortunately, he'd had the foresight to prepare an extra package. This time we both climbed to apartment 306, and Hong was pleased no end, although he kept apologizing for having nothing to reciprocate.

57   As we rode to our next destination, my father said, "Don't tell your mother about this. I'll never hear the end of it."

58   The next Christmas, my father had fine tuned his plan. We bought the chickens in late October so they could be fattened longer. Business improved, so instead of Johnny Walker he decided on Haig Pinch, and he wrote in English right under the Chinese. We still delivered on Christmas Eve, and like Good King Wenceslaus and his faithful page, we trekked in the snow.

59   This time, however, the recipients were ready for Santa and his helper. Even before the boxed hen left my hands, they would be full of return gifts. A box of Tuero cigars, or a fine bottle of expensive liquor, or packaged Chinese cookies from Hong Kong. We were piling up the car as much as we were unloading it. My father had started something grand in the Chinese community.

60   "So Christmas is nothing more than giving and receiving gifts," my mother commented afterwards. "We Chinese do that all the time anyway. Even when it isn't Christmas."

61   "It's the thought," my father quoted from something he had heard.

62   "It seems to me," my mother observed critically, "that we are doing too much. Every year now, you and Hardy start Christmas shopping for hens. They smell up the house for three months. It takes another six months to get rid of the stink and disinfect the basement. We spend money on feed. Then when the chickens are nice and plump, you give them away to someone else's dinner table. And what do you get? Bottles of liquor and cigars, Chinatown tins of dried-out cookies. Why can't we give store-bought things?"

63   "*Lai! Lai!* Tradition!" my father answered loudly. "I have started a tradition. It has been going on for six years. We will lose face if we stop."

64   By the look on my mother's face, I knew she wasn't convinced. She dropped the subject with her characteristic tightly pursed lips, but I knew what was in her heart.

65   My father was pleased when I got my driver's licence. Now I could play Santa Claus all by myself. By this time, my father's Christmas Chinese-style was an accepted fact in Thibeault Falls' Chinese community.

His list had changed as families moved away and new ones came. Still, some names and addresses remained constant. Mr. Hong was still in apartment 306.

One year, Mr. Hong's Christmas package was my last delivery. The temperature had fallen into a deep freeze; not even the highest setting on the car heater was enough to ward off the bone-chilling cold. The boxed hen was in the trunk the whole time. While I was climbing the stairs, the hen flapped lamely and gurgled, sounding like a death rattle.

Mr. Hong's wife came to the door and we exchanged gifts. Her small children, curious about the hen, started opening the box under the mild protest of Mrs. Hong. They wanted to see a live chicken. She expected the bird to entertain and occupy the two unruly eight-year-olds, but the Rhode Island Red lay in a corner of the cardboard box, unmoving. I knew it wouldn't live through the hour.

I saw the panic in Mrs. Hong's eyes and paling face. It was a bad omen to have a live gift die, especially near a holy day. This incident would be gossiped about for years.

"Maybe I should prepare the chicken for you," I blurted.

Mrs. Hong didn't know what to do. She gave me a faint nod, and I took the bird to the tiny kitchen. I slaughtered it, draining the blood into a bowl with a mixture of salt and water. Then I plucked the feathers and dressed it in the Chinese style: a thick salt rubdown, then rinse and dry. Throughout this procedure, Mrs. Hong and her children watched, fascinated.

"So that's how you do it, *Amah!*" one of the kids said.

Later, I heard that the hen was the best poultry the Hongs had ever eaten. I earned a place in the anecdotes of the Hong family, a saga embellished with each successive telling. My mother was pleased with the way I'd salvaged the situation.

Even when I went to university, my father's tradition continued. When I'd return for Thanksgiving weekend, before I could even unload my bags, my father would hurry me into the car and off we would go to Powassan for the Rhode Island Reds. By Christmastime the hens were all fattened, and I was Santa's helper once more. But then my father's Christmas Chinese-style faced another obstacle.

My father died.

His Christmas tradition had had its run. Even when my father sold his interest in the Panama Cafe and promptly bought himself a Mom-Pop-and-Son diner, he argued for his little piece of Christmas. Throughout the tempestuous years of the tradition, my mother often grumbled, "We are not Christian, we Chinese!"

76   Now he was gone, and we sold the diner to a cousin. In September, I returned to university and my mother secluded herself in the house that she'd toiled for twenty years to pay off. The chicken coop had served its purpose. I marvelled at how it had survived the scratches and constant peckings over the years. My father had built it to last. The coop would now sit idle, to gather dust and memories.

77   As the only son, I returned home during the university break to look after my mother's finances and utility payments, and to keep her company.

78   "We go to Powassan," she declared that Thanksgiving weekend.

79   "Why?"

80   Normally, I would drive her to all the plazas in Thibeault Falls where we would spend hours shopping for household necessities. She looked at me disapprovingly. I had not read her mind.

81   "Chickens, my son, chickens!"

82   "Why? You've got a freezer full."

83   "Christmas Chinese-style!" she explained. "Your father's tradition must carry on."

84   So that Christmas Eve, I wore my ratty red Santa toque with pompom still intact and drove to all the destinations. My last stop was the Hong family.

85   "You know, Hardy," he said, "your family doesn't need to do this after..." He paused; it was not proper in Chinese to remind me of our recent loss. "This tradition is good — after all these years, I must confess."

86   "Confess?"

87   "All those years, all those hens," Mr. Hong said slowly.

88   "Yes?" I prompted.

89   "That Christmas Eve when you prepared the bird was the only time we ate farm-fresh chicken."

90   "The other years?"

91   "I — we gave the hens away. I can't prepare live chicken."

92   "And you a chef!"

93   "My wife and I just can't do the —" His index finger slashed across his throat.

94   I laughed. The irony of it all! My father had assumed that any cook from China knew how to slaughter a chicken. I wondered what he would say if he knew. Twenty some years of giving a Christmas gift that the recipient didn't know what to do with! If and when I'd tell my mother, I wondered what kind of laughter she would have.

"Well, Mr. Hong," I said as I carried the Christmas hen into the   95
kitchen. I sharpened the cleaver. "Maybe I should add something new to
my father's tradition of Christmas Chinese-style."

2000

NOTES

Garry Engkent is a Chinese-Canadian writer. His best-known story is
"Why My Mother Can't Speak English."

Fan gwei A Chinese term for white Canadians; literally, it means "return
demon, ghost, or devil." It is a word from one of the many Cantonese
dialects. Other phrases are *fan gwei lo*, *lo fan*, and *gwei lo*.

Gum san A Chinese term for Canada; literally, it means "gold mountain."

Giving a live chicken on special occasions is traditional in Chinese culture.

The red envelope with lucky money, or *lai shi*, is another Chinese tradition.
Usually it is given to children, especially at Chinese New Year.

Tueros Expensive cigars, packaged in boxes of 25.

Amah A Chinese word for "mother" or "mom." Sometimes it is transliter-
ated as "Ah-mah."

COMPREHENSION AND DISCUSSION

1. Why does the father want to start a Christmas tradition in his household?
2. Why does the mother object to a Christmas tradition? (Note: there are
   different reasons at different times in the story.)
3. Briefly explain the father's scheme for Christmas Chinese-style.
4. What relevance has the Christmas carol "Good King Wenceslaus" to
   the story?
5. Why does the mother continue the tradition after the father's death?
6. What does the son discover at the Hong apartment?
7. Will he tell his mother what he has learned? Why or why not?
8. Which phrases indicate that time has passed between scenes?
9. What are some gift-giving traditions that you follow?
10. What do you do with gifts that you don't want but must accept, or gifts
    that you don't know how to use?

LITERARY TECHNIQUES

A story that stretches over time requires the writer to give clues to each period so that the reader will not be lost or confused. The writer here cues the reader in different ways: the mention of years, the growth of the narrator at different stages of his life, and the passing of the father.

Writers often use words and expressions from other languages even though readers may not be familiar with the terms. These phrases give colour and authenticity to the story. The term is either immediately translated in an appositive form or left for the reader to catch in context. Longer passages are usually translated. Look at the clues Engkent gives to help readers understand the Chinese phrases.

Autobiographical fiction Writers write what they know, and often in fiction they incorporate personal experiences and observations in the story. (See David Arnason's "A Girl's Story" [p. 20] and Tim O'Brien's "The Man I Killed" [p. 174] for examples of autobiographical fiction.) However, not every element of a story is always personal or based on real life. Things may be added to enhance the literary and artistic quality of the story. Reality is much more complex than the ordered and simplified arrangement of incidents in fiction. In short, literature is art; life is chaos.

Irony A literary device that reveals absolute contrast or contradiction, and often the unexpected. For example, in the story, the father assumes that a chef would know how to slaughter a chicken and, for twenty years, he gives a live bird to the Hongs. Only much later does the son discover the truth.

ASSIGNMENTS

1. Compare this story with Stephen Leacock's "How We Kept Mother's Day" (p. 142). You can examine the irony or the humour.
2. How should immigrants adapt traditions from their new homeland? What makes a tradition important to keep or to discard? Suggest guidelines.
3. Compare this short story with Rosie DiManno's "Growing Up on Grace" (p. 246), a non-fictional account of an immigrant family in Canada. Discuss the common experiences of both narrators. Or contrast the fictional treatment and the non-fictional.
4. Read "Rediscovering Christmas" (p. 346) by Almas Zakiuddin. Write an essay describing the universality of the Christmas celebration with references to Zakiuddin's article and Engkent's story.

The Cowherd

a Chinese folktale, retold by Garry Engkent

Once upon a time there was a poor cowherd. His father died, and he had to work to support himself and his widowed mother. 1

He tended cows several leagues away from his home. Every day, rain or shine, his mother would bring him a hot midday meal. She would travel across the rugged fields, over a bridge where the deep river swiftly flowed, and to the spot under the tree where he would eat. 2

Now this cowherd was a peevish lad. Whenever his mother came early with his lunch, he would scold her for being so early. Whenever she came late, he would beat her with the long switch he used to train wayward calves. Whenever she came on time, he would say how cold or hot his lunch was. 3

This went on for a long time. The cowherd's widowed mother never complained, and bore her pains to herself. 4

One day the heavens opened up, and rain poured all morning. 5

The cowherd took shelter under his favourite tree. By chance, he heard the sound of chirping. He spotted a mother bird feeding her babies. She would fly out into the slashing rain again and again, and bring back food to her hungry brood. 6

Suddenly it dawned on him. This was exactly what his widowed mother was doing for him day in and day out. Remorse engulfed him. 7

That day, he vowed to change his ways. When his mother brought him his meal, he would fall upon her feet and beg forgiveness. He would become a good son. 8

Then in the distance he saw his mother. Almost bent double from the pounding rain, she trudged on, sheltering his lunch. 9

The cowherd cried out, "Mother!" He dashed from his dry shelter into the rain. His arms flailed about as he ran to meet her. 10

As she reached the middle of the bridge, the cowherd's mother saw her son running madly towards her. She could hear his loud voice above the crackling thunder. She could see in his hand the stick. 11

At another time she might have borne it. But today she was tired of another scolding and of another beating. 12

She put his lunch down, and jumped into the swift flowing river. And perished. 13

Date unknown

NOTES

Many Western folktales or fairy tales have changed to suit the tastes of a contemporary audience; however, the Chinese folktale retains its harsh bite. For example, in "Little Red Riding Hood" the original ending, in which the wolf wins, has been changed so that the girl and grandmother are rescued. Chinese folktales lack such sentimentality. Their driving force is to reiterate a basic lesson about life.

Stories translated from one language into another often lose the texture and subtlety of the originals. A translation can never hope to duplicate everything.

COMPREHENSION AND DISCUSSION

1. What makes the cowherd angry?
2. What incident changed him? How? Why?
3. How do you know that this story is not real?
4. How has the storyteller prepared you for the ending?
5. What is the lesson in this folktale?
6. Why do you like or dislike this story?
7. Would this story be as effective if it had a happy ending? Does it need an uplifting conclusion?
8. What is the difference between a folktale and a parable? Are urban legends just updated folktales?

LITERARY TECHNIQUES

A folktale is a story that originates in the oral tradition. Its authorship is unknown as the tale is handed down through the generations. The narrative is simple in construction and contains little detail. Description is kept to a minimum. The starkness of its telling becomes part of its charm and power. Often the purpose is not so much to entertain as it is to give a moral lesson.

Didactic stories Literary works that provide a lesson or instruction. One theory is that all literature has an implicit or explicit lesson to impart. The intent of the author determines whether the didactic quality is strong or mild. Most Chinese tales are didactic.

Like the fairy tale, the folktale is told simply. Note the similarity in the opening: "Once upon a time...," "Once there was...," "There was a...," or "A long time ago..." The setting is stark, and the characters are generically named for universal appeal.

ASSIGNMENTS

1. Retell a favourite folktale or fairy tale in your own words with a specific audience in mind.
2. How does this story compare with Hans Christian Andersen's original "Little Mermaid" or "The Little Match Girl"?
3. Compare the Disney version of "Cinderella" with the version by the Brothers Grimm.
4. Which is more important in storytelling—entertainment value or moral lesson? Write a persuasive paper discussing this question.
5. Read "Sedna, The Witch under the Sea," by Marion Wood (p. 210). How does it compare with this story? What is the difference between a folktale and a myth?
6. Compare the insight and the ending of this story with Morley Callaghan's "All the Years of Her Life" (p. 45).

The Moose and the Sparrow
Hugh Garner

1   From the very beginning Moose Maddon picked on him. The kid was bait for all of Maddon's cruel practical jokes around the camp. He was sent back to the toolhouse for left-handed saws, and down to the office to ask the pay cheater if the day's mail was in, though the rest of us knew it was only flown out every week. *(Spar*

2   The kid's name was Cecil, and Maddon used to mouth it with a simpering mockery, as if it pointed to the kid being something less than a man. I must admit though that the name fitted him, for Cecil was the least likely lumberjack I've seen in over twenty-five years in lumber camps. Though we knew he was intelligent enough, and a man too, if smaller than most of us, we all kidded him, in the good-natured way a bunkhouse gang will. Maddon however always lisped the kid's name as if it belonged to a woman.

3   Moose Maddon was as different from Cecil as it is possible for two human beings to be and still stay within the species. He was a big moose of a man, even for a lumber stiff, with a round flat unshaven face that looked down angrily and dourly at the world. Cecil on the other hand was hardly taller than an axe-handle, and almost as thin. He was about nineteen years old, with the looks of an inquisitive sparrow behind his thick horn-rimmed glasses. He had been sent out to the camp for the summer months by a distant relative who had a connection with the head office down in Vancouver.

4   That summer we were cutting big stuff in an almost inaccessible stand of Douglas fir about fifty miles out of Nanaimo. The logs were catted five miles down to the river where they were bunked waiting for the drive. Cecil had signed on as a whistle punk, but after a few days of snarling the operation with wrong signals at the wrong time and threatening to hang the rigging-slingers in their own chokers, he was transferred to Maddon's gang as a general handyman. Besides going on all the ridiculous and fruitless errands for Moose, he carried the noon grub to the gangs from the panel truck that brought it out from camp, made the tea and took the saws and axes in to old Bobbins, the squint eye, to be sharpened.

5   For the first two weeks after he arrived, the jokes were the usual ones practised on a greenhorn, but when they seemed to be having little or no effect on his bumbling habits and even temper Moose devised more cruel and intricate ones. One night Moose and a cohort of his called Lefevre car-

ried the sleeping Cecil, mattress and all, down to the river and threw him in. The kid almost drowned, but when he had crawled up on shore and regained his breath he merely smiled at his tormentors and ran back to the bunkhouse, where he sat shivering in a blanket on the springs of his bunk till the sun came up.

Another time Moose painted a wide mustache with tar on Cecil's face 6
while he slept. It took him nearly a week to get it all off, and his upper lip was red and sore-looking for longer than that.

Nearly all of us joined in the jokes on Cecil at first, putting a young 7
raccoon in his bunk, kicking over his tea water, hiding his clothes or tying them in knots, all the usual things. It wasn't long though until the other men noticed that Moose Maddon's jokes seemed to have a grim purpose. You could almost say he was carrying out a personal vendetta against the kid for refusing to knuckle under or cry "Uncle." From then on everybody but Moose let the kid alone.

One evening as a few of us sat outside the bunkhouse shooting the 8
guff, Moose said, "Hey, Cecil dear, what do you do over on the mainland?"

"Go to school," Cecil answered. 9

Moose guffawed. "Go to school? At your age!" 10

Cecil just grinned. 11

"What school d'ya go to, Cecil? Kindergarten?" Moose asked him, 12
guffawing some more.

"No." 13

"Well, what school d'ya go to?" 14

"U.B.C." 15

"What's that, a hairdressin' school?" 16

"No, the university." 17

"University! You!" 18

Moose, who was probably a Grade Four dropout himself, was flabber- 19
gasted. I'm sure that up until that minute he'd been living in awe of any-body with a college education.

"What you takin' up?" he asked, his face angry and serious now. 20

"Just an arts course," Cecil said. 21

"You mean paintin' pictures an' things?" 22

"No, not quite," the kid answered. 23

For once Moose had nothing further to say. 24

From then on things became pretty serious as far as Moose and Cecil 25
were concerned. On at least two occasions the other men on the gang had to prevent Moose from beating the boy up, and old Bobbins even went so far as to ask Mr. Semple, the walking boss, to transfer the youngster to

another gang. Since learning that Cecil was a college boy, Moose gave him no peace at all, making him do jobs that would have taxed the strength of any man in the camp, and cursing him out when he was unable to do them, or do them fast enough.

26   The kid may not have been an artist, as Moose had thought, but he could make beautiful things out of wire. Late in the evenings he would sit on his bunk and fashion belt-buckles, rings and tie-clips from a spool of fine copper wire he'd found in the tool shed. He made things for several of the men, always refusing payment for them. He used to say it gave him something to do, since he couldn't afford to join in the poker games.

27   One evening late in the summer as I was walking along the river having an after-supper pipe, I stumbled upon Cecil curled up on a narrow sandy beach.

28   His head was buried in his arms and his shoulders were heaving with sobs. I wanted to turn around without letting him know he'd been seen, but he looked so lonely crying there by himself that I walked over and tapped him on the shoulder.

29   He jumped as if I'd prodded him with a peavey, and swung around, his eyes nearly popping from his head with fright. The six weeks he'd spent working under Moose Maddon hadn't done his nerves any good.

30   "It's all right kid," I said.

31   "Oh! Oh, it's you, Mr. Anderson!"

32   He was the only person in camp who ever called me anything but "Pop."

33   "I don't mean to butt in," I said. "I was just walking along here, and couldn't help seeing you. Are you in trouble?"

34   He wiped his eyes on his sleeve before answering me. Then he turned and stared out across the river.

35   "This is the first time I broke down," he said, wiping his glasses.

36   "Is it Moose?"

37   "Yes."

38   "What's he done to you now?"

39   "Nothing more than he's been doing to me all along. At first I took it — you know that, Mr. Anderson, don't you?"

40   I nodded.

41   "I thought that after I was out here a couple of weeks it would stop," he said. "I expected the jokes that were played on me at first. After all I was pretty green when I arrived here. When they got to know me the other men stopped, but not that — that Moose."

42   He seemed to have a hard time mouthing the other's name.

"When are you going back to school?" I asked him.   43

"In another couple of weeks."   44

"Do you think you can stand it until then?"   45

"I need all the money I can make, but it's going to be tough."   46

I sat down on the sand beside him and asked him to tell me about him-   47
self. For the next ten or fifteen minutes he poured out the story of his life;
he was one of those kids who are kicked around from birth. His mother and
father had split up while he was still a baby, and he'd been brought up in a
series of foster homes. He'd been smart enough, though, to graduate from
high school at seventeen. By a miracle of hard work and self-denial he'd
managed to put himself through the first year of university, and his ambition was to continue on to law school. The money he earned from his
summer work here at the camp was to go towards his next year's tuition.

When he finished we sat in silence for a while. Then he asked, "Tell   48
me, Mr. Anderson, why does Maddon pick on me like he does?"

I thought about his question for a long time before answering it. Finally   49
I said, "I guess that deep down Moose knows you are smarter than he is in
a lot of ways. I guess he's — well, I guess you might say he's jealous of
you."

"No matter what I do, or how hard I try to please him, it's no good."   50

"It never is," I said.   51

"How do you mean?"   52

I had to think even longer this time. "There are some men, like Moose   53
Maddon, who are so twisted inside that they want to take it out on the
world. They feel that most other men have had better breaks than they've
had, and it rankles inside them. They try to get rid of this feeling by
working it out on somebody who's even weaker than they are. Once they
pick on you there's no way of stopping them short of getting out of their
way or beating it out of their hide."

Cecil gave me a wry grin. "I'd never be able to beat it out of the — the   54
Moose's hide."

"Then try to keep out of his way."   55

"I can't for another two weeks," he said. "I'm afraid that before then   56
he'll have really hurt me."

I laughed to reassure him, but I was afraid of the same thing myself. I   57
knew that Moose was capable of going to almost any lengths to prevent
Cecil leaving the camp without knuckling under at least once; his urge
seemed to me to be almost insane. I decided to talk to George Semple
myself in the morning, and have the boy flown out on the next plane.

"I don't think Moose would go as far as to really hurt you," I told him.   58

59   "Yes he would! He would, Mr. Anderson, I know it! I've seen the way he's changed. All he thinks about any more are ways to make me crawl. It's no longer a case of practical jokes; he wants to kill me!"

60   My reassuring laugh stuck in my throat this time. "In another two weeks, son, you'll be back in Vancouver, and all this will seem like a bad dream."

61   "He'll make sure I leave here crippled," Cecil said.

62   We walked back to the camp together, and I managed to calm him down some.

63   The next day I spoke to Semple, the walking boss, and convinced him we should get the boy out of there. There was never any thought of getting rid of Moose, of course. Saw bosses were worth their weight in gold, and the top brass were calling for more and more production all the time. Whatever else Moose was, he was the best production foreman in the camp. When Semple spoke to Cecil, however, the kid refused to leave. He said he'd made up his mind to stick it out until his time was up.

64   Though my gang was working on a different site than Maddon's, I tried to keep my eye on the boy from then on. For a week things went on pretty much as usual, then one suppertime Cecil came into the dining hall without his glasses. Somebody asked him what had happened, and he said there'd been an accident, and that Moose had stepped on them. We all knew how much of an accident it had been; luckily the kid had an old spare pair in his kit. Few of his gang had a good word for Moose any more, which only seemed to make him more determined to take his spite out on the kid.

65   That evening I watched Cecil fashioning a signet ring for one of the men out of wire and a piece of quartz the man had found. The way he braided the thin wire and shaped it around a length of thin sapling was an interesting thing to see. Moose was watching him too, but pretending not to. You could see he hated the idea of Cecil getting along so well with the other men.

66   "I was going to ask you to make me a new watch strap before you left," I said to Cecil. "But it looks like you're running out of wire."

67   The kid looked up. "I still have about twenty-five feet of it left," he said. "That'll be enough for what I have in mind. Don't worry, Mr. Anderson, I'll make you the watch strap before I leave."

68   The next afternoon there was quite a commotion over where Maddon's gang were cutting, but I had to wait until the whistle blew to find out what had happened. Cecil sat down to supper with his right hand heavily bandaged.

69   "What happened?" I asked one of Maddon's men.

"Moose burned the kid's hand," he told me. "He heated the end of a 70
saw blade in the tea fire, and then called the kid to take it to the squint eye
to be sharpened. He handed the hot end to Cecil, and it burned his hand
pretty bad."

"But — didn't any of you — " 71

"None of us was around at the time. When we found out, big Chief 72
went after Moose with a cant hook, but the rest of us held him back. He
would have killed Moose. If Maddon doesn't leave the kid alone, one of us
is going to have to cripple him for sure."

Moose had been lucky that The Chief, a giant Indian called Danny 73
Corbett, hadn't caught him. I made up my mind to have Cecil flown out in
the morning without fail, no matter how much he protested.

That evening the kid turned in early, and we made sure there was 74
always one of us in the bunkhouse to keep him from being bothered by
anybody. He refused to talk about the hand-burning incident at all, but
turned his head to the wall when anybody tried to question him about it.
Moose left shortly after supper to drink and play poker in Camp Three,
about a mile away through the woods.

I woke up during the night to hear a man laughing near the edge of the 75
camp, and Maddon's name being called. I figured it was Moose and
Lefevre coming home drunk from Camp Three, where the bull cook boot-
legged homebrew.

When I got up in the morning, Cecil was already awake and dressed, 76
sitting on the edge of his bunk plaiting a long length of his copper wire,
using his good hand and the ends of the fingers of the one that was burned.

"What are you doing up so early?" I asked him. 77

"I went to bed right after chow last night, so I couldn't sleep once it got 78
light." He pointed to the plaited wire. "This is going to be your watch
strap."

"But you didn't need to make it now, Cecil," I said. "Not with your 79
hand bandaged and everything."

"It's all right, Mr. Anderson," he assured me. "I can manage it okay, 80
and I want to get it done as soon as I can."

Just as the whistle blew after breakfast one of the jacks from Camp 81
Three came running into the clearing shouting that Moose Maddon's body
was lying at the bottom of a deep narrow ravine outside the camp. This
ravine was crossed by means of a fallen log, and Moose must have lost his
footing on it coming home drunk during the night. There was a free fall of
more than forty feet down to a rocky stream bed.

82   None of us were exactly broken-hearted about Moose kicking off that way, but the unexpectedness of it shocked us. We all ran out to the spot, and the boys rigged a sling from draglines and hauled the body to the top of the ravine. I asked Lefevre if he'd been with Moose the night before, but he told me he hadn't gone over to Camp Three. Later in the day the district coroner flew out from Campbell River or somewhere, and after inspecting the log bridge made us rig a handline along it. He made out a certificate of accidental death.

83   When they flew the body out, Cecil stood with the rest of us on the river bank, watching the plane take off. If I'd been in his place I'd probably have been cheering, but he showed no emotion at all, not relief, happiness, or anything else.

84   He worked on my watch strap that evening, and finished it the next day, fastening it to my watch and attaching my old buckle to it. It looked like a real professional job, but when I tried to pay him for it he waved the money aside.

85   It was another week before Cecil packed his things to leave. His hand had begun to heal up nicely, and he was already beginning to lose the nervous twitches he'd had while Moose was living. When he rowed out to the company plane, all the boys from his bunkhouse were on the river bank to see him go. The last we saw of Cecil was his little sparrow smile, and his hand waving to us from the window.

86   One day in the fall I went out to the ravine to see how the handline was making it. It still shocked me to think that Maddon, who had been as sure-footed as a chipmunk, and our best man in a log-rolling contest, had fallen to his death the way he had. Only then did I notice something nobody had looked for before. In the bark of the trunks of two small trees that faced each other diagonally across the fallen log were burn marks that could have been made by wire loops. A length of thin wire rigged from one to the other would have crossed the makeshift footbridge just high enough to catch a running man on the shin, and throw him into the ravine. Maddon could have been running across the log that night, if he'd been goaded by the laughter and taunts of somebody waiting at the other end. I remembered the sound of laughter and the shouting of Maddon's name.

87   I'm not saying that's what happened, you understand, and for all I know nobody was wandering around outside the bunkhouses on the night of Maddon's death, not Cecil or anybody else. Still, it gives me a queer

feeling sometimes, even yet, to look down at my wrist. For all I know I may be the only man in the world wearing the evidence of a murder as a wristwatch strap.

1966

NOTES

Hugh Garner (1913–1979) is a renowned Canadian writer, acclaimed for his short stories.

Logging terminology Garner uses logging jargon to give flavour to the story. Some of the words are outdated. It's not necessary to understand what each term means precisely, but here are some definitions:

Bull cook An assistant cook who tends the stoves and water supply.

Catted Moved on a Caterpillar (cat) trailer.

Choker A short noose of wire rope used for hauling logs.

Pay cheater A person who handles the money in the camp.

Peavey A pointed stick with a hook, used for rolling and handling logs floating in water.

Whistle punk A person who gives whistle signals to lumberjacks to control the operation.

COMPREHENSION AND DISCUSSION

1. Describe Cecil, Moose, and Pop Anderson. Why do their names and nicknames suit them?
2. Why is this story entitled "The Moose and the Sparrow"? What characteristics are suggested in the characters?
3. Why did Moose Maddon bully Cecil? Why didn't he stop? Explain how and why the bullying progressed.
4. How did the rest of the crew feel about the bullying? Why wasn't it stopped by someone in authority?
5. How did Cecil react to the bullying? Should he have behaved differently? Could he have stopped Maddon?

6. Who is the story narrated by? Why is this effective? Why couldn't the story be narrated by one of the two main characters?
7. What did Cecil fear would happen? Do you think he was right?
8. Did Cecil murder Moose? Would it be considered justifiable homicide?
9. What evidence puts in doubt that Cecil could have planned and executed the "death by misadventure" as stated by the local coroner? What evidence says that he did the deed?

LITERARY TECHNIQUES

Jargon Writers sometimes use jargon, technical terms, or vocabulary for a specific profession. This story is peppered with logging jargon that the average reader would be unfamiliar with. It is appropriate because the narrator is a logger. It gives the story some colour.

First-person narration In this story, the first-person point of view comes not from one of the main characters, but from a secondary character, Pop Anderson. He tells the story, and he is involved in the story, but not so directly as to take out the mystery in the plot. Anderson remains objective, and readers can trust his observations. However, because he doesn't know everything, we know only what he tells us. We cannot get into the minds of Cecil and Moose, and that is what Garner wanted.

Inconclusive ending Sometimes the ending to a story is uncertain, much as in real life. Although Pop suspects a murder was committed, he's not sure, and so neither is the reader. Garner leaves throughout the story clues that the reader can use to draw or justify a certain conclusion. This type of ending can frustrate those readers who prefer a neat, clear-cut conclusion to a story, and delight those who want to choose their own ending.

ASSIGNMENTS

1. Read Lawrence Hill's "So What Are You, Anyway?" (p. 100), which is a story about a different kind of bullying. Compare the bullies or the types of bullying.
2. Read the story of David and Goliath (1 Samuel 17:1–58). Compare this biblical story with Garner's.
3. Find some company guidelines or rules on workplace harassment and compare them to what happens in this story.

4. Research the subject of bullying. To limit your scope, classify the kinds of bullying or harassment. For example, you could just write about schoolyard bullying, sexual harassment, or workplace harassment. Write an essay on causes or effects.

5. How is alcohol used as a plot device in this story? Read T. Coraghessan Boyle's "Greasy Lake" (p. 33), Alice Munro's "An Ounce of Cure" (p. 156), David Arnason's "A Girl's Story" (p. 20), and Edgar Allan Poe's "The Cask of Amontillado" (p. 181), and speculate how different the plots would be without alcohol.

The Immaculate Conception Photography Gallery

Katherine Govier

1   Sandro named the little photography shop on St. Clair Avenue West, between Lord's Shoes and Bargain Jimmies, after the parish church in the village where he was born. He had hankered after wider horizons, the rippled brown prairies, the hard-edged mountains. But when he reached Toronto he met necessity in the form of a wife and babies, and, never having seen a western sunset, he settled down in Little Italy. He photographed the brides in their fat lacquered curls and imported lace and their quick babies in christening gowns brought over from home. Blown up to near life size on cardboard cutouts, their pictures filled the windows of his little shop.

2   Sandro had been there ten years already when he first really saw his sign and the window. He stood still in front of it and looked. A particularly buxom bride with a lace bodice and cap sleeves cut in little scallops shimmered in a haze of concupiscence under the sign reading IMMACULATE CONCEPTION PHOTOGRAPHY GALLERY. Sandro was not like his neighbours any more, he was modern, a Canadian. He no longer went to church. As he stared, one of the street drunks shuffled into place beside him. Sandro knew them all, they came into the shop in winter. (No one ought to have to stay outside in that cold, Sandro believed.) But he especially knew Becker. Becker was a smart man; he used to be a philosopher at a university.

3   "Immaculate conception," said Sandro to Becker. "What do you think?"

4   Becker lifted his eyes to the window. He made a squeezing gesture at the breasts. "I never could buy that story," he said.

5   Sandro laughed, but he didn't change the sign that year or the next, and he got to be forty-five and then fifty and it didn't seem worth it. The Immaculate Conception Photography Gallery had a reputation. Business came in from as far away as Rosedale and North Toronto, because Sandro was a magician with a camera. He also had skill with brushes and lights and paint, he reshot his negatives, he lined them with silver, he had tricks even new graduates of photography school couldn't (or wouldn't) copy.

6   Sandro was not proud of his tricks. They began in a gradual way, fixing stray hairs and taking wrinkles out of dresses. He did it once, then twice, then people came in asking for it. Perhaps he'd have gone on this way, with

small lies, but he met with a situation that was larger than most; it would have started a feud in the old country. During a very large and very expensive wedding party, Tony the bridegroom seduced Alicia the bridesmaid in the basketball storage room under the floor of the parish hall. Six months later, Tony confessed, hoping perhaps to be released from his vows. But the parents judged it was too late to dissolve the union: Diora was used, she was no longer a virgin, there was a child coming. Tony was reprimanded, Diora consoled, the mothers became enemies, the newlyweds made up. Only Alicia remained to be dealt with. The offence became hers.

In Italy, community ostracism would have been the punishment of 7 choice. But this was Canada, and if no one acknowledged Alicia on the street, if no one visited her mother, who was heavy on her feet and forced to sit on the sofa protesting her daughter's innocence, if no one invited her father out behind to drink home-made wine, Alicia didn't care. She went off to her job behind the till in a drugstore with her chin thrust out much as before. The in-laws perceived that the young woman could not be subdued by the old methods. This being the case, it was better she did not exist at all.

Which was why Diora's mother turned up at Sandro's counter with the 8 wedding photos. The pain Alicia had caused! she began. Diora's mother's very own miserable wages, saved these eighteen years, had paid for these photographs! She wept. The money was spent, but the joy was spoiled. When she and Diora's father looked at the row of faces flanking the bride and groom there she was — Alicia, the whore! She wiped her tears and made her pitch.

"You can solve our problem, Sandro. I will get a new cake, we will all 9 come to the parish hall. You will take the photographs again. Of course," she added, "we can't pay you again."

Sandro smiled, it was so preposterous. "Even if I could afford to do all 10 that work for nothing, I hate to say it, but Diora's out to here."

"Don't argue with me." 11

"I wouldn't be so bold," said Sandro. "But I will not take the photo- 12 graphs over."

The woman slapped the photographs where they lay on the counter. 13 "You will! I don't care how you do it!" And she left.

Sandro went to the back and put his negatives on the light box. He 14 brought out his magic solution and his razor blades and his brushes. He circled Alicia's head and shoulders in the first row and went to work. He felt a little badly, watching the bright circle of her face fade and swim, darken down to nothing. But how easily she vanished! He filled in the white spot with a bit of velvet curtain trimmed from the side.

15   "I'm like a plastic surgeon," he told his wife. "Take that patch of skin from the inner thigh and put it over the scar on the face. Then sand the edges. Isn't that what they do? Only it isn't a face I'm fixing, it's a memory."

16   His wife stood on two flat feet beside the sink. She shook the carrot she was peeling. "I don't care about Alicia," she said, "but Diora's mother is making a mistake. She is starting them off with a lie in their marriage. And why is she doing it? For her pride! I don't like this, Sandro."

17   "You're missing the point," said Sandro.

18   The next day he had another look at his work. Alicia's shoulders and the bodice of her dress were still there, in front of the chest of the uncle of the bride. He couldn't remove them; it would leave a hole in Uncle. Sandro had nothing to fill the hole, no spare male torsos in black tie. He considered putting a head on top, but whose head? There was no such thing as a free face. A stranger would be questioned, a friend would have an alibi. Perhaps Diora's mother would not notice the black velvet space, as where a tooth had been knocked out, between the smiling faces.

19   Indeed she didn't but kissed his hand fervently and thanked him with tears in her eyes. "Twenty-five thousand that wedding cost me. Twenty-five thousand to get this photograph, and you have rescued it."

20   "Surely you got dinner and a dance, too?" said Sandro.

21   "The wedding was one day. This is forever," said Diora's mother.

22   "I won't do that again," said Sandro, putting the cloth over his head and looking into his camera lens to do a passport photo. In the community the doctored photograph had been examined and re-examined. Alicia's detractors enjoyed the headless shoulders as evidence of a violent punishment. "No, I won't do that again at all," said Sandro to himself, turning aside compliments with a shake of his head. But there was another wedding. After the prosciutto e melone, the veal piccata, the many-tiered cake topped with swans, the father of the bride drew Sandro aside and asked for a set of prints with the groom's parents removed.

23   "My God, why?" said Sandro.

24   "He's a bastard. A bad man."

25   "Shouldn't have let her marry his son, then," said Sandro, pulling a cigarette out of the pack in his pocket. These conversations made him nervous.

26   The father's weathered face was dark, his dinner jacket did not button around his chest. He moaned and ground his lower teeth against his uppers. "You know how they are, these girls in Canada. I am ashamed to say it, but I couldn't stop her."

Sandro said nothing. 27

"Look, I sat here all night long, said nothing, did nothing. I don't 28
wanna look at him for the next twenty years."

Sandro drew in a long tube of smoke. 29

"I paid a bundle for this night. I wanna remember it nice-like." 30

The smoke made Sandro nauseous. He dropped his cigarette and 31
ground it into the floor with his toe, damning his own weakness. "So what
am I going to do with the table?"

The father put out a hand like a tool, narrowed his eyes, and began to 32
saw where the other man sat.

"And leave it dangling, no legs?" 33

"So make new legs." 34

"I'm a photographer, not a carpenter," said Sandro. "I don't make table 35
legs."

"Where you get legs is your problem," said the father. "I'm doing well 36
here. I've got ten guys working for me. You look like you could use some
new equipment."

And what harm was it after all, it was only a photograph, said Sandro 37
to himself. Then, too, there was the technical challenge. Waiting until they
all got up to get their bonbonnière, he took a shot of the head table empty.
Working neatly with his scalpel, he cut the table from this second negative,
removed the in-laws and their chairs from the first one, stuck the empty
table-end onto the table in the first picture, blended over the join neatly,
and printed it. Presto! Only one set of in-laws.

"I don't mind telling you, it gives me a sick feeling," said Sandro to his 38
wife. "I was there. I saw them. We had a conversation. They smiled for me.
Now . . ." He shrugged. "An empty table. Lucky I don't go to church any
more."

"Let the man who paid good money to have you do it confess, not 39
you," she said. "A photograph is a photograph."

"That's what I thought, too," said Sandro. 40

The next morning Sandro went to the Donut House, got himself a take- 41
out coffee and stood on the street beside his window.

"Why do people care about photographs so much?" he asked Becker. 42
Becker had newspaper stuffed in the soles of his shoes. He had on a pair of
stained brown pants tied up at the waist with a paisley necktie. His bottle
was clutched in a paper bag gathered around the neck.

"You can put them on your mantel," said Becker. "They don't talk 43
back."

"Don't people prefer life?" said Sandro. 44

45   "People prefer things," said Becker.

46   "Don't they want their memories to be true?"

47   "No," said Becker.

48   "Another thing. Are we here just to get our photograph taken? Do we have a higher purpose?"

49   Becker pulled one of the newspapers out of his shoe. There were Brian and Mila Mulroney having a gloaty kiss. They were smeared by muddy water and depressed by the joint in the ball of Becker's foot.

50   "I mean real people," said Sandro. "Have we no loyalty to the natural?"

51   "These are existential questions, Sandro," said Becker. "Too many more of them and you'll be out here on the street with the rest of us."

52   Sandro drained the coffee from his cup, pitched it in the bin painted "Keep Toronto Clean" and went back into his gallery. The existential questions nagged. But he did go out and get the motor drive for the camera. In the next few months he eradicated a pregnancy from a wedding photo, added a daughter-in-law who complained of being left out of the Christmas shots, and made a groom taller. Working in the darkroom, he was hit by vertigo. He was on a slide, beginning a descent. He wanted to know what the bottom felt like.

53   After a year of such operations a man from the Beaches came in with a tiny black and white photo of a long-lost brother. He wanted it coloured and fitted into a family shot around a picnic table on Centre Island.

54   "Is this some kind of joke?" said Sandro. It was the only discretion he practised now: he wanted to talk about it before he did it.

55   "No. I'm going to send it to Mother. She thinks Christopher wrote us all off."

56   "Did he?" said Sandro.

57   "Better she should not know."

58   Sandro neglected to ask if Christopher was fat or thin. He ended up taking a medium-sized pair of shoulders from his own cousin and propping them up behind a bush, with Christopher's head on top. Afterward, Sandro lay sleepless in his bed. Suppose that in the next few months Christopher should turn up dead, say, murdered. Then Mother would produce the photograph stamped Immaculate Conception Photography Gallery, 1816 St. Clair Avenue West. Sandro would be implicated. The police might come.

59   "I believe adding people is worse than taking them away," he said to his wife.

60   "You say yes to do it, then you do it. You think it's wrong, you say no."

"Let me try this on you, Becker," said Sandro the next morning. "To   61
take a person out is only half a lie. It proves nothing except that he was not
in that shot. To add a person is a whole lie: it proves that he was there,
when he was not."

"You haven't proven a thing, you're just fooling around with celluloid.   62
Have you got a buck?" said Becker.

"It is better to be a murderer than a creator. I am playing God, out-   63
playing God at His own game." He was smarter than Becker now. He knew
it was the photographs that lasted, not the people. In the end the proof was
in the proof. Though he hadn't prayed in thirty years, Sandro began to pray.
It was like riding a bicycle: he got the hang of it again instantly. "Make me
strong," he prayed, "strong enough to resist the new equipment that I might
buy, strong enough to resist the temptation to expand the gallery, to buy a
house in the suburbs. Make me say no to people who want alterations."

But Sandro's prayers were not answered. When people offered him   64
money to dissolve an errant relative, he said yes. He said yes out of
curiosity. He said yes out of a desire to test his skills. He said yes out of
greed. He said yes out of compassion. "What is the cost of a little happiness?" he said. "Perhaps God doesn't count photographs. After all, they're
not one of a kind."

Sandro began to be haunted, in slow moments behind the counter in the   65
Immaculate Conception, by the faces of those whose presence he had tam-
pered with. He kept a file — Alicia the lusty bridesmaid, Antonia and
Marco, the undesired in-laws. Their heads, their shoes and their hands,
removed from the scene with surgical precision, he saved for the moment
when, God willing, a forgiving relative would ask him to replace them. But
the day did not come. Sandro was not happy.

"Becker," he said, for he had a habit now of buying Becker a coffee   66
first thing in the morning and standing out if it was warm, or in if it was
cold, for a chat. "Becker, let's say it's a good service I'm doing. It makes
people happy, even if it tells lies."

"Sandro," said Becker, who enjoyed his coffee, "these photographs,   67
doctored by request of the subjects, reflect back the lives they wish to have.
The unpleasant bits were removed, the wishes are added. If you didn't do
it, someone else would. Memory would. It's a service."

"It's also money," said Sandro. He found Becker too eager to make   68
excuses now. He liked him better before.

"You're like Tintoretto, painting in his patron, softening his greedy   69
profile, lifting the chin of his fat wife. It pays for the part that's true art."

70   "Which part is that?" said Sandro, but Becker didn't answer. He was
still standing there when Diora came in. She'd matured, she'd gained
weight, and her twins, now six years old, were handsome and strong.
Sandro's heart flew up in his breast. Perhaps she had made friends with
Alicia, perhaps Diora had come to have her bridesmaid re-instated.

71   "The long nightmare is over," said Diora. "I've left him."

72   The boys were running from shelf to shelf lifting up the photographs
with their glass frames and putting them down again. Sandro watched them
with one eye. He knew what she was going to say.

73   "I want you to take him out of those pictures," she said.

74   "You'd look very foolish as a bride with no groom," he said severely.

75   "No, no, not those," she said. "I mean the kids' birthday shots."

76   They had been particularly fine, those shots, taken only two weeks
ago, Tony tall and dark, Diora and the children radiant and blond.

77   "Be reasonable, Diora," he said. "I never liked him myself. But he balances the portrait. Besides, he was there."

78   "He was not there!" cried Diora. Her sons went on turning all the pictures to face the walls. "He was never there. He was running around, in his
heart he was not with me. I was alone with my children."

79   "I'll take another one," said Sandro. "Of you and the boys. Whenever
you like. This one stays like it is."

80   "We won't pay."

81   "But Diora," said Sandro, "everyone knows he's their father."

82   "They have no father," said Diora flatly.

83   "It's immaculate conception," said Becker gleefully.

84   But Diora did not hear. "It's our photograph, and we want him out. You
do your job. The rest of it's none of your business." She put one hand on
the back of the head of each of her twins and marched them out the door.

85   Sandro leaned on his counter idly flipping the pages of a wedding
album. He had a vision of a great decorated room with a cake on the table.
Everyone had had his way, the husband had removed the wife, the wife the
husband, the bridesmaid her parents, and so forth. There was no one there.

86   "We make up our lives out of the people around us," he said to Becker.
"When they don't live up to standard, we can't just wipe them out."

87   "Don't ask me," said Becker. "I just lit out for the streets. Couldn't live
up to a damn thing." Then he, too, went out the door.

88   "Lucky bugger," said Sandro.

89   Alone, he went to his darkroom. He opened the drawer of bits and
pieces. His disappeared ones, the inconvenient people. His body parts, his
halves of torsos, tips of shiny black shoes. Each face, each item of clothing

punctured him a little. He looked at his negatives stored in drawers. They were scarred, pathetic things. I haven't the stomach for it, not any more, thought Sandro.

As he walked home, St. Clair Avenue seemed very fine. The best part was, he thought, there were no relationships. Neither this leaning drunk nor that window-shopper was so connected to any other as to endanger his or her existence. The tolerance of indifference, said Sandro to himself, trying to remember it so that he could tell Becker.

But Sandro felt ill at ease in his own home, by its very definition a dangerous and unreliable setting. His wife was stirring something, with her lips tight together. His children, almost grown up now, bred secrets as they looked at television. He himself only posed in the doorway, looking for hidden seams and the faint hair-lines of an airbrush.

That night he stood exhausted by his bed. His wife lay on her side with one round shoulder above the sheet. Behind her on the wall was the photo he'd taken of their village before he left Italy. He ought to reshoot it, take out that gas station and clean up the square a little. His pillow had an indentation, as if a head had been erased. He slept in a chair.

In the morning he went down to the shop. He got his best camera and set up a tripod on the sidewalk directly across the street. He took several shots in the solid bright morning light. He locked the door and placed the CLOSED sign in the window. In the darkroom he developed the film, floating the negatives in the pungent fluid until the row of shop fronts came through clearly, the flat brick faces, the curving concrete trim, the two balls on the crowns. Deftly he dissolved each brick of his store, the window and the sign. Deftly he reattached each brick of the store on the west side to the bricks of the store to the east.

I have been many things in my life, thought Sandro, a presser of shutters, a confessor, a false prophet. Now I am a bricklayer, and a good one. He taped the negatives together and developed them. He touched up the join and then photographed it again. He developed this second negative and it was perfect. Number 1812, Lord's Shoes, joined directly to 1820, Bargain Jimmies: the Immaculate Conception Photography Gallery at 1816 no longer existed. Working quickly, because he wanted to finish before the day was over, he blew it up to two feet by three feet. He cleared out his window display of brides and babies and stood up this new photograph — one of the finest he'd ever taken, he thought. Then he took a couple of cameras and a bag with the tripod and some lenses. He turned out the light, pulling the door shut behind him, and began to walk west.

1988

NOTES

In addition to writing fiction, Katherine Govier has published anthologies of travel writing. This story won the CBC Literary Contest for short fiction.

In Christian belief, the Immaculate Conception refers to Mary, the mother of Jesus. According to religious dogma, she was born without original sin. (Some people erroneously believe that the reference is to Jesus's birth.) Becker, Sandro's mentor and friend, uses this term mockingly (paragraph 83). Note also the irony in the title of this story.

Prosciutto e melone   Italian ham with melon, a traditional appetizer.

Bonbonnière   Sugared almond wrapped in netting, given as wedding favours.

Brian and Mila Mulroney   Brian Mulroney was the prime minister of Canada (1984 – 1993); his wife is Mila. Sandro dismisses them as not being "real people" (paragraph 50).

Tintoretto   (1518 – 1594) An Italian painter of the mannerist style. The suggestion here is that Tintoretto deliberately falsified his portraits of his wealthy patrons, as Sandro does with his photographs.

COMPREHENSION AND DISCUSSION

1. How old is Sandro? How long has he had the store when the story begins? Why is his Italian heritage important to the story?
2. Why did the community want to punish Alicia? What do you think of the way she was treated? Was it fair?
3. What is Becker's role in this story?
4. Why does Sandro doctor the photographs despite his objections?
5. What finally makes Sandro quit his profession? Why does he tamper with his last photograph in which he removes his own place of business?
6. Explain this statement that Sandro makes: "It is better to be a murderer than a creator. I am playing God, outplaying God at His own game" (paragraph 63).
7. Explain the religious subtext in this story. In short, why are the store and the story called "The Immaculate Conception Photography Gallery"? What purpose is served by religious references such as Lord's Shoes?
8. Explain the comments on human relationships in this story. Are they too cynical?

LITERARY TECHNIQUES

Confidant Usually, a secondary character to whom the protagonist reveals inner thoughts and confidences. Sandro pitches his questions to Becker, who gives back philosophical answers.

Foil A contrasting character who helps show up opposite traits or actions of the main character. Again, Becker is a foil to Sandro and to other affluent people in Canadian society.

Ironic juxtapositioning Irony is the sense of contrast or contradiction, and juxtapositioning is the deliberate placing of ideas, scenes, and such to create an effect. Govier subtly employs this device by having Sandro's shop sandwiched between Lord's Shoes and Bargain Jimmies. The focus of attention is on the two words and ideas "Lord" and "Bargain." Throughout the story, Sandro is forever caught between taking wedding pictures ("Lord" because of the sanctity of marriage) and removing people from the originals as requested by family members ("Bargain" because of Sandro's complicity and the fact that they try to negotiate a lower fee).

ASSIGNMENTS

1. Computers have made it much easier to change photographs. Write an essay on the repercussions or ethics of digital photography. You could write about the use of photographs as evidence in a criminal trial. Or, you could detail guidelines to be used in the media and advertising for altering such images. For example, is it ethical to alter a view of scenery in order to create a more picturesque image for a travel brochure?
2. Can memory be as easily altered as Sandro's photographs? (If you can no longer trust a photograph, can you still trust your memory?)
3. Why do people take photographs or have their picture taken? What does a photograph represent?
4. With cellphones that take and send pictures, is photography becoming less of an art?
5. Read Margaret Wente's "If We're So Rich, Why Aren't We Happy?" (p. 342). Compare Wente's article and this story on the concept of happiness.

Stolen Chocolates

Ursula Hegi

1   My first love has tripled in size. I didn't recognize him, though I noticed him when he entered the Greek restaurant, because the waiter replaced his armchair with a piano bench before he let him sit down. He was with a woman who wore apple-green silk and was heavy too, though not nearly his weight.

2   "Vera," he called out across the restaurant, and hoisted himself from the piano bench. His bulk drifted toward me as if carried by the scent of the exotic spices, surprisingly agile, fleshy hands leading.

3   I glanced behind me, searching for an escape or some other woman named Vera, though I know it's not a common name. All through school, I was the only Vera in my class.

4   "Vera, sweetie, it's me — Eddie," he said as if accustomed to identifying himself to people he hadn't seen in a long time. His suit looked expensive, made to order, and in the amber flow of the fringed ceiling lamps, his hair was blond and curly as ever.

5   "Eddie," I said, trying to reconcile this man with the image of the wiry boy I'd followed around the neighborhood at fourteen. I would wait at the end of his street for hours, heart pounding, just to get a glimpse of him, and when he finally started noticing me, he blotted all the questions and uncertainties I'd felt up to that day about my future. Whenever he helped me with my chores in my grandparents' grocery store, I rewarded him with stolen chocolates that we ate until we both felt as though we were about to explode.

6   "We will always be together," we said the afternoon he kissed me. "We will always be together," we promised each other in our letters for nearly half a year after his family moved to Cleveland.

7   "You look good, Vera. Real good." The voice was the same, though the fat had changed his features and stretched his skin so tightly there wasn't space for a single wrinkle. "How long has it been?"

8   "Almost thirty years, Eddie."

9   "How's the food here?"

10   I felt ill at the thought of him squeezing anything else into that body. "I sold them the restaurant."

11   "It was yours?"

12   "No, no. I'm selling real estate now. The new owner, Mr. Fariopoulos, gave me a bonus — two hundred dollars' worth of meals."

"I hear their buffet is famous. All you can eat for twelve ninety-five."   13

"I usually just order a vegetarian dish."   14

"My first wife died seven years ago." He said it as if her death had   15
been the result of being a vegetarian. He motioned to his table. "Bonnie
over there — we got married the year after."

"Sorry about your first wife. And congratulations on—"   16

"I don't like weddings."   17

"Okay."   18

"But that's what we're in Albany for. Another wedding. My cousin's   19
boy. Come, sit with us."

I hesitated.   20

"You're probably waiting for someone."   21

"Not really."   22

"No argument, then." One hand on my elbow, the other balancing my   23
plate and wineglass, he led me toward his table like a trophy, his hips
brushing dangerously close to other tables.

Certain that everyone was staring at us, I felt ashamed of my embar-   24
rassment to be seen with him.

He introduced me to his wife, Bonnie. "This is Vera." He beamed.   25
"You know, the Vera of my youth." He made me sound mysterious and
glamorous, and I wondered what he'd told his wife about me.

She tucked her handbag under her arm and greeted me with the cau-   26
tious smile of heavy women who don't trust thin women. Her face had the
natural look you can only achieve with skilful makeup.

Eddie sat down, his knees spread to accommodate his enormous   27
thighs. "My cousin says you married a dentist."

"That was finished a long time ago."   28

"Sorry to hear that."   29

"Don't. I was ready."   30

"Any kids?"   31

"A daughter. She's at the University of New Hampshire."   32

"Good for you. Bonnie and I, we have our own pharmacy. In a mall.   33
She handles the cosmetics and over-the-counter stuff, I get to count the
pills." He laughed. "Amazing . . . Remember how I used to hate math?" He
leaned over to his wife, one hand across his tie to keep it from falling into
my glass. "Vera let me copy her homework."

"And you helped me in the store."   34

But he didn't hear me. He was frowning at my plate of eggplant and   35
rice. "I think I'll go for the buffet, Bonnie."

"Me too."   36

37   His enormous backside blocked out half the buffet table as he loaded up his plate. Oh, Eddie, I thought, Eddie, unable to continue my meal as I watched him eat silently, shoveling his food into his mouth at an alarming speed, giving shape to my deepest fears. To think I used to eat like that as a girl. To think I sometimes still longed to eat like that.

38   "How long are you staying in Albany, Eddie?" I asked, wishing he hadn't come back at all.

39   "Hold that question, Vera. I'll be right back." His breath had taken on the rich aroma of the food. Pushing the piano bench back, he headed for the buffet.

40   Bonnie only kept up with him for three trips, and then she sank into her chair, tiny beads of moisture between her perfect eyebrows; but Eddie kept returning for more, and with each bite he swallowed, I felt my stomach distend, harden.

41   It was on Eddie's fifth approach to the buffet that the owner of the restaurant, Mr. Fariopoulos, stepped into his way. He was nearly a head shorter than Eddie, and he raised one lean hand and held it up in front of Eddie's chest to stop him. Without lowering his voice, he informed Eddie that he had eaten enough. "More than enough," Mr. Fariopoulos said.

42   His face purple-red, Eddie stood there like a boy caught stealing chocolates, and I felt his humiliation as though it were my own. Nearly everyone in the restaurant was watching him, except Bonnie, who was staring at the white tablecloth, her face rigid. Eddie opened his mouth — not to say something, but to breathe easier. He did not move — neither toward the buffet nor toward our table.

43   I had no idea what I was about to say when I got up and walked toward Eddie and Mr. Fariopoulos. My stomach was aching as if I'd eaten far too much, and my heart was beating as fiercely as all those time I'd waited for Eddie to appear in the door of his house.

44   I linked my arm through his and gave a nod to Mr. Fariopoulos. "I'm glad you've had a chance to meet my friend, Eddie."

45   "Vera —" Mr. Fariopoulos started.

46   "The menu," I asked, "what do you have printed next to the word 'buffet'? Is it 'all you can eat'? Or 'all we let you eat'?"

47   "You and your friends are always welcome here."

48   "All we let you eat?"

49   "All you can eat. You know that. But we can't afford to keep this place open if everyone eats like him."

50   "Then I'll be glad to put it back on the market for you."

51   "Vera," Eddie said, "you don't have to —"

"But I do," I said, and turned to Mr. Fariopoulos. "Tell me" — now I was going — "how many of your customers stop after the first trip to the buffet? Do you give them a discount? A doggie bag?" 52

It ended up with Mr. Fariopoulos apologizing to Eddie and telling him there would be no bill at all. In the parking lot, Eddie was rather quiet, and his hands felt cold when I grasped them to say goodbye, but Bonnie told me to visit them if I ever got to Cleveland. What I didn't expect was the dream I had that night, a wonderfully erotic dream about Eddie — not the way he used to look as a boy, when I'd suffered that first, glorious crush on him, but the way he was now. He drew me into his huge embrace, sheltered me against his solid chest. We were lying in the meadow behind my grandparents' store, and spread in front of us were all the pastries and cakes I had ever denied myself. We ate together — passionately, joyfully — letting each other taste the most satisfying delicacies without remorse. Eddie's breath was sweet as he consumed me with his hungry mouth, replenished me with his hungry mouth. My arms were long enough to reach around him. His body felt light as he enveloped me into his soft vastness, so light that he took us all the way up to the sky. 53

2001

NOTES

Ursula Hegi was born and raised in Germany and now lives in the United States.

Food has always been a useful metaphor in storytelling. It suggests the quality of consumption — the desire to eat up, to possess, to dominate, to satisfy the appetites whatever they may be.

COMPREHENSION AND DISCUSSION

1. What is the setting, and why is it important to the story?
2. What was Vera's first reaction to seeing Eddie, and why did she change her attitude?
3. What evidence is there in the story that shows Vera is thin? Why is this trait important?
4. Explain why the author gives details about Vera and Eddie's past.
5. Do the present occupations of Vera, Bonnie, and Eddie have anything to do with the story? Explain.

6. How effective is the first sentence? Did it catch your attention?
7. Using a baby-name book, look up the meanings of Vera, Bonnie, and Eddie. Do the names have relevance to the story?
8. Why does Vera feel she needs to defend Eddie even though she disapproves of his eating habits?
9. Does the restaurateur have the right to stop Eddie from taking more food? How do you know that this incident with Eddie and the buffet has happened before?
10. Why do people prefer buffets or smorgasbords? Why do some restaurants offer this array of foods in an "all you can eat" offering?
11. Is denial and self-sacrifice better than letting go and gorging — whether it be food or some other temptation?
12. Why is the story entitled "Stolen Chocolates"? What do these two words suggest, individually and collectively?
13. At the end, Vera admits to having an erotic fantasy about Eddie. What do sex and food have in common?
14. Explain the ending of this story.

LITERARY TECHNIQUES

Metaphor A metaphor is a comparison to another object or sometimes to an abstraction. It draws on similarities, and only selective similarities, so that the reader can see a connection between the two things. For example, "He is a lion among men" attributes the qualities of a lion — majestic, respected, powerful, ferocious, fearless — to the person. Second, a metaphor can be used as a one-time parallel, or it can be extended to cover the entire passage or story. In "Stolen Chocolates," eating abundantly becomes a metaphor for indulging in life's pleasures, whereas dieting becomes a metaphor for denial of living one's life to its fullest.

Flashback A flashback is a literary technique in which the writer stops the flow of the plot to give the reader some past event important to the present situation. Some flashbacks are long and involved; others are brief. In this story, the writer establishes the relationship between Eddie and Vera, and prepares the reader both for Vera's defence of Eddie at the food bar and for her fantasy at the end.

ASSIGNMENTS

1. Sexism and racism are socially unacceptable. Discrimination and prejudice against overweight people still runs rampant, however. Is this discrimination justified? What is fuelling it?
2. Explore various diet fads and advice.
3. Explore the medical problems of anorexia nervosa and bulimia. Why are these illnesses more prevalent in the West than in other parts of the world?
4. Read "The Patterns of Eating" by Peter Farb and George Armelagos (p. 254). Is the smorgasbord or buffet an extension of current dining habits?

So What Are You, Anyway?

Lawrence Hill

1   Carole settles in Seat 12A, beside the window, puts her doll on a vacant seat and snaps open her purse. She holds up a mirror. She looks into her own dark eyes. She examines her handful of freckles, which are tiny ink spots dotting her cheeks. She checks for pimples, but finds none. Only the clear complexion that her father sometimes calls "milk milk milk milk chocolate" as he burrows into her neck with kisses.

2   "This is yours, I believe." A big man with a sunburnt face is holding her doll upside down.

3   "May I have her, please?" Carole says.

4   He turns the doll right side up. "A black doll! I never saw such a thing!"

5   "Her name's Amy. May I have her, please?"

6   "Henry Norton!" cries the man's wife. "Give that doll back this instant!"

7   Carole tucks the doll close to the window.

8   The man sits beside Carole. The woman takes the aisle seat.

9   "Don't mind him," the woman says, leaning towards Carole. "By the way, I'm Betty Norton, and he's my husband, Henry."

10   The man next to Carole hogs the armrest. His feet sprawl onto her side. And he keeps looking at her.

11   The stewardess passes by, checking seat belts. "Everything okay?"

12   "May I go to the bathroom?" Carole asks.

13   "Do you think you could wait? We're about to take off."

14   "Okay."

15   Carole looks out the window, sees the Toronto airport buildings fall behind and wonders if her parents are watching. Say goodbye, she instructs Amy, waving the doll's hand, say goodbye to Mom and Dad. The engines charge to life. Her seat hums. They taxi down the runway. She feels a hollowness in her stomach when they lift into the air. Her ears plug and stay that way until the plane levels out over pillows of cotton. They burn as bright as the sun. So that is what the other side of clouds look like!

16   "Excuse me. *Excuse me!*" The man is talking to her. "You can go to the bathroom now, you know."

17   "No, that's all right," Carole says.

18   "Travelling all alone, are you?"

19   Carole swallows with difficulty.

"Where do you live?" he asks.   20

"Don Mills."   21

"Oh, really?" he says. "Were you born there?"   22

"Yes."   23

"And your parents?"   24

"My mother was born in Chicago and my father was born in Tucson."   25

"And you're going to visit your grandparents?"   26

She nods.   27

"And you parents let you travel alone!"   28

"It's only an airplane! And I'm a big girl."   29

The man lowers the back of his seat, chuckling. He whispers to his   30
wife. "No!" Carole hears her whisper back, "*You* ask her!"

Carole yawns, holds Amy's hand and goes to sleep. The clinking of sil-   31
verware wakens her, but she hears the man and woman talking about her,
so she keeps her eyes shut.

"I don't know, Henry," says the woman. "Don't ask me. Ask *her*."   32

"I'm kind of curious," he says. "Aren't you?"   33

Carole can't make out the woman's answer. But then she hears her say: 34

"I just can't see it. It's not fair to children. I don't mind them mixed,   35
but the world isn't ready for it. They're neither one thing nor the other.
Henry, wake that child and see if she wants to eat."

When the man taps her shoulder, Carole opens her eyes. "I have to go   36
to the bathroom," she says.

"But they're going to serve the meal," the man says.   37

"Henry! If she wants out, let her out. She's only a child."   38

Carole grimaces. She is definitely not a child. She is a young lady! She   39
can identify Drambuie, Kahlua, and Grand Marnier by smell!

Once in the aisle, Carole realizes she has forgotten Amy.   40

Henry Norton hands her the doll. "There you go. And don't fall out of   41
the plane, now. There's a big hole down by the toilet."

"There is not!" Carole says. "There isn't any such thing!" She heads   42
down the aisle with an eye out just in case there is a hole, after all.

Coming out of the toilet, Carole finds the stewardess. "Excuse me,   43
miss. Could I sit somewhere else?"

The woman frowns. "Why?"   44

"I don't like the window."   45

"Is that it? Is that the only reason?"   46

"Well . . . yes."   47

"I'm sorry, but we don't have time to move you now. We're serving a   48
meal. Ask me later, if you like."

49   After Carole had eaten and had her tray taken and been served a hot face towel, the man says: "What are you, anyway? My wife and I were wondering."

50   Carole blinks, sees the man's clear blue eyes and drops her head.

51   "What do you mean?" she says.

52   "You know, what are you? What race?"

53   Carole's mouth drops. Race? What is that? She doesn't understand. Yet she senses that the man is asking a bad question. It is as if he is asking her something dirty, or touching her in a bad place. She wishes her Mom and Dad were there. They could tell her what "race" meant.

54   "That doll of yours is black," Henry Norton says. "That's a Negro doll. That's race. Negro. What's your race?"

55   The question still confuses her.

56   "Put it this way," the man says. "What is your father?"

57   The question baffles her. What is her father? He is her Dad! He is her Dad and every Sunday morning he makes pancakes for the whole family and lets Carole pour hot syrup on them and afterwards he sits her on his lap and tells stories.

58   Mrs. Norton leans towards Carole. "Say you had a colouring book. What colour would you make your Dad?"

59   "I never use just one colour."

60   "Okay. What colour would you make his face?"

61   "Brown."

62   "And your mother?"

63   Carole imagines a blank page. What would she put in her mother's face? She has to put something in there. She can't just leave it blank. "I don't know."

64   "Sure you do," Mrs. Norton says. "How would you colour your mother's face?"

65   "Yellow."

66   Carole sees Mr. and Mrs. Norton look at each other.

67   "Is your mother Chinese?" Mrs. Norton asks.

68   "No."

69   "Are you sure you'd colour her yellow?"

70   "No."

71   "What else might you colour her?"

72   What else? Carole feels ashamed at her stupidity. A tear races down her cheek. "Red," she says, finally.

73   "Red! You can't colour a face red! Is your mother white? Is she like me? Her face! Is it the same colour as mine?"

"Yes."   74

"And your father's brown?"   75

Carole nods.   76

"When you say brown, do you mean he is a Negro?"   77

"Yes." Of course her father is a Negro. If Mrs. Norton wanted to know   78
all along if her Dad was a Negro, why didn't she just ask?

"So you're mixed?" Mrs. Norton says. "You're a mulatto!"   79

Carole's lip quivers. What is mulatto? Why do they keep asking her   80
what she is? She isn't anything!

"So is that it? You're a mulatto? You know what a mulatto is, don't   81
you? Haven't your parents taught you that word?"

Approaching with a cart of juice, the stewardess looks up and smiles   82
at Carole. That gives her a rush of courage.

"Leave me alone!" she screams at Mrs. Norton.   83

Passengers stare. The stewardess spills a drink. Mrs. Norton sits back   84
hard in her seat, her hands raised, fingers spread. Carole sees people
watching.

"Why do you keep asking me if my Dad is Negro? Yes, he's a Negro!   85
Okay? okay? Negro Negro Negro!"

"Calm down," Mrs. Norton says, reaching over.   86

"Don't touch her," the stewardess says.   87

"Who are these people?" someone says from across the aisle.   88
"Imagine, talking to a child like that, and in 1970!"

One woman sitting in front of Carole stands up and turns around.   89

"Would you like to come and sit with me, little girl?"   90

"No!" Carole shouts. "I don't like all these questions. She keeps asking 91
me how I would colour my parents in a colouring book! Why do you keep
asking me that?"

Mrs. Norton pleads with Carole to stop.   92

"How would you like it if that happened to you?" Carole says. "So   93
what are you, anyway? What are your parents? How would you colour
them? Well, I don't care! I don't even care!"

"How would you like to come and sit with me?" the stewardess says,   94
smiling. "I'll make you a special drink. Have you ever had a Shirley Temple?"

Carole nods enthusiastically. Already she feels better. Clutching Amy,   95
she passes by the Nortons, who swing their legs to let her out.

"My God," Carole hears Mrs. Norton tell her husband, "talk about   96
sensitive."

1992

NOTES

Lawrence Hill writes primarily about the African-Canadian experience. His personal story is told in *Black Berry, Sweet Juice: On Being Black and White in Canada* (2001).

Don Mills A suburb of Toronto.

Negro A term that was once considered a euphemism and is now considered a racial slur. Accepted terms have changed from "coloured," to "Negro," to "black," to "Afro-American."

Shirley Temple A non-alcoholic drink served in a cocktail glass, named after a child actress.

COMPREHENSION AND DISCUSSION

1. How old do you think Carole is? How does the writer provide you with this information?
2. Who are the Nortons? Describe them.
3. How do you know the Nortons are imposing on Carole? Why do they persist on asking her personal questions when they realize she is uncomfortable talking to them?
4. Are the Nortons racist, just curious, or adult bullies?
5. Explain Mrs. Norton's statement: "It's not fair to children. I don't mind them mixed, but the world isn't ready for it. They're neither one thing nor the other" (paragraph 35).
6. What is proper etiquette in such encounters? How would you have handled the situation? What do you think Carole should have done?
7. Explain how Hill sets up the situation. How does he lead up to the Nortons' questioning?
8. Why does Hill set the story in 1970? Have racial attitudes changed in the last thirty years? Do you think racially mixed children are more accepted now?

LITERARY TECHNIQUES

Point of view The story is told in third person; however, the focus stays on Carole, not the Nortons. Throughout the story, then, Hill maintains the child's point of view. Her innocence and vulnerability are like an island surrounded by adults. Thus, the reader is able to sense that the couple are intruders into Carole's life and privacy.

Present tense The writer uses the present tense rather than the simple past. This technique simulates immediacy as if the action is happening now and the reader is right there with Carole and the Nortons.

Foreshadowing An arrangement of clues to prepare for later action or events. An author who uses this technique plays fair with readers by enabling them to anticipate the outcome. For example, Hill informs the reader about Carole's racial heritage when he refers to her complexion as "milk chocolate" in the opening paragraph (paragraph 1). He also reveals Henry Norton's character by describing him as red-faced ("sunburnt") to suggest "redneck" or bigot, and by having him hold the doll upside down (paragraph 2).

Dialogue Much of the story is carried by dialogue rather than by description and extended narration. In general, dialogue gives the story a rapid movement because the speeches of the characters are usually kept short. Second, it shows character traits: how a person says something defines that person. In this case, Carole sounds like a small, vulnerable young child in the way she responds to the Nortons. Third, dialogue draws readers into the story as if we were overhearing a conversation.

ASSIGNMENTS

1. What questions do you consider improper to ask a stranger? Explain why.
2. Define the following words: racism, bigotry, discrimination, prejudice, stereotype. First use the dictionary meanings; then add your own in the form of observation, anecdote, or feelings.
3. Can anyone ever be totally free of prejudice? Can a society be free of discrimination? What are some causes of racial prejudice?
4. Compare Carole to Piquette in Margaret Laurence's "The Loons" (p. 130). How do they handle their respective problems with a prejudiced society? How are their situations similar?

5. While talking about breeding in animals is acceptable, it is a controversial subject when applied to human beings. Eugenics (the study of controlled breeding in the human race to improve certain hereditary traits), for example, is associated with the Nazis and with forced sterilization. Some people argue for racial purity, while others say that mixing races is an important step to eliminating prejudice. Research one of the issues associated with this topic, and write an explanation of the controversy.

The Lottery
Shirley Jackson

The morning of June 27th was clear and sunny, with the fresh warmth of a full-summer day; the flowers were blossoming profusely and the grass was richly green. The people of the village began to gather in the square, between the post office and the bank, around ten o'clock; in some towns there were so many people that the lottery took two days and had to be started on June 26th, but in this village, where there were only about three hundred people, the whole lottery took less than two hours, so it could begin at ten o'clock in the morning and still be through in time to allow the villagers to get home for noon dinner. 1

The children assembled first, of course. School was recently over for the summer, and the feeling of liberty sat uneasily on most of them; they tended to gather together quietly for a while before they broke into bois-terous play, and their talk was still of the classroom and the teacher, of books and reprimands. Bobby Martin had already stuffed his pockets full of stones, and the other boys soon followed his example, selecting the smoothest and roundest stones; Bobby and Harry Jones and Dickie Delacroix — the villagers pronounced this name "Dellacroy" — eventually made a great pile of stones in one corner of the square and guarded it against the raids of the other boys. The girls stood aside, talking among themselves, looking over their shoulders at the boys, and the very small children rolled in the dust or clung to the hands of their older brothers or sisters. 2

Soon the men began to gather, surveying their own children, speaking of planting and rain, tractors and taxes. They stood together, away from the pile of stones in the corner, and their jokes were quiet and they smiled rather than laughed. The women, wearing faded house dresses and sweaters, came shortly after their menfolk. They greeted one another and exchanged bits of gossip as they went to join their husbands. Soon the women, standing by their husbands, began to call to their children, and the children came reluctantly, having to be called four or five times. Bobby Martin ducked under his mother's grasping hand and ran, laughing, back to the pile of stones. His father spoke up sharply, and Bobby came quickly and took his place between his father and his oldest brother. 3

The lottery was conducted — as were the square dances, the teen club, the Halloween program — by Mr. Summers, who had time and energy to devote to civic activities. He was a round-faced, jovial man and he ran the 4 coal business, and people were sorry for him, because he had no children and his wife was a scold. When he arrived in the square, carrying the black wooden box, there was a murmur of conversation among the villagers, and he waved and called, "Little late today, folks." The postmaster, Mr. Graves, followed him, carrying a three-legged stool, and the stool was put in the centre of the square and Mr. Summers set the black box down on it. The villagers kept their distance, leaving a space between themselves and the stool, and when Mr. Summers said, "Some of you fellows want to give me a hand?" there was a hesitation before two men, Mr. Martin and his oldest son, Baxter, came forward to hold the box steady on the stool while Mr. Summers stirred up the papers inside it.

5   The original paraphernalia for the lottery had been lost long ago, and the black box now resting on the stool had been put into use even before Old Man Warner, the oldest man in town, was born. Mr. Summers spoke frequently to the villagers about making a new box, but no one liked to upset even as much tradition as was represented by the black box. There was a story that the present box had been made with some pieces of the box that had preceded it, the one that had been constructed when the first people settled down to make a village here. Every year, after the lottery, Mr. Summers began talking again about a new box, but every year the subject was allowed to fade off without anything's being done. The black box grew shabbier each year; by now it was no longer completely black but splintered badly along one side to show the original wood colour, and in some places faded or stained.

6   Mr. Martin and his oldest son, Baxter, held the black box securely on the stool until Mr. Summers had stirred the papers thoroughly with his hand. Because so much of the ritual had been forgotten or discarded, Mr. Summers had been successful in having slips of paper substituted for the chips of wood that had been used for generations. Chips of wood, Mr. Summers had argued, had been all very well when the village was tiny, but now that the population was more than three hundred and likely to keep on growing, it was necessary to use something that would fit more easily into the black box. The night before the lottery, Mr. Summers and Mr. Graves made up the slips of paper and put them in the box, and it was then taken to the safe of Mr. Summers' coal company and locked up until Mr. Summers was ready to take it to the square next morning. The rest of the year, the box was put way, sometimes one place, sometimes another; it had spent one year in Mr. Graves's barn and another year underfoot in the post office, and sometimes it was set on a shelf in the Martin grocery and left there.

There was a great deal of fussing to be done before Mr. Summers   7
declared the lottery open. There were the lists to make up—of heads of
families, heads of households in each family, members of each household
in each family. There was the proper swearing-in of Mr. Summers by the
postmaster, as the official of the lottery; at one time, some people remembered, there had been a recital of some sort, performed by the official of the
lottery, a perfunctory, tuneless chant that had been rattled off duly each
year; some people believed that the official of the lottery used to stand just
so when he said or sang it, others believed that he was supposed to walk
among the people, but years and years ago this part of the ritual had been
allowed to lapse. There had been, also, a ritual salute, which the official of
the lottery had had to use in addressing each person who came up to draw
from the box, but this also had changed with time, until now it was felt necessary only for the official to speak to each person approaching. Mr.
Summers was very good at all this; in his clean white shirt and blue jeans,
with one hand resting carelessly on the black box, he seemed very proper
and important as he talked interminably to Mr. Graves and the Martins.

Just as Mr. Summers finally left off talking and turned to the assem-   8
bled villagers, Mrs. Hutchinson came hurriedly along the path to the
square, her sweater thrown over her shoulders, and slid into place in the
back of the crowd. "Clean forgot what day it was," she said to Mrs.
Delacroix, who stood next to her, and they both laughed softly. "Thought
my old man was out back stacking wood," Mrs. Hutchinson went on, "and
then I looked out the window and the kids was gone, and then I remembered it was the twenty-seventh and came a-running." She dried her hands
on her apron, and Mrs. Delacroix said, "You're in time, though. They're
still talking away up there."

Mrs. Hutchinson craned her neck to see through the crowd and found her   9
husband and children standing near the front. She tapped Mrs. Delacroix on
the arm as a farewell and began to make her way through the crowd. The
people separated good-humouredly to let her through; two or three people
said, in voices just loud enough to be heard across the crowd, "Here comes
your Missus, Hutchinson," and "Bill, she made it after all." Mrs. Hutchinson
reached her husband, and Mr. Summers, who had been waiting, said cheer-
fully, "Thought we were going to have to get on without you, Tessie." Mrs.
Hutchinson said, grinning, "Wouldn't have me leave m'dishes in the sink,
now, would you, Joe?" and soft laughter ran through the crowd as the people
stirred back into position after Mrs. Hutchinson's arrival.

"Well, now," Mr. Summers said soberly, "guess we better get started,   10
get this over with, so's we can go back to work. Anybody ain't here?"

11   "Dunbar," several people said. "Dunbar, Dunbar."

12   Mr. Summers consulted his list. "Clyde Dunbar," he said. "That's right. He's broke his leg, hasn't he? Who's drawing for him?"

13   "Me. I guess," a woman said, and Mr. Summers turned to look at her. "Wife draws for her husband," Mr. Summers said. "Don't you have a grown boy to do it for you, Janey?" Although Mr. Summers and everyone else in the village knew the answer perfectly well, it was the business of the official of the lottery to ask such questions formally. Mr. Summers waited with an expression of polite interest while Mrs. Dunbar answered.

14   "Horace's not but sixteen yet," Mrs. Dunbar said regretfully. "Guess I gotta fill in for the old man this year."

15   "Right," Mr. Summers said. He made a note on the list he was holding. Then he asked, "Watson boy drawing this year?"

16   A tall boy in the crowd raised his hand. "Here," he said. "I'm drawing for m'mother and me." He blinked his eyes nervously and ducked his head as several voices in the crowd said things like "Good fellow, Jack," and "Glad to see your mother's got a man to do it."

17   "Well," Mr. Summers said, "guess that's everyone. Old Man Warner make it?"

18   "Here," a voice said, and Mr. Summers nodded.

19   A sudden hush fell on the crowd as Mr. Summers cleared his throat and looked at the list. "All ready?" he called. "Now, I'll read the names — heads of families first — and the men come up and take a paper out of the box. Keep the paper folded in your hand without looking at it until everyone has had a turn. Everything clear?"

20   The people had done it so many times that they only half listened to the directions; most of them were quiet, wetting their lips, not looking around. Then Mr. Summers raised one hand high and said, "Adams." A man disengaged himself from the crowd and came forward. "Hi, Steve," Mr. Summers said, and Mr. Adams said, "Hi, Joe." They grinned at one another humourlessly and nervously. Then Mr. Adams reached into the black box and took out a folded paper. He held it firmly by one corner as he turned and went hastily back to his place in the crowd, where he stood a little apart from his family, not looking down at his hand.

21   "Allen," Mr. Summers said. "Anderson . . . Bentham."

22   "Seems like there's no time at all between lotteries any more," Mrs. Delacroix said to Mrs. Graves in the back row. "Seems like we got through with the last one only last week."

23   "Time sure goes fast," Mrs. Graves said.

24   "Clark . . . Delacroix."

"There goes my old man," Mrs. Delacroix said. She held her breath   25
while her husband went forward.

"Dunbar," Mr. Summers said, and Mrs. Dunbar went steadily to the   26
box while one of the women said. "Go on, Janey," and another said, "There
she goes."

"We're next," Mrs. Graves said. She watched while Mr. Graves came   27
around from the side of the box, greeted Mr. Summers gravely, and
selected a slip of paper from the box. By now, all through the crowd there
were men holding the small folded papers in their large hands, turning
them over and over nervously. Mrs. Dunbar and her two sons stood
together, Mrs. Dunbar holding the slip of paper.

"Harburt...Hutchinson."   28

"Get up there, Bill," Mrs. Hutchinson said, and the people near her   29
laughed.

"Jones."   30

"They do say," Mr. Adams said to Old Man Warner, who stood next to   31
him, "that over in the north village they're talking of giving up the lottery."

Old Man Warner snorted. "Pack of crazy fools," he said. "Listening to   32
the young folks, nothing's good enough for *them*. Next thing you know,
they'll be wanting to go back to living in caves, nobody work any more,
live *that* way for a while. Used to be a saying about 'Lottery in June, corn
be heavy soon.' First thing you know, we'd all be eating stewed chickweed
and acorns. There's *always* been a lottery," he added petulantly. "Bad
enough to see young Joe Summers up there joking with everybody."

"Some places have already quit lotteries," Mrs. Adams said.   33

"Nothing but trouble in *that*," Old Man Warner said stoutly. "Pack of   34
young fools."

"Martin." And Bobby Martin watched his father go forward.   35
"Overdyke...Percy."

"I wish they'd hurry," Mrs. Dunbar said to her older son. "I wish   36
they'd hurry."

"They're almost through," her son said.   37

"You get ready to run tell Dad," Mrs. Dunbar said.   38

Mr. Summers called his own name and then stepped forward precisely   39
and selected a slip from the box. Then he called, "Warner."

"Seventy-seventh year I been in the lottery," Old Man Warner said as   40
he went through the crowd. "Seventy-seventh time."

"Watson." The tall boy came awkwardly through the crowd. Someone   41
said, "Don't be nervous, Jack," and Mr. Summers said, "Take your time, son."

"Zanini."   42

43   After that, there was a long pause, a breathless pause, until Mr. Summers, holding his slip of paper in the air, said, "All right, fellows." For a minute, no one moved, and then all the slips of paper were opened. Suddenly, all the women began to speak at once, saying, "Who is it?," "Who's got it?," "Is it the Dunbars?," "Is it the Watsons?" Then the voices began to say, "It's Hutchinson. It's Bill," "Bill Hutchinson's got it."

44   "Go tell your father," Mrs. Dunbar said to her older son.

45   People began to look around to see the Hutchinsons. Bill Hutchinson was standing quiet, staring down at the paper in his hand. Suddenly, Tessie Hutchinson shouted to Mr. Summers, "You didn't give him time enough to take any paper he wanted. I saw you. It wasn't fair!"

46   "Be a good sport, Tessie," Mrs. Delacroix called, and Mrs. Graves said, "All of us took the same chance."

47   "Shut up, Tessie," Bill Hutchinson said.

48   "Well, everyone," Mr. Summers said, "that was done pretty fast, and now we've got to be hurrying a little more to get done in time." He consulted his next list. "Bill," he said, "you draw for the Hutchinson family. You got any other households in the Hutchinsons?"

49   "There's Don and Eva," Mrs. Hutchinson yelled, "Make *them* take their chance!"

50   "Daughters draw with their husbands' families, Tessie," Mr. Summers said gently. "You know that as well as anyone else."

51   "It wasn't *fair*," Tessie said.

52   "I guess not, Joe," Bill Hutchinson said regretfully. "My daughter draws with her husband's family, that's only fair. And I've got no other family except the kids."

53   "Then, as far as drawing for families is concerned, it's you," Mr. Summers said in explanation, "and as far as drawing for households is concerned, that's you, too. Right?"

54   "Right," Bill Hutchinson said.

55   "How many kids, Bill?" Mr. Summers asked formally.

56   "Three," Bill Hutchinson said. "There's Bill, Jr., and Nancy, and little Dave. And Tessie and me."

57   "All right, then," Mr. Summers said. "Harry, you got their tickets back?"

58   Mr. Graves nodded and held up the slips of paper. "Put them in the box, then," Mr. Summers directed. "Take Bill's and put it in."

59   "I think we ought to start over," Mrs. Hutchinson said, as quietly as she could. "I tell you it wasn't *fair*. You didn't give him time enough to choose. *Every*body saw that."

Mr. Graves had selected the five slips and put them in the box, and he   60
dropped all the papers but those onto the ground, where the breeze caught
them and lifted them off.

"Listen, everybody," Mrs. Hutchinson was saying to the people around   61
her.

"Ready, Bill?" Mr. Summers asked, and Bill Hutchinson, with one   62
quick glance around at his wife and children, nodded.

"Remember," Mr. Summers said, "take the slips and keep them folded   63
until each person has taken one. Harry, you help little Dave." Mr. Graves
took the hand of the little boy, who came willingly with him up to the box.
"Take a paper out of the box, Davy," Mr. Summers said. Davy put his hand
into the box and laughed. "Take just *one* paper," Mr. Summers said.
"Harry, you hold it for him." Mr. Graves took the child's hand and removed
the folded paper from the tight fist and held it while little Dave stood next
to him and looked at him wonderingly.

"Nancy next," Mr. Summers said. Nancy was twelve, and her school   64
friends breathed heavily as she went forward, switching her skirt, and took
a slip daintily from the box. "Bill, Jr.," Mr. Summers said, and Billy, his
face red and his feet overlarge, near knocked the box over as he got a paper
out. "Tessie," Mr. Summers said. She hesitated for a minute, looking
around defiantly, and then set her lips and went up to the box. She snatched
a paper out and held it behind her.

"Bill," Mr. Summers said, and Bill Hutchinson reached into the box   65
and felt around, bringing his hand out at last with the slip of paper in it.

The crowd was quiet. A girl whispered, "I hope it's not Nancy," and the   66
sound of the whisper reached the edges of the crowd.

"It's not the way it used to be," Old Man Warner said clearly. "People   67
ain't the way they used to be."

"All right," Mr. Summers said. "Open the papers. Harry, you open little   68
Dave's."

Mr. Graves opened the slip of paper and there was a general sigh   69
through the crowd as he held it up and everyone could see that it was blank.
Nancy and Bill, Jr., opened theirs at the same time, and both beamed and
laughed, turning around to the crowd and holding their slips of paper above
their heads.

"Tessie," Mr. Summers said. There was a pause, and then Mr.   70
Summers looked at Bill Hutchinson, and Bill unfolded his paper and
showed it. It was blank.

"It's Tessie," Mr. Summers said, and his voice was hushed. "Show us   71
her paper, Bill."

72   Bill Hutchinson went over to his wife and forced the slip of paper out of her hand. It had a black spot on it, the black spot Mr. Summers had made the night before with the heavy pencil in the coal-company office. Bill Hutchinson held it up, and there was a stir in the crowd.

73   "All right, folks," Mr. Summers said. "Let's finish quickly."

74   Although the villagers had forgotten the ritual and lost the original black box, they still remembered to use stones. The pile of stones the boys had made earlier was ready; there were stones on the ground with the blowing scraps of paper that had come out of the box. Mrs. Delacroix selected a stone so large she had to pick it up with both hands and turned to Mrs. Dunbar. "Come on," she said. "Hurry up."

75   Mrs. Dunbar had small stones in both hands, and she said, gasping for breath, "I can't run at all. You'll have to go ahead and I'll catch up with you."

76   The children had stones already, and someone gave little Davy Hutchinson a few pebbles.

77   Tessie Hutchinson was in the centre of a cleared space by now, and she held her hands out desperately as the villagers moved in on her. "It isn't fair," she said. A stone hit her on the side of the head.

78   Old Man Warner was saying, "Come on, come on, everyone." Steve Adams was in the front of the crowd of villagers, with Mrs. Graves beside him.

79   "It isn't fair, it isn't right," Mrs. Hutchinson screamed, and then they were upon her.

1948

NOTES

"The Lottery" is a classic and is considered one of the most famous short stories in English. Shirley Jackson (1919–1965) is also known for the book *The Haunting of Hill House*, which has been made into two films, both called *The Haunting* (1963, 1999).

The word "lottery" comes from the drawing of lots. A "lot" is an object, a chit, or a piece of paper used to make a choice, often about a person's fortune or fate. The verb form is "allot."

Stoning is an ancient and inexpensive method of punishment. Death resulting from it is quite agonizing and protracted. Often the act is a communal one in which all members participate in the condemning of the victim. One of the first martyred saints was St. Stephen, who was stoned to death for his beliefs.

Fertility rituals, including those asking for a bountiful harvest from the land, can be found in all cultures and societies, particularly in earlier times. Often these rites involve human sacrifice. The purpose of a ritual is to appease forces greater than humanity in the hope that these powers may help the tribe to survive (or, at least, refrain from hindering the tribe's survival). Many fertility rituals were later transformed into religious rituals.

There have been many kinds of lotteries throughout history. For example, the ancient Athenians used a lottery system to banish undesirable citizens. From this practice, we have the words "ostracize" and "ostracism."

COMPREHENSION AND DISCUSSION

1. What is so special about June 27?
2. What is the importance of the black box? Why does the box have to be black? Why old?
3. How do you know that this ceremony or ritual is in decline?
4. Explain how the lottery is conducted.
5. Is the process democratic and fair? What is Tessie Hutchinson's objection to the lottery?
6. Why are there so many names in this story? What is the symbolic importance of names like Mr. Graves, Mr. Summers, Old Man Warner, Dickie Delacroix, and Tessie Hutchinson?
7. What are Old Man Warner's reasons for continuing the lottery? Why does he disparage the young for joking about the lottery, and other communities for abandoning the tradition?
8. Will this lottery really help the village to harvest a bumper crop? Why would the villagers continue with this practice if they are so impatient to have the process concluded?
9. Were you surprised at the ending? How did Jackson prepare you for it?

LITERARY TECHNIQUES

The surprise ending is a popular strategy in writing short stories. It makes the reader go through the story again just to see what clues he or she may have missed. Surprise endings require the writer to use foreshadowing and to drop clues for the astute reader. Note how Jackson innocently mentions the piles of stones in the beginning.

Jackson uses the third-person objective point of view. She does not reveal the thoughts of the characters, but reports only what they say and what they do. In a sense, the strategy is crucial to the surprise ending.

A symbol represents meanings greater than and outside of the object itself. It is something concrete that represents something abstract. For example, although a flag is just a piece of cloth with a colourful design, it also represents a country. In this inanimate object, recognition of state, love of country, respect for its existence, and other ideals are all woven. Symbols are important to Jackson's story, especially the stones, the old box, and the colour black. On the surface, Old Man Warner is just another long survivor of the lottery in this community, but symbolically he represents the unchanging tradition to which others also adhere.

Microcosmic view Writers often use a smaller unit or number of characters in a story to give focus and suggest a larger picture. An example of a small unit is a village; an even smaller unit is the family. As the story progresses, we see what happens to the Hutchinson family in particular. In theory, the microcosm reflects the macrocosm, or the larger unit. Therefore, if this type of ritual occurs in the Hutchinsons' neighbourhood, then it may also be performed across the state, the country, and the world.

ASSIGNMENTS

1. Research the concept of "scapegoating" as a religious or social practice and write a short explanation.
2. Read the story of Abraham and Isaac (Genesis 22:1–19). How is this story the same as or different from Jackson's?
3. Define the terms "sacrifice" and "lottery."
4. Write an essay explaining why rituals are important in a society. You may wish to examine the following: the marriage ceremony, graduations, courtship rituals in different cultures, handshakes, burial services, and baptisms.

5. Speculate on the aftermath of Tessie Hutchinson's death. You can focus on the entire town or just on the Hutchinson family at the dinner table that evening.
6. Violence and brutality are within each human soul. We like to hurt people; hurting others gives us pleasure, satisfaction, and entertainment. Is this statement valid? Explain.
7. "The Lottery" has been turned into a play and several films. The 1996 TV movie expands on the story and takes liberties with the plot. Write a critique of the film.
8. Compare this story with Edgar Allan Poe's "The Cask of Amontillado" (p. 181). Which story do you think is more horrific? Why?

Generation Y

Nancy Kilpatrick

1   "I'm *not* 'menacing'!"

2   "Rand, I'm sure he didn't mean to upset you. I think he just meant that, well, under the circumstances . . . " The Psychiatrist turns her palms up, and scans the prison's interview room. "Your statement about being a sensitive male *is* odd." The Psychiatrist crosses her short legs and leans forward, resting both forearms on her thigh, clasping her hands together as if she is pleading.

3   Rand likes the shape of her thigh, the way the pastel silk skirt clings to the taut skin and just lies there, passive, resting, waiting for fingers to reach out and separate fabric from flesh.

4   "Can you elaborate?" The Psychiatrist asks. "How do you see yourself as a sensitive young man?"

5   "There's lots of guys like me. Regular guys. Sensitive. Decent," Rand says.

6   "Yeah. A regular, sensitive, decent serial killer!" The Reporter's remarks are aggressive. Hostile. Violent.

7   Rand focuses on The Reporter. "A lot of guys are serial killers. More and more every day. You see it on TV. In the news. Guys like you write about guys like me. Guys who are trying to help."

8   "Help? Right!" The Reporter stabs symbols into his notebook, barely glancing down. The carved lines of his face deepen under the glare of brilliant TV lights. He starts to say, "Look, you little sh —"

9   "You created me."

10   The Reporter looks disgusted. His skin is tight, but with no appealing insulation beneath his cheeks. Just bone, nothing but bone. Hard, not subtle. Holding up a face with limited flexibility. He starts to say, "Look, you little sh —"

11   "Rand, I think what you're trying to get at," The Psychiatrist interrupts, "is that the media portrays violence and that in turn encourages violence in young people like yourself, with a predisposition."

12   "Fuck!" The Reporter mutters under his breath, low enough that the microphone will not pick it up. Rand watches him glance at The Guard by the door, whose eyes are non-committal, but whose mouth — the one that spits saliva when he talks, that opens and closes like the jaws of a vice, that utters sound bytes that Rand breaks into chunks and swallows whole — whose mouth twitches at the left corner. Nice touch, Rand thinks. But too far in the background to be effective.

"Well, Rand?" The Psychiatrist says, "Do you see yourself as a victim 13 of media violence?"

"Oh, come on!" The Reporter says. "Tell us why you mutilated all 14 those —"

"Let him answer the question," The Psychiatrist interrupts again. 15

The Reporter crashes back against the chair. Rand knows The Reporter 16 would love to jump to his feet and punch The Prisoner in the face. The Reporter is violent by nature, that's clear. His turn to ask the questions is coming. They are supposed to take turns. Politely. That's the way it's supposed to go.

"I love television," Rand says. His voice is not as sincere as he wants 17 it to sound, so he concentrates on lowering his eyes, dropping his head down a fraction. He looks up through his long lashes at The Psychiatrist. The dark eyelid hairs cut her body into strips. "And newspapers. It's important to know what's going on in the world around you."

Her face softens. She reminds him of The Teacher, and The Minister's 18 Wife. The Others in the room wouldn't notice that her face has changed, but Rand does. She understands. "Tell us about your childhood," The Psychiatrist says gently.

This script is familiar. He has repeated these lines many times and 19 knows them by heart. He wants to sigh, but that would not be the right thing to do. In a moment of inspiration, he tilts his head and looks away. If only his hands were free, but the chain keeps them six inches apart, which means he cannot rely on his hands to speak for him, and they speak eloquently.

"I had a very normal life," he says matter-of-factly, repeating by rote 20 what he has said so often. Why won't they believe him? "My parents were divorced, but that wasn't a problem. Mom was great. She took real good care of me."

"How so?" asks The Psychiatrist. 21

"From when I was a baby. She had a monitor in the nursery and every- 22 thing. So nothing bad would happen."

He remembers the monitor, even when he got old enough to go to 23 school. His mother hovered just in the next room, always listening, waiting, as if for a sign.

"And there were home movies, then videos," he adds. Many. Endless 24 tapes. She recorded them from before he could walk; Rand strapped into his cradle, the television set on — he still remembers his favourite show, the cartoon with the blood-red lion that chomped off the heads of its enemies; moving images of Rand eating meatloaf with his hands in front of the

TV in a highchair; wandering the mall in his toddler harness, so he wouldn't get lost, or be stolen or be violated by some sick man. "She liked to shoot me. She said I was a natural on tape."

25   The Psychiatrist smiles.

26   The Reporter scribbles more notes.

27   The Guard shifts his weight to his other leg.

28   This room is small, like the set at a television station Rand saw once on a school tour. They had been broadcasting the news. The set, the size of a bathroom, consisted mainly of a plywood desk, the front veneered so it looked like real wood on tape. Two cameras. A control room with a bank of monitors before The Reporters. The Class visited the control room. The Technicians sat at the panels of switches and buttons and levers, wearing headsets, sending and receiving instructions as directed, zeroing in on The Female Reporter, then The Male Reporter. Back and forth, back and forth. Then The Weatherperson. The Technical Director controlled how everyone looked, what they said and how they said it. It was just like a movie.

29   "I'm sorry," he says when he realizes The Psychiatrist has asked a question.

30   "I asked if you would try to explain your motivation. Why you did what you did, to all those people . . . You must have felt very angry —"

31   "I never feel angry."

32   The Reporter leans forward.

33   The Psychiatrist sits back.

34   "Who's the first person you killed?" The Reporter demands.

35   "I never killed a person."

36   "Your DNA matches the DNA found at the scene of six murders. Six mutilations. And the jury found you guilty of —"

37   "They were wrong. I'm innocent. DNA can be wrong, you know. I saw a show on *60 Minutes* —"

38   "Yeah, kid, I know the stats. If you're not an identical twin, it's one in a million —"

39   "Two million. One in two million, depending on the tests used. But two million and one could be a match —"

40   "How did it feel to just tear off —"

41   "Please!" The Psychiatrist grips The Reporter's arm, tempering him. Reluctantly, he moves back in his chair. His face tightens. The Psychiatrist moves forward. This is her territory.

42   "Rand, I read the reports and evaluations. What you told the court. What you told the other doctors. You said you never felt the slightest bit of anger toward anyone."

"That's right," Rand agrees. "I don't believe in getting angry. That's   43
how Mom raised me."

"But you must have been angry at your mother now and again. And   44
your father—"

"Nope." He knows he's answered too quickly. It sounds like he is   45
trying to hide something, but he isn't. Not at all. There's nothing to hide.

"My father wasn't around, so why would I get angry at him?"   46

"He was around until you were ten."   47

"I didn't notice. He was always at work."   48

"Rand, there's a history of domestic violence, your father assaulting   49
your mother, and—"

"Yeah, well, she divorced him. Besides, she protected me. I didn't   50
know about it until later. I was busy."

"You played a lot of video games," The Reporter says, struggling to get   51
with the program at last.

"Sure. Some D&D stuff, then Nintendo when I got older. Doesn't   52
everybody?"

"Yeah, but everybody doesn't—"   53

"I mean, doesn't everybody like video games? All the kids at my   54
school did."

"Rand . . ." The Psychiatrist searches for another avenue, as though if   55
she keeps probing he'll split apart, spill what's inside him. Bleed for the
camera. But there is nothing to say that he hasn't said before. "Some of
those games get pretty violent, don't they?"

"I guess."   56

"After you played them, you went out and played them in real life,   57
didn't you?" The Reporter interjects, blurring the picture again.

"No."   58

"Sure you did!"   59

"Why should I? I had the games."   60

"And the urges—"   61

"Nope."   62

Rand looks up, presenting the face of The Innocent to The   63
Videographer, a slim-bodied young woman with the head of a camera.
How many hundreds of thousands, maybe millions of people will watch
this drama unfold? he wonders. Most, he is certain, will understand. Most
are against violence.

The Lawyer sits beside him, prepared to nip any compromising ques-   64
tions or answers in the bud. So far she has said nothing. Now she does.

65   "My client's answers to these questions are a matter of record. It's all in the trial transcripts."

66   "What's the basis of your final appeal?" The Reporter asks.

67   The Videographer shifts the camera to the left, to capture The Reporter's profile.

68   "Evidence that should never have been admissible," The Lawyer says.

69   "The video tapes?"

70   "Yes, the tapes."

71   A flash-fire races through Rand—The Reporter isn't supposed to steal the limelight! Rand is The Prisoner. The-Juvenile-Sentenced-To-Death. The one who has agreed to this three-way exclusive. The *only* one the camera should be focused on!

72   Rand knows he should say nothing but he needs to regain control.

73   "The only urges I have are to get rid of The Evil."

74   The Lawyer jumps in.

75   "Don't say another word—"

76   "What is The Evil?" The Psychiatrist asks, leaning far forward, until Rand can smell her perfume.

77   "You mean evil, like you?" The Reporter says sharply.

78   Rand smiles slightly and gazes seductively into the impassive camera eye. For effect, he fingers the white ribbon he always wears on his prison shirt, over his name. "I just mean, the world is full of violence. I wish it wasn't, but it is."

79   "That's enough, Rand! My client is—"

80   "Men are the violent ones. Everybody says so. The TV, the newspapers. So men have got to stop the violence. 'A man's gotta do what a man's gotta do.' John Wayne said that, you know. My mother used to quote him."

81   "Rand, have you heard of the psychiatric term 'projection'? It's—"

82   "If men don't do it, who will? The good guys have to stop the bad guys, or there's gonna be violence."

83   "Listen, kid, I've been a reporter for twenty years, and I know BS when I smell it—"

84   "My mother didn't raise me to be violent. She didn't want me to be like my father."

85   "As your counsel, Rand, I must advise you—"

86   "Most men are violent, don't you think so doctor? You're a woman."

87   "Rand, people can project feelings they have onto someone else—the way a camera projects an image. Angry feelings, or feelings of wanting to harm someone we fear will harm us—"

But Rand tunes her out. He directs his remarks exclusively toward The   88
Videographer, to her cold, precise eye, studying him, controlling him,
never letting him slide out of her objective sight.

"If there were no men in the world, there wouldn't be any violence.   89
Isn't that right?"

Silence cuts the air for barely a second.   90

"I'm sorry, people, but as Rand's attorney, I must protect my client's   91
interests. This interview is—"

"Deny it! Go ahead and deny it!" Rand shouts at the retreating camera,   92
using emotional charge to lure it back. "You say it all the time, all of you.
How can you say something different now? You're phonies!"

"Rand, do you feel attacked? No one here is attacking you—"   93

"All of you! You want all males dead!"   94

"Turn off the camera, or I'll file a civil action—"   95

"So do I! Then there won't be any more violence."   96

"Listen, you little shithead, *you're* the violent male!"   97

Rand lunges. He is aware of the camera zooming in on his hands. The   98
chain from the wrist cuffs is hooked to a waist chain and his reach stops
inches from his grasp.

Silence clutches the air. The Videographer has captured all. The   99
shocked looks. The gasp from The Lawyer. The cry of "No!" from The
Psychiatrist. The Guard drawing his gun. The Reporter, struggling to protect his genitals, what would have been seconds too late, but for The
Prisoner's restraints.

Rand stares down at his hands. They are bony and thin, "sensitive" his   100
mother always said. The fingers stretch like talons, ready to claw The Evil
from its roots. Ready to deposit it into his hungry mouth, where powerful
jaws can pulverize and razor teeth rend. Where what should not exist, by
being devoured, can be eliminated forever.

That would have made a great shot. His mom would have loved it.   101
Rand sits back and smiles into the camera's eye. He just hopes that The
Videographer had the lens in sharp focus when she captured him.

1999

NOTES

Nancy Kilpatrick is an award-winning Canadian horror writer who is best
known for her vampire stories. She lives in Montreal.

Generation Y The term Generation X was coined by Vancouver writer Douglas Coupland to refer to late baby boomers — those born in the early 1960s. This term has been mistakenly used for other groups, especially those born after the baby boom (1947–1965). Post-boomers, born in the 1970s and 1980s, have been referred to as Generation Y.

D&D Dungeons and Dragons is a popular role-playing game in which players become characters such as wizards and dwarfs.

COMPREHENSION AND DISCUSSION

1. What is Rand's crime?
2. Where is this story set? What details or clues enable you to come to this conclusion?
3. Why does the writer need to give us Rand's childhood, especially about his mother and father?
4. Why does Rand tell The Reporter, "You created me" (paragraph 9)?
5. Why is it important that a videographer be present? Would Rand behave differently if she were not there?
6. How does the writer deceive the reader as to who the victims are? Why does Kilpatrick do this?
7. Why do The Psychiatrist, The Lawyer, and The Videographer have to be women? Why are The Reporter and The Guard men?
8. Does this story make you re-evaluate capital punishment? Should heinous, multiple-victim killers be executed?
9. Why is the title appropriate? Can you think of a better one?

LITERARY TECHNIQUES

Present tense Most stories are written in the simple past tense to simulate action that is happening "in real time," just like a movie camera following the characters. There is a sense of immediacy. Everything is now. Note how this sense is achieved in "Generation Y."

Dialogue Dialogue or direct speech made by the characters has several advantages in storytelling. First, it reveals character traits of the speaker. Second, it moves the story along, often faster than narration or description. Third, it breaks up the monotony of lengthy narration and adds variety to the reading diet. Some writers depend on dialogue more than on recounting the action to create suspense. For example, Kilpatrick hides information and misdirects the reader in The Reporter's dialogue: "Tell us why you mutilated all those—" Here the writer makes the reader assume that The Reporter means women.

Profanity Swear words in print still have some shock value, although many have become rather commonplace in speech. Newspapers often use asterisks (*) to avoid printing profanity in full. The use of such words in short stories gives the dialogue authenticity.

Generic characters In a short story, minor characters serve a function but are not fully developed characters. Sometimes they are not identified by a name. Kilpatrick has gone a step further by de-personalizing these characters. She identifies them by profession and uses capital letters to emphasize this further. When these titles are capitalized, they are specific to one character and not to any psychiatrist or reporter. These people in their occupations have their role to play in that capacity; moreover, they collectively draw attention to the person who does possess a name: Rand. He becomes the centre of attention, just as the character draws attention to himself throughout.

Suspense A suspense story creates an atmosphere of uncertainty and mystery. The reader is left wondering what will happen, rather than, as in a mystery story, how the detective will solve the crime or expose the killer. In this story, the killer has already been caught. The questions to be answered are why he killed and what he did to his victims.

ASSIGNMENTS

1. "Big Brother" is a term coined by George Orwell in *1984*, a satiric novel in which everyone is under surveillance, whether it be human or technological. In "Generation Y," Rand speaks of his early life being recorded or taped. In homes, stores, banks, and government institutions, surveillance cameras are gathering information about individuals. Even cellphones now have video capability. Is this kind of surveillance a good or even moral phenomenon in our society?
2. Andy Warhol, a pop icon of the 1960s, stated that everyone would have fifteen minutes of fame in life. Rand is aware of the camera and he poses for television and its millions of viewers. Should criminals be accorded celebrity status?
3. Kalle Lasn talks about the bad influence of television in "Toxic Culture Syndrome" (p. 293). How does Rand's case relate to what Lasn says?

4. How do video games and violent TV shows and movies affect children? Note that most video games have become more and more violent in story line and graphics. Speculate on a society based on that kind of technology as entertainment.

5. Write an essay on the effectiveness of dialogue to tell a story, using "Generation Y" as your main example. Consider what David Arnason's "A Girl's Story" (p. 20) says about using dialogue (paragraph 24). You can compare "Generation Y" to another story that uses a lot of dialogue, such as Lawrence Hill's "So, What Are You Anyway?" (p. 100), or to a story with little or no dialogue, such as Stephen Leacock's "How We Kept Mother's Day" (p. 142).

Girl

Jamaica Kincaid

Wash the white clothes on Monday and put them on the stone heap; wash   1
the color clothes on Tuesday and put them on the clothesline to dry; don't
walk barehead in the hot sun; cook pumpkin fritters in very hot sweet oil;
soak your little cloths right after you take them off; when buying cotton to
make yourself a nice blouse, be sure that it doesn't have gum on it, because
that way it won't hold up well after a wash; soak salt fish overnight before
you cook it; is it true that you sing benna in Sunday school?; always eat your
food in such a way that it won't turn someone else's stomach; on Sundays
try to walk like a lady and not like the slut you are so bent on becoming;
don't sing benna in Sunday school; you mustn't speak to wharf-rat boys, not
even to give directions; don't eat fruits on the street — flies will follow you;
but I don't sing benna on Sundays at all and never in Sunday school; this is
how to sew on a button; this is how to make a buttonhole for the button you
have just sewed on; this is how to hem a dress when you see the hem
coming down and so to prevent yourself from looking like the slut I know
you are so bent on becoming; this is how you iron your father's khaki shirt
so that it doesn't have a crease; this is how you grow okra — far from the
house, because okra tree harbors red ants; when you are growing dasheen,
make sure it gets plenty of water or else it makes your throat itch when you
are eating it; this is how you sweep a corner; this is how you sweep a whole
house; this is how you sweep a yard; this is how you smile to someone you
don't like too much; this is how you smile to someone you don't like at all;
this is how you smile to someone you like completely; this is how you set
a table for tea; this is how you set a table for dinner; this is how you set a
table for dinner with an important guest; this is how you set a table for
lunch; this is how you set a table for breakfast; this is how to behave in the
presence of men who don't know you very well, and this way they won't
recognize immediately the slut I have warned you against becoming; be
sure to wash every day, even if it is with your own spit; don't squat down to
play marbles — you are not a boy, you know; don't pick people's flowers —
you might catch something; don't throw stones at blackbirds, because it
might not be a blackbird at all; this is how to make a bread pudding; this is
how to make doukona; this is how to make pepper pot; this is how to make
a good medicine for a cold; this is how to make a good medicine to throw
away a child before it even becomes a child; this is how to catch a fish; this
is how to throw back a fish you don't like, and that way something bad
won't fall on you; this is how to bully a man; this is how a man bullies you;

this is how to love a man, and if this doesn't work there are other ways, and if they don't work don't feel too bad about giving up; this is how to spit up in the air if you feel like it, and this is how to move quick so that it doesn't fall on you; this is how to make ends meet; always squeeze bread to make sure it's fresh; *but what if the baker won't let me feel the bread?*; you mean to say that after all you are really going to be the kind of woman who the baker won't let near the bread?

1983

NOTES

Jamaica Kincaid is an American writer who was born and raised in Antigua.

Benna Popular music, calypso.

Dasheen A variety of taro, a tuberous plant.

Doukona A spicy Caribbean dish, often made from plantain.

COMPREHENSION AND DISCUSSION

1. Who are the two characters?
2. Categorize the subjects on which the mother instructs her daughter.
3. Where is this story set? Give some evidence from the story to support your answer.
4. What is the speaker's recurring fear concerning her daughter? How does she express it?
5. Is this a story? What are the elements of a story?
6. Is "Girl" criticism or instruction? When is the line crossed between parental advice and criticism or nagging?
7. Is this a proper way to teach a child? How would you teach a child about life, duties, and responsibilities?
8. How do you know that time passes, or that the child is growing up?
9. What is the narrator's tone? (Tone may be defined as the feelings behind the expressions and words. For example, tone can be warm, cold, sarcastic, angry, despairing, and so on.)
10. What makes you believe that the child is being coy in her question at the end?
11. What does the parent mean by this line: "you mean to say that after all you are really going to be the kind of woman who the baker won't let near the bread?" How many ways can you interpret this statement?

12. Is this story sexist?
13. Speculate about why this story is written in one continuous sentence and in one paragraph.

LITERARY TECHNIQUES

Dramatic monologue Refined to an art by Robert Browning in his many poems, the dramatic monologue is basically one person speaking aloud to an identifiable silent listener. The monologue is dramatic in the sense that there is drama; that is, the telling is vivid, striking, and even theatrical in presentation. In the course of the monologue, the speaker reveals more than what she wants to tell; involuntarily, she exposes her soul to the other character, and thus to the reader. Moreover, throughout, the reader comes to understand the setting and the occasion on which the monologue is predicated. However, in "Girl," Kincaid changes the basic elements of the dramatic monologue. In italics she gives the daughter first a rebuttal to the mother's accusation, and second a coy question in response to the mother's final instruction. Furthermore, the story is prose instead of poetry.

The short short story The length of a story determines its classification. Usually, a story under a 1000 words is called a short short story, while a story beyond 5000 words is called a novella or long short story. (These classifications are often inexact and arbitrary.) A short short story must still have all the elements of storytelling: plot, characters, setting, conflict, dialogue, theme or subject matter, a beginning and end.

ASSIGNMENTS

1. In "Are Goody Bags a Good Thing?" (p. 334), Rita Sirignano questions Canadian parents' penchant for spoiling children with material goods. In "Girl," the mother does not spoil her daughter at all. How should children be treated?
2. Should children do housework? Why or why not?
3. In the monologue, the mother hints at birth control and abortion. Should children receive their sex education at home, at school, or on the streets? Debate the pros and cons.
4. Compare the mother in "Girl" with the mother in Morley Callaghan's "All the Years of Her Life" (p. 45), "The Cowherd" (p. 71), Garry Engkent's "Chickens for Christmas" (p. 61), or Alice Munro's "An Ounce of Cure" (p. 156).

The Loons
Margaret Laurence

1   Just below Manawaka, where the Wachakwa River ran brown and noisy over the pebbles, the scrub oak and grey-green willow and chokecherry bushes grew in a dense thicket. In a clearing at the centre of the thicket stood the Tonnerre family's shack. The basis of this dwelling was a small square cabin made of poplar poles and chinked with mud, which had been built by Jules Tonnerre some fifty years before, when he came back from the Batoche with a bullet in his thigh, the year that Riel was hung and the voices of the Métis entered their long silence. Jules had only intended to stay the winter in the Wachakwa Valley, but the family was still there in the thirties, when I was a child. As the Tonnerres had increased, their settlement had been added to, until the clearing at the foot of the town hill was a chaos of lean-tos, wooden packing cases, warped lumber, discarded car tires, ramshackle chicken coops, tangled strands of barbed wire and rusty tin cans.

2   The Tonnerres were French halfbreeds, and among themselves they spoke a *patois* that was neither Cree nor French. Their English was broken and full of obscenities. They did not belong among the Cree of the Galloping Mountain reservation, further north, and they did not belong among the Scots-Irish and Ukrainians of Manawaka, either. They were, as my Grandmother MacLeod would have put it, neither flesh, fowl, nor good salt herring. When their men were not working at odd jobs or as section hands on the C.P.R., they lived on relief. In the summers, one of the Tonnerre youngsters, with a face that seemed totally unfamiliar with laughter, would knock at the doors of the town's brick houses and offer for sale a lard-pail full of bruised wild strawberries, and if he got as much as a quarter he would grab the coin and run before the customer had time to change her mind. Sometimes old Jules, or his son Lazarus, would get mixed up in a Saturday-night brawl, and would hit out at whoever was nearest, or howl drunkenly among the offended shoppers on Main Street, and then the Mountie would put them for the night in the barred cell underneath the Court House, and the next morning they would be quiet again.

3   Piquette Tonnerre, the daughter of Lazarus, was in my class at school. She was older than I, but she had failed several grades, perhaps because her attendance had always been sporadic and her interest in schoolwork negligible. Part of the reason she had missed a lot of school was that she had had

tuberculosis of the bone, and had once spent many months in hospital. I knew this because my father was the doctor who had looked after her. Her sickness was almost the only thing I knew about her, however. Otherwise, she existed for me only as a vaguely embarrassing presence, with her hoarse voice and her clumsy limping walk and her grimy cotton dresses that were always miles too long. I was neither friendly nor unfriendly towards her. She dwelt and moved somewhere within my scope of vision, but I did not actually notice her very much until that peculiar summer when I was eleven.

"I don't know what to do about that kid," my father said at dinner one evening. "Piquette Tonnerre, I mean. The damn bone's flared up again. I've had her in hospital for quite a while now, and it's under control all right, but I hate like the dickens to send her home again." 4

"Couldn't you explain to her mother that she has to rest a lot?" my mother said. 5

"The mother's not there," my father replied. "She took off a few years back. Can't say I blame her. Piquette cooks for them, and she says Lazarus would never do anything for himself as long as she's there. Anyway, I don't think she'd take much care of herself, once she got back. She's only thirteen, after all. Beth, I was thinking — what about taking her up to Diamond Lake with us for the summer? A couple of months rest would give that bone a much better chance." 6

My mother looked stunned. 7

"But Ewen — what about Roddie and Vanessa?" 8

"She's not contagious," my father said. "And it would be company for Vanessa." 9

"Oh dear," my mother said in distress, "I'll bet anything she has nits in her hair." 10

"For Pete's sake," my father said crossly, "do you think Matron would let her stay in the hospital for all this time like that? Don't be silly, Beth." 11

Grandmother MacLeod, her delicately featured face as rigid as a cameo, now brought her mauve-veined hands together as though she were about to begin a prayer. 12

"Ewen, if that half-breed youngster comes along to Diamond Lake, I'm not going," she announced. "I'll go to Morag's for the summer." 13

I had trouble in stifling my urge to laugh, for my mother brightened visibly and quickly tried to hide it. If it came to a choice between Grandmother MacLeod and Piquette, Piquette would win hands down, nits or not. 14

15   "It might be quite nice for you, at that," she mused. "You haven't seen Morag for over a year, and you might enjoy being in the city for a while. Well, Ewen dear, you do what you think best. If you think it would do Piquette some good, then we'll be glad to have her, as long as she behaves herself."

16   So it happened that several weeks later, when we all piled into my father's old Nash, surrounded by suitcases and boxes of provisions and toys for my ten-month-old brother, Piquette was with us and Grandmother MacLeod, miraculously, was not. My father would only be staying at the cottage for a couple of weeks, for he had to get back to his practice, but the rest of us would stay at Diamond Lake until the end of August.

17   Our cottage was not named, as many were, "Dew Drop Inn" or "Bide-a-Wee," or "Bonnie Doon." The sign on the roadway bore in austere letters only our name, MacLeod. It was not a large cottage, but it was on the lake-front. You could look out the windows and see, through the filigree of the spruce trees, the water glistening greenly as the sun caught it. All around the cottage were ferns, and sharp-branched raspberry bushes, and moss that had grown over fallen tree trunks. If you looked carefully among the weeds and grass, you could find wild strawberry plants which were in white flower now and in another month would bear fruit, the fragrant globes hanging like miniature scarlet lanterns on the thin hairy stems. The two grey squirrels were still there, gossiping at us from the tall spruce beside the cottage, and by the end of the summer they would again be tame enough to take pieces of crust from my hands. The broad moose antlers that hung above the back door were a little more bleached and fissured after the winter, but otherwise everything was the same. I raced joyfully around my kingdom, greeting all the places I had not seen for a year. My brother, Roderick, who had not been born when we were here last summer, sat on the car rug in the sunshine and examined a brown spruce cone, meticulously turning it round and round in his small and curious hands. My mother and father toted the luggage from car to cottage, exclaiming over how well the place had wintered, no broken windows, thank goodness, no apparent damage from storm-felled branches or snow.

18   Only after I had finished looking around did I notice Piquette. She was sitting on the swing, her lame leg held stiffly out, and her other foot scuffling the ground as she swung slowly back and forth. Her long hair hung black and straight around her shoulders, and her broad coarse-featured face bore no expression — it was blank, as though she no longer dwelt within her own skull, as though she had gone elsewhere. I approached her very hesitantly.

"Want to come and play?"   19

Piquette looked at me with a sudden flash of scorn.   20

"I ain't a kid," she said.   21

Wounded, I stamped angrily away, swearing I would not speak to her   22
for the rest of the summer. In the days that followed, however, Piquette
began to interest me, and I began to want to interest her. My reasons did
not appear bizarre to me. Unlikely as it may seem, I had only just realized
that the Tonnerre family, whom I had always heard called half-breeds, were
actually Indians, or as near as made no difference. My acquaintance with
Indians was not extensive. I did not remember ever having seen a real
Indian, and my new awareness that Piquette sprang from the people of Big
Bear and Poundmaker, of Tecumseh, of the Iroquois who had eaten Father
Brébeuf's heart — all this gave her an instant attraction in my eyes. I was
a devoted reader of Pauline Johnson at this age, and sometimes would orate
aloud in an exalted voice, *West Wind, blow from your prairie nest; Blow
from the mountains, blow from the west* — and so on. It seemed to me that
Piquette must be in some way a daughter of the forest, a kind of junior
prophetess of the wilds, who might impart to me, if I took the right
approach, some of the secrets which she undoubtedly knew — where the
whippoorwill made her nest, how the coyote reared her young, or whatever
it was that it said in Hiawatha.

I set about gaining Piquette's trust. She was not allowed to go swim-   23
ming, with her bad leg, but I managed to lure her down to the beach — or
rather, she came because there was nothing else to do. The water was
always icy, for the lake was fed by springs, but I swam like a dog, thrashing
my arms and legs around at such a speed and with such an output of energy
that I never grew cold. Finally, when I had had enough, I came out and sat
beside Piquette on the sand. When she saw me approaching, her hand
squashed flat the sand castle she had been building, and she looked at me
sullenly, without speaking.

"Do you like this place?" I asked, after a while, intending to lead on   24
from there into the question of forest lore.

Piquette shrugged. "It's okay. Good as anywhere."   25

"I love it," I said. "We come here every summer."   26

"So what?" Her voice was distant, and I glanced at her uncertainly,   27
wondering what I could have said wrong.

"Do you want to come for a walk?" I asked her. "We wouldn't need to   28
go far. If you just walk around the point there, you come to a bay where
great big reeds grow in the water, and all kinds of fish hang around there.
Want to? Come on."

29   She shook her head.

30   "Your dad said I ain't supposed to do no more walking than I got to."

31   I tried another line.

32   "I bet you know a lot about the woods and all that, eh?" I began respectfully.

33   Piquette looked at me from her large dark unsmiling eyes.

34   "I don't know what in hell you're talkin' about," she replied. "You nuts or somethin'? If you mean where my old man, and me, and all them live, you better shut up, by Jesus, you hear?"

35   I was startled and my feelings were hurt, but I had a kind of dogged perseverance. I ignored her rebuff.

36   "You know something, Piquette? There's loons here, on this lake. You can see their nests just up the shore there, behind those logs. At night, you can hear them even from the cottage, but it's better to listen from the beach. My dad says we should listen and try to remember how they sound because in a few years when more cottages are built at Diamond Lake and more people come in, the loons will go away."

37   Piquette was picking up stones and snail shells and then dropping them again.

38   "Who gives a good goddamn?" she said.

39   It became increasingly obvious that, as an Indian, Piquette was a dead loss. That evening I went out by myself, scrambling through the bushes that overhung the steep path, my feet slipping on the fallen spruce needles that covered the ground. When I reached the shore, I walked along the firm damp sand to the small pier that my father had built, and sat down there. I heard someone else crashing through the undergrowth and the bracken, and for a moment I thought Piquette had changed her mind, but it turned out to be my father. He sat beside me on the pier and we waited, without speaking.

40   At night the lake was like black glass with a streak of amber which was the path of the moon. All around, the spruce trees grew tall and close-set, branches blackly sharp against the sky, which was lightened by a cold flickering of stars. Then the loons began their calling. They rose like phantom birds from the nests on the shore, and flew out onto the dark still surface of the water.

41   No one can ever describe that ululating sound, the crying of the loons, and no one who has heard it can ever forget it. Plaintive, and yet with a quality of chilling mockery, those voices belonged to a world separated by eons from our neat world of summer cottages and the lighted lamps of home.

"They must have sounded just like that," my father remarked, "before 42
any person ever set foot here."

Then he laughed. "You could say the same, of course, about sparrows, 43
or chipmunks, but somehow it only strikes you that way with the loons."

"I know," I said. 44

Neither of us suspected that this would be the last time we would ever 45
sit here together on the shore, listening. We stayed for perhaps half an hour,
and then we went back to the cottage. My mother was reading beside the fire-
place. Piquette was looking at the burning birch log, and not doing anything.

"You should have come along," I said, although in fact I was glad she 46
had not.

"Not me," Piquette said. "You wouldn' catch me walkin' way down 47
there jus' for a bunch of squawkin' birds."

Piquette and I remained ill at ease with one another. I felt I had 48
somehow failed my father, but I did not know what was the matter, nor
why she would not or could not respond when I suggested exploring the
woods or playing house. I thought it was probably her slow and difficult
walking that held her back. She stayed most of the time in the cottage with
my mother, helping her with the dishes or with Roddie, but hardly ever
talking. Then the Duncans arrived at their cottage, and I spent my days
with Mavis, who was my best friend. I could not reach Piquette at all, and
I soon lost interest in trying. But all that summer she remained as both a
reproach and a mystery to me.

That winter, my father died of pneumonia, after less than a week's ill- 49
ness. For some time I saw nothing around me, being completely immersed
in my own pain and my mother's. When I looked outward once more, I
scarcely noticed that Piquette Tonnerre was no longer at school. I do not
remember seeing her at all until four years later, one Saturday night when
Mavis and I were having Cokes in the Regal Café. The jukebox was
booming like tuneful thunder, and beside it, leaning lightly on its chrome
and its rainbow glass, was a girl.

Piquette must have been seventeen then, although she looked about 50
twenty. I stared at her, astounded that anyone could have changed so much.
Her face, so stolid and expressionless before, was animated now with a
gaiety that was almost violent. She laughed and talked very loudly with the
boys around her. Her lipstick was bright carmine, and her hair was cut short
and frizzily permed. She had not been pretty as a child, and she was not
pretty now, for her features were still heavy and blunt. But her dark and
slightly slanted eyes were beautiful, and her skin-tight skirt and orange
sweater displayed to enviable advantage a soft and slender body.

51   She saw me, and walked over. She teetered a little, but it was not due to her once-tubercular leg, for her limp was almost gone.

52   "Hi, Vanessa." Her voice still had the same hoarseness. "Long time no see, eh?"

53   "Hi," I said. "Where've you been keeping yourself, Piquette?"

54   "Oh, I been around," she said. "I been away almost two years now. Been all over the place — Winnipeg, Regina, Saskatoon. Jesus, what I could tell you! I come back this summer, but I ain't stayin'. You kids goin' to the dance?"

55   "No," I said abruptly, for this was a sore point with me. I was fifteen, and thought I was old enough to go to the Saturday-night dances at the Flamingo. My mother, however, thought otherwise.

56   "Y'oughta come," Piquette said. "I never miss one. It's just about the on'y thing in this jerkwater town that's any fun. Boy, you couldn' catch me stayin' here. I don' give a shit about this place. It stinks."

57   She sat down beside me, and I caught the harsh over-sweetness of her perfume.

58   "Listen, you wanna know something, Vanessa?" she confided, her voice only slightly blurred. "Your dad was the only person in Manawaka that ever done anything good to me."

59   I nodded speechlessly. I was certain she was speaking the truth. I knew a little more than I had that summer at Diamond Lake, but I could not reach her now any more than I had then. I was ashamed, ashamed of my own timidity, the frightened tendency to look the other way. Yet I felt no real warmth towards her — I only felt that I ought to, because of that distant summer and because my father had hoped she would be company for me, or perhaps that I would be for her, but it had not happened that way. At this moment, meeting her again, I had to admit that she repelled and embarrassed me, and I could not help despising the self-pity in her voice. I wished she would go away. I did not want to see her. I did not know what to say to her. It seemed that we had nothing to say to one another.

60   "I'll tell you something else," Piquette went on. "All the old bitches an' biddies in this town will sure be surprised. I'm gettin' married this fall — my boyfriend, he's an English fella, works in the stockyards in the city there, a very tall guy, got blond wavy hair. Gee, is he ever handsome. Got this real classy name. Alvin Gerald Cummings — some handle, eh? They call him Al."

61   For the merest instant, then, I saw her. I really did see her, for the first and only time in all the years we had both lived in the same town. Her

defiant face, momentarily, became unguarded and unmasked, and in her eyes there was a terrifying hope.

"Gee, Piquette—" I burst out awkwardly, "that's swell. That's really wonderful. Congratulations—good luck—I hope you'll be happy—" 62

As I mouthed the conventional phrases, I could only guess how great her need must have been, that she had been forced to seek the very things she so bitterly rejected. 63

When I was eighteen, I left Manawaka and went away to college. At the end of my first year, I came back home for the summer. I spent the first few days in talking non-stop with my mother, as we exchanged all the news that somehow had not found its way into letters—what had happened in my life and what had happened here in Manawaka while I was away. My mother searched her memory for events that concerned people I knew. 64

"Did I ever write to you about Piquette Tonnerre, Vanessa?" she asked one morning. 65

"No, I don't think so," I replied. "Last I heard of her, she was going to marry some guy in the city. Is she still there?" 66

My mother looked perturbed, and it was a moment before she spoke, as though she did not know how to express what she had to tell and wished she did not need to try. 67

"She's dead," she said at last. Then, as I stared at her, "Oh, Vanessa, when it happened, I couldn't help thinking of her as she was that summer—so sullen and gauche and badly dressed. I couldn't help wondering if we could have done something more at that time—but what could we do? She used to be around in the cottage there with me all day, and honestly, it was all I could do to get a word out of her. She didn't even talk to your father very much, although I think she liked him, in her way." 68

"What happened?" I asked. 69

"Either her husband left her, or she left him," my mother said. "I don't know which. Anyway, she came back here with two youngsters, both only babies—they must have been born very close together. She kept house, I guess, for Lazarus and her brothers, down the valley there, in the old Tonnerre place. I used to see her on the street sometimes, but she never spoke to me. She'd put on an awful lot of weight, and she looked a mess, to tell you the truth, a real slattern, dressed any old how. She was up in court a couple of times—drunk and disorderly, of course. One Saturday night last winter, during the coldest weather, Piquette was alone in the shack with the children. The Tonnerres made home brew all the time, so I've heard, and Lazarus said later she'd been drinking most of the day 70 when he and the boys went out that evening. They had an old woodstove there — you know the kind, with exposed pipes. The shack caught fire. Piquette didn't get out, and neither did the children."

71   I did not say anything. As so often with Piquette, there did not seem to be anything to say. There was a kind of silence around the image in my mind of the fire and the snow, and I wished I could put from my memory the look that I had seen once in Piquette's eyes.

72   I went up to Diamond Lake for a few days that summer, with Mavis and her family. The MacLeod cottage had been sold after my father's death, and I did not even go to look at it, not wanting to witness my long-ago kingdom possessed now by strangers. But one evening I went down to the shore by myself.

73   The small pier which my father had built was gone, and in its place there was a large and solid pier built by the government, for Galloping Mountain was now a national park, and Diamond Lake had been re-named Lake Wapakata, for it was felt that an Indian name would have a greater appeal to tourists. The one store had become several dozen, and the settlement had all the attributes of a flourishing resort — hotels, a dance-hall, cafés with neon signs, the penetrating odours of potato chips and hot dogs.

74   I sat on the government pier and looked out across the water. At night the lake at least was the same as it had always been, darkly shining and bearing within its black glass the streak of amber that was the path of the moon. There was no wind that evening, and everything was quiet all around me. It seemed too quiet, and then I realized that the loons were no longer here. I listened for some time, to make sure, but never once did I hear that long-drawn call, half mocking and half plaintive, spearing through the stillness across the lake.

75   I did not know what happened to the birds. Perhaps they had gone away to some far place of belonging. Perhaps they had been unable to find such a place, and had simply died out, having ceased to care any longer whether they lived or not.

76   I remembered how Piquette had scorned to come along, when my father and I sat there and listened to the lake birds. It seemed to me now that in some unconscious and totally unrecognized way, Piquette might have been the only one, after all, who had heard the crying of the loons.

1974

NOTES

Margaret Laurence (1926 – 1987) is one of Canada's most famous writers. This story is part of the Manawaka series of short stories and novels and may be found in the Vanessa MacLeod collection of stories, *A Bird in the House*.

Piquette and the Tonnerre family play prominent roles in the Manawaka stories. Piquette's tragic life is recounted in Laurence's novels *The Stone Angel* and *The Diviners*.

Louis Riel (1844 – 1885) A Métis leader who formed a provisional government in Manitoba, led two rebellions, and was executed for treason. The Métis were people of mixed Native and European parentage.

Batoche, Saskatchewan The capital of Louis Riel's provisional government for the Northwest.

C.P.R. Canadian Pacific Railway. The railway that joins Canada from east coast to west coast.

Nash The make of a car that is no longer manufactured.

Big Bear (1825 – 1888) Cree leader in the North-West Rebellion of 1885. He was tried for treason and imprisoned.

Poundmaker (1842 – 1886) Cree chief who also participated in the North-West Rebellion.

Tecumseh (1768 – 1813) Shawnee chief who fought beside the British in the War of 1812 against the Americans. He died in battle.

Father Brébeuf (1593 – 1649) A Jesuit missionary to the Hurons. He was tortured and killed by the Iroquois near what is now Midland, Ontario. This martyr was made a saint in 1930.

Pauline Johnson (1861 – 1913) Born Tekahionwake, this Mohawk poet's work celebrated her Native heritage.

Hiawatha An epic poem, *The Song of Hiawatha*, written by Henry Wadsworth Longfellow in 1885.

COMPREHENSION AND DISCUSSION

1. Why doesn't Grandmother MacLeod go to Diamond Lake with the family?
2. What sort of person is Ewen MacLeod?

3. Why is Piquette's sickness, tuberculosis of the bone, important to the story? How is this disease significant symbolically about the girl herself?
4. What does Vanessa first believe Piquette possesses? How is Vanessa disappointed? What lesson does she learn?
5. Recount at least three ways in which Piquette tries to fit into white Anglo-Saxon society.
6. What does Vanessa learn about her mother from the way she talks about Piquette?
7. What makes Piquette a stereotype? What makes her an individual?
8. Is Piquette's life tragic, especially in the manner of her death? Would her life have improved had she lived longer?
9. Explain the last line in the story.

LITERARY TECHNIQUES

Although Laurence uses the first-person point of view, the narrator, Vanessa MacLeod, is not actually the main character. The story is really about Piquette Tonnerre. By using this particular technique, we see the episodes unfold from Vanessa's perspective, and we learn about Piquette only through Vanessa.

Symbol Something concrete that represents something abstract. To illustrate, a ring is just a small, round ornament that a person wears on a finger; however, worn in marriage, a ring represents the love two people have for each other. In this story, the loons represent the wilderness, which is fast disappearing with white society's progress.

ASSIGNMENTS

1. In this story, the Tonnerres are called "half-breeds": "neither flesh, fowl, nor good salt herring" (paragraph 2). In Laurence Hill's "So What Are You, Anyway?", Mrs. Norton says, "I don't mind them mixed, but the world isn't ready for it. They're neither one thing nor the other" (paragraph 35). Explain these attitudes about mixed-raced children and discuss how relevant these views are in today's world.
2. Vanessa thinks that "Piquette must be in some way a daughter of the forest, a kind of junior prophetess of the wilds" (paragraph 22). Read the three articles about Grey Owl (pp. 232, 236, and 327). Discuss this view of Native people and its implications.

3. Research one of the historical figures mentioned in the story. Write a short biography.
4. Compare Piquette to Mike or Chris in Barbara Scott's "Lifeguard" (p. 190). Consider both the situations they find themselves in and how they deal with them.
5. In a short essay, explain the attraction of summer cottages.
6. In the last paragraphs of the story, Vanessa describes the changes to the lake area where her family had a cottage. Should such development be restricted? For example, should national and provincial parks remain undeveloped? What kind of restrictions, if any, should be imposed?
7. Look up *The Song of Hiawatha* or the poems of Pauline Johnson. Choose an excerpt and write a literary analysis of it.

How We Kept Mother's Day
Stephen Leacock

1   Of all the different ideas that have been started lately, I think that the very best is the notion of celebrating once a year "Mother's Day." I don't wonder that May the eleventh is becoming such a popular date all over America and I am sure the idea will spread to England too.

2   It is especially in a big family like ours that such an idea takes hold. So we decided to have a special celebration of Mother's Day. We thought it a fine idea. It made us all realize how much Mother had done for us for years, and all the efforts and sacrifice that she had made for our sake.

3   So we decided that we'd make it a great day, a holiday for all the family, and do everything we could to make Mother happy. Father decided to take a holiday from his office, so as to help in celebrating the day, and my sister Anne and I stayed home from college classes, and Mary and my brother Will stayed home from high school.

4   It was our plan to make it a day just like Xmas or any big holiday, and so we decided to decorate the house with flowers and with mottoes over the mantelpieces, and all that kind of thing. We got Mother to make mottoes and arrange the decorations, because she always does it at Xmas.

5   The two girls thought it would be a nice thing to dress in our very best for such a big occasion, and so they both got new hats. Mother trimmed both the hats, and they looked fine, and Father had bought four-in-hand silk ties for himself and us boys as a souvenir of the day to remember Mother by. We were going to get Mother a new hat too, but it turned out that she seemed to really like her old grey bonnet better than a new one, and both the girls said that it was awfully becoming to her.

6   Well, after breakfast we had it arranged as a surprise for Mother that we would hire a motor car and take her for a beautiful drive away into the country. Mother is hardly ever able to have a treat like that, because we can only afford to keep one maid, and so Mother is busy in the house nearly all the time. And of course the country is so lovely now that it would be just grand for her to have a lovely morning, driving for miles and miles.

7   But on the very morning of the day we changed the plan a little bit, because it occurred to Father that a thing it would be better to do even than to take Mother for a motor drive would be to take her fishing. Father said that as the car was hired and paid for, we might just as well use it for a drive up into hills where the streams are. As Father said, if you just go out driving without any object, you have a sense of aimlessness, but if you are going to fish, there is a definite purpose in front of you to heighten the enjoyment.

So we all felt that it would be nicer for Mother to have a definite pur- 8
pose; and anyway, it turned out that Father had just got a new rod the day
before, which made the idea of fishing all the more appropriate, and he said
that Mother could use it if she wanted to; in fact, he said it was practically
for her, only Mother said she would much rather watch him fish and not try
to fish herself.

So we got everything arranged for the trip, and we got Mother to cut 9
up some sandwiches and make up a sort of lunch in case we got hungry,
though of course we were to come back home again to a big dinner in the
middle of the day, just like Xmas or New Year's Day. Mother packed it all
up in a basket for us ready to go in the motor.

Well, when the car came to the door, it turned out that there hardly 10
seemed as much room in it as we had supposed, because we hadn't reck-
oned on Father's fishing basket and the rods and the lunch, and it was plain
enough that we couldn't all get in.

Father said not to mind him, he said that he could just as well stay 11
home, and that he was sure that he could put in the time working in the
garden; he said that there was a lot of rough dirty work that he could do,
like digging a trench for the garbage, that would save hiring a man, and so
he said that he'd stay home; he said that we were not to let the fact of his
not having had a real holiday for three years stand in our way; he wanted
us to go right ahead and be happy and have a big day, and not to mind him.
He said that he could plug away all day, and in fact he said he'd been a fool
to think there'd be any holiday for him.

But of course we all felt that it would never do to let Father stay home, 12
especially as we knew he would make trouble if he did. The two girls,
Anne and Mary, would gladly have stayed and helped the maid get dinner,
only it seemed such a pity to, on a lovely day like this, having their new
hats. But they both said that Mother had only to say the word, and they'd
gladly stay home and work. Will and I would have dropped out, but unfortunately we wouldn't have been any use in getting the dinner.

So in the end it was decided that Mother would stay home and just 13
have a lovely restful day round the house, and get the dinner. It turned out
anyway that Mother doesn't care for fishing, and also it was just a little bit
cold and fresh out of doors, though it was lovely and sunny, and Father was
rather afraid that Mother might take cold if she came.

He said he would never forgive himself if he dragged Mother round the 14
country and let her take a severe cold at a time when she might be having
a beautiful rest. He said it was our duty to try and let Mother get all the rest
and quiet that she could, after all that she had done for all of us, and he said

that that was principally why he had fallen in with this idea of a fishing trip, so as to give Mother a little quiet. He said that young people seldom realize how much quiet means to people who are getting old. As to himself, he could still stand the racket, but he was glad to shelter Mother from it.

15   So we all drove away with three cheers for Mother, and Mother stood and watched us from the verandah for as long as she could see us, and Father waved his hand back to her every few minutes till he hit his hand on the back edge of the car, and then said that he didn't think Mother could see us any longer.

16   Well, we had the loveliest day up among the hills that you could possibly imagine, and Father caught such big specimens that he felt sure that Mother couldn't have landed them anyway, if she had been fishing for them, and Will and I fished too, though we didn't get so many as Father, and the two girls met quite a lot of people that they knew as we drove along, and there were some young men friends of theirs that they met along the stream and talked to, and so we all had a splendid time.

17   It was quite late when we got back, nearly seven o'clock in the evening, but Mother had guessed that we would be late, so she had kept back the dinner so as to have it just nicely ready and hot for us. Only first she had to get towels and soap for Father and clean things for him to put on, because he always gets so messed up with fishing, and that kept Mother busy for a little while, that and helping the girls get ready.

18   But at last everything was ready, and we sat down to the grandest kind of dinner — roast turkey and all sorts of things like on Xmas Day. Mother had to get up and down a good bit during the meal fetching things back and forward, but at the end Father noticed it and said she simply mustn't do it, that he wanted her to spare herself, and he got up and fetched the walnuts over from the sideboard himself.

19   The dinner lasted a long while, and was great fun, and when it was over all of us wanted to help clear the things up and wash the dishes, only Mother said that she would really much rather do it, and so we let her, because we wanted just for once to humour her.

20   It was quite late when it was all over, and when we all kissed Mother before going to bed, she said it had been the most wonderful day in her life, and I think there were tears in her eyes. So we all felt awfully repaid for all that we had done.

1926

NOTES

Stephen Leacock (1869 – 1944) is one of Canada's most famous writers. He has an award for humorous writing named after him.

The observance of Mother's Day has been standardized as the second Sunday in May. However, when the holiday first originated, in about 1910, the day was set and moved accordingly with each year. For example, in Leacock's story, the set date is May 11, so if Mother's Day occurs on Tuesday one year, the next year it would fall on Wednesday.

Note the word "kept" in the story title. It means observed, celebrated, or paid close attention to.

Xmas Note the use of the short form for Christmas. The "X" is not an English X to cross something out but the Greek letter chi (χ), which looks like an "X" but is written "ch" in English.

COMPREHENSION AND DISCUSSION

1. The family members have good intentions of making the day easier for the mother. What do they do? Then what really happens?
2. What evidence in the story tells you that the setting and time are in the early 20th century?
3. Are the father and children selfish in their celebration or are they just unaware of what they do?
4. Recount the various changes in the plan that cause the mother to end up staying at home.
5. List all the extra work, beyond the normal running of the house, that the family members make for the mother.
6. How does the mother take all this?
7. Explain the concluding paragraph to the story: "It was quite late when it was all over, and when we all kissed Mother before going to bed, she said it had been the most wonderful day in her life, and I think there were tears in her eyes. So we all felt awfully repaid for all that we had done" (paragraph 20).
8. Would you accept this treatment of the mother as normal? Why or why not?
9. What would you do for your mother to celebrate Mother's Day?

LITERARY TECHNIQUES

Note how this story lacks dialogue; there is no direct speech from any of the characters. There is, however, indirect speech. With this strategy, Leacock blurs the distinction between a fictional story and a remembrance of the past. Unless the reader is aware of the writer's biography, he or she could take this piece as an article, a non-fiction account.

Leacock uses irony to create humour. Irony may be defined in several ways. First, what is said and what is done are diametrically opposed; for example, the sisters in the story want their mother to rest, but she ends up trimming the girls' newly bought hats. Second, irony has the element of the unexpected; for instance, the father's fishing tackle takes up so much space in the car that the family decides to leave the mother at home.

Humour depends on recognition. A situation is funny only if the reader understands what is going on or has had a similar experience. Leacock relies on common experiences that most readers have had sometime in their lives. For example, most of us can identify with the father in this story, who offers to sacrifice his chance to go fishing and instead stay at home and do work around the house while at the same time drawing attention to his sad plight.

ASSIGNMENTS

1. How should family roles and responsibilities be divided? Write a persuasive essay.
2. Write a dialogue based on one of the conversational exchanges in the story.
3. Describe a holiday, such as Father's Day, Halloween, or Canada Day, and explain how it is celebrated. Research the background.
4. In 1994, the National Film Board of Canada (NFB) produced a ten-minute animated film of this story. Watch the film and compare it with the written version.

The Prodigal Son

Luke 15:11 – 32

from The King James Authorized Version of the Holy Bible

And he said, A certain man had two sons: 11

And the younger of them said to *his* father, Father, give me the portion   12
of goods that falleth *to me*. And he divided unto them *his* living.

And not many days after the younger son gathered all together, and   13
took his journey into a far country, and there wasted his substance with
riotous living.

And when he had spent all, there arose a mighty famine in that land;   14
and he began to be in want.

And he went and joined himself to a citizen of that country; and he sent   15
him into his fields to feed swine.

And he would fain have filled his belly with the husks that the swine   16
did eat: and no man gave unto him.

And when he came to himself, he said, How many hired servants of my   17
father's have bread enough and to spare, and I perish with hunger!

I will arise and go to my father, and will say unto him, Father, I have   18
sinned against heaven, and before thee,

And am no more worthy to be called thy son: make me as one of thy   19
hired servants.

And he arose, and came to his father. But when he was yet a great way   20
off, his father saw him, and had compassion, and ran, and fell on his neck,
and kissed him.

And the son said unto him, Father, I have sinned against heaven, and   21
in thy sight, and am no more worthy to be called thy son.

But the father said to his servants, Bring forth the best robe, and put it   22
on him; and put this ring on his hand, and shoes on *his* feet:

And bring hither the fatted calf, and kill *it*; and let us eat, and be merry: 23

For this my son was dead, and is alive again; he was lost, and is found.   24
And they began to be merry.

Now his elder son was in the field: and as he came and drew nigh to   25
the house, he heard musick and dancing.

And he called one of the servants, and asked what these things meant.   26

And he said unto him, Thy brother is come; and thy father had killed   27
the fatted calf, because he hath received him safe and sound.

28   And he was angry, and would not go in: therefore came his father out, and intreated him.

29   And he answering said to *his* father, Lo, these many years do I serve thee, neither transgressed I at any time thy commandment: and yet thou never gavest me a kid, that I might make merry with my friends:

30   But as soon as this thy son was come, which hath devoured thy living with harlots, thou hast killed for him this fatted calf.

31   And he said unto him, Son, thou art ever with me, and all that I have is thine.

32   It was meet that we should make merry, and be glad: for this thy brother was dead, and is alive again; and was lost, and is found.

around A.D. 30, translated 1611

NOTES

A parable is a story that illustrates a moral lesson. Often a parable has more than just surface meaning. It resonates with spiritual teachings. In the West, the most famous and memorable parables are those told by Jesus. In his short ministry, Jesus was often asked questions, and he would reply by telling a parable. Thus, this story begins with the phrase "And he said." Other famous parables are "The Good Samaritan" and "The Lost Lamb."

"Prodigal" means wasteful and lavish. From this story it gained the additional meaning of someone who returns to a family, and this is the most common meaning today.

To tend swine is an insulting and humiliating task, especially for a Jew. The young man has fallen quite low socially, financially, and spiritually. According to the dietary and divine laws in the Bible, the pig is a prohibited animal: "And the swine, though he divide the hoof, and be clovenfooted, yet he cheweth not the cud; he *is* unclean to you. Of their flesh shall ye not eat, and their carcase shall ye not touch; they *are* unclean to you" (Leviticus 11:7–8).

A fattened animal is kept for special occasions. The father has deemed the return of his son a time to celebrate.

COMPREHENSION AND DISCUSSION

1. Why does the son want his inheritance?
2. At what point does the young man realize his mistake?

3. What is the moral of this story? In other words, what is the point that Jesus makes in telling this story to the Pharisees and scribes?
4. Does an adult child have the right to demand a share of the inheritance from parents who are still living?
5. How do you know whether your friends are true or merely fair-weather ones?
6. Does the other son have legitimate reason to complain? Should people who break the rules be given greater consideration than those who are "good"?

LITERARY TECHNIQUES

This well-known parable was translated from the original Greek during the reign of King James I of England, 1603–1625. The translators attempted to preserve not only the veracity of the message but also the simple style of the original.

The parable is meant to be spoken rather than read. It imitates speech, albeit an archaic 17th-century pattern of speaking. The constant use of "and" to begin the verses suggests a chaining of ideas.

This parable has stark sentences that move the story along. In each verse or paragraph, there are no more than two sentences. There is little description, and there are no quotation marks to distinguish speech from narration.

Note that the moral lesson is not explicit. Unlike Aesop's fables, in which the moral is reiterated, the parable lets the listener or reader come to realize the point.

ASSIGNMENTS

1. How does this parable differ from the folktale "The Cowherd" (p. 71)?
2. Read the other well-known parable, "The Good Samaritan" (Luke 10:25–37). Which one do you prefer and why?
3. Rewrite the story in modern English. You can write it from the same point of view, or that of the parent or the brother who remains at home.
4. Compare the son in this parable and the son in Morley Callaghan's "All the Years of Her Life" (p. 45) or the son in "The Cowherd" (p. 71).
5. Read "The Ant and the Grasshopper" by W. Somerset Maugham (p. 150). Write an essay comparing the two sets of brothers.

The Ant and the Grasshopper

W. Somerset Maugham

1   When I was a very small boy I was made to learn by heart certain of the fables of La Fontaine, and the moral of each was carefully explained to me. Among those I learnt was "The Ant and the Grasshopper," which is devised to bring home to the young the useful lesson that in an imperfect world industry is rewarded and giddiness punished. In this admirable fable (I apologize for telling something which everyone is politely, but inexactly, supposed to know) the ant spends a laborious summer gathering its winter store, while the grasshopper sits on a blade of grass singing to the sun. Winter comes and the ant is comfortably provided for, but the grasshopper has an empty larder: he goes to the ant and begs for a little food. Then the ant gives him her classic answer:

2   "What were you doing in the summer time?"

3   "Saving your presence, I sang, I sang all day, all night."

4   "You sang. Why, then go and dance."

5   I do not ascribe it to perversity on my part, but rather to the inconsequence of childhood, which is deficient in moral sense, that I could never quite reconcile myself to the lesson. My sympathies were with the grasshopper and for some time I never saw an ant without putting my foot on it. In this summary (and as I have discovered since, entirely human) fashion I sought to express my disapproval of prudence and common sense.

6   I could not help thinking of this fable when the other day I saw George Ramsay lunching by himself in a restaurant. I never saw anyone wear an expression of such deep gloom. He was staring into space. He looked as though the burden of the whole world sat on his shoulders. I was sorry for him: I suspected at once that his unfortunate brother had been causing trouble again. I went up to him and held out my hand.

7   "How are you?" I asked.

8   "I'm not in hilarious spirits," he answered.

9   "Is it Tom again?"

10   He sighed.

11   "Yes, it's Tom again."

12   "Why don't you chuck him? You've done everything in the world for him. You must know by now that he's quite hopeless."

13   I suppose every family has a black sheep. Tom had been a sore trial to his for twenty years. He had begun life decently enough: he went into busi-

ness, married, and had two children. The Ramsays were perfectly respectable people and there was every reason to suppose that Tom Ramsay would have a useful and honourable career. But one day, without warning, he announced that he didn't like work and that he wasn't suited for marriage. He wanted to enjoy himself. He would listen to no expostulations. He left his wife and his office. He had a little money and he spent two happy years in the various capitals of Europe. Rumours of his doings reached his relations from time to time and they were profoundly shocked. He certainly had a very good time. They shook their heads and asked what would happen when his money was spent. They soon found out: he borrowed. He was charming and unscrupulous. I have never met anyone to whom it was more difficult to refuse a loan. He made a steady income from his friends and he made friends easily. But he always said that the money you spent on necessities was boring; the money that was amusing to spend was the money you spent on luxuries. For this he depended on his brother George. He did not waste his charm on him. George was a serious man and insensible to such enticements. George was respectable. Once or twice he fell to Tom's promises of amendment and gave him considerable sums in order that he might make a fresh start. On these Tom bought a motor-car and some very nice jewellery. But when circumstances forced George to realize that his brother would never settle down and he washed his hands of him, Tom, without a qualm, began to blackmail him. It was not very nice for a respectable lawyer to find his brother shaking cocktails behind the bar of his favourite restaurant or to see him waiting on the box-seat of a taxi outside his club. Tom said that to serve in a bar or to drive a taxi was a perfectly decent occupation, but if George could oblige him with a couple of hundred pounds he didn't mind for the honour of the family giving it up. George paid.

Once Tom nearly went to prison. George was terribly upset. He went into the whole discreditable affair. Really Tom had gone too far. He had been wild, thoughtless, and selfish, but he had never before done anything dishonest, by which George meant illegal; and if he were prosecuted he would assuredly be convicted. But you cannot allow your only brother to go to gaol. The man Tom had cheated, a man called Cronshaw, was vindictive. He was determined to take the matter into court; he said Tom was a scoundrel and should be punished. It cost George an infinite deal of trouble and five hundred pounds to settle the affair. I have never seen him in such a rage as when he heard that Tom and Cronshaw had gone off together to Monte Carlo the moment they cashed the cheque. They spent a happy month there.

14

15   For twenty years Tom raced and gambled, philandered with the pret-
tiest girls, danced, ate in the most expensive restaurants, and dressed beautifully. He always looked as if he had just stepped out of a bandbox.
Though he was forty-six you would never have taken him for more than
thirty-five. He was a most amusing companion and though you knew he
was perfectly worthless you could not but enjoy his society. He had high
spirits, an unfailing gaiety, and incredible charm. I never grudged the contributions he regularly levied on me for the necessities of his existence. I
never lent him fifty pounds without feeling that I was in his debt. Tom
Ramsay knew everyone and everyone knew Tom Ramsay. You could not
approve of him, but you could not help liking him.

16   Poor George, only a year older than his scapegrace brother, looked
sixty. He had never taken more than a fortnight's holiday in the year for a
quarter of a century. He was in his office every morning at nine-thirty and
never left it till six. He was honest, industrious, and worthy. He had a good
wife, to whom he had never been unfaithful even in thought, and four
daughters to whom he was the best of fathers. He made a point of saving a
third of his income and his plan was to retire at fifty-five to a little house
in the country where he proposed to cultivate his garden and play golf. His
life was blameless. He was glad that he was growing old because Tom was
growing old too. He rubbed his hands and said:

17   "It was all very well when Tom was young and good-looking, but he's
only a year younger than I am. In four years he'll be fifty. He won't find
life so easy then. I shall have thirty thousand pounds by the time I'm fifty.
For twenty-five years I've said that Tom would end in the gutter. And we
shall see how he likes that. We shall see if it really pays best to work or be
idle."

18   Poor George! I sympathized with him. I wondered now as I sat down
beside him what infamous thing Tom had done. George was evidently very
much upset.

19   "Do you know what's happened now?" he asked me.

20   I was prepared for the worst. I wondered if Tom had got into the hands
of the police at last. George could hardly bring himself to speak.

21   "You're not going to deny that all my life I've been hardworking,
decent, respectable, and straightforward. After a life of industry and thrift
I can look forward to retiring on a small income in gilt-edged securities.
I've always done my duty in that state of life in which it has pleased
Providence to place me."

22   "True."

"And you can't deny that Tom has been an idle, worthless, dissolute, 23
and dishonourable rogue. If there were any justice he'd be in the work-
house."

"True." 24

George grew red in the face. 25

"A few weeks ago he became engaged to a woman old enough to be 26
his mother. And now she's died and left him everything she had. Half a million pounds, a yacht, a house in London, and a house in the country."

George Ramsay beat his clenched fist on the table. 27

"It's not fair, I tell you, it's not fair. Damn it, it's not fair." 28

I could not help it. I burst into a shout of laughter as I looked at 29
George's wrathful face, I rolled in my chair, I very nearly fell on the floor.
George never forgave me. But Tom often asks me to excellent dinners in
his charming house in Mayfair, and if he occasionally borrows a trifle from
me, that is merely from force of habit. It is never more than a sovereign.

1938

NOTES

W. Somerset Maugham (1874 – 1965) wrote plays, short stories, and
novels, including *Of Human Bondage*. He served in the British secret
service and drew on those experiences in his works, starting the tradition
of the modern spy story.

"The Ant and the Grasshopper" is one of Aesop's fables, retold by Jean de
La Fontaine. A fable is a short moral tale, often with animals acting out
human characteristics. Aesop was a Greek slave and famed storyteller who
lived around 600 B.C. La Fontaine was a 17th-century French poet who
retold many of Aesop's fables.

COMPREHENSION AND DISCUSSION

1. Is the narrator the main character in this story? If not, who is? How is
   this effective?
2. Why does the narrator recount the La Fontaine story for the reader?
3. Describe the characters of the two brothers.
4. Briefly summarize what happens in the story.

5. Consider Tom's "blackmail" of George. In today's society, would many people care if a relative entered a less than respectable profession? Who would care? What if the relative embarked on a life of crime?
6. What words, phrases, or clues tell you this story is British?
7. How does this story differ from the fable?
8. Explain the humour in the plot twist.
9. What moral lesson has Maugham inverted? Why?
10. Whom do you identify with more — George or Tom Ramsay? Why?
11. How important is the work ethic in modern society?

LITERARY TECHNIQUES

Point of view Although this story is told from the first-person point of view, the narrator is not the main character or protagonist. He is a secondary character. There are several advantages to this method. The point of view is objective. The speaker balances the characterization of Tom and George. Second, he can make comments on the action. Moreover, he can participate in the action (plot); in this way, the narrator becomes integral to the telling of the story.

Using fables and folktales Writers often borrow, steal, or adapt a plot from a well-known old story. For example, the basic story line of Cinderella, where a poor but good girl makes good by marrying a prince, can be found in everything from romance novels to teen movies. The story of two star-crossed lovers in *Romeo and Juliet* was updated in the movie *West Side Story*. Often the writer, like Maugham, updates the details and gives a contemporary retelling or twist.

Contrast Antithesis is the literary term for showing contrast. Like Maugham's use of George and Tom, sharp differences between two characters or two things work better in storytelling than non-distinct contrasts. Parallelism in the contrasts is important to the structure of a story.

Irony In this story, irony is found in the twist ending. It is not what we expect, especially in comparison to the original fable. Tom does not have a sad ending like the grasshopper's. Moreover, irony creates humour; even though George follows society's rules and works hard, he ends up the loser and the butt of the joke.

ASSIGNMENTS

1. Write a paragraph or an essay comparing the Ramsay brothers to the two brothers in "The Prodigal Son."
2. Choose another fable by Aesop or La Fontaine, and explain why it is relevant to modern life. Some well-known fables are "The Tortoise and the Hare," "The Fox and the Grapes," "The North Wind and the Sun," "The Crow and the Pitcher," and "The Town Mouse and the Country Mouse."
3. What does our society need more — people like George or people like Tom? Explain in an essay.
4. Research the meaning of the term "Protestant work ethic." What are the virtues in such belief? What is wrong with this belief? Is it applicable to our society today?
5. Frank Stockton's "The Lady or the Tiger?" (p. 202) deals with fate or the unknown factor that governs life. A person cannot foresee the future in order to avoid the pitfalls or to embrace the advantages. Would George have changed his life or his attitude had he known what would happen thirty years in the future?
6. Write a comparison essay on how Maugham in "The Ant and the Grasshopper" and Stephen Leacock in "How We Kept Mother's Day" (p. 142) use irony to achieve humour.

An Ounce of Cure

Alice Munro

1   My parents didn't drink. They weren't rabid about it, and in fact I remember that when I signed a pledge in grade seven, with the rest of that superbly if impermanently indoctrinated class, my mother said, "It's just nonsense and fanaticism, children of that age." My father would drink a beer on a hot day, but my mother did not join him, and — whether accidentally or symbolically — this drink was always consumed *outside* the house. Most of the people we knew were the same way, in the small town where we lived. I ought not to say that it was this which got me into difficulties, because the difficulties I got into were a faithful expression of my own incommodious nature — the same nature that caused my mother to look at me, on any occasion which traditionally calls for feelings of pride and maternal accomplishment (my departure for my first formal dance, I mean, or my hellbent preparations for a descent on college) with an expression of brooding and fascinated despair, as if she could not possibly expect, did not ask, that it should go with me as it did with other girls; the dreamed-of spoils of daughters — orchids, nice boys, diamond rings — would be borne home in due course by the daughters of her friends, but not by me; all she could do was hope for a lesser rather than a greater disaster — an elopement, say, with a boy who could never earn his living, rather than an abduction into the White Slave trade.

2   But ignorance, my mother said, ignorance, or innocence if you like, is not always such a fine thing as people think and I am not sure it may not be dangerous for a girl like you; then she emphasized her point, as she had a habit of doing, with some quotation which had an innocent pomposity and odour of mothballs. I didn't even wince at it, knowing full well how it must have worked wonders with Mr. Berryman.

3   The evening I baby-sat for the Berrymans must have been in April. I had been in love all year, or at least since the first week in September, when a boy named Martin Collingwood had given me a surprised, appreciative, and rather ominously complacent smile in the school assembly. I never knew what surprised him; I was not looking like anybody but me; I had an old blouse on and my home-permanent had turned out badly. A few weeks after that he took me out for the first time, and kissed me on the dark side of the porch — also, I ought to say, on the mouth; I am sure it was the first time anybody had ever kissed me effectively, and I know that I did not wash my face that night or the next morning, in order to keep the imprint

NEL

of those kisses intact. (I showed the most painful banality in the conduct of this whole affairs, as you will see.) Two months, and a few amatory stages later, he dropped me. He had fallen for the girl who played opposite him in the Christmas production of *Pride and Prejudice*.

I said I was not going to have anything to do with that play, and I got   4 another girl to work on Makeup in my place, but of course I went to it after all, and sat down in front with my girl friend Joyce, who pressed my hand when I was overcome with pain and delight at the sight of Mr. Darcy in white breeches, silk waistcoat, and sideburns. It was surely seeing Martin as Darcy that did for me; every girl is in love with Darcy anyway, and the part gave Martin an arrogance and male splendour in my eyes which made it impossible to remember that he was simply a high-school senior, passably good-looking and of medium intelligence (and with a reputation slightly tainted, at that, by such preferences as the Drama Club and the Cadet Band) who appeared to be the first boy, the first really presentable boy, to take an interest in me. In the last act they gave him a chance to embrace Elizabeth (Mary Bishop, with a sallow complexion and no figure, but big vivacious eyes) and during this realistic encounter I dug my nails bitterly into Joyce's sympathetic palm.

That night was the beginning of months of real, if more or less self-   5 inflicted, misery for me. Why is it a temptation to refer to this sort of thing lightly, with irony, with amazement even, at finding oneself involved with such preposterous emotions in the unaccountable past? That is what we are apt to do, speaking of love; with adolescent love, of course, it's practically obligatory; you would think we sat around, dull afternoons, amusing ourselves with these tidbit recollections of pain. But it really doesn't make me feel very gay—worse still, it doesn't really surprise me—to remember all the stupid, sad, half-ashamed things I did, that people in love always do. I hung around the places where he might be seen, and then pretended not to see him; I made absurdly roundabout approaches, in conversation, to the bitter pleasure of casually mentioning his name. I daydreamed endlessly; in fact if you want to put it mathematically, I spent perhaps ten times as many hours thinking about Martin Collingwood—yes, pining and weeping for him—as I ever spent with him; the idea of him dominated my mind relentlessly and, after a while, against my will. For if at first I had dramatized my feelings, the time came when I would have been glad to escape them; my well-worn daydreams had become depressing and not even temporarily consoling. As I worked my math problems I would torture myself, quite mechanically and helplessly, with an exact recollection of Martin kissing my throat. I had an exact recollection of *everything*. One night I had an impulse to swallow all the aspirins in the bathroom cabinet, but stopped after I had taken six.

6   My mother noticed that something was wrong and got me some iron pills. She said, "Are you sure everything is going all right at school?" *School!* When I told her that Martin and I had broken up all she said was, "Well so much the better for that. I never saw a boy so stuck on himself." "Martin has enough conceit to sink a battleship," I said morosely and went upstairs and cried.

7   The night I went to the Berrymans was a Saturday night. I baby-sat for them quite often on Saturday nights because they liked to drive over to Baileyville, a much bigger, livelier town about twenty miles away, and perhaps have supper and go to a show. They had been living in our town only two or three years — Mr. Berryman had been brought in as plant manager of the new door-factory — and they remained, I suppose by choice, on the fringes of its society; most of their friends were youngish couples like themselves, born in other places, who lived in new ranch-style houses on a hill outside town where we used to go tobogganing. This Saturday night they had two other couples in for drinks before they all drove over to Baileyville for the opening of a new supper-club; they were all rather festive. I sat in the kitchen and pretended to do Latin. Last night had been the Spring Dance at the High School. I had not gone, since the only boy who had asked me was Millerd Crompton, who asked so many girls that he was suspected of working his way through the whole class alphabetically. But the dance was held in the Armouries, which was only half a block away from our house; I had been able to see the boys in dark suits, the girls in long pale formals under their coats, passing gravely under the street-lights, stepping around the last patches of snow. I could even hear the music and I have not forgotten to this day that they played "Ballerina," and — oh, song of my aching heart — "Slow Boat to China." Joyce had phoned me up this morning and told me in her hushed way (we might have been discussing an incurable disease I had) that yes, M.C. *had* been there with M.B., and she had on a formal that must have been made out of somebody's old lace tablecloth, it just *hung*.

8   When the Berrymans and their friends had gone I went into the living room and read a magazine. I was mortally depressed. The big softly lit room, with its green and leaf-brown colours, made an uncluttered setting for the development of the emotions, such as you would get on a stage. At home the life of the emotions went on all right, but it always seemed to get

buried under the piles of mending to be done, the ironing, the children's jigsaw puzzles and rock collections. It was the sort of house where people were always colliding with one another on the stairs and listening to hockey games and Superman on the radio.

I got up and found the Berrymans' "Danse Macabre" and put it on the record player and turned out the living-room lights. The curtains were only partly drawn. A street light shone obliquely on the windowpane, making a rectangle of thin dusty gold, in which the shadows of bare branches moved, caught in the huge sweet winds of spring. It was a mild black night when the last snow was melting. A year ago all this — the music, the wind and darkness, the shadows of the branches — would have given me tremendous happiness; when they did not do so now, but only called up tediously familiar, somehow humiliatingly personal thoughts, I gave up my soul for dead and walked into the kitchen and decided to get drunk. 9

No, it was not like that. I walked into the kitchen to look for a coke or something in the refrigerator, and there on the front of the counter were three tall beautiful bottles, all about half full of gold. But even after I had looked at them and lifted them to feel their weight I had not decided to get drunk; I had decided to have a drink. 10

Now here is where my ignorance, my disastrous innocence, comes in. It is true that I had seen the Berrymans and their friends drinking their highballs as casually as I could drink a coke, but I did not apply this attitude to myself. No; I thought of hard liquor as something to be taken in extremities, and relied upon for extravagant results, one way or another. My approach could not have been less casual if I had been the Little Mermaid drinking the witch's crystal potion. Gravely, with a glance at my set face in the black window above the sink, I poured a little whisky from each of the bottles (I think now there were two brands of rye and an expensive Scotch) until I had my glass full. For I had never in my life seen anyone pour a drink and I had no idea that people frequently diluted their liquor with water, soda, et cetera, and I had seen that the glasses the Berrymans' guests were holding when I came through the living room were nearly full. 11

I drank it off as quickly as possible. I set the glass down and stood looking at my face in the window, half expecting to see it altered. My throat was burning, but I felt nothing else. It was very disappointing, when I had worked myself up to it. But I was not going to let it go at that. I poured another full glass, then filled each of the bottles with water to approximately the level I had seen when I came in. I drank the second glass only a little more slowly than the first. I put the empty glass down on the 12

counter with care, perhaps feeling in my head a rustle of things to come, and went and sat down on a chair in the living room. I reached up and turned on a floor lamp beside the chair, and the room jumped on me.

13 When I say that I was expecting extravagant results I do not mean that I was expecting this. I had thought of some sweeping emotional change, an upsurge of gaiety and irresponsibility, a feeling of lawlessness and escape, accompanied by a little dizziness and perhaps a tendency to giggle out loud. I did not have in mind the ceiling spinning like a great plate somebody had thrown at me, nor the pale green blobs of the chairs swelling, converging, disintegrating, playing with me a game full of enormous senseless inanimate malice. My head sank back; I closed my eyes. And at once opened them, opened them wide, threw myself out of the chair and down the hall and reached — thank God, thank God! — the Berrymans' bathroom, where I was sick everywhere, everywhere, and dropped like a stone.

14 From this point on I have no continuous picture of what happened; my memories of the next hour or two are split into vivid and improbable segments, with nothing but murk and uncertainty between. I do remember lying on the bathroom floor looking sideways at the little six-sided white tiles, which lay together in such an admirable and logical pattern, seeing them with the brief broken gratitude and sanity of one who has just been torn to pieces with vomiting. Then I remember sitting on the stool in front of the hall phone, asking weakly for Joyce's number. Joyce was not home. I was told by her mother (a rather rattlebrained woman, who didn't seem to notice a thing the matter — for which I felt weakly, mechanically grateful) that she was at Kay Stringer's house. I didn't know Kay's number so I just asked the operator; I felt I couldn't risk looking down at the telephone book.

15 Kay Stringer was not a friend of mine but a new friend of Joyce's. She had a vague reputation for wildness and a long switch of hair, very oddly, though naturally, coloured — from soap-yellow to caramel-brown. She knew a lot of boys more exciting than Martin Collingwood, boys who had quit school or been imported into town to play on the hockey team. She and Joyce rode around in these boys' cars, and sometimes went with them — having lied of course to their mothers — to the Gay-la dance hall on the highway north of town.

16 I got Joyce on the phone. She was very keyed-up, as she always was with boys around, and she hardly seemed to hear what I was saying.

17 "Oh, I can't tonight," she said. "Some kids are here. We're going to play cards. You know Bill Kline? He's here. Ross Armour — "

"I'm *sick*," I said trying to speak distinctly; it came out an inhuman   18
croak. "I'm *drunk*. Joyce!" Then I fell off the stool and the receiver dropped
out of my hand and banged for a while dismally against the wall.

I had not told Joyce where I was, so after thinking about it for a   19
moment she phoned my mother, and using the elaborate and unnecessary
subterfuge that young girls delight in, she found out. She and Kay and the
boys — there were three of them — told some story about where they were
going to Kay's mother, and got into the car and drove out. They found me
still lying on the broadloom carpet in the hall; I had been sick again, and
this time I had not made it to the bathroom.

It turned out that Kay Stringer, who arrived on this scene only by acci-   20
dent, was exactly the person I needed. She loved a crisis, particularly one
like this, which had a shady and scandalous aspect and which must be kept
secret from the adult world. She became excited, aggressive, efficient; that
energy which was termed wildness was simply the overflow of a great
female instinct to manage, comfort and control. I could hear her voice
coming at me from all directions, telling me not to worry, telling Joyce to
find the biggest coffeepot they had and make it full of coffee (*strong*
coffee, she said), telling the boys to pick me up and carry me to the sofa.
Later, in the fog beyond my reach, she was calling for a scrub-brush.

Then I was lying on the sofa, covered with some kind of crocheted   21
throw they had found in the bedroom. I didn't want to lift my head. The
house was full of the smell of coffee. Joyce came in, looking very pale;
she said that the Berryman kids had wakened up but she had given them
a cookie and told them to go back to bed, it was all right; she hadn't let
them out of their room and she didn't believe they'd remember. She said
that she and Kay had cleaned up the bathroom and the hall though she was
afraid there was still a spot on the rug. The coffee was ready. I didn't
understand anything very well. The boys had turned on the radio and were
going through the Berrymans' record collection; they had it out on the
floor. I felt there was something odd about this but I could not think what
it was.

Kay brought me a huge breakfast mug full of coffee.   22

"I don't know if I can," I said. "Thanks."   23

"Sit up," she said briskly, as if dealing with drunks was an everyday   24
business for her, I had no need to feel myself important. (I met, and recognized, that tone of voice years later, in the maternity ward.) "Now drink,"
she said. I drank, and at the same time realized that I was wearing only my
slip. Joyce and Kay had taken off my blouse and skirt. They had brushed
off the skirt and washed out the blouse, since it was nylon; it was hanging

in the bathroom. I pulled the throw up under my arms and Kay laughed. She got everybody coffee. Joyce brought in the coffeepot and on Kay's instructions she kept filling my cup whenever I drank from it. Somebody said to me with interest, "You must have really wanted to tie one on."

25   "No," I said rather sulkily, obediently drinking my coffee. "I only had two drinks."

26   Kay laughed, "Well it certainly gets to you, I'll say that. What time do you expect *they'll* be back?" she said.

27   "Late. After one, I think."

28   "You should be all right by that time. Have some more coffee."

29   Kay and one of the boys began dancing to the radio. Kay danced very sexily, but her face had the gently superior and indulgent, rather cold look it had when she was lifting me up to drink the coffee. The boy was whispering to her and she was smiling, shaking her head. Joyce said she was hungry, and she went out to the kitchen to see what there was — potato chips or crackers, or something like that, that you could eat without making too noticeable a dint. Bill Kline came over and sat on the sofa beside me and patted my legs through the crocheted throw. He didn't say anything to me, just patted my legs and looked at me with what seemed to me a very stupid, half-sick, absurd and alarming expression. I felt very uncomfortable; I wondered how it had ever got around that Bill Kline was so good-looking, with an expression like that. I moved my legs nervously and he gave me a look of contempt, not ceasing to pat me. Then I scrambled off the sofa, pulling the throw around me, with the idea of going to the bathroom to see if my blouse was dry. I lurched a little when I started to walk, and for some reason — probably to show Bill Kline that he had not panicked me — I immediately exaggerated this, and calling out, "Watch me walk a straight line!" I lurched and stumbled, to the accompaniment of everybody's laughter, towards the hall. I was standing in the archway between the hall and the living room when the knob of the front door turned with a small matter-of-fact click and everything became silent behind me except the radio of course and the crocheted throw inspired by some delicate malice of its own slithered down around my feet and there — oh, delicious moment in a well-organized farce! — there stood the Berrymans, Mr. and Mrs., with expressions on their faces as appropriate to the occasion as any old-fashioned director of farces could wish. They must have been preparing those expressions, of course; they could not have produced them in the first moment of shock; with the noise we were making, they had no doubt heard us as soon as they got out of the car; for the same reason, we had not heard them. I don't think I ever knew what

brought them home so early—a headache, an argument—and I was not really in a position to ask.

Mr. Berryman drove me home. I don't remember how I got into that car, or   30
how I found my clothes and put them on, or what kind of a good-night, if any, I said to Mrs. Berryman. I don't remember what happened to my friends, though I imagine they gathered up their coats and fled, covering up the ignominy of their departure with a mechanical roar of defiance. I remember Joyce with a box of crackers in her hand, saying that I had become terribly sick from eating—I think she said *sauerkraut*—for supper, and that I had called them for help. (When I asked her later what they made of this she said, "It wasn't any use. You *reeked*.") I remember also her saying, "Oh, no, Mr. Berryman I beg of you, my mother is a terribly nervous person I don't know what the shock might do to her. I will go down on my knees to you if you like but *you must not phone my mother*." I have no picture of her down on her knees—and she would have done it in a minute—so it seems this threat was not carried out.

Mr. Berryman said to me, "Well, I guess you know your behaviour   31
tonight is a pretty serious thing." He made it sound as if I might be charged with criminal negligence or something worse. "It would be very wrong of me to overlook it," he said. I suppose that besides being angry and disgusted with *me*, he was worried about taking me home in this condition to my strait-laced parents, who could always say I got the liquor in his house. Plenty of Temperance people would think that enough to hold him responsible, and the town was full of Temperance people. Good relations with the town were very important to him from a business point of view.

"I have an idea it wasn't the first time," he said. "If it was the first time,   32
would a girl be smart enough to fill three bottles up with water? No. Well in this case, she *was* smart enough, but not smart enough to know I could spot it. What do you say to that?" I opened my mouth to answer and although I was feeling quite sober the only sound that came out was a loud, desolate-sounding giggle. He stopped in front of our house. "Light's on," he said. "Now go in and tell your parents the straight truth. And if you don't, remember I will." He did not mention paying me for my babysitting services of the evening and the subject did not occur to me either.

I went into the house and tried to go straight upstairs but my mother   33
called to me. She came into the front hall, where I had not turned on the light, and she must have smelled me at once for she ran forward with a cry of pure amazement, as if she had seen somebody falling, and caught me by the shoulders as I did indeed fall down against the bannister, overwhelmed

by my fantastic lucklessness, and I told her everything from the start, not omitting even the name of Martin Collingwood and my flirtation with the aspirin bottle, which was a mistake.

34   On Monday morning my mother took the bus over to Baileyville and found the liquor store and bought a bottle of Scotch whisky. Then she had to wait for a bus back, and she met some people she knew and was not quite able to hide the bottle in her bag; she was furious with herself for not bringing a proper shopping-bag. As soon as she got back she walked out to the Berrymans'; she had not even had lunch. Mr. Berryman had not gone back to the factory. My mother went in and had a talk with both of them and made an excellent impression and then Mr. Berryman drove her home. She talked to them in the forthright and unemotional way she had, which was always agreeably surprising to people prepared to deal with a mother, and she told them that although I seemed to do well enough at school I was extremely backward — or perhaps eccentric — in my emotional development. I imagine that this analysis of my behaviour was especially effective with Mrs. Berryman, a great reader of Child Guidance books. Relations between them warmed to the point where my mother brought up a specific instance of my difficulties, and disarmingly related the whole story of Martin Collingwood.

35   Within a few days it was all over town and the school that I had tried to commit suicide over Martin Collingwood. But it was already all over school and the town that the Berrymans had come home on Saturday night to find me drunk, staggering, wearing nothing but my slip, in a room with three boys, one of whom was Bill Kline. My mother had said that I was to pay for the bottle she had taken the Berrymans out of my baby-sitting earnings, but my clients melted away like the last April snow, and it would not be paid for yet if newcomers to town had not moved in across the street in July, and needed a baby-sitter before they talked to any of their neighbours.

36   My mother also said that it had been a great mistake to let me go out with boys and that I would not be going out again until well after my sixteenth birthday, if then. This did not prove to be a concrete hardship at all, because it was at least that long before anybody asked me. If you think that news of the Berrymans' adventure would put me in demand for whatever gambols and orgies were going on in and around that town, you could not be more mistaken. The extraordinary publicity which attended my first debauch may have made me seemed marked for a special kind of ill luck, like the girl whose illegitimate baby turns out to be triplets: nobody wants to have anything to do with her. At any rate I had at the same time one of the most silent telephones and positively the most sinful reputation in the

whole High School. I had to put up with this until the next fall, when a fat blonde girl in Grade Ten ran away with a married man and was picked up two months later, living in sin—though not with the same man—in the city of Sault Ste. Marie. Then everybody forgot about me.

But there was a positive, a splendidly unexpected, result of this affair: I got completely over Martin Collingwood. It was not only that he at once said, publicly, that he had always thought I was a nut; where he was concerned I had no pride, and my tender fancy could have found a way around that, a month, a week, before. What was it that brought me back into the world again? It was the terrible and fascinating reality of my disaster; it was *the way things happened.* Not that I enjoyed it; I was a self-conscious girl and I suffered a good deal from all this exposure. But the development of events on that Saturday night—that fascinated me; I felt that I had had a glimpse of the shameless, marvellous, shattering absurdity with which the plots of life, though not of fiction, are improvised. I could not take my eyes off it.

And of course Martin Collingwood wrote his Senior Matric that June, and went away to the city to take a course at a school for Morticians, as I think it is called, and when he came back he went into his uncle's undertaking business. We lived in the same town and we would hear most things that happened to each other but I do not think we met face to face or saw one another, except at a distance, for years. I went to a shower for the girl he married, but then everybody went to everybody else's showers. No, I do not think I really saw him again until I came home after I had been married several years, to attend a relative's funeral. Then I saw him; not quite Mr. Darcy but still very nice-looking in those black clothes. And I saw him looking over at me with an expression as close to a reminiscent smile as the occasion would permit, and I knew that he had been surprised by a memory either of my devotion or my little buried catastrophe. I gave him a gentle uncomprehending look in return. I am a grown-up woman now; let him unbury his own catastrophes.

1968

NOTES

Alice Munro is one of Canada's internationally acclaimed short-story writers. Another of her best-known stories is "Boys and Girls."

White Slave trade The kidnapping of young, white girls for the purpose of prostitution and slavery.

Pride and Prejudice A romantic novel written by Jane Austen (1775–1817). It is a story about young women trying to find wealthy husbands. Mr. Darcy is the main male character and Elizabeth Bennett is the protagonist who is pursued by Mr. Darcy.

Danse Macabre Literally, "dance of death" (French). The recording of the same title is probably that of a symphony by Saint-Saëns (1835–1921).

The Little Mermaid A fairy tale written by Hans Christian Andersen (1805–1875). A young mermaid falls in love with a mortal prince and trades her soul in order to be human and secure his love. She sacrifices her own happiness for the prince's. (Note that the Disney version changes the story to include a happy ending.)

Temperance Avoidance of alcohol.

COMPREHENSION AND DISCUSSION

1. What is the significance of the first sentence? Why does the narrative begin that way?
2. For whom does the narrator babysit? How is this family different from the other neighbours?
3. Why is the narrator infatuated with Martin Collingwood?
4. What happens when Joyce and her friends come to rescue the narrator? Are they helpful?
5. What does the mother do to make amends to the Berrymans? What does she do to her daughter, the narrator? How would you have handled the situation?
6. What rumours begin to circulate about this incident? What are the results?
7. Has the narrator learned anything from her experience at the Berrymans and its aftermath? How do you know?
8. Why does Munro have Martin Collingwood become a mortician? Is this significant to the story?
9. Describe Kay Stringer in your own words. What kind of adult would she become? What would be a likely career for her?
10. Is Munro's portrayal of teenage love realistic?
11. A proverb says, "An ounce of prevention is worth a pound of cure." Discuss the meaning of the title of the story.

LITERARY TECHNIQUES

The "I" narrator remains unnamed throughout the story. The narrator is not the author. Often writers prefer an anonymous narrator in order to make her "everywoman," in this case the generic teenager who has had experiences with infatuation and drunkenness similar to those of many teenagers. In addition, the first-person point of view restricts the perspective to the unnamed narrator.

In the first paragraph, Munro writes a very long sentence beginning with "I ought not to say . . ." and ending with " . . . into the White Slave trade." In this instance, the rambling quality of the sentence shows the narrator's state of mind, her views on life, and her relationship with her family all at once. The sentence employs, in a minor way, the stream-of-consciousness method in which the writer attempts to show the progress of a character's thoughts.

Time shifts One of Munro's favourite techniques is to jump ahead several years after the events narrated in the story. The ending then gives a different perspective: the narrator can evaluate her youthful follies and comment on her maturity. Note that Martin Collingwood has become an undertaker. His occupation allows for a play on the words "unbury" and "catastrophe" (paragraph 38).

ASSIGNMENTS

1. Compare this story with T. Coraghessan Boyle's "Greasy Lake" (p. 33). You can examine the themes of maturity, adolescent angst, teenage rites of passage, influence of alcohol, or lessons.
2. The narrator says that Martin Collingwood has "a reputation slightly tainted, at that, by such preferences as the Drama Club and the Cadet Band" (paragraph 4). Discuss the qualities teenagers value in their peers. What makes a person "cool," for example? You can also consider the characters in "Greasy Lake" (p. 33) to answer this question.
3. How are the problems of teenage boys different from those of teenage girls? What problems do both share? Write an expository paper.
4. Write a set of guidelines for babysitters.
5. What immature acts have you done that you later regretted? What were the consequences?
6. Atlantis Television made a 1983 film based on this story. Compare the film with the original story.

7. Compare the characters and events in this story with what would likely happen to today's teenagers.
8. Compare the mother in this story with the mother in Jamaica Kincaid's "Girl" (p. 127).

One Rejection Too Many

Patricia Nurse

Dear Dr. Asimov: 1

Imagine my delight when I spotted your new science fiction magazine 2
on the newsstands. I have been a fan of yours for many, many years, and I
naturally wasted no time in buying a copy. I wish you every success in this
new venture.

In your second issue I read with interest your plea for stories from new 3
authors. While no writer myself, I have had a time traveller living with me
for the past two weeks (he materialized in the bathtub without clothes or
money, so I felt obliged to offer him shelter), and he has written a story of
life on earth as it will be in the year 5000.

Before he leaves this time frame, it would give him great pleasure to see 4
his story in print—I hope you will feel able to make this wish come true.

Yours sincerely, 5
Nancy Morrison (Miss)

Dear Miss Morrison: 6

Thank you for your kind letter and good wishes. 7

It is always refreshing to hear from a new author. You have included 8
some most imaginative material in your story; however, it is a little short
on plot and human interest—perhaps you could rewrite it with this thought
in mind.

Yours sincerely, 9
Isaac Asimov

Dear Dr. Asimov: 10

I was sorry that you were unable to print the story I sent you. Vahl (the 11
time traveller who wrote it) was quite hurt as he tells me he is an author of
some note in his own time. He has, however, rewritten the story and this
time has included plenty of plot and some rather interesting mating rituals
which he has borrowed from the year 3000. In his own time (the year 5015)
sex is no longer practised, so you can see that it is perfectly respectable
having him in my house. I do wish, though, that he could adapt himself to
our custom of wearing clothes—my neighbours are starting to talk!

12   Anything that you can do to expedite the publishing of Vahl's story would be most appreciated, so that he will feel free to return to his own time.

13   Yours sincerely,
                    Nancy Morrison (Miss)

14 Dear Miss Morrison:

15   Thank you for your rewritten short story.

16   I don't want to discourage you but I'm afraid you followed my suggestions with a little too much enthusiasm — however, I can understand that having an imaginary nude visitor from another time is a rather heady experience. I'm afraid that your story now rather resembles a far-future episode of "Mary Hartman, Mary Hartman" or "Soap."

17   Could you tone it down a bit and omit the more bizarre sex rituals of the year 3000 — we must remember that *Isaac Asimov's Science Fiction Magazine* is intended to be a family publication.

18   Perhaps a little humour would improve the tale too.

19   Yours sincerely,
                    Isaac Asimov

20 Dear Dr. Asimov:

21   Vahl was extremely offended by your second rejection — he said he has never received a rejection slip before, and your referring to him as "imaginary" didn't help matters at all. I'm afraid he rather lost his temper and stormed out into the garden — it was at this unfortunate moment that the vicar happened to pass by.

22   Anyway, I managed to get Vahl calmed down and he has rewritten the story and added plenty of humour. I'm afraid my subsequent meeting with the vicar was not blessed with such success! I'm quite sure Vahl would not understand another rejection.

23   Yours truly,
                    Nancy Morrison (Miss)

24 Dear Miss Morrison:

25   I really admire your persistence in rewriting your story yet another time. Please don't give up hope — you can become a fairly competent writer in time, I feel sure.

26   I'm afraid the humour you added was not the kind of thing I had in mind at all — you're not collaborating with Henny Youngman by any

chance are you? I really had a more sophisticated type of humour in mind.
Yours truly,

Isaac Asimov

27

P.S. Have you considered reading your story, as it is, on "The Gong Show"?

Dear Dr. Asimov:

28

    It really was very distressing to receive the return of my manuscript once again—Vahl was quite speechless with anger.

29

    It was only with the greatest difficulty that I prevailed upon him to refine the humour you found so distasteful, and I am submitting his latest rewrite herewith.

30

    In his disappointment, Vahl has decided to return to his own time right away. I shall be sorry to see him leave as I was getting very fond of him—a pity he wasn't from the year 3000 though. Still, he wouldn't have made a very satisfactory husband; I'd have never known where (or when) he was. It rather looks as though my plans to marry the vicar have suffered a severe setback too. Are you married, Dr. Asimov?

31

    I must close this letter now as I have to say good-bye to Vahl. He says he has just finished making some long overdue improvements to our time frame as a parting gift—isn't that kind of him?

32

Yours sincerely,

Nancy Morrison (Miss)

33

Dear Miss Morrison:

34

    I am very confused by your letter. Who is Isaac Asimov? I have checked with several publishers and none of them has heard of *Isaac Asimov's Science Fiction Magazine*, although the address on the envelope was correct for *this* magazine.

35

    However, I was very impressed with your story and will be pleased to accept it for our next issue. Seldom do we receive a story combining such virtues as a well-conceived plot, plenty of human interest, and a delightfully subtle brand of humour.

36

Yours truly,

George H. Scithers,

Editor,

Arthur C. Clarke's Science Fiction Magazine

37

1978

NOTES

Isaac Asimov (1920–1992) A prolific writer of science fiction and other genres, and a biochemistry professor at Boston University. He is the author of "The Fun They Had" (p. 28). *Isaac Asimov's Science Fiction Magazine* is a real publication, not a fictional creation.

Mary Hartman, Mary Hartman (1976–1977) A TV comedy show mocking soap operas (overly dramatic continuing television series, usually shown in the afternoon).

Soap (1977–1981) A popular TV series, also spoofing soap operas.

Henny Youngman (1960–1998) An American comedian known for such one-liners as "Take my wife…please!"

The Gong Show A 1970s TV series in which contestants displayed their various and often limited talents until they were stopped by the sound of a gong.

George H. Scithers A real-life editor of *Isaac Asimov's Science Fiction Magazine*.

Arthur C. Clarke A renowned writer of science and science fiction. His best-known work is a collaboration with director Stanley Kubrick on *2001: A Space Odyssey* (1968). He does not have a science fiction magazine in his name.

COMPREHENSION AND DISCUSSION

1. Explain what happens in this story.
2. What are some of Miss Morrison's hopes and dreams?
3. What year does Vahl come from? How do you picture him?
4. How does Isaac Asimov keep offending Miss Morrison more unkindly with each reply?
5. How does Vahl get his revenge? What clues does the writer give to foreshadow this conclusion?
6. Explain how Patricia Nurse creates humour in this story.
7. This was Nurse's first published story. Do you think she made several attempts to be published before? How can you tell?
8. How is this story similar to other time travel stories you are familiar with?

9. Discuss the letter technique used here. How else could this story have been told? Why is the use of letters effective?

LITERARY TECHNIQUES

Letter form Using a series of letters, the writer concocts a story line or plot, often with parts left out to be filled in by the reader's imagination. For example, the letters hint at Vahl's subject matter but never completely tell of it; Miss Morrison includes asides about her desire for marriage and companionship ("Are you married, Dr. Asimov?" [paragraph 31]).

Time travel One of the most popular themes in science fiction, it offers not only adventurous and imaginative story lines but also social commentary. Here, the time traveller Vahl becomes vital to the conclusion of the story.

Plausibility By using real names and transforming these people into fictional story characters (such as Isaac Asimov and Arthur C. Clarke), the writer lends a credible note to the story. In short, the letters seem like real correspondence. The content (although outrageous) is delivered matter-of-factly and in all seriousness.

Surprise ending A conclusion to a story that the reader is not expecting. Often the ending has a twist. When the reader rereads the story, he or she discovers that the writer has inserted clues throughout to play fair with the astute reader.

ASSIGNMENTS

1. Read "The Fun They Had" by Isaac Asimov (p. 28). What do you think Asimov's opinion was of Nurse's story?
2. What is the difference between science fiction and fantasy? Read Charles de Lint's story (p. 52) and compare the two works.
3. If time travel were possible, which time period would you visit? Why?
4. Explain the benefits and/or problems of time travel.
5. Read David Arnason's "A Girl's Story" (p. 20) and Charles de Lint's "Mr. Truepenny's Book Emporium and Gallery" (p. 52). Explain what these two stories, and "One Rejection Too Many," tell about being a writer.

The Man I Killed

Tim O'Brien

1   His jaw was in his throat, his upper lip and teeth were gone, his one eye was shut, his other eye was a star-shaped hole, his eyebrows were thin and arched like a woman's, his nose was undamaged, there was a slight tear at the lobe of one ear, his clean black hair was swept upward into a cowlick at the rear of the skull, his forehead was lightly freckled, his fingernails were clean, the skin at his left cheek was peeled back in three ragged strips, his right cheek was smooth and hairless, there was a butterfly on his chin, his neck was open to the spinal cord and the blood there was thick and shiny and it was this wound that had killed him. He lay face-up in the centre of the trail, a slim, dead, almost dainty young man. He had bony legs, a narrow waist, long shapely fingers. His chest was sunken and poorly muscled — a scholar, maybe. His wrists were the wrists of a child. He wore a black shirt, black pajama pants, a grey ammunition belt, a gold ring on the third finger of his right hand. His rubber sandals had been blown off. One lay beside him, the other a few metres up the trail. He had been born, maybe, in 1946 in the village of My Khe near the central coastline of Quang Ngai Province, where his parents farmed, and where his family had lived for several centuries, and where, during the time of the French, his father and two uncles and many neighbours had joined in the struggle for independence. He was not a Communist. He was a citizen and a soldier. In the village of My Khe, as in all of Quang Ngai, patriotic resistance had the force of tradition, which was partly the force of legend, and from his earliest boyhood the man I killed had listened to stories about the heroic Trung sisters and Tran Hung Dao's famous rout of the Mongols and Le Loi's final victory against the Chinese at Tot Dong. He had been taught that to defend the land was a man's highest duty and highest privilege. He accepted this. It was never open to question. Secretly, though, it also frightened him. He was not a fighter. His health was poor, his body small and frail. He liked books. He wanted someday to be a teacher of mathematics. At night, lying on his mat, he could not picture himself doing the brave things his father had done, or his uncles, or the heroes of other stories. He hoped in his heart that he would never be tested. He hoped the Americans would go away. Soon, he hoped. He kept hoping and hoping, always, even when he was asleep.

2   "Oh, man, you fuckin' trashed the fucker," Azar said. "You scrambled his sorry self, look at that, you *did*, you laid him out like Shredded fuckin' Wheat."

"Go away," Kiowa said.   3

"I'm just saying the truth. Like oatmeal."   4

"Go," Kiowa said.   5

"Okay, then, I take it back," Azar said. He started to move away, then   6
stopped and said, "Rice Krispies, you know? On the dead test, this particular individual gets A-plus."

Smiling at this, he shrugged and walked up the trail toward the village   7
behind the trees.

Kiowa kneeled down.   8

"Just forget that crud," he said. He opened up his canteen and held it   9
out for a while and then sighed and pulled it away. "No sweat, man. What
else could you do?"

Later, Kiowa said, "I'm serious. Nothing *anybody* could do. Come on,   10
Tim, stop staring."

The trail junction was shaded by a row of trees and tall brush. The slim   11
young man lay with his legs in the shade. His jaw was in his throat. His one
eye was shut and the other was a star-shaped hole.

Kiowa glanced at the body.   12

"All right, let me ask a question," he said. "You want to trade places   13
with him? Turn it all upside down — you *want* that? I mean, be honest."

The star-shaped hole was red and yellow. The yellow part seemed to   14
be getting wider, spreading out at the centre of the star. The upper lip and
gum and teeth were gone. The man's head was cocked at a wrong angle, as
if loose at the neck, and the neck was wet with blood.

"Think it over," Kiowa said.   15

Then later he said, "Tim, it's a *war*. The guy wasn't Heidi — he had   16
a weapon, right? It's a tough thing, for sure, but you got to cut out that
staring."

Then he said, "Maybe you better lie down a minute."   17

Then after a long empty time he said, "Take it slow. Just go wherever   18
the spirit takes you."

The butterfly was making its way along the young man's forehead,   19
which was spotted with small dark freckles. The nose was undamaged. The
skin on the right cheek was smooth and fine-grained and hairless. Frail-
looking, delicately boned, the young man had never wanted to be a soldier
and in his heart had feared that he would perform badly in battle. Even as
a boy growing up in the village of My Khe, he had often worried about this.
He imagined covering his head and lying in a deep hole and closing his
eyes and not moving until the war was over. He had no stomach for violence. He loved mathematics. His eyebrows were thin and arched like a

woman's, and at school the boys sometimes teased him about how pretty he was, the arched eyebrows and long shapely fingers, and on the playground they would mimic a woman's walk and make fun of his smooth skin and his love for mathematics. He could not make himself fight them. He often wanted to, but he was afraid, and this increased his shame. If he could not fight little boys, he thought, how could he ever become a soldier and fight the Americans with their airplanes and helicopters and bombs? It did not seem possible. In the presence of his father and uncles, he pretended to look forward to doing his patriotic duty, which was also a privilege, but at night he prayed with his mother that the war might end soon. Beyond anything else, he was afraid of disgracing himself, and therefore his family and village. But all he could do, he thought, was wait and pray and try not to grow up too fast.

20   "Listen to me," Kiowa said. "You feel terrible, I know that."

21   Then he said, "Okay, maybe I *don't* know."

22   Along the trail there were small blue flowers shaped like bells. The young man's head was wrenched sideways, not quite facing the flowers, and even in the shade a single blade of sunlight sparkled against the buckle of his ammunition belt. The left cheek was peeled back in three ragged strips. The wounds at his neck had not yet clotted, which made him seem animate even in death, the blood still spreading out across his shirt.

23   Kiowa shook his head.

24   There was some silence before he said, "Stop *staring.*"

25   The young man's fingernails were clean. There was a slight tear at the lobe of one ear, a sprinkling of blood on the forearm. He wore a gold ring on the third finger of his right hand. His chest was sunken and poorly muscled — a scholar, maybe. For years, despite his family's poverty, the man I killed had been determined to continue his education in mathematics. The means for this were arranged, perhaps, through the village liberation cadres, and in 1964 the young man began attending classes at the university in Saigon, where he avoided politics and paid attention to the problems of calculus. He devoted himself to his studies. He spent his nights alone, wrote romantic poems in his journal, took pleasure in the grace and beauty of differential equations. The war, he knew, would finally take him, but for the time being he would not let himself think about it. He had stopped praying; instead, now, he waited. And as he waited, in his final year at the university, he fell in love with a classmate, a girl of seventeen, who one day told him that his wrists were like the wrists of a child, so small and delicate, and who admired his narrow waist and the cowlick that rose up like

a bird's tail at the back of his head. She liked his quiet manner; she laughed at his freckles and bony legs. One evening, perhaps, they exchanged gold rings.

Now one eye was a star. 26

"You okay?" Kiowa said. 27

The body lay almost entirely in the shade. There were gnats at the 28
mouth, little flecks of pollen drifting above the nose. The butterfly was gone. The bleeding had stopped except for the neck wounds.

Kiowa picked up the rubber sandals, clapping off the dirt, then bent 29
down to search the body. He found a pouch of rice, a comb, a fingernail clipper, a few soiled piastres, a snapshot of a young woman standing in front of a parked motorcycle. Kiowa placed these items in his rucksack along with the grey ammunition belt and rubber sandals.

Then he squatted down. 30

"I'll tell you the straight truth," he said. "The guy was dead the second 31
he stepped on the trail. Understand me? We all had him zeroed. A good kill — weapon, ammunition, everything." Tiny beads of sweat glistened at Kiowa's forehead. His eyes moved from the sky to the dead man's body to the knuckles of his own hands. "So listen, you have to pull your shit together. Can't just sit there all day."

Later he said, "Understand?" 32

Then he said, "Five minutes, Tim. Five more minutes and we're 33
moving out."

The one eye did a funny twinkling trick, red to yellow. His head was 34
wrenched sideways, as if loose at the neck, and the dead young man seemed to be staring at some distant object beyond the bell-shaped flowers along the trail. The blood at the neck had gone to a deep purplish black. Clean fingernails, clean hair — he had been a soldier for only a single day. After his years at the university, the man I killed returned with his new wife to the village of My Khe, where he enlisted as a common rifleman with the 48th Vietcong Battalion. He knew he would die quickly. He knew he would see a flash of light. He knew he would fall dead and wake up in the stories of his village and people.

Kiowa covered the body with a poncho. 35

"Hey, Tim, you're looking better," he said. "No doubt about it. All you 36
needed was time — some mental R & R."

Then he said, "Man, I'm sorry." 37

Then later he said, "Why not talk about it?" 38

Then he said, "Come on, man, talk." 39

40   He was a slim, dead, almost dainty young man of about twenty. He lay with one leg bent beneath him, his jaw in his throat, his face neither expressive nor inexpressive. One eye was shut. The other was a star-shaped hole.

41   "Talk to me," Kiowa said.

1991

NOTES

Tim O'Brien served as an infantryman in the Vietnam War. He is best known for his collection of short stories *The Things They Carried* and has written many novels.

O'Brien uses some of his own war experiences as the foundation for this story and for others in the collection *The Things They Carried.* He even uses his own name for the character of the storyteller. He adds a wrinkle here. The dead Vietcong's life as imagined by the soldier Tim is really what happened to Tim O'Brien the writer. If you remove local references, the core is autobiographical.

Tim the soldier is projecting his own story onto the dead Vietcong. Projection is a psychological term that describes how a person having certain experiences or feelings attributes them to someone or something else.

Although the title is "The Man *I* Killed" (emphasis added), you will find the "I" used only twice, both times in the repetition of the title phrase. There is a certain detachment or objectivity in the telling when the narrator hides the self ("I"). The focus is on the dead soldier.

R & R   Rest and recreation.

Heidi   A female character in the classic children's story *Heidi* (1881) by Johanna Spyri (1829–1901). She is sweet, friendly, and helpful.

Quang Ngai   A province in Vietnam.

Trung sisters   Two widows, Trung Trac and Trung Nhi, who led an uprising against foreign rule in A.D. 39.

Tran Hung Dao   The Vietnamese general (1213–1300) who defeated Kublai Khan's army of Mongols.

Le Loi   A Vietnamese emperor (1428–1433) who was considered a hero because of his fight against the Chinese.

COMPREHENSION AND DISCUSSION

1. What is the theme of this story?
2. Who are the two friends of the protagonist? How are they different from one another?
3. How are the three characters' attitudes revealed? What are their attitudes toward the dead man?
4. What story does the protagonist create about the dead man? Why does he make up such a story? Who is the narrator really talking about?
5. Observe Kiowa's speech. How does he change? How does the writer make this obvious?
6. Why does the writer have the character repeat certain details in his description of the dead soldier?
7. Why does the writer choose to open the story with the aftermath of an ambush? Should the writer have described the attack in detail?
8. What is the tone of this story?

LITERARY TECHNIQUES

Autobiographical fiction is a literary category in which the writer recounts aspects of his life in fictional form. However, these events probably did not occur exactly as the writer presents them in the story. It is important to realize that the story is fictional even though it may contain biographical events.

This story is static in that Tim the soldier does not move; even Kiowa and Azar have limited movement and action. The extended paragraphs reveal Tim's thoughts; the dialogue is reserved for his two buddies. The story is, therefore, a psychological study.

Sentence structure The opening sentence beginning with "His jaw..." and concluding with "...this wound that had killed him" is not only long but also detailed in its description of the dead soldier. Long sentences tend to be descriptive and informative, while short sentences are emphatic, attention-getting, and succinct. Notice the shorter sentences near the end of the paragraph. Because of their brevity, the sentences sound choppy, thus changing the rhythm or flow.

Paragraphing O'Brien has three very long paragraphs in which he talks about the dead enemy. This technique merits mentioning. First, like the long sentence, the lengthy paragraph reveals the workings of Tim the soldier's mind. Second, Tim the soldier imagines a life that the dead Vietcong never had. The first half of a long paragraph is description and the last half is the invented life Tim gives to the fallen soldier. In the first paragraph, the word "maybe" begins the imagined biography. Each successive long paragraph adds different details to the Vietcong's "life."

Repetition Repeating words and ideas shows Tim the soldier's preoccupation with his first kill. The recurring images of the butterfly, the star-shaped wound, and fingers gain symbolic value: the delicacy of the man and the fragility of life.

Language There is sharp contrast in the thoughts of Tim the soldier and in the speeches by his two buddies, especially Azar's. In Tim's mind, the diction and vocabulary are almost formalized, whereas in the dialogues the expletive words and phrases reveal a coarse reality.

ASSIGNMENTS

1. What does this story say about war and combat, or about soldiers?
2. This story has no action in the traditional sense. Analyze the story to show how the writer captures the reader's attention and interest.
3. Explain the ending in which Kiowa says: "Talk to me." How has he changed even though Tim never spoke to him at all?
4. David Arnason's "A Girl's Story" (p. 20) is metafiction, writing that refers to the process of writing. Does O'Brien's story have elements of this technique? If so, how?
5. Read George Orwell's "Shooting an Elephant" (p. 305). How do both stories focus on states of mind? Explain the similarities.

The Cask of Amontillado
Edgar Allan Poe

The thousand injuries of Fortunato I had borne as I best could, but when he ventured upon insult I vowed revenge. You, who so well know the nature of my soul, will not suppose, however, that I gave utterance to a threat. *At length* I would be avenged; this was a point definitely settled — but the very definitiveness with which it was resolved precluded the idea of risk. I must not only punish but punish with impunity. A wrong is unredressed when retribution overtakes its redresser. It is equally unredressed when the avenger fails to make himself felt as such to him who has done the wrong. 1

It must be understood that neither by word nor deed had I given Fortunato cause to doubt my goodwill. I continued, as was my wont, to smile in his face, and he did not perceive that my smile *now* was at the thought of his immolation. 2

He had a weak point — this Fortunato — although in other regards he was a man to be respected and even feared. He prided himself on his connoisseurship in wine. Few Italians have the true virtuoso spirit. For the most part their enthusiasm is adopted to suit the time and opportunity, to practise imposture upon the British and Austrian *millionaires*. In painting and gemmary, Fortunato, like his countrymen, was a quack, but in the matter of old wines he was sincere. In this respect I did not differ from him materially; — I was skillful in the Italian vintages myself, and bought largely whenever I could. 3

It was about dusk, one evening during the supreme madness of the carnival season, that I encountered my friend. He accosted me with excessive warmth, for he had been drinking much. The man wore motley. He had on a tight-fitting parti-striped dress, and his head was surmounted by the conical cap and bells. I was so pleased to see him that I thought I should never have done wringing his hand. 4

I said to him — "My dear Fortunato, you are luckily met. How remarkably well you are looking today! But I have received a pipe of what passes for Amontillado, and I have my doubts." 5

"How?" said he. "Amontillado? A pipe? Impossible! And in the middle of the carnival!" 6

"I have my doubts," I replied; "and I was silly enough to pay the full Amontillado price without consulting you in the matter. You were not to be found, and I was fearful of losing a bargain." 7

"Amontillado!" 8

9 "I have my doubts."

10 "Amontillado!"

11 "And I must satisfy them."

12 "Amontillado!"

13 "As you are engaged, I am on my way to Luchresi. If anyone has a critical turn it is he. He will tell me —"

14 "Luchresi cannot tell Amontillado from Sherry."

15 "And yet some fools will have it that his taste is a match for your own."

16 "Come, let us go."

17 "Whither?"

18 "To your vaults."

19 "My friend, no; I will not impose upon your good nature. I perceive you have an engagement. Luchresi —"

20 "I have no engagement; — come."

21 "My friend, no. It is not the engagement, but the severe cold with which I perceive you are afflicted. The vaults are insufferably damp. They are encrusted with nitre."

22 "Let us go, nevertheless. The cold is merely nothing. Amontillado! You have been imposed upon. And as for Luchresi, he cannot distinguish Sherry from Amontillado."

23 Thus speaking, Fortunato possessed himself of my arm; and putting on a mask of black silk and drawing a *roquelaure* closely about my person, I suffered him to hurry me to my palazzo.

24 There were no attendants at home; they had absconded to make merry in honour of the time. I had told them that I should not return until the morning, and had given them explicit orders not to stir from the house. These orders were sufficient, I well knew, to insure their immediate disappearance, one and all, as soon as my back was turned.

25 I took from their sconces two flambeaux, and giving one to Fortunato, bowed him through several suites of rooms to the archway that led into the vaults. I passed down a long and winding staircase, requesting him to be cautious as he followed. We came at length to the foot of the descent, and stood together on the damp ground of the catacombs of the Montresors.

26 The gait of my friend was unsteady, and the bells upon his cap jingled as he strode.

27 "The pipe," said he.

28 "It is farther on," said I; "but observe the white webwork which gleams from these cavern walls."

29 He turned towards me, and looked into my eyes with two filmy orbs that distilled the rheum of intoxication.

30 "Nitre?" he asked at length.

"Nitre," I replied. "How long have you had that cough?" 31

"Ugh! ugh! ugh!—ugh! ugh! ugh!—ugh! ugh! ugh!—ugh! ugh! ugh!—ugh! ugh! ugh!" 32

My poor friend found it impossible to reply for many minutes. 33

"It is nothing," he said at last. 34

"Come," I said, with decision, "we will go back; your health is precious. You are rich, respected, admired, beloved; you are happy, as once I was. You are a man to be missed. For me it is no matter. We will go back; you will be ill, and I cannot be responsible. Besides, there is Luchresi—" 35

"Enough," he said; "the cough is a mere nothing; it will not kill me. I shall not die of a cough." 36

"True—true," I replied; "and, indeed, I had no intention of alarming you unnecessarily—but you should use all proper caution. A draught of this Médoc will defend us from the damps." 37

Here I knocked off the neck of a bottle which I drew from a long row of its fellows that lay upon the mould. 38

"Drink," I said, presenting him the wine. 39

He raised it to his lips with a leer. He paused and nodded to me familiarly, while his bells jingled. 40

"I drink," he said, "to the buried that repose around us." 41

"And I to your long life." 42

He again took my arm, and we proceeded. 43

"These vaults," he said, "are extensive." 44

"The Montresors," I replied, "were a great and numerous family." 45

"I forget your arms." 46

"A huge human foot d'or, in a field azure; the foot crushes a serpent rampant whose fangs are imbedded in the heel." 47

"And the motto?" 48

"Nemo me impune lacessit." 49

"Good!" he said. 50

The wine sparkled in his eyes and the bells jingled. My own fancy grew warm with the Médoc. We had passed through long walls of piled skeletons, with casks and puncheons intermingling, into the inmost recesses of the catacombs. I paused again, and this time I made bold to seize Fortunato by an arm above the elbow. 51

"The nitre!" I said; "see, it increases. It hangs like moss upon the vaults. We are below the river's bed. The drops of moisture trickle among the bones. Come, we will go back ere it is too late. Your cough—" 52

"It is nothing," he said; "let us go on. But first, another draught of the Médoc." 53

54   I broke and reached him a flagon of De Grâve. He emptied it at a breath. His eyes flashed with a fierce light. He laughed and threw the bottle upward with a gesticulation I did not understand.

55   I looked at him in surprise. He repeated the movement—a grotesque one.

56   "You do not comprehend?" he said.

57   "Not I," I replied.

58   "Then you are not of the brotherhood."

59   "How?"

60   "You are not of the masons."

61   "Yes, yes," I said; "yes, yes."

62   "You? Impossible! A mason?"

63   "A mason," I replied.

64   "A sign," he said, "a sign."

65   "It is this," I answered, producing from beneath the folds of my *roquelaure* a trowel.

66   "You jest," he exclaimed, recoiling a few paces. "But let us proceed to the Amontillado."

67   "Be it so," I said, replacing the tool beneath the cloak and again offering him my arm. He leaned upon it heavily. We continued our route in search of the Amontillado. We passed through a range of low arches, descended, passed on, and descending again, arrived at a deep crypt, in which the foulness of the air caused our flambeaux rather to glow than flame.

68   At the most remote end of the crypt there appeared another less spacious. Its walls had been lined with human remains, piled to the vault overhead, in the fashion of the great catacombs of Paris. Three sides of this interior crypt were still ornamented in this manner. From the fourth the bones had been thrown down, and lay promiscuously upon the earth, forming at one point a mound of some size. Within the wall thus exposed by the displacing of the bones, we perceived a still interior crypt or recess, in depth about four feet, in width three, in height six or seven. It seemed to have been constructed for no especial use within itself, but formed merely the interval between two of the colossal supports of the roof of the catacombs, and was backed by one of their circumscribing walls of solid granite.

69   It was in vain that Fortunato, uplifting his dull torch, endeavoured to pry into the depth of the recess. Its termination the feeble light did not enable us to see.

70   "Proceed," I said; "herein is the Amontillado. As for Luchresi—"

"He is an ignoramus," interrupted my friend, as he stepped unsteadily   71
forward, while I followed immediately at his heels. In an instant he had
reached the extremity of the niche, and finding his progress arrested by the
rock, stood stupidly bewildered. A moment more and I had fettered him to
the granite. In its surface were two iron staples, distant from each other
about two feet, horizontally. From one of these depended a short chain,
from the other a padlock. Throwing the links about his waist, it was but the
work of a few seconds to secure it. He was too much astounded to resist.
Withdrawing the key I stepped back from the recess.

"Pass your hand," I said, "over the wall; you cannot help feeling the   72
nitre. Indeed it is *very* damp. Once more let me *implore* you to return. No?
Then I must positively leave you. But I must first render you all the little
attentions in my power."

"The Amontillado!" ejaculated my friend, not yet recovered from his   73
astonishment.

"True," I replied; "the Amontillado."   74

As I said these words I busied myself among the pile of bones of which   75
I have before spoken. Throwing them aside, I soon uncovered a quantity of
building stone and mortar. With these materials and with the aid of my
trowel, I began vigorously to wall up the entrance of the niche.

I had scarcely laid the first tier of the masonry when I discovered that   76
the intoxication of Fortunato had in a great measure worn off. The earliest
indication I had of this was a low moaning cry from the depth of the recess.
It was *not* the cry of a drunken man. There was a long and obstinate
silence. I laid the second tier, and the third, and the fourth; and then I heard
the furious vibrations of the chain. The noise lasted for several minutes,
during which, that I might hearken to it with the more satisfaction, I ceased
my labours and sat down upon the bones. When at last the clanking sub-
sided, I resumed the trowel, and finished without interruption the fifth, the
sixth, and the seventh tier. The wall was now nearly upon a level with my
breast. I again paused, and holding the flambeaux over the masonwork,
threw a few feeble rays upon the figure within.

A succession of loud and shrill screams, bursting suddenly from the   77
throat of the chained form, seemed to thrust me violently back. For a brief
moment I hesitated, I trembled. Unsheathing my rapier, I began to grope
with it about the recess; but the thought of an instant reassured me. I placed
my hand upon the solid fabric of the catacombs, and felt satisfied. I reap-
proached the wall; I replied to the yells of him who clamoured. I re-echoed,
I aided, I surpassed them in volume and in strength. I did this, and the
clamourer grew still.

78   It was now midnight, and my task was drawing to a close. I had completed the eighth, the ninth, and the tenth tier. I had finished a portion of the last and the eleventh; there remained but a single stone to be fitted and plastered in. I struggled with its weight; I placed it partially in its destined position. But now there came from out the niche a low laugh that erected the hairs upon my head. It was succeeded by a sad voice, which I had difficulty in recognizing as that of the noble Fortunato. The voice said—

79   "Ha! ha! ha!—he! he! he!—a very good joke, indeed—an excellent jest. We will have many a rich laugh about it at the palazzo—he! he! he!—over our wine—he! he! he!"

80   "The Amontillado!" I said.

81   "He! he! he!—he! he! he!—yes, the Amontillado. But is it not getting late? Will not they be awaiting us at the palazzo, the Lady Fortunato and the rest? Let us be gone."

82   "Yes," I said, "let us be gone."

83   *"For the love of God, Montresor!"*

84   "Yes," I said, "for the love of God!"

85   But to these words I hearkened in vain for a reply. I grew impatient. I called aloud—

86   "Fortunato!"

87   No answer. I called again—

88   "Fortunato!"

89   No answer still. I thrust a torch through the remaining aperture and let it fall within. There came forth in return only a jingling of the bells. My heart grew sick; it was the dampness of the catacombs that made it so. I hastened to make an end of my labour. I forced the last stone into its position; I plastered it up. Against the new masonry I re-erected the old rampart of bones. For the half of a century no mortal has disturbed them. *In pace requiescat!*

1846

NOTES

Edgar Allan Poe (1809–1849) was an American writer; he is known for horror stories and poems, such as "The Raven," "The Fall of the House of Usher," and "The Purloined Letter."

Roquelaure A knee-length cloak of the 18th century. It was a popular garment, often adorned with silk and fur.

Palazzo Italian for "a stately home, a palace."

D'or French for "of gold."

Nemo me impune lacessit Latin for "no one hurts me without penalty." Poe has taken this motto from the royal arms of Scotland and the Order of the Thistle.

Fortunato's reference to the masons' brotherhood is to the Free and Accepted Masons, popularly known as Freemasons, an international organization with secret signs and rituals. This secret society has a long and colourful history. Because Montresor is not a member, he has reason to fear reprisals should the masons discover his crime.

Montresor shows the trowel to Fortunato and declares himself a mason. The avenger's meaning is different from the victim's. This trowel foreshadows events to follow.

Catacomb An underground cemetery with long tunnels and recesses for graves. During the persecution of early Christians by the Romans, catacombs were popular places of sanctuary and made convenient burial grounds.

In pace requiescat! Latin for "May he rest in peace!" Note the irony as Montresor says this prayer.

COMPREHENSION AND DISCUSSION

1. What kind of insult would make Montresor plot his revenge?
2. Show the various steps that Montresor has taken to secure vengeance.
3. Does Montresor know human behaviour? Cite at least three examples of this knowledge.
4. Explain the importance of Fortunato's costume to the story.
5. Does Fortunato deserve his fate?
6. How do you know that this story is told in flashback? Why is this technique effective?
7. To whom is Montresor confessing this dastardly crime? Why? What punishment does he wish to evade, now at his deathbed?
8. Is there a surprise ending here? If not, why are you not surprised? Is there suspense?

LITERARY TECHNIQUES

The names of characters are important to the telling of the story. *Montresor* means "my treasure" in French, and everything about him shows that his treasure is himself. He and his whole family are vain and egotistical. Note the declaration in the Montresors' coat of arms. On the other hand, *Fortunato*, which means "the lucky one," is used ironically; he is a most unlucky man.

The Latin mottoes and expressions lend authenticity to setting, show the social status of the characters, and imply a classical education.

To create an atmosphere of dread, Poe has both Montresor and Fortunato descend deeper into the catacombs. This downward movement can be a metaphor for the depths of hell or of the human soul. In addition, the dampness and Fortunato's persistent cough suggest it is an unhealthy place to be.

Poe uses first-person narration. The speaker and main character is Montresor, the villain. Usually, in first-person point of view, the protagonist is good or virtuous so that the reader can identify with the hero. However, Poe gives a twist to this convention; by having Montresor as the narrator, the author reveals the twisted mind of his character.

The "you" addressed in the opening does not refer to the reader, although that is the usual interpretation upon first reading. "You" is made clear at the end when Montresor confesses his crime to a priest. This sleight of hand is deliberate so that the story sounds more intimate than it is.

For fifty years, Montresor has successfully evaded punishment on earth for his heinous crime. He is at least seventy years old now, and may be close to death. To escape damnation in heaven, he confesses to a priest. In Roman Catholicism, a priest has the power to absolve all sins for someone who confesses freely. Poe makes this point obvious when Montresor says *"in pace requiescat"* ("rest in peace") for himself.

ASSIGNMENTS

1. Discuss the common elements of horror stories present in this story.
2. Explain the concept of revenge. When is it justified? There is a saying that revenge is a dish best enjoyed cold. Discuss the validity of this saying.

3. A short film has been made of this story. Watch it and write a critique.
4. Read another of Poe's stories and compare it with this one.
5. Research the Freemasons and write a short explanatory essay.
6. Read Pico Iyer's "Of Weirdos an Eccentrics" (p. 282). Is Montresor an eccentric or a weirdo? Why?

The Lifeguard

Barbara Scott

1   I'm not all that crazy about small kids. That might seem strange coming from a guy who's a lifeguard at the Bridgeland Community Swimming Pool, but the job gives me free pool time, and I'm training for the city try-outs. Keeping snot-nosed kids from drowning themselves and one another is the only price I have to pay. I made it pretty clear to the kids the first couple days that I wasn't hired as their babysitter or their buddy, and most of them gave me a wide berth after that. Fine by me. I had my own problems that summer.

2   For one thing, my mom got this great job offer that she couldn't turn down, never mind that this was the year I finally had a chance to make the city team. After four years of being told, You're too small, too thin, not strong enough. Four years of push-ups and sit-ups in the dark of my bedroom after Mom said lights out, of countless lengths in the mornings before school. So I flat out refused to move, and wound up living on my own in Calgary while she and my kid brother lived in Vancouver and kept in touch through weekly phone calls that all went pretty much the same way. Mom would ask how I was doing, and then she'd start to cry and remind me that none of this was her fault, that the Vancouver job paid almost twice as much as her old job and if Dad hadn't run off like he did everything would be just great. Which, when I thought about the time before he took off, made me wonder whether her mind hadn't been cracked by the move. I suppose the good thing about it was that there wasn't much room for me to get too upset, what with her getting upset enough for the both of us. I'd tell her about practice and how my time was really improving and she'd ask if I was remembering to eat right. A few words with the kid bro and that was it for another week.

3   All of which I was OK with, for the most part. But then, right out of the blue, my dad shows up. After running out on us six years before, I had to look twice to be sure it was him behind the glass in the viewing area, watching me. Watching me watching him. And he doesn't wave or move or even crack a smile. Typical.

4   I'd been diving before they opened up the pool for the free swim. I get a kick out of doing my dives then, surfacing to catch the kids staring at me with open mouths. I hadn't told anybody, not even my mom, but I wasn't only trying out for the swim team. My real goal was to be on the diving team. High diving. I like everything about it, the swing of my back as I

climb the ladder, the metal steps and rungs cold under my feet and hands. I even like the way my stomach falls away when I get to the top and feel the pebbly rain of the platform under my feet. And no matter how many times I dive, my gut always does fall away. Butterflies, my mom calls it. "Butterflies," she used to sing out into the back seat whenever we hit a big bump driving down into the States on holidays. And my kid brother, who was practically a baby still, would laugh like crazy, with his snorty little laugh that sounds like a sneeze, and try to say, "Butterflies," with her while she reached over from the front seat to tickle his tummy. That was when we were all still a family. I don't remember much about my dad, even though I was old enough to remember. I guess he was just there, hands on the wheel, eyes on the road. I don't really know. I try to picture him doing anything else and that's the best I can do.

I stand at the edge of the platform for a minute, smelling the chlorine and staring into the blue-green square, gathering everything I've got into the centre of my body. A couple of bends at the knee, then up and out, with all the tension in my legs pouring through my chest and straight out the top of my head. Try to hang there forever, stretched out and motionless, then make the body arrow-straight and knife-steady and slice open that pool like it was a melon. There isn't anything like it. When the dive is right it's just you and the air racing away from everything, even from your body.

So anyway, I sploosh out of the pool after a dive and there's a whole bunch of kids jostling in the viewing room. And Dad. We barely lock eyeballs when the doors burst open and all the little buggers cannonball into the pool, yelling fit to break glass. And I'm blowing my whistle and yelling too, so I don't have a lot of time to think about why he's here and what exactly I'm supposed to do about it.

I just get things slightly under control when a finger pokes my arm. I look down and there's Mike. Ever since he first saw me dive, that kid stuck to me like a leech no matter how hard I tried to shake him loose. He was always after me, "How's my crawl doin', Chris?" and "Watch me do the butterfly." So every once in a while, to get some peace, I'd watch him thrash his way around the shallow end of the pool. He was lousy, but no amount of telling him so would get him off my back.

Mike was so scrawny he barely had enough ass to hang swim trunks on, and without his glasses, his eyes were always slightly out of focus, like he was looking at something just beyond you. For all the times I saw him at the pool, and that was almost every day for the whole summer, I don't think I ever saw him swim with anybody — he was always off by himself, puffing and blowing like a baby whale. His mom would drop him off at the gate. She looked a bit like my mom. First time I saw her, I thought for a minute Mom had changed her mind about taking the job in Vancouver. After his mom left, Mike spent all his time paddling in the shallow end. And bugging me. Like I didn't have better things to do with my time.

9   So I'm scanning the viewing room to see if my dad's still there, only my eyes keep getting snagged on one of the babes that hang out at the pool in a bathing suit that's a clear signal they don't come for the swimming, and she looks away and laughs with her friends and I'm hoping she was watching when I made that dive. I hadn't taken my eyes off the pool for more than a few minutes but all of a sudden I see Mike splashing around in the deep end. So I'm in the pool like a flash, hauling him to the surface and throwing him onto the edge like a dead mackerel. "You dumb little shit! What do you think you're doing down this end of the pool? You could've drowned!"

10   He stands there streaming with water and this weird, shining kind of look.

11   "Wow! That is so cool!"

12   I glance over to the viewing area. No sign of my dad, and the girls have moved on too.

13   I poke Mike in the chest, hard. "Cut the crap, man. What the hell were you doing down in the deep end?"

14   "You gotta try it, Chris."

15   "Try what?" The little snot has gone off the deep end in more ways than one.

16   "Look, I'll show you." And he starts back to where I've just finished hauling him out. Some people you have to hit over the head with a sledge-hammer. I yank him back by the arm.

17   "Haven't you heard a word I've been saying? You're not allowed down there unless you can swim a length."

18   "Why should I have to swim a length?" the kid asks. "Anybody knows that even if you fall in the middle of the pool, the most you'd have to swim is half a width."

19   "Yeah, well, for you that'd still be pushing it."

20   "If I swim the width will you let me show you?"

21   "Show me what?"

22   He answered with the slow patience you'd treat someone with who wasn't wrapped too tight. "If I have to show you, I can't tell you, can I?" And then before I can say anything, in he dives — into the deep end again, couldn't prove his point in the shallow end, not Mike. Well, he's moving like an eggbeater, churning up the water and looking like he'll go down any

minute. But I have to admit that he's made it when he comes back up to me.

"Now watch," he says, like he's going to open me up to some kind of   23
miracle.

What I see convinces me that the little squirt is definitely a little bent.   24
He crouches down at the edge of the pool and rolls himself up into a ball,
then slowly tips himself off the edge backwards, gradually unfolding as he
sinks deeper and deeper into the water. I keep waiting for some sort of
trick. But all he does is a limp deadman's float underneath the surface of
the water, not moving, only wafting like a fleshy seaweed. The longer he
stays there the more nervous I get, and I'm just thinking I'm going to have
to go in after him a second time when he slowly rises to the surface,
bursting through near the ladder. He comes running up to me with the same
goofy expression, like a pup that figures it's been really clever. "Did you
see, Chris? Did you see?"

"See *what*?"   25

He stares at me like *I'm* the moron.   26

"It's like . . . like falling into a . . . a cloud, and it . . . " I tap my   27
forehead with one finger and draw circles in the air. Mike's voice fizzles.
"I guess you have to do it yourself to figure it out." He tugs at my finger.
"Why don't you try it, Chris? It feels really neat."

"I have to get back to work, kid. I can't stand around all day listening   28
to weirdos." I start to walk away. But he's a persistent guy and you've got
to admit he doesn't take an insult. He tags along, saying, "Yeah, but you
will try it, won't you, Chris?"

"Yeah, yeah, sure, kid." I keep walking.   29

That Sunday the usual phone call took an unusual turn.   30

"Dad came by the pool last week."   31

"How on earth did he find you? After six years!" Mom clamps down   32
on this outburst and there's a long, murky pause; then she says, too carefully. "What did you two talk about?"

"We didn't. He just stood there. He watched me practise and then he   33
left."

"If that isn't exactly like him, to wait for you to make the . . . " She   34
reins in her voice hard, and takes a minute before going on. "What do you
think you'll do about it?"

"I don't know. He left."   35

"He'll be back." Her voice is too neutral, gives nothing away, and I feel   36
like I'm straining to see her face, to find out what she thinks I should do,
but all I can see is the blank wall of the kitchen.

37   "Shit, Mom, I don't know."

38   "Don't swear, Chris," but she says it automatically, not like she's mad. "Honey, I don't know either. You have to do what's best for you."

39   Thanks a lot, I think. All the times she couldn't keep her nose out of my business, telling me what to do, and for the first time in ages, when I'd actually like at least a hint, now I'm grown up enough to decide for myself.

40   "Yeah, well. I guess I'll let you know."

41   "OK, dear." Another pause and then, almost like a question, "I love you."

42   "I know, Mom. I know."

43   "Do you want to talk to your brother?"

44   "Naw, I'll catch him next time. I gotta go."

45   She was right of course. He came back. Every few days I'd look up from the water and see him behind the glass. He never came beyond it and I never waved or motioned in any way. And I knew that he was leaving it up to me to decide. The asshole, I thought. Serve him right if one of these days I walk up to that viewing room, shove open the door and pop him one right in the mouth. Tell him exactly what I've been thinking of him in the years he's been gone. I had a lot of fantasies like that, and they got my blood boiling pretty good, but the ones that made me even madder were the ones that snuck in when I was off my guard, the ones where he looked at me and half smiled, a little nervous, and said he was sorry for everything.

46   "So how does he look?" Mom asked on one of my calls.

47   Old, I think. Seeing not only the greying hair that dipped across his forehead, but the lines around the eyes and mouth, deep enough to see even through glass. "He looks OK, I guess." For a minute I think, why not tell the truth, dummy? You don't have to protect him. And then I realize it's not him I'm protecting. I remember what it was like when he was around. Mom talking all the time, especially towards the end. Dad barely talking at all. Me shunted between the two of them, Mom pushing Dad to take me to the park, then pulling me aside and asking me what he said, whether he left me alone there. It was almost a relief when he took off. Almost but not quite. The first couple years I used to see him everywhere, only it was never him. It was so typical that he'd finally show up once I got used to the fact that he was gone. And that thought would get me boiling all over again.

48   Mike was at the pool almost every day, not swimming, just playing his strange little game. Every so often he'd bug me to watch him, but my temper was not the best and usually I told him to buzz off. I was spending

every spare minute at the pool, even helping to clean up after the last Belly-Burner Aquacise class ended at eleven. I'd come back early in the morning and spend hours swimming lengths, paring precious seconds off my time. At the end of one of these sessions I could barely stand. I pushed myself with my diving too, leaping harder, trying to go higher, come down faster, cleaner, deeper. One day, Keith, one of the older lifeguards who also did some diving yelled at me to get out of the pool and then dragged me into the office, wet and shivering. Didn't even give me time to get my towel. He glared at me and plugged in a video of the Olympic Games a few years back. A Russian diver miscalculated his dive and hit the platform on his way down. The moment of impact didn't look like anything much; he barely glanced off the edge, nothing dramatic at all. But you could tell he was in trouble the minute he hit. His body. It just dropped, like there was no one inside it any more. And then the water bloomed red from the bottom of the pool. I felt sick. Keith switched off the VCR. "I don't know what you're thinking about out there, kid," he said, "but it isn't diving. And if you're not thinking about diving, stay the hell off the platform."

I barely opened my mouth to say something when he stared me down and said, "I don't want to hear it. Stop assing around out there or I'll have you banned from this pool." 49

It's hard to try for righteous indignation when you're practically naked and shaking with cold and anger, so I slammed out of the office, and straight into Mike. 50

"Hi, Chris. You OK? Did he ream you out?" 51

I swear, I tried to keep walking and not talk to him, but he grabbed my hand and something snapped. I turned around with my fist raised, like I was going to smack him, and yelled straight into his nerdy face. "Leave me the hell alone, you little geek. Just fuck off and leave me alone!" I stomped off to the changing rooms without even a glance at the viewing area. Just my luck my dad'd be there in time to see me practically cream some kid a quarter my size. Well, I didn't want to know about it, thank you very much. 52

So naturally, when Mike stopped coming to the pool, I figured it had to be because I'd yelled at him. I felt pretty bad but, honestly, he was such a pain in the neck, and I figured he'd get over it. Then one day I overheard a couple of parents talking while their kids were getting showered. Talking about Mike's family, in that hush-hush, greedy voice people use when they go over gory details. Mike and his parents had been driving up to Saskatchewan to see some relatives. Just out of Drumheller they'd been hit head-on by a kid out joyriding, playing chicken with another guy. Asshole 53 pulled out to pass on a curve and hit Mike's family doing about a hundred klicks. His buddy didn't even stop, but a Greyhound bus driver saw the whole thing and radioed the police. When they got there Mike's mom was squashed like an accordion under the dashboard, and his dad was walking in big crazy circles all over the road, muttering to himself in gibberish and flapping his arms like a chicken. Mike had crawled into the corner farthest from his mom, in the back seat, and was staring from behind his shattered glasses, from one parent to the other, folded in on himself like a tight, hard ball.

54   Well, you can imagine what a shit I felt then. The pool is right near the hospital they had Mike at, so I went over to see him after work. I talked to a nurse there, and she filled me in on the rest of the story. Mike's mom was killed on impact; his dad took a few days more to go. They did a whole bunch of tests on Mike, and apart from some cuts and a big bruise on his forehead he was OK. Physically.

55   Since they'd brought him in he hadn't said a word or looked like he could hear anyone. They couldn't even tell if he knew his parents were dead. He didn't move, didn't speak, barely blinked. There wasn't a friend or relative who could take him — he had to be dressed and changed like a baby — so they were sending him to a Home a few blocks away.

56   I went up to his room and it was spooky the way he just sat there, staring at nothing. He didn't even look at me. I felt funny trying to talk to him, so I only stayed a few minutes that day. But the Home was even closer to the pool than the hospital, so I got into the habit of dropping in on him every couple of days. He got on pretty well there. In a few weeks he was walking again, and going to the toilet himself. But nobody could get a peep out of him. I almost gave up going, but I couldn't get him out of my head, he looked so scrawny and small behind his glasses. And apart from feeling sorry for the guy, I found out it's actually pretty cool talking to somebody who can't talk back. Easier to open up when the person doesn't say anything stupid to shut you back down again. Or when they don't have a stake in what's on your mind. It got so I'd talk to Mike a lot, and I even looked forward to it.

57   Things went on this way for most of the summer. The last week in August were my tryouts. The swimming one went great. All those lengths stood me in good stead and I was solidly in the middle range for the team. But my diving tryout was a total bomb. I got to the edge of the platform and nothing went the way it usually does. No butterflies, no rush from the smell of chlorine. The pool looked too close, too real, my legs and arms felt too big, gangly, in the way. And what clinched it was my dad. There again,

behind the viewing glass. No smile, no wave. You bastard, I thought, I'll show you, and I flung myself into my dive like a knife-thrower. It was a disaster. No hang-time, in fact I felt so rushed I barely had time to straighten out and avoid the total humiliation, not to mention pain, of a belly-flop. I knew as soon as I got out of the water that I'd blown it. I wanted to ask for a second chance, but I was afraid I'd start blubbering all over the place if I opened my mouth, so I had to just stand there tight-lipped, my chest clenched like a fist, while the coach told me really nicely that I was trying too hard, I had to learn to let go and let the dive take me with it. I couldn't even thank her when she suggested I come to some training sessions she was giving at the Y. By the time I headed for the showers my dad was gone.

I didn't go to see Mike for five days after that. I showed up for work 58 and went home and that was about it. My dad didn't show up either. I was watching for him. Then the nurse called me. She'd gotten my name from the sign-in sheet and looked up my number in the phone book. Just wanted to know how I was doing, she said, but I knew she wanted to know why I'd suddenly stopped visiting. Christ, I thought, even when he can't speak the kid finds a way to hassle me. But I told her I'd be by the next day.

I stopped at the door of his room, and watched him for a minute, 59 breathing that pale, washed-out smell you get in hospitals. Lying in that big white square of a bed he looked like he had been swallowed whole. The fist in my chest squeezed tighter and I thought, it's too much, I can't do it. But I pasted a big smile on my face, walked to the side of the bed and sat down.

"Hey, Mikey," I said. 60

He looked at me. Turned his head and looked at me. And when I fig- 61 ured out he really was in there somewhere, I couldn't help it, I started to cry. And I told him about the tryouts and my dad and how crappy it was, what with my mom being no help at all and me not knowing whether I wanted to talk to him or kill him. And the whole time I was thinking, good going, Chris, the kid just lost both his parents and may never get a chance at a normal life, and you're busy telling him all your pissant little problems, but I just couldn't help it.

Finally I scrubbed my face and said, "Sorry, kid. Guess you've got 62 problems of your own, eh?" But he was gone again, not a flicker in his eyes, staring beyond me. "Well, at least I still have my day job. They've asked me to teach swimming a couple nights a week. Most of the kids are worse swimmers than you, and boy, is that saying something." Still nothing. And suddenly it became the most important thing in the world to get him to look at me again. "Listen, Mikey, they're putting in a whirlpool for sports injury therapy. Looks pretty neat. Why don't you come to the pool sometime? Would you like that?"

63   He touched my face with one finger.

64   Well, I was like a crazy man, running up to the nurse all excited, shouting my head off. And she was just as bad. So that was how he started coming to the pool again, only this time a volunteer attendant brought him. The guy would sit Mike in the shallow end and kind of play with him, splashing him lightly with water, letting him walk around. Mike seemed to be quite happy just to sit or paddle. He was tired and old-looking, too feeble to resist when the attendant steered him away from the deep end. I began to think that this might be the best he'd ever do.

65   Then one day, while the attendant is talking to one of the girls in the new Jacuzzi, I see Mike head for the deep end, walking close to the edge, jerkily, like he's on automatic pilot. The deep end is near the Jacuzzi and I figure it's only a matter of moments before the volunteer sees what the kid's up to and hauls him away, so I casually wander over to the whirlpool and block his view. All the time I'm watching Mike out of the corner of my eye and trying to convince myself that if he starts to get into trouble I can get him out of it, but I'm still pretty nervous. How the hell do I really know why he's off to that end of the pool, anyway? But another part of me, lower down, is drumming out this message over and over, telling him to go for it, go for it, and I don't even know what I mean. Well, Mike gets to the deep end and, sure enough, the attendant looks over my shoulder and freaks. He leaps out of the whirlpool as Mike crouches down, but I hold him back by one arm. "Leave him alone, man."

66   "Are you crazy?" he says. "You're gonna get me fired."

67   "Fuck off," I say, eyes glued to the kid.

68   Mike tips himself backwards into the pool.

69   "Jesus H. Christ!" yells the volunteer and hurls himself towards the pool, only to come smack up against me. I'm ready to punch him out if he takes one more step towards that kid, so help me God. Mike is floating like a dead man, loose and motionless beneath the water. My heart is thrashing the inside of my chest when I think of what could be happening if I'm wrong. The attendant is staring at me like I'm a murderer, and I'm grunting with the strain of holding him back when suddenly I realize I haven't been keeping track of my breathing. I don't know how long he's been in there.

70   Maybe this is what he intended all along. Maybe he figured he could trust me to let him go.

Maybe he's two steps above vegetable and whatever's left of him is 71
somewhere in there screaming for help.

"MIKEY!" I yell at the pool. But I don't move one step closer. 72

The attendant is practically crying, and a ragged group is forming 73
behind us, trying to figure out what's happening, what we're staring at.

Mike's arms and legs start to move. He looks like he's feeling his way 74
through some invisible tunnel, then he bursts through into the open air,
climbs out of the pool and walks back to the same spot, more confidently,
almost eagerly. He tips himself backwards again, eyes closed.

My hands are still digging into the attendant's arms — he'll have a hell 75
of a bruise, and I think I've strained a muscle in my wrist. We breathe in
our first wild gulps, and stand there panting for a few seconds after I let
him go. "See," I say while he rubs the red spots, "it's just his game. He's
OK. I'll watch him." We dance around a little, 'cause I've wounded the
guy's pride, but basically he's cool.

I turn away to check the rest of the pool, and there's my dad in the 76
viewing room. He's seen the whole thing. I can tell because his face is
twisted like he's in pain, and he looks like he's ready to step through the
glass like it's nothing but air. Our eyes lock, and his hands rise to the glass
and press against it, fingers spread wide open. And it's like what he's
feeling is so strong it pulls my hand towards it all by itself. But that's where
it ends. Every muscle in my body aches. I need to sit down, rub my wrists.
I need. And all he does is stand there.

I still spend a lot of time at the pool. My dad comes by, but not so often, 77
and I find myself looking for him less and less. When he does show, I don't
make a move to go talk to him. I figure there are some things you have to
work out on your own. Maybe he will, maybe he won't. Maybe he'll just
disappear again. But that's up to him. In the meantime, I have things to get
on with. My diving lessons at the Y. And Mike. Like I promised, I watch
him, every day, while he tips himself into the depths of that big fluffy cloud
or living pool or hands of God or whatever his bent little brain thinks is
there. Most days he doesn't give any sign that he knows I'm here. But I
know I am, and I guess that's what matters. And I'll tell you something
else. Every time he breaks water it's like some kind of underwater flower
bursting into the sunlight, and I swear I can feel the touch of something
warm on my face.

1989

NOTE

Barbara Scott is the author of *The Quick*, a collection of short stories.

COMPREHENSION AND DISCUSSION

1. Who is the narrator of the story? What is his name? What does he do? Does he like his job?
2. What problems is the narrator facing? What is his living situation?
3. Do you think Chris is old enough to live away from his parents? Is he mature enough? At what age should children leave home?
4. How successful is the author at conveying the narrator's voice? Do you believe it is a teenage boy talking?
5. What is the setting for this story? Why is it important to the entire story?
6. Why and how does the narrator become interested in Mike in the beginning and then later in the story?
7. How does Mike's life parallel the narrator's? How do they differ, especially with respect to family?
8. Why does the narrator visit Mike in the Home? What happens there?
9. What is Chris's relationship with his father? Is it similar to his relationship with Mike?
10. What is heroism? What is hero worship? What does Chris do that may be considered heroic?
11. What if Chris's gambit had failed (and Mike had drowned)? Speculate on the consequences.
12. Could this story be told from Mike's point of view? How would that change the plot, situation, and crisis?
13. Have you ever experienced the kind of freedom Chris and Mike feel in the water in one of your sports? How can sport become a cathartic experience?

LITERARY TECHNIQUES

Author vs. narrator A common misconception some readers have about first-person point of view is that only a male author can write from a male voice and make it sound authentic, and vice versa. This is patently not true, as proven in this story. The author is a middle-aged woman while the narrator is Chris, a teenage boy. It is important not to confuse the author of the story and the narrator.

Colloquial language Because the story is told from the point of view of a sixteen year old, Scott chooses appropriate vocabulary and diction that such a character would use, including profanity. This technique gives authenticity to the speaker. For example, "my eyes keep getting snagged on one of the babes that hang out at the pool in a bathing suit that's a clear signal they don't come for the swimming" (paragraph 9) has colloquial speech patterns, improper grammar, and slang. These touches make readers believe they are hearing a teenager, not Scott the writer. Note that this type of language can date quickly and that some of the expressions Scott uses sound old-fashioned even though the story was written as recently as 1989.

ASSIGNMENTS

1. Write an essay comparing the character of Chris with the narrator of "Greasy Lake" by T. Coraghessan Boyle (p. 33) or with Rand from "Generation Y" by Nancy Kilpatrick (p. 118).
2. Lifeguarding is a time-honoured job for teenagers. Research the qualifications for the job and write an essay discussing the advantages or disadvantages of this kind of work.
3. Read Morley Callaghan's "All the Years of Her Life" (p. 45). As in Scott's story, the main character learns something about himself and his situation. Compare the situations of the two characters. How does this insight change the character? Will it make him a better human being?
4. Read Margaret Laurence's "The Loons" (p. 130). Like Mike in Scott's story, Piquette is a damaged person. Compare the effects of physical injury on the mental health of these two teenagers.

The Lady or the Tiger?
Frank R. Stockton

1   In the very olden time, there lived a semi-barbaric king, whose ideas, though somewhat polished and sharpened by the progressiveness of distant Latin neighbors, were still large, florid, and untrammeled, as became the half of him which was barbaric. He was a man of exuberant fancy, and, withal, of an authority so irresistible that, at his will, he turned his varied fancies into facts. He was greatly given to self-communing, and, when he and himself agreed upon anything, the thing was done. When every member of his domestic and political systems moved smoothly in its appointed course, his nature was bland and genial; but whenever there was a little hitch, and some of his orbs got out of their orbits, he was blander and more genial still, for nothing pleased him so much as to make the crooked straight and crush down uneven places.

2   Among the borrowed notions by which his barbarism had become semified was that of the public arena, in which, by exhibitions of manly and beastly valor, the minds of his subjects were refined and cultured.

3   But even here the exuberant and barbaric fancy asserted itself. The arena of the king was built, not to give the people an opportunity of hearing the rhapsodies of dying gladiators, nor to enable them to view the inevitable conclusion of a conflict between religious opinions and hungry jaws, but for purposes far better adapted to widen and develop the mental energies of the people. This vast amphitheater, with its encircling galleries, its mysterious vaults, and its unseen passages, was an agent of poetic justice, in which crime was punished, or virtue rewarded, by the decrees of an impartial and incorruptible chance.

4   When a subject was accused of a crime of sufficient importance to interest the king, public notice was given that on an appointed day the fate of the accused person would be decided in the king's arena — a structure which well deserved its name, for, although its form and plan were borrowed from afar, its purpose emanated solely from the brain of this man, who, every barleycorn a king, knew no tradition to which he owed more allegiance than pleased his fancy, and who ingrafted on every adopted form of human thought and action the rich growth of his barbaric idealism.

5   When all the people had assembled in the galleries, and the king, surrounded by his court, sat high up on his throne of royal state on one side of the arena, he gave a signal, a door beneath him opened, and the accused subject stepped out into the amphitheater. Directly opposite him, on the

other side of the enclosed space, were two doors, exactly alike and side by side. It was the duty and the privilege of the person on trial to walk directly to these doors and open one of them. He could open either door he pleased. He was subject to no guidance or influence but that of the aforementioned impartial and incorruptible chance. If he opened the one, there came out of it a hungry tiger, the fiercest and most cruel that could be procured, which immediately sprang upon him and tore him to pieces as a punishment for his guilt. The moment that the case of the criminal was thus decided, doleful iron bells were clanged, great wails went up from the hired mourners posted on the outer rim of the arena, and the vast audience, with bowed heads and downcast hearts, wended slowly their homeward way, mourning greatly that one so young and fair, or so old and respected, should have merited so dire a fate.

But if the accused person opened the other door, there came forth from   6 it a lady, the most suitable to his years and station that His Majesty could select among his fair subjects, and to this lady he was immediately married, as a reward of his innocence. It mattered not that he might already possess a wife and family, or that his affections might be engaged upon an object of his own selection. The king allowed no such subordinate arrangements to interfere with his great scheme of retribution and reward. The exercises, as in the other instance, took place immediately, and in the arena. Another door opened beneath the king, and a priest, followed by a band of choristers and dancing maidens blowing joyous airs on golden horns and treading an epithalamic measure, advanced to where the pair stood, side by side, and the wedding was promptly and cheerily solemnized. Then the gay brass bells rang forth their merry peals, the people shouted glad hurrahs, and the innocent man, preceded by children strewing flowers on his path, led his bride to his home.

This was the king's semi-barbaric method of administering justice. Its   7 perfect fairness is obvious. The criminal could not know out of which door would come the lady. He opened either he pleased, without having the slightest idea whether, in the next instant, he was to be devoured or married. On some occasions the tiger came out of one door, and on some out of the other. The decisions of this tribunal were not only fair — they were positively determinate. The accused person was instantly punished if he found himself guilty, and, if innocent, he was rewarded on the spot, whether he liked it or not. There was no escape from the judgments of the king's arena.

The institution was a very popular one. When the people gathered   8 together on one of the great trial days, they never knew whether they were to witness a bloody slaughter or a hilarious wedding. This element of uncertainty lent an interest to the occasion which it could not otherwise have attained. Thus the masses were entertained and pleased, and the thinking part of the community could bring no charge of unfairness against this plan, for did not the accused person have the whole matter in his own hands?

9   This semi-barbaric king had a daughter as blooming as his most florid fancies, and with a soul as fervent and imperious as his own. As is usual in such cases, she was the apple of his eye and was loved by him above all humanity. Among his courtiers was a young man of that fineness of blood and lowness of station common to the conventional heroes of romance who love royal maidens. This royal maiden was well satisfied with her lover, for he was handsome and brave to a degree unsurpassed in all this kingdom, and she loved him with an ardor that had enough of barbarism in it to make it exceedingly warm and strong. This love affair moved on happily for many months, until one day the king happened to discover its existence. He did not hesitate nor waver in regard to his duty in the premises. The youth was immediately cast into prison, and a day was appointed for his trial in the king's arena. This, of course, was an especially important occasion, and His Majesty, as well as all the people, was greatly interested in the workings and development of this trial. Never before had such a case occurred; never before had a subject dared to love the daughter of the king. In after years such things became commonplace enough, but then they were, in no slight degree, novel and startling.

10   The tiger-cages of the kingdom were searched for the most savage and relentless beasts, from which the fiercest monster might be selected for the arena; and the ranks of maiden youth and beauty throughout the land were carefully surveyed by competent judges, in order that the young man might have a fitting bride in case fate did not determine for him a different destiny. Of course, everybody knew that the deed with which the accused was charged had been done. He had loved the princess, and neither he, she, nor anyone else thought of denying the fact; but the king would not think of allowing any fact of this kind to interfere with the workings of the tribunal, in which he took such great delight and satisfaction. No matter how the affair turned out, the youth would be disposed of, and the king would take an aesthetic pleasure in watching the course of events, which would determine whether or not the young man had done wrong in allowing himself to love the princess.

11   The appointed day arrived. From far and near the people gathered and thronged the great galleries of the arena; and crowds, unable to gain admit-

tance, massed themselves against its outside walls. The king and his court were in their places, opposite the twin doors — those fateful portals, so terrible in their similarity.

All was ready. The signal was given. A door beneath the royal party 12 opened, and the lover of the princess walked into the arena. Tall, beautiful, fair, his appearance was greeted with a low hum of admiration and anxiety. Half the audience had not known so grand a youth had lived among them. No wonder the princess loved him! What a terrible thing for him to be there!

As the youth advanced into the arena he turned, as the custom was, to 13 bow to the king. But he did not think at all of that royal personage; his eyes were fixed upon the princess, who sat to the right of her father. Had it not been for the moiety of barbarism in her nature, it is probable that lady would not have been there. But her intense and fervid soul would not allow her to be absent on an occasion in which she was so terribly interested. From the moment that the decree had gone forth that her lover should decide his fate in the king's arena, she had thought of nothing, night or day, but this great event and the various subjects connected with it. Possessed of more power, influence, and force of character than anyone who had ever before been interested in such a case, she had done what no other person had done — she had possessed herself of the secret of the doors. She knew in which of the two rooms behind those doors stood the cage of the tiger, with its open front, and in which waited the lady. Through these thick doors, heavily curtained with skins on the inside, it was impossible that any noise or suggestion should come from within to the person who should approach to raise the latch of one of them; but gold, and the power of a woman's will, had brought the secret to the princess.

Not only did she know in which room stood the lady, ready to emerge 14 all blushing and radiant, should her door be opened, but she knew who the lady was. It was one of the fairest and loveliest of the damsels of the court who had been selected as the reward of the accused youth, should he be proved innocent of the crime of aspiring to one so far above him; and the princess hated her. Often had she seen, or imagined that she had seen, this fair creature throwing glances of admiration upon the person of her lover, and sometimes she thought these glances were perceived and even returned. Now and then she had seen them talking together; it was but for a moment or two, but much can be said in a brief space; it may have been on most unimportant topics, but how could she know that? The girl was lovely, but she had dared to raise her eyes to the loved one of the princess; and, with all the intensity of the savage blood transmitted to her through long lines of wholly barbaric ancestors, she hated the woman who blushed and trembled behind that silent door.

15   When her lover turned and looked at her, and his eye met hers as she sat there paler and whiter than anyone in the vast ocean of anxious faces about her, he saw, by that power of quick perception which is given to those whose souls are one, that she knew behind which door crouched the tiger and behind which stood the lady. He had expected her to know it. He understood her nature, and his soul was assured that she would never rest until she had made plain to herself this thing, hidden to all other lookers-on, even to the king. The only hope for the youth in which there was any element of certainty was based upon the success of the princess in discovering this mystery; and the moment he looked upon her, he saw she had succeeded, as in his soul he knew she would succeed.

16   Then it was that his quick and anxious glance asked the question: "Which?" It was as plain to her as if he shouted it from where he stood. There was not an instant to be lost. The question was asked in a flash; it must be answered in another.

17   Her right arm lay on the cushioned parapet before her. She raised her hand and made a slight, quick movement toward the right. No one but her lover saw her. Every eye but his was fixed on the man in the arena.

18   He turned, and with a firm and rapid step he walked across the empty space. Every heart stopped beating, every breath was held, every eye was fixed immovably upon that man. Without the slightest hesitation, he went to the door on the right and opened it.

19   Now, the point of the story is this: did the tiger come out of that door, or did the lady?

20   The more we reflect upon this question, the harder it is to answer. It involves a study of the human heart which leads us through devious mazes of passion, out of which it is difficult to find our way. Think of it, fair reader, not as if the decision of the question depended upon yourself, but upon that hot-blooded, semi-barbaric princess, her soul at a white heat beneath the combined fires of despair and jealousy. She had lost him, but who should have him?

21   How often, in her waking hours and in her dreams, had she started in wild horror and covered her face with her hands as she thought of her lover opening the door on the other side of which waited the cruel fangs of the tiger!

But how much oftener had she seen him at the other door! How in her   22
grievous reveries had she gnashed her teeth and torn her hair when she saw
his start of rapturous delight as he opened the door of the lady! How her
soul had burned in agony when she had seen him rush to meet that woman,
with her flushing cheek and sparkling eye of triumph; when she had seen
him lead her forth, his whole frame kindled with the joy of recovered life;
when she had heard the glad shouts from the multitude and the wild ringing
of the happy bells; when she had seen the priest, with his joyous followers,
advance to the couple and make them man and wife before her very eyes;
and when she had seen them walk away together upon their path of
flowers, followed by the tremendous shouts of the hilarious multitude, in
which her one despairing shriek was lost and drowned!

Would it not be better for him to die at once and go to wait for her in   23
the blessed regions of semi-barbaric futurity?

And yet, that awful tiger, those shrieks, that blood!   24

Her decision had been indicated in an instant, but it had been made   25
after days and nights of anguished deliberation. She had known she would
be asked, she had decided what she would answer, and, without the
slightest hesitation, she had moved her hand to the right.

The question of her decision is one not to be lightly considered, and it   26
is not for me to presume to set myself up as the one person able to answer
it. And so I leave it with all of you: which came out of the opened door —
the lady or the tiger?

1886

NOTES

Frank R. Stockton is an American writer who lived from 1834 to 1902.
This story was such a hit for Stockton that its success dogged him for the
rest of his life. People would beg him to reveal the ending of the story, even
trying to trick him at parties into choosing food moulded like a lady or a
tiger. Some of his later work was even refused by publishers because they
believed it did not come up to the standards set by this story.

Semified Words can be both constructed and deconstructed from Latin-
and Greek-based roots, prefixes, and suffixes. Here, in Stockton's word,
"semi" means "half" (as in "semicircle"). The suffix "-fy" means "to
make" and is used to form verbs (for example, "beautify"). So "semify"
means "to make half."

COMPREHENSION AND DISCUSSION

1. Why does Stockton call the king "semi-barbaric"?
2. Why is the king's method of justice called "impartial and incorruptible chance"? Do you think it is fair and just?
3. Describe the king in your own words. Why does he like his method of trying people?
4. Why do the king's subjects enjoy this method of justice?
5. Describe the princess in your own words. How important is it that she is also "semi-barbaric"?
6. What do you think happened? Was it the lady or the tiger that came out the door the young man chose? Support your answer.
7. What does this story say about the human heart or mind? ("If I can't have it, nobody else can either!" "Bread and circuses.")
8. Would the story have the same effect if the author said what the outcome was?
9. This story was written 150 years ago. Could the same story be told in the context of today's sensibilities?

LITERARY TECHNIQUES

Ornate writing style Just as furniture and clothing styles have moved from elaborate styles to simpler lines, writing style has changed. The way words, phrases, and sentences are put together reveals the manner of the times. For example, contemporary writers generally write shorter sentences and shorter paragraphs; moreover, their word choice and vocabulary respond to current tastes. Similarly, in the 19th century a writer such as Frank Stockton wrote for his readership. People then tended to have more time for reading and delighted in the construction of long sentences and ornate phrases.

Addressing the reader A classic method of storytelling is to engage readers by making them participate in the story. It comes from the more traditional technique of reciting or orally delivering a story to a live audience. For example, David Arnason in "A Girl's Story" (p. 20) draws female readers in by making them part of the plot. Similarly, Stockton challenges his readers to decide on the young man's fate.

Open-ended stories Sometimes writers leave readers to draw their own conclusions as to what happens at the end of a story. Often readers can come up with alternative endings, based either on interpreting the clues in the plot or on their own life experiences. Stories that are set up in this manner are made memorable by the fact that readers are required to mull over and decide what ending they believe in.

ASSIGNMENTS

1. Read "Sedna, The Witch under the Sea" by Marion Wood (p. 210). In an essay, compare the princess in "The Lady or the Tiger?" with Sedna. You can look at the characters themselves and/or their relative situations, such as father–daughter relationships.
2. Another story with an open-ended conclusion is "The Moose and the Sparrow" (p. 74). Compare how Stockton and Hugh Garner use this technique.
3. In groups, create a paraphrase of the story that incorporates more modern language. Each group can paraphrase a small section of the text.
4. Write a brief summary of the story.
5. Write an essay on which outcome is more likely.
6. In an essay, compare Stockton's style of writing with that of a contemporary writer, such as Nancy Kilpatrick in "Generation Y" (p. 118).

Sedna, The Witch under the Sea

Marion Wood

1   Sedna, the Sea Spirit, was once a mortal girl, living with her father by the seashore. She was very beautiful and many men came to court her, bringing gifts to win her favour. But Sedna was very proud and haughty and would have none of them. Always she found some fault. This one was too short or that one had bad teeth. She spurned their gifts and turned her back on them, refusing even to speak.

2   This behaviour infuriated her father. "Why can you not take a husband like other girls?" he asked impatiently. "Now that I am old, I need a son-in-law to help me with hunting."

3   Sedna only shrugged carelessly and turned away, brushing her long dark hair and humming.

4   Finally, when yet another young man had gone away, hurt and saddened by Sedna's cruelty, her father lost his temper. "The very next man who comes here," he stormed, "you shall marry! Next time I will make you! You will not refuse again!"

5   He did not have long to wait. The very next day a strange kayak appeared at the water's edge. In it sat a tall young man dressed in rich, dark furs. A heavy hood covered his head and his face was half-hidden by his wooden snow-goggles.

6   Sedna's father hurried down to the shore, dragging his struggling, protesting daughter behind him. Even before the stranger had time to disembark, the old man shouted, "Do you seek a wife? Here is my daughter Sedna! She is young and beautiful, and can cook and sew. She will make you an excellent wife."

7   The young man smiled. "I have heard much of your daughter's beauty," he nodded, "and have come with the purpose of making her acquaintance." Turning to Sedna, he went on. "I have a large and splendid house in my own country, hung with furs to keep out the elements. If you marry me, you will sleep on soft bearskins and eat only the finest food."

8   Sedna looked at the young man sitting tall and straight in his kayak. "Well, if I must take a husband, I suppose I must," she thought grudgingly. "He seems kind and not too ugly. I could do worse."

9   Indeed she had little choice in the matter, for her father's mind was made up and without more ado he bundled her into the kayak. The young man picked up his paddle and pushed off from the shore.

For many miles they travelled across the ice-cold sea. Sedna, cross and   10
sulky, said nothing, nor did the young man seem inclined for conversation.
Only the lapping of the water against the kayak or the occasional cry of a
solitary bird disturbed the silence. On and on they went until at last a rocky
island loomed out of the mists.

"Look!" said the young man. "There is my home."   11

Sedna was filled with dismay. The island seemed a bleak and inhos-   12
pitable place. Nothing grew on its stony shores and sea birds swooped
about the cliffs, filling the air with their wild, mournful cries.

The young man brought the kayak into the shallows and leaped ashore.   13
He threw back his hood and pulled off his goggles. Sedna looked at him
aghast. He was very ugly, short and squat, with tiny, red-rimmed eyes. He
had seemed tall before only because of the high seat of his kayak. He saw
Sedna's horrified face and burst into harsh, cackling laughter.

"Come!" he cried, roughly seizing her arm. "Come and see my fine   14
house — your new home!"

But it was not at all fine. It was nothing but a heap of twigs and drift-   15
wood perched on a high rocky ledge. There were no soft furs as the young
man had promised, only a few miserable fish skins thrown on the rough
floor. Sedna looked at her new husband and, before her eyes, he turned into
a small, soot-black bird. Too late she realized the truth. This was no young
man whom she had married, but a storm petrel in human disguise.

Sedna regretted bitterly the foolish pride which had brought her to this   16
terrible place. The cliff-top nest was cold and uncomfortable and there was
only fish to eat, but there was no way of escape and so for a long time
Sedna lived with the storm petrel on the rocky island. During the day he
left the nest in his bird form and flew over the sea in search of food. When
he returned in the evening he became a man once more.

Meanwhile, Sedna's father, repenting his hasty temper, decided to go   17
in search of her and, after many days' travel, he too came to the lonely rock
where the storm petrel lived. When he saw his daughter's misery, he was
stricken with remorse. "Oh my poor child," he cried, "I did not mean you
to suffer such a fate. Surely you have been punished enough! Let us return
home at once."

They climbed hastily into his kayak and set off, but, even before the   18
island had faded from view, Sedna, looking back, saw a black speck
appear. "Father! Father!" she screamed. "My husband is returning! When
he finds me gone, he is sure to follow us. What shall we do?"

19   The old man pushed her down into the bottom of the kayak and covered her over with skins. Urged on by fear, he paddled as fast as he could and the kayak flew over the waves.

20   Out of the darkening skies came the storm petrel, swooping low, his wings stiff and outstretched. Although Sedna was hidden under the pile of skins, he knew she was there. He flew round and round the kayak, shrieking wildly. At first the old man paid no heed, but again the bird swooped low, beating at the sea with his wings so that it grew black and angry and great waves began to wash over the kayak. The old man shouted and struck out at him with his paddle, but the bird dodged the blows and, skimming the surface of the water, beat his wings so furiously that the storm raged even more fiercely and the sea became a churning whirlpool, tossing and spinning the kayak like a child's toy, threatening to engulf it completely.

21   Fearing for his life, the old man lost his reason and dragged the trembling Sedna from her hiding place. "Here is your wife!" he cried. "Take her for yourself," and he hurled her into the sea.

22   Screaming in terror, Sedna clung to the kayak, but her father, maddened with fear, struck at her hands with his paddle, and the first joints of her fingers, frozen with cold, broke off like icicles and fell into the sea. As they bobbed away, they changed miraculously into seals, diving and twisting in the waves.

23   Again Sedna clung to the kayak, pleading for her life, but again her father tried to make her release her grasp, this time cutting off the second joints of her fingers. These, too, fell into the sea and became the first walrus. With her bleeding stumps, Sedna made one last despairing attempt to seize hold of the kayak, but her father had no pity and struck off the remaining joints, which took the form of whales and followed the seals and walrus down into the depths of the ocean.

24   Now Sedna had no more fingers and she sank to the bottom of the sea. The storm petrel circled the kayak, lamenting his lost wife. Then he turned and flew back to his bleak island home.

25   But Sedna was not drowned. Instead, she became the Spirit of the Sea and Mother of the Sea Beasts. Legend says that she lives still at the bottom of the sea, jealously guarding the creatures which came from her fingers. Because of her father's cruelty, she has no love for human beings. Their wicked deeds trouble her, affecting her body with sores and infesting her hair like lice. Lacking fingers, she cannot brush her hair and it becomes tangled and matted. In revenge, she calls up storms to prevent men from hunting, or keeps the sea creatures to herself.

At such times shamans must travel to the land below the sea to confess   26
men's sins and to beg her forgiveness. Only the most powerful, who fear
nothing, can undertake this journey for the way is long and dangerous,
blocked by great rolling boulders, and evil spirits guard the entrance to the
Sea Mother's sealskin tent. To sooth Sedna's rage and pain, the shaman
must first comb her hair until it hangs clean and smooth once more. Then
Sedna may feel more kindly and release the whale, walrus and seal from
the great pool below her lamp, so that for a time, until they forget and sin
again, people may hunt freely and without fear.

Date of the myth unknown.

NOTES

This story is a retelling of an Inuit creation myth.

COMPREHENSION AND DISCUSSION

1. What kind of girl is Sedna in the beginning? Has she changed by the
   end?
2. Why does her father want her to marry?
3. Why does Sedna agree to run away with the stranger in the kayak?
4. What does she discover about her new husband?
5. Explain the actions of Sedna's father. Is he a weak person? How do you
   know?
6. Who is worse: Sedna's father or her storm petrel husband?
7. Why does the writer include the graphic descriptions of violence done
   to Sedna?
8. Using this story as benchmark, what makes it an Inuit tale?
9. What does this story attempt to explain in the natural world?
10. Is there a moral lesson in this myth? What is it?
11. Why are transformations important to myths? For example, in different
    stories the storm petrel becomes a man; a prince is turned into a frog
    and back; or a beast becomes a prince. Explain the appeal to story-
    telling. What is the relationship between human and animals?

LITERARY TECHNIQUES

Retold stories Popular cultural or folk stories are often retold by various writers. Because these stories have no known authorship (other than that they belong to a certain group, culture, or race) or because they originated long ago in the oral tradition, they tend to be recast in print by folklorists. Sometimes these retold stories are written simply for young readers, other times for posterity. No matter the reason for preserving them, these stories are powerful and have universal appeal. The story of Sedna, the innocent but betrayed young woman who becomes a capricious sea goddess, transcends its Inuit roots. It evokes raw emotions in readers and offers a mythical explanation of the forces of nature in human terms.

Creation myth "Where do we come from?" "Why are we here on this earth?" "Who made us?" "How did these things come about?" These are basic questions people ask. Creation stories or myths try to satisfy that yearning to know. Every culture or race has its own way of telling about the beginnings of existence. For example, in Asian stories, the universe begins as a gigantic egg that hatched; in Norse sagas, a cow dies and from its parts flows the creation of natural elements and life.

Metamorphosis In many folktales and myths, human beings can morph into animal form, and vice versa. For example, the werewolf is really a human being doomed at full moon to change into a savage animal. Such relationships between man and beast become not only plot devices but also metaphors about how close we are to being animals. We all have the beast within.

ASSIGNMENTS

1. Compare Sedna with the princess in "The Lady or the Tiger?" (p. 202). How are the characters and their situations similar? How are they different?
2. Folktales and myths do not always have a happy ending. Read "The Cowherd" (p. 71), a Chinese folktale. Is there a point to unhappy endings?
3. Consider Jay Ingram's "Once Upon a Time, A Story Meant Survival" (p. 278). Is the story of Sedna useful storytelling? Why or why not?
4. Find another Canadian Native myth and compare it with the story of Sedna.

part two | reading non-fiction

READING NON-FICTION

INTRODUCTION

The world of books is divided into fiction and non-fiction. The library and the bookstore both use this essential classification. In television, fiction is in the form of dramas and comedies, while non-fiction is in the form of documentaries and news programs. The term "fiction" comes from the Latin *fictio*, "the act of shaping, a feigning, that which is feigned." In English, then, fiction is something made up, imaginary; so non-fiction is, essentially, reality. The writer may be expressing a strange view of the subject matter, but the events he or she is discussing are true ones.

Most writing is non-fiction. Every day, we give information, express our thoughts, or share our experiences with others. You may want to tell your friend about the wonderful movie you saw, so you e-mail him or write a letter. On the other hand, you may want to complain about the widget that does not work properly and demand a replacement from the manufacturer. At work, you may need to write up monthly reports or develop in-house manuals for employees. What you have written is non-fiction. The message you have sent is grounded in reality and is true. The purpose of writing, then, is to inform, persuade, or entertain.

You read different kinds of non-fiction. A newspaper story reports an accident, the results of a study, or a political situation. An essay or an editorial gives the writer's opinions on the news story. A textbook gives you information on the subject you are studying and directs your learning. A manual tells you how to operate your car, appliances, or electronic gadget. A biography tells the story of a person's life.

DISTINGUISHING FICTION AND NON-FICTION

While the world of literature is divided into fiction and non-fiction, sometimes it is not easy to tell the difference. For example, Garry Engkent's short stories, like "Chickens for Christmas" (p. 61), have often been incorrectly classified as non-fiction essays because they are based on true events and because the narrator is a person similar to the author. However, if you compare this story with Rosie DiManno's "Growing Up on Grace" (p. 246), you can see the difference. Engkent uses dialogue to tell his story, whereas reminiscences are rarely presented with so much dialogue. How many of us could remember the exact words our mother said to us when we were children?

The line between fiction and non-fiction today is often blurred. Docudramas on television re-create real events, but they are still "re-creations." Reality TV is manipulated and edited to present what the producers judge to be good television. Journalists sometimes make up a character that represents several real people to give sharper focus to the article or column, even though that person does not exist. Essay writers may go off on a flight of fancy that has more in common with creative fiction. For instance, Philip Marchand imagines cops at his door (p. 300) and Robert Arnason creates a hypothetical example (p. 224). Colin Ross takes this even further in his satire of the Grey Owl story (p. 327). Sometimes a fictional character like Scrooge seems real because so many people have heard of him so often that they want him to be fact.

Non-fiction writers borrow techniques from fiction writers, and vice versa. Essayists can use narrative to tell a story, as Rosie DiManno and George Orwell do. Truman Capote's book *In Cold Blood* is called a non-fiction novel. A celebrity biography may stretch the truth so much that the book seems to belong on the fiction shelves. Two history books can have very different versions of reality. Old science and medical books can be based on so much inaccurate information that they resemble works of fiction. It is even said that truth is stranger than fiction.

However, even though the fiction/non-fiction distinction may not always hold fast, it is still a useful one. The majority of works you read will clearly belong to one camp or the other, and the more experience you have as a reader, the easier it will be to see the difference.

TYPES OF NON-FICTION

Writing can be categorized according to different rhetorical modes or types. Essay writers generally use more than one rhetorical mode in a piece. For instance, to describe a process, the writer uses definition and description to make the process clear. These types of essays are discussed again, from a writing point of view, in Chapter 6 of Part Three.

Exposition Explaining something that the writer knows. "Exposition" means to expose or show ideas and information. Often it is an umbrella term that includes all other modes of writing. Examples from this text include:

"Grey Owl's Magnificent Masquerade" (p. 232)
"A Cell of Our Own Making" (p. 260)
"Don't You Think It's Time to Start Thinking?" (p. 264)

"No Offence" (p. 269)
"No Idol Industry Here" (p. 273)
"Once Upon a Time, A Story Meant Survival" (p. 278)
"Toxic Culture Syndrome" (p. 293)

Example/illustration Giving specific models or details to support ideas or to give readers a clearer picture. Readings that use illustration include:
"Toothpaste" (p. 241)
"Mess Up Your Kid's Education in 10 Easy Steps" (p. 287)

Definition Giving clear meanings of concepts, words, or practices. Readings that use definition include:
"The Mathematics of Relationships" (p. 224)
"Don't You Think It's Time to Start Thinking?" (p. 264)
"No Offence" (p. 269)

Classification/division Separating items or concepts into categories for easier identification. It is a kind of definition. For example, writing may be separated into fiction and non-fiction: the work of imagination and the work of reality. Moreover, it may be further broken down into kinds of fiction or kinds of non-fiction, such as detective stories and romances in fiction, and cookbooks and literary critiques in non-fiction. Examples of classification can be found in:
"Techno Dummies Need Not Suffer in Silence" (p. 300)
"Drugs in Sports: Why the Fuss?" (p. 322)

Compare and contrast Drawing similarities or differences between two or more items. Examples appear in:
"No Offence" (p. 269)
"Drugs in Sports: Why the Fuss?" (p. 322)

Cause and effect Demonstrating relationships and consequences so that readers can see connections. Examples can be found in:
"Truth and Consequences" (p. 236)
"Are Goody Bags a Good Thing?" (p. 334)

Description Detailing information, usually visual information, so that readers can make a mental picture of the item or get a good idea of what it is like. You can find examples of description in:
"Where Do the Children Play?" (p. 228)
"Shooting an Elephant" (p. 305)
"If We're So Rich, Why Aren't We Happy?" (p. 342)

Narration Telling a story, describing an incident or action. Examples of narration in the reading selections include all the short stories and the following essays:

"Where Do the Children Play?" (p. 228)

"Truth and Consequences" (p. 236)

"Growing Up on Grace" (p. 246)

"The Patterns of Eating" (p. 254)

"Shooting an Elephant" (p. 305)

"Have Wheels, Will Go A-Wooing" (p. 318)

"The Story of Grey Owl" (p. 327)

"Rediscovering Christmas" (p. 346)

Argumentation/persuasion Trying to make readers accept a certain point of view. The readings that use argument include:

"Where Do the Children Play?" (p. 228)

"Grey Owl's Magnificent Masquerade" (p. 232)

"Don't You Think It's Time to Start Thinking?" (p. 264)

"Never Give in, Never" (p. 313)

"Have Wheels, Will Go A-Wooing" (p. 318)

"Drugs in Sports: Why the Fuss?" (p. 322)

"Are Goody Bags a Good Thing?" (p. 334)

"Rediscovering Christmas" (p. 346)

Process/instruction Showing how something works, and telling readers how to perform certain tasks. The readings that use process/instruction include:

"The Mathematics of Relationships" (p. 224)

"Toothpaste" (p. 241)

"The Patterns of Eating" (p. 254)

"No Offence" (p. 269)

"Mess Up Your Kid's Education in 10 Easy Steps" (p. 287)

DETERMINING MAIN IDEAS

When you read an essay, you will be asked to determine the author's main point or thesis. Ask yourself why the writer wrote the article, what message he or she is trying to communicate to the audience. You should be able to express the main idea in one complete sentence, which could also be called a summary statement. Do not confuse the thesis with the topic. If you say something like "this article is about...," you are probably going to give the topic, not the main point.

In "Pet-o-philia," Judith Timson talks about people and their pets. (topic)

In "Pet-o-philia," Judith Timson argues that some people care more for pets than for people. (thesis)

As you read the non-fiction articles, determine the main idea of each. Write it down in your reading notes. Next, look for secondary or supporting ideas that make the case for the thesis. Often they come in the form of examples, illustrations, and explanations.

ANALYZING ESSAYS

Just as you examine the techniques used by short-story writers, you can analyze essays. You can start by determining the rhetorical modes used, the author's purpose (the main idea), and the intended audience of the piece. You look carefully at the content—what is said and how it is organized. How does the writer support the statements? What kind of background information is given? Is the essay clear?

In addition to looking at content, you must examine tone and style. Is the article conversational or academic? Do the words carry strong connotations? For instance, an anti-abortionist might use the term "baby-killer" to refer to doctors who perform abortions. Does the author have a distinctive style—favouring puns or word play, for example?

Some patterns of organization are typical for certain kinds of writing. Magazine articles, for example, often start with an anecdote or story before they move on to more general information. Newspaper stories are arranged in a spiral: the headline tells the story briefly, the first paragraph or two tells the story again (but in full sentences), and the rest of the article repeats the story with more information. News stories rarely have proper conclusions because sometimes they must be chopped off at the end in order to fit the space.

ANSWERING READING COMPREHENSION QUESTIONS

Reading requires more than just the ability to pass your eyes over a piece of text and recognize all the words. You must be able to absorb ideas and information from the printed page. You must understand what you read. You must be able to follow the logic of the information. To find out whether you have understood something, your instructor will test you. This testing can be as simple as answering a few questions orally in class, or it can be a written exam or assignment.

Paraphrasing is an important test of reading comprehension. You can't put something in your own words if you do not understand it. In an assignment or exercise, you may be asked to paraphrase a particular passage. Other times, in a test, you may just have to put the author's ideas in your own words. It is not sufficient simply to copy the words directly from the text; this tells the instructor little about your understanding of the text.

For example, here are two possible answers to the question, "What is Judith Timson's opinion about today's treatment of pets by their owners?" ("Pet-o-philia," p. 338).

1. Timson thinks that owners treat their pets beyond the bounds of mere animal love. These pets are seen as humans or as children, and they have the same civil liberties and other rights as humans.

2. Timson objects to giving pets the status of a family member or a citizen. After all, pets are animals, not people, and they should be treated as such.

Answer 1 uses too many words and phrases from the original text: "beyond the bounds of mere animal love" and "have the same civil liberties." Moreover, it is wordy. Answer 2 makes the same points with conciseness and clarity.

In addition to such short-answer questions, you might be asked multiple choice or true-or-false questions. While some questions may focus on content, others might require you to analyze and interpret the text. You may have to identify the writer's thesis or comment on the techniques used in the essay. Writing a summary is also a test of reading comprehension.

SKIMMING AND SCANNING

Skimming and scanning are useful reading techniques when you need to get the general idea of a piece or are looking for a specific piece of information. When you skim a text, you let your eyes pass quickly over the words. You don't worry about understanding everything; you are just trying to get the gist of what is said. In scanning, you look for specific words. For instance, you might look for the name of a place or a specific date.

Skimming and scanning also include selective reading. You can read subtitles, the first sentences of paragraphs, and chapter introductions and summaries to get an idea of what material is covered. The table of contents and index can help you find specific points.

Learning to skim and scan effectively will help you deal with the volume of reading that is required in college courses. It lets you use your time to advantage. These skills are just part of your arsenal of reading tools. The more you read, the easier it will become. You will be able to understand the relationship between ideas better, have a larger vocabulary, and see the context of readings.

The Mathematics of Relationships

Robert Arnason

1   E=MC squared: Einstein's equation to convert mass into energy, and the most famous equation in the world until now.

2   There is a new equation on the block that is seeking fame, and maybe fortune. Its creator, me, is not as famous as Einstein, but my equation does have a catchy name. I call it the Relationship Equation.

3   Like all great discoveries, the equation came in a flash of brilliance. I was lying awake in my bed alone two weeks after a six-month relationship ended and was reviewing the reasons for the breakup.

4   Then it hit me. The cause of our breakup was not many little things, like the time I refused to go see *Divine Secrets of the Ya-Ya Sisterhood*. It could be explained by one simple mathematical equation: WM, 0.25.

5   This is how you use the equation: Take the amount of energy a woman puts into the relationship (W), then subtract the amount of energy a man puts into the relationship (M). If the difference between W and M is less than 25 per cent, the relationship can be a success.

6   As you know, there is only so much time in the day. You have to work. You have to play. But my relationship with my ex-girlfriend failed because we never satisfied the Relationship Equation. She wanted a boyfriend who would commit 99.99 per cent of his energy to the relationship and lazy ol' me just wanted to commit a very reasonable 55 per cent. Okay, okay. She wanted 70 per cent, and I could give only 40 per cent.

7   Now that you understand the math, I'll explain the theory behind the Relationship Equation.

8   In the equation, it's assumed that the woman will put more energy into the relationship. The argument behind this assumption is that most men spend 20 per cent of their energy on golf, 10 per cent on hockey pools, and 5 per cent on making up excuses. When your maximum score is 65 per cent, it's tough to outscore women.

9   The maximum difference of 25 per cent was chosen because I thought 25 per cent was a nice round number.

10   Now that I have introduced the theory, there is an outside chance that you may still be skeptical. So, I will subdue your skepticism with a real-world example to demonstrate how the equation works.

In this example, we have two guys, one girl and one dead goldfish.   11

One guy we will call Mr. 75 Per Cent, the other guy Mr. 40 Per Cent,   12
and we'll call the girl Sarah. The goldfish's name is Pete. Was Pete.

Pete was Sarah's goldfish for six years until tragedy struck one   13
Saturday afternoon. Sarah knocked over Pete's bowl while vacuuming and
Pete got sucked into the vacuum. Pete, as you probably can guess, did not
survive the sucking. Sarah is distraught and needs someone to talk to; she
calls her boyfriend.

Now let's pretend that Mr. 75 Per Cent is Sarah's boyfriend and we'll   14
study his reaction to her phone call.

Mr. 75 Per Cent listens carefully to the tragic tale of Pete's demise,   15
then immediately jumps into his car and drives to Sarah's apartment. To
comfort her, he draws a hot bath for Sarah, makes her some peppermint tea,
and then tells her how much Pete meant to him and sheds a few tears while
sharing some of his favourite memories of Pete.

The next day, he digs a small hole outside and gives a brief eulogy   16
during the burial ceremony. (Tip for the fashion conscious: Vogue says
smart casual attire is suitable for pet funerals.)

Okay. Well done, Mr. 75 Per Cent.   17

Now let's pretend Mr. 40 Per Cent is Sarah's boyfriend and we'll study   18
his response when Sarah calls.

Mr. 40 Per Cent doesn't answer the phone. He's home but doesn't feel   19
like talking. Sarah leaves a heartbreaking message explaining Pete's
untimely death, and Mr. 40 Per Cent rolls his eyes as he listens. But since
he's not totally heartless, he decides to drive over to Sarah's to see how
she is.

He stops to pick up a pizza because he's hungry. When he arrives at   20
Sarah's, he sees her red eyes and gives her a one-armed hug while holding
the pizza box with the other arm. Then he says something comforting, "So,
your fish died, eh? What was its name, Mike?"

He then sits down in front of the TV, turns on *Hockey Night in Canada*   21
and opens the pizza box.

So what can we learn from this?   22

That Mr. 40 Per Cent is a jerk? That Sarah should dump him for Mr.   23
75 Per Cent? That smart casual attire is suitable for many social occasions?

The important lesson is this: You would think that Sarah's hypothetical   24
relationship with Mr. 75 Per Cent is much more likely to be successful, but,
my friend, the Relationship Equation says women should date men who
put slightly less energy into the relationship.

25   Sarah is a 70-per-cent girl. She puts lots into her relationships, but not all of her energy and not all of her time. She works as an accountant, she's a volunteer Big Sister, and she used to have a goldfish. All these take time and energy. She doesn't want Mr. 75 Per Cent smothering her.

26   Mr. 75 Per Cent is probably a better match for Sarah's friend Jenny. Who puts 90 per cent of her time and energy into relationships and would expect her boyfriend to build a goldfish memorial.

27   So Sarah and Mr. 40 Per Cent might just work out. Mr. 40 Per Cent is willing to make the effort and bump up his percentage to 50 per cent, because he likes Sarah and she's a great girl.

28   And don't be so hard on Mr. 40 Per Cent. I mean, I did bring pizza after all.

2003

NOTES

Robert Arnason lives in Winnipeg.

Divine Secrets of the Ya-Ya Sisterhood is a 2002 movie about mothers and daughters, the type of movie commonly referred to as a "chick flick."

COMPREHENSION AND DISCUSSION

1. Explain in your own words what Arnason's formula means and how he derived it.
2. What point is Arnason making when he starts with Einstein's equation?
3. Why did Arnason's relationship with his previous girlfriend end?
4. Summarize Arnason's actions when Sarah's fish died.
5. Explain the difference between Sarah and Jenny and why Mr. 40 Per Cent is a better match for Sarah than Mr. 75 Per Cent.
6. Paraphrase (write in your own words): "Now that I have introduced the theory, there is an outside chance that you may still be skeptical. So, I will subdue your skepticism with a real-world example to demonstrate how the equation works."
7. Arnason says that women put more time and effort into relationships than men generally do. Is his premise correct? Explain why or why not.
8. What factors determine how much time and effort people should put into a relationship?

9. Explain how you know that this article was written with tongue firmly in cheek.
10. How does Arnason create humour in this essay? Which statements are particularly funny? What is the effect?

LITERARY TECHNIQUES

Hypothetical situation A hypothetical situation is one that is not real. It is a construct made to support an argument or illustrate a point. Arnason's "two guys, a girl and one dead goldfish" example serves to explain his theory of the Relationship Equation. He uses phrases such as "let's pretend" to show that it is not a true story. While a hypothetical situation is supposed to be entirely made up, it is often based on a real case.

Twist ending To make the content of an article truly memorable or delightful, a writer may create a twist or surprise ending akin to that used in fiction. For example, Arnason has already primed the reader in the beginning by using himself; however, as he explains his theory he develops an objective narrative of Mr. 75 Per Cent and Mr. 40 Per Cent. The reader then assumes that the writer is no longer talking about himself. At the end, the reader discovers that Mr. 40 Per Cent is Arnason, when the writer slyly reveals: "And don't be so hard on Mr. 40 Per Cent. I mean, I did bring the pizza after all."

ASSIGNMENTS

1. In academic English, write a summary of Arnason's theory and how it works.
2. Write an analysis of Arnason's use of humour in his essay.
3. What is the key to a succesful relationship? Write an essay on the most important factors.
4. In the article "Have Wheels, Will Go A-Wooing" (p. 318), Kurt Preinsperg describes how he buys a car to improve his love life. Where would Preinsperg's actions fit into Arnason's theory? Is Preinsperg likely to invest too much time and energy in a relationship? Write a paragraph supporting your view.
5. Find another article on the relationships between the sexes and compare the article with Arnason's. You can discuss point of view or technique. Popular magazines often have articles that give advice on dating relationships.

Where Do the Children Play?

Deborah Banks

1 *Where Do the Children Play?* In what seems like a lifetime ago, I remember those words from a Cat Stevens song. Back then, it seemed incomprehensible to me that this could be a real question that would merit serious consideration. Thirty years ago, we knew where to play, how to allow our little young bodies to find the natural world, be it through a swim in the river, chasing fireflies at dusk in the summer or building a snowman out of the new-fallen snow that would beckon through the living-room window until we heeded the call.

2 I have been teaching for 20 years now and my career has taken me from the Arctic to the Eastern Townships of Quebec and finally to Montreal, where I now work. The transition in terms of geography has been nothing short of dramatic. I used to hold the fantasy that children were children no matter where you went but, in the past few years, I have started to question that belief.

3 That is why: Last week one of my students shook me up with her journal entry. She wrote: "I've never climbed a tree before though I dearly want to. I want to climb it and watch the sun set." This revelation stunned and silenced me. How can we have come to this? It wasn't simply this journal confession that was troubling me; it was a mounting catalogue of discoveries I had made since the start of the school year.

4 On my first day with my new class, we read a Mary Oliver poem about a summer day and the simple pleasure of strolling through a field, paying attention to the humble gifts of nature. This engendered more confessions. I was rendered speechless by the number of hands that were raised in response to my question, "Has anyone not walked through a field?"

5 The following week, we took our students on a nature exploration of Mont Royal, guided by a naturalist. My students demonstrated, time and again, their fear of nature with the tentative approach of curious squirrels, the lazy buzzing of late summer wasps, or the accidental bumping up against a burr which attached itself to a piece of clothing, subsequently releasing a stream of screams that reverberated over the entire mountain. If it wasn't so tragic, it almost could have been funny.

6 What is happening to our urban children? Many of them seem to have lost any connection that ever existed between themselves and nature. But for the artificial excursions to the country to ski or attend a tennis camp, this next generation does not know what the natural world could possibly

mean to them. They have not explored their own potentially deep connection with trees or plants, or considered the fragility of the precious resource of water.

How can we possibly expect them to have any concerns that ensure the perpetuity of green spaces, clean air and water if their lives have so little to do with the earth that sustains us? What hope is there for their children's children if they have not held a horse chestnut in their fist and contemplated its remarkable spikiness, or climbed into the canopy of a maple tree and imagined other worlds, or studied the metamorphosis of a dragonfly along a riverbed? Many of our urban children cannot imagine that being idle on a lazy summer afternoon while bathing in a cacophony of insect melodies could add anything of value to their lives. 7

It behooves parents to be more vigilant, to ensure that their sons and daughters walk in the natural world and learn to feel the peace that can only come when one makes meaningful connections with the planet that sustains us. In a society that seemingly has everything, we have not given our children nature. In fact, we are actually perpetuating its disappearance. We have not invited our youngest generation to climb a tree and feel the firm rub of old bark that allows us to know humility. We have not pulled them away from the television or computer and brought them out into the lawn to gaze at the stars after night has fallen. We have not taken them to an orchard (where those same lazy wasps buzz), to pick a family's supply of McIntosh or Lobo or Cortland apples for their lunches for the weeks to come. 8

We have done them a terrible disservice, and we have shortchanged our own society. 9

I'm really worried, and I'm really sad. What will our children remember about their childhood? They will not remember the countless hours in front of a screen. Those days will blur into one grey mass. But they will remember the time they listened to the cicadas sing their late summer dirge, held a perfect oak leaf in their hand, considered the complicated beauty of a spider's web or sat in the tall grass just learning to be still. How many more children do we want to send into adulthood who, when asked at the tender age of 11, admit wistfully that they have never climbed a tree? 10

Where do the children play? The answer is they don't. 11

2003

NOTES

Deborah Banks lives in Dorval, Quebec.

Cat Stevens is a folksinger of the 1970s. One of his more famous songs is "Morning Has Broken."

The title of Mary Oliver's poem is "Little Summer Poem Touching the Subject of Faith." Oliver's poems are written with children as the main readership in mind. You can find her poems on the Internet.

COMPREHENSION AND DISCUSSION

1. What is the thesis (main idea) of this essay?
2. Why is Banks worried about the children she teaches? How did she learn that these children lived differently than she expected?
3. Why is Banks concerned about children's lack of experience with nature? What could this lead to?
4. Why would an experience with nature be more memorable than the experience of sitting in front of a screen?
5. Why are some children afraid of nature?
6. What does Banks mean when she describes the "excursions to the country to ski or attend a tennis camp" as "artificial"?
7. Lack of activity among children today is leading to health problems such as obesity. What are the causes of such inactivity, and how can the problem be solved?
8. Is a life lived in front of a computer or TV screen less of a life?

LITERARY TECHNIQUES

Rhetorical question Essay writers often ask questions that are used for rhetorical effect, rather than to elicit an actual reply. In doing so, the speaker evokes thought in the audience and emphasizes the point more strongly. Generally, the answer is obvious. Note that Banks begins paragraphs 6 and 7 with rhetorical questions and uses two more in her conclusion. Rhetorical questions can be effective when they are used judiciously.

ASSIGNMENTS

1. Write a personal essay explaining what you have learned and experienced in the outdoors.
2. Interview a parent or grandparent about his or her childhood. Write an essay comparing childhood today with childhood one or two generations ago.
3. Use the Internet to find the lyrics for "Where Do the Children Play?" by Cat Stevens. Compare the message of the song with that of the article.
4. Cat Stevens gave up his successful singing career when he converted to Islam. Look up his biography on the Internet. In your opinion, was this a wise decision? Is spirituality more vital to human existence than fame and fortune?
5. Experts say that middle-class children today are over-programmed with adult-run activities such as league sports, and that children need leisure time in order to develop creativity and to learn how to entertain themselves. Write a research essay on what the experts say about the importance of play and how modern children are being short-changed.
6. Write a counterargument to Banks's article. Show that she is out of touch with contemporary society.
7. Kalle Lasn ("Toxic Culture Syndrome," p. 293) also talks about the problems of the modern lifestyle. Compare the points Lasn and Banks make about too much television.

Grey Owl's Magnificent Masquerade

John Barber

1   The colourful lies and personal failures that marked the career of the pseudo-Native Grey Owl did nothing to diminish his reputation when they flashed into view after his premature death in 1938. "Grey Owl had cockney accent and four wives," one headline read. As many of his eulogists accurately predicted, the fabrications served mainly to enhance his legacy.

2   "His attainments as a writer and naturalist will survive," *The Ottawa Citizen* editorialized at the time, "and when in later years our children's children are told of the strange masquerade — if it was a masquerade — their wonder and their appreciation will grow."

3   The time of those children's children has now come. Beginning tomorrow, they will be munching popcorn in front of a frankly hagiographic blockbuster devoted to the life and times of Grey Owl — a film that never would have been made had Archie Belaney not "written" his life according to the improbable conventions of Hollywood melodrama.

4   Grey Owl's many champions say that he misrepresented himself in order to attract attention to the causes of animal rights and wilderness conservation. No one would have paid attention to a plain old Englishman gone native in the Canadian North, they say; but a mystical "Red Indian" could really put it across. So, despite his lies, he did good.

5   In fact, there is no "despite" about it. The lies and the message are inextricable. The truth is, Grey Owl did good because he lied. Or, to make that statement more palatable, incorporate the euphemism favoured for lies we approve of: Grey Owl helped create the mythology that made the modern environmental movement possible.

6   The most powerful myth he created was that Native North Americans are the exemplars of environmental consciousness. Of all the variants of the "noble savage" cultural stereotype, invented by 18th-century Europeans for their own political and cultural purposes, it is by far the most durable. Despite what we know — and there is basically no anthropological evidence to support the notion — we can't let it go.

7   The best example is that of Chief Seattle, famous for an inspiring speech that brilliantly and poetically captures all the core beliefs of modern environmentalism. ("The Earth does not belong to man; man belongs to the Earth,"

et cetera.) Supposedly delivered in 1854, it was actually written around 1970 by U.S. screenwriter Ted Perry—and based on a poetic rendition that itself was based on an "improved" version of a highly dubious transcription made by a romantic Englishman 30 years after the actual words were uttered.

"Why are we so willing to accept a text like that if it's attributed to a   8
Native American?" Mr. Perry has wondered. More to the point, why do so many people still vehemently insist on its authenticity?

Reading Grey Owl today, it is blazingly obvious (as many of his Native   9
friends knew at the time) that he was no half-Apache wanderer who lacked formal education and, as late as his teenage years, had nothing better than pidgin English. His contemporary readers engaged in a suspension of disbelief that was more than willing—it was fierce.

It is less obvious, but equally true, that Grey Owl was no Canadian. The   10
movement that he joined included many Canadians, most prominently the artists of the Group of Seven; and he learned his entire shtick from the writings of Ernest Thompson Seton (especially *Two Little Savages*, a manual on living like an Indian that Archie Belaney read as a boy and put into practice brilliantly). But to modern readers, his preoccupations seem wholly English.

Until Grey Owl, for instance, issues of animal rights were basically   11
unknown on this side of the pond. (Even the famous John James Audubon shot every bird he ever painted.) In extolling the virtues of the "little folk" of the forest, especially the beavers he made into pets, Grey Owl was clearly following the example of his English grandfather and namesake, a crusading anti-vivisectionist—and not, as he claimed, traditional Native ways.

Grey Owl was surely the only Ojibwa of the 1930s to hold passionate   12
views on the morality of English fox hunting.

None of that matters now. Grey Owl endures as a true Canadian hero,   13
a foreigner who helped reveal the beauty of a magnificent landscape to scandalously blinkered nationals. He endures as a Native hero, not in his blood but in attitudes and beliefs that we still believe to be authentic. More than anything, he is an environmental hero, one who helped change the "real world" fundamentally through a magnificent act of the imagination.

1999

NOTES

John Barber is a columnist for *The Globe and Mail*.

Hagiographic blockbuster A huge Hollywood movie that portrays its hero as a saint. Barber is referring to the 1999 film *Grey Owl* starring Pierce Brosnan, which was just due to come out when this article was written.

Archie Belaney (1888–1938) An Englishman who lived in Canada, adopted the name Grey Owl, and wrote about environmental issues.

Red Indian A term to distinguish Native North Americans from East Indians, people from India. European settlers kept the generic misnomer of "Indian" for the North American Native peoples but distinguished them by the colour of their skin, which they saw as "red." This term is now considered a racial slur.

Noble savage A term coined in the 17th century by European writers and philosophers who idealized the North American Indian as being in touch with nature and unspoiled by civilization.

Chief Seattle (1786–1866) A famous Suquamish Native American who befriended settlers in the Pacific Northwest. He is revered as an environmentalist because of the speech he supposedly made.

Group of Seven (1920–1933) Famous Canadian artists who painted the wilderness of Canada.

Ernest Thompson Seton (1860–1946) A Canadian writer who wrote about animals and nature. His best-known works are *Wild Animals I Have Known* (1898) and *Two Little Savages: Being the Adventures of Two Boys Who Lived as Indians and What They Learned* (1906).

John James Audubon (1785–1851) An American naturalist and artist, famous for his study of birds.

Anti-vivisectionist Someone who is against experimentation on live animals.

COMPREHENSION AND DISCUSSION

1. What is Barber's attitude toward Grey Owl?
2. Does the writer try to balance his article with pros and cons about his subject? How?
3. Explain the paradox: "The truth is, Grey Owl did good because he lied" (paragraph 5). When is a lie acceptable? Do you believe that the end justifies the means?

4. Why did Grey Owl's words mean more than Archie Belaney's words would have? In other words, why was the masquerade necessary?
5. Why would modern readers be less likely to believe the masquerade?
6. Put this statement in your own words: "His contemporary readers engaged in a suspension of disbelief that was more than willing — it was fierce" (paragraph 9).

LITERARY TECHNIQUES

Barber makes his opinion clear by the positive words he uses, right from the title phrase "magnificent masquerade." Although he does not omit Belaney's character faults, he deals with them lightly and emphasizes the man's good deeds.

Oxymoron A literary device, a deliberate joining of two contradictory words or ideas, such as true lies or a healthy illness, to draw attention. Sometimes an oxymoron is used to create humour, at other times to heighten the truth in the contradiction. For example, Barber states: "The truth is, Grey Owl did good because he lied" (paragraph 5). Since Grey Owl's life is full of such contraries, the oxymoron is appropriate.

ASSIGNMENTS

1. Make a vocabulary list for this article. Write down the words you are not familiar with and find definitions and synonyms.
2. One of the greatest impostors in recent history is Ferdinand Demara. Research his story. Find out his Canadian connections. Write a brief account of his exploits and life.
3. Read "Truth and Consequences" (p. 236) and "The Story of Grey Owl" (p. 327). How do the three writers differ in their tone and approach to the topic?
4. Read "The Loons" (p. 130). In this short story, Vanessa thinks that Piquette knows the secrets of nature because of the stereotype of Native people. Discuss the stereotype and explain what impact it has in our society.
5. Charlotte Gray's "No Idol Industry Here" (p. 273) discusses the lack of Canadian heroes. Would Grey Owl fit the criteria of a hero?
6. Read Chief Seattle's speech (available on the Internet) and analyze its effectiveness as an environmental message.

Truth and Consequences

Brian Bethune

1   Almost as soon as the man known as Grey Owl died in a Prince Albert, Saskatchewan, hospital on April 13, 1938, his many secrets began to emerge into the open air. That same day, *The North Bay Nugget* ran a story it had sat on for three years, revealing that the famous Indian naturalist was actually an Englishman named Archie Belaney. And not just any Englishman, it eventually turned out, but a binge-drinking bigamist who had had five "wives." His closest supporters, especially Lovat Dickson, the Canadian-born London publisher who had made Grey Owl a household name in Britain, were devastated. They were desperately worried that all the good Grey Owl had done the cause of conservation would now be interred with his bones. But the twists and turns of Archie Belaney's strange saga by no means ended with his death.

2   Belaney was born in the English Channel port of Hastings in 1888, the son of a teenage bride and a reprobate father who soon left his family. Raised by two strict maiden aunts, Archie early on began to develop elaborate fantasies about his absent father, entwining the elder Belaney with his own love of animals and fascination with North American Natives. Those fantasies became the basis of Grey Owl's imaginary ancestry as the Mexican-born son of a Scots frontiersman and an Apache woman — Belaney's standard account of himself within two years of his arrival alone at age 17 in Northern Ontario in 1906. In 1910, Belaney married an Ojibwa woman, Angele Egwuna, his first and only legal wife. The next year, already drinking heavily, he abandoned her and their daughter, Alice.

3   During the next four poorly documented years of his life, Belaney strove to eradicate his English accent. He also had a son with a Métis woman, who died of tuberculosis soon after giving birth. Belaney next emerged in Digby, Nova Scotia, in May 1915, when he enlisted in the Canadian army. There he told the army recruiters that he was unmarried, thereby depriving Angele and Alice of government financial support. Belaney was out of the trenches in a year, after losing a toe to a possibly self-inflicted rifle wound. While convalescing near his aunts' home in Hastings, he re-met a childhood friend, Ivy Holmes, and married her in February 1917. When he returned to Canada that September, he told Ivy he would send for her. They never saw each other again.

After the war, Belaney continued to fine-tune his identity as an Indian. 4
He dyed his hair black and coloured his skin with henna. His disgust with
civilization, made almost complete by his combat experience, only deep-
ened his concern for the shrinking forests of the North and the disappearing
beaver. Under the influence of his fourth wife, an Iroquois variously called
Pony or Anahareo, Belaney abandoned trapping. In 1929, he wrote a successful article for the British magazine *Country Life* about the passing
wilderness way of life. The magazine's editors suggested he write a book.
During the two years he worked on *The Men of the Last Frontier*, Belaney
told his editors first that he lived among Indians, next that he had been
adopted by Indians, and finally, in 1931, that he *was* an Indian. After a stab
at the name White Owl, he settled on Grey Owl. From the book's publication until his death from pneumonia seven years later, he was an international superstar, one of the most famous Canadians of his day.

During his glory years, Grey Owl wrote more best-sellers, two of 5
which — *Pilgrims of the Wild* and *The Adventures of Sajo and Her Beaver
People* — are still regarded as classics. He made movies. Yousuf Karsh
photographed him, even though Grey Owl missed a dinner engagement
with Karsh and a clutch of Ottawa VIPs because of his involvement in a
drunken brawl in a hotel bar. Grey Owl did manage to dine with Prime
Minister William Lyon Mackenzie King, and he conducted two triumphant
lecture tours of the British Isles, culminating in a three-hour audience with
the Royal Family, including the future Queen Elizabeth II.

All the ironies of Archie Belaney's deceptive life came into play in that 6
time. Certainly his key message of preservation of wilderness and wildlife
struck a responsive chord, especially in animal-loving Britain. And in the
time-honoured Canadian fashion, success in Britain brought acclaim back
home. But what gained him a hearing in the first place was his assumed
identity as an exotic noble savage, buttressed by his compelling storytelling power, itself polished through years of lying. His real upbringing
provided him with his graceful prose. Grey Owl may have looked and
sounded Indian, at least to urban audiences, but he wrote like the Hastings
Grammar School graduate he was. (Only one contemporary critic noticed
Grey Owl's rarefied English, however, and enraged Belaney — who could
not admit the truth — by suggesting the untutored Native had had the aid
of a ghostwriter.)

Throughout the 1930s, dozens of people, including almost every 7
Indian who encountered him, knew the truth about Archie Belaney. Yet
none ever exposed him publicly. Angele willingly admitted the facts to
anyone who asked, including a *North Bay Nugget* reporter in 1935, but she

did not initiate an open scandal. Those who knew Belaney either liked him—even the abandoned wives—or like the *Nugget*'s city editor and Indian leaders who appreciated Grey Owl's support for Natives, thought his message too important to risk harming. And when his death freed the *Nugget* to publish, setting off an international media frenzy, the Canadian response was surprisingly positive. "Of course, the value of his work is not jeopardized. His attainments as a writer and naturalist will survive," concluded *The Ottawa Citizen*, in an opinion widely shared in the national press.

8   That didn't stop a generation of neglect, however, as another world war and unprecedented economic growth pushed wilderness Canada out of the public consciousness. But the dawning environmental movement of the late 1960s found inspiration in Grey Owl's work. "Grey Owl was a superb propagandist for the natural world," says University of Calgary historian Donald Smith, author of *From the Land of Shadows: The Making of Grey Owl.* "He was the first to get it right—our uniqueness, our wonderful forests and rivers, what we were doing wrong—the first to tell mainstream Canada, 'Remember you belong to Nature, not it to you.'"

9   In the early 1970s, Grey Owl's books came out in new editions and in 1972 CBC-TV aired a documentary on him. His books remain in print, and new works about their author continue to appear, including Smith's 1990 biography and Jane Billinghurst's lavishly illustrated *Grey Owl* (1999). Even Parks Canada, which had allowed Grey Owl's last home, Beaver Lodge in Prince Albert National Park, to fall into disrepair, was roused to action. It made the area around Beaver Lodge a protected wilderness sanctuary and restored the cabin itself. That was a gesture that might have moved the enigmatic Archie Belaney. In a lifetime of deceit, love of the wilderness may have been his only genuine emotion.

1999

NOTES

Brian Bethune is a senior editor for *Maclean's* magazine.

Bigamist A person who is married to more than one spouse at the same time. Bigamy is illegal.

The North Bay Nugget A newspaper published in North Bay, Ontario.

Yousuf Karsh (1908–2002) A famous Canadian photographer, renowned for his photographs of famous people.

Noble savage A term invented and used by Europeans at the beginning of the 17th century to denote an Aboriginal person with high principles, who lives in the wilds but is civilized.

The Ottawa Citizen A daily newspaper published in Ottawa.

COMPREHENSION AND DISCUSSION

1. Who is Archie Belaney? (Summarize his biography as given in this article.)
2. How did he hone his Native persona? (A persona is a voice or character developed by a writer, or a role that one assumes in public.)
3. What did he do for Canada?
4. Why did people who knew him not expose him as a fraud?
5. Why is he still controversial?
6. What is Bethune's view of Archie Belaney?
7. Why does Bethune begin the essay with Grey Owl's death?
8. How do you view Grey Owl — as a hero or a fraud? What is the most important aspect of his life?

LITERARY TECHNIQUES

Biography The story of a person's life. This article is biographical, more so than the articles by John Barber and Colin Ross. Note how the biography begins with Grey Owl's death. This technique is a common one. From here the writer can review Grey Owl's life and evaluate his contributions or achievements.

Chronology The sequence of events in a time line. Bethune goes from birth to death and elaborates the significant events in Grey Owl's life. Note that the writer does not jump back and forth at this time because doing so may confuse the reader. In addition, the references to dates help the reader get a bearing as Bethune gathers events together.

Quotations Actual words spoken or written about someone or something. Quotations inserted in an article tend to authenticate and advance the writer's views on the subject. They lend credence to opinions and explanations; they also offer another point of view. Sometimes writers pepper their articles with quotations to show that they have done extensive research on this subject and that the reader can depend on the article's veracity.

Slant This term refers to a bias or point of view in the writing. It can be favourable or unfavourable, depending on the approach the writer takes to the topic. Although most expository writing tends to be neutral or objective, a writer cannot help but put a bias or slant in it. Sometimes this bias occurs with the choice of material or point of view; sometimes the leaning is unintentional. When the slant is decidedly one way, the writer intends it to be so (as in Colin Ross's article on Grey Owl, p. 327).

ASSIGNMENTS

1. Read the other two articles on Grey Owl: John Barber's "Grey Owl's Magnificent Masquerade" (p. 232) and Colin Ross's "The Story of Grey Owl" (p. 327). Explain the viewpoints each writer holds about Grey Owl.
2. Read Pico Iyer's "Of Weirdos and Eccentrics" (p. 282). Does Grey Owl qualify as eccentric? Support your view in a brief essay.
3. Research and write a short biography of another controversial Canadian, such as William Lyon Mackenzie King, Sir John A. Macdonald, Louis Riel, Margaret Trudeau, Amor De Cosmos, Nellie McClung, or Gerta Munsinger. Evaluate the person's place in history.
4. Research the story of a famous Native Canadian and write a brief report. Consider such people as Joseph Brant, Tekakwitha, Tecumseh, Louis Riel, Pauline Johnson, Tom Longboat, Shawnadithit, Graham Greene, Thomas King, Dudley George, or Tomson Highway.
5. Watch the motion picture *Grey Owl* (1999), starring Pierce Brosnan. Write a critique of the movie. What do you think Archie Belaney would think of the movie?

Toothpaste
David Bodanis

Into the bathroom goes our male resident, and after the most pressing need   1
is satisfied it's time to brush the teeth. The tube of toothpaste is squeezed, its pinched metal seams are splayed, pressure waves are generated inside, and the paste begins to flow. But what's in this toothpaste, so carefully being extruded out?

Water mostly, 30 to 45 percent in most brands: ordinary, everyday   2
simple tap water. It's there because people like to have a big gob of toothpaste to spread on the brush, and water is the cheapest stuff there is when it comes to making big gobs. Dripping a bit from the tap onto your brush would cost virtually nothing; whipped in with the rest of the toothpaste the manufacturers can sell it at a neat and accountant-pleasing $2 per pound equivalent. Toothpaste manufacture is a very lucrative occupation.

Second to water in quantity is chalk: exactly the same material that   3
schoolteachers use to write on blackboards. It is collected from the crushed remains of long-dead ocean creatures. In the Cretaceous seas chalk particles served as part of the wickedly sharp outer skeleton that these creatures had to wrap around themselves to keep from getting chomped by all the slightly larger other ocean creatures they met. Their massed graves are our present chalk deposits.

The individual chalk particles—the size of the smallest mud particles   4
in your garden—have kept their toughness over the eons, and now on the toothbrush they'll need it. The enamel outer coating of the tooth they'll have to face is the hardest substance in the body—tougher than skull, or bone, or nail. Only the chalk particles in toothpaste can successfully grind into the teeth during brushing, ripping off the surface layers like an abrading wheel grinding down a boulder in a quarry.

The craters, slashes, and channels that the chalk tears into the teeth   5
will also remove a certain amount of built-up yellow in the carnage, and it is for that polishing function that it's there. A certain amount of unduly enlarged extra-abrasive chalk fragments tear such cavernous pits into the teeth that future decay bacteria will be able to bunker down there and thrive; the quality control people find it almost impossible to screen out these errant super-chalk pieces, and government regulations allow them to stay in.

6   In case even the gouging doesn't get all the yellow off, another substance is worked into the toothpaste cream. This is titanium dioxide. It comes in tiny spheres, and it's the stuff bobbing around in white wall paint to make it come out white. Splashed onto your teeth during the brushing, it coats much of the yellow that remains. Being water soluble it leaks off in the next few hours and is swallowed, but at least for the quick glance up in the mirror after finishing it will make the user think his teeth are truly white. Some manufacturers add optical whitening dyes—the stuff more commonly found in washing machine bleach—to make extra sure that that glance in the mirror shows reassuring white.

7   These ingredients alone would not make a very attractive concoction. They would stick in the tube like a sloppy white plastic lump, hard to squeeze out as well as revolting to the touch. Few consumers would savour rubbing in a mixture of water, ground-up blackboard chalk, and the whitener from latex paint first thing in the morning. To get around that finicky distaste the manufacturers have mixed in a host of other goodies.

8   To keep the glop from drying out, a mixture including glycerine glycol—related to the most common car anti-freeze ingredient—is whipped in with the chalk and water, and to give *that* concoction a bit of substance (all we really have so far is wet coloured chalk) a large helping is added of gummy molecules from the seaweed *Chondrus crispus*. This seaweed ooze spreads in among the chalk, paint, and anti-freeze, then stretches itself in all directions to hold the whole mass together. A bit of paraffin oil (the fuel that flickers in camping lamps) is pumped in with it to help the moss ooze keep the whole substance smooth.

9   With the glycol, ooze, and paraffin we're almost there. Only two minor chemicals are left to make the refreshing, cleansing substance we know as toothpaste. The ingredients so far are fine for cleaning, but they wouldn't make much of the satisfying foam we have come to expect in the morning brushing.

10   To remedy that, every toothpaste on the market has a big dollop of detergent added too. You've seen the suds detergent will make in a washing machine. The same substance added here will duplicate that inside the mouth. It's not particularly necessary, but it sells.

11   The only problem is that by itself this ingredient tastes, well, too like detergent. It's horribly bitter and harsh. The chalk put in toothpaste is pretty foul-tasting too for that matter. It's to get around that gustatory discomfort that the manufacturers put in the ingredient they tout perhaps the most of all. This is the flavouring, and it has to be strong. Double rectified peppermint

oil is used—a flavourer so powerful that chemists know better than to sniff it in the raw state in the laboratory. Menthol crystals and saccharin or other sugar simulators are added to complete the camouflage operation.

Is that it? Chalk, water, paint, seaweed, anti-freeze, paraffin oil, deter- 12
gent, and peppermint? Not quite. A mix like that would be irresistible to the hundreds of thousands of individual bacteria lying on the surface of even an immaculately cleaned bathroom sink. They would get in, float in the water bubbles, ingest the ooze and paraffin, maybe even spray out enzymes to break down the chalk. The result would be an uninviting mess. The way manufacturers avoid that final obstacle is by putting something in to kill the bacteria. Something good and strong is needed, something that will zap any accidentally intrudant bacteria into oblivion. And that something is formaldehyde—the disinfectant used in anatomy labs.

So it's chalk, water, paint, seaweed, anti-freeze, paraffin oil, detergent, 13
peppermint, formaldehyde, and fluoride (which can go some way towards preserving children's teeth)—that's the usual mixture raised to the mouth on the toothbrush for a fresh morning's clean. If it sounds too unfortunate, take heart. Studies show that thorough brushing with just plain water will often do as good a job.

1986

NOTES

David Bodanis, an American based in Britain, is a technology consultant. This article is from his bestselling book, *The Secret House*.

Cretaceous The last period of the Mesozoic era, about seventy million years ago.

COMPREHENSION AND DISCUSSION

1. Why does Bodanis want to give you all this information about tooth-paste? Can you see the broader ramifications?
2. How does Bodanis arrange the information for you? Why does he choose this method?
3. Explain how the ingredients work together to clean your teeth.
4. What can you do with this information? How does it affect you?
5. What qualities in toothpaste are important to you, and which could you do without?

6. How does this information make you look at other products you use? Which products would you like to know more about?
7. Is this too much information? Would you prefer not to know what is in toothpaste? Why or why not?

LITERARY TECHNIQUES

Bodanis begins his thesis with a rhetorical question: "But what's in this toothpaste, so carefully being extruded out?" (paragraph 1). He answers this question in the rest of the article. A rhetorical question grabs the attention and curiosity of the reader.

Process analysis or description is a rhetorical mode that explains in detail how something works or how something is made or done. Its purpose is to give you an understanding of the workings of the subject. It is methodical in that it is a step-by-step explanation.

Classification/division Classification and division are two other methods used in this article. Division is the categorizing of ideas or things into smaller units. For example, a large company may divide itself up into the electronics division, the parts division, and so on. Classification is the breakdown of one unit into smaller components. For example, Bodanis uses one unit — toothpaste — and separates it into its components: water, chalk, detergent, and so on.

Diction Diction is the choice of words used in an article. In this case, Bodanis prefers informal, plain English rather than technical language because his audience does not require it. Moreover, scientific jargon might frustrate or confuse his readers. Appropriate vocabulary is important in writing.

ASSIGNMENTS

1. Research another cosmetic product and write an essay about its ingredients.
2. Write a process analysis paragraph or essay on how a food product goes from original ingredients to your table. For example, track coffee from the plantation to your cup.
3. How much do consumers really need to know about what they eat or use? Consider, for example, hot dogs, trans fats, and herbal remedies.

4. Food manufacturers must list their ingredients on the package. No such stipulation exists for cosmetic manufacturers, however. Write an argument essay on whether cosmetic manufacturers should list ingredients.

Growing Up on Grace

Rosie DiManno

1   I was about 6 years old when I discovered that I was a Canadian.

2   This came as a rude shock.

3   Insofar as I had a vague image of a huge world with a bunch of different countries in it, I thought I was an American.

4   My parents are Italian immigrants and I was born in Toronto, grew up on Grace St. downtown, but didn't learn English until I started school. In my household, whenever the adults spoke of leaving their old country for this new one, it was always put in these terms: We came to *America.* They made no distinction between the United States and Canada, or maybe I just didn't grasp it.

5   *America.* Sometimes it was said with regret and sadness, other times in terms of a bold adventure, but never with a sense of belonging. It was always this alien place in which they found themselves, and to which they were grateful for whatever comforts they had acquired. But their suspicions and their sense of isolation lingered. It's why they — and every other ethnic group that ventures to this city — clustered in self-contained, unilingual neighbourhoods, both to shun and to defend themselves from shunning. They weren't cultural ghettos; they were outposts of the familiar, like pioneer forts in a hostile land. The land of the *Inglese.*

6   It was the early '60s. I watched American TV beamed from Buffalo: *Captain Kangaroo* and *Commander Tom.* Sitcoms like *Petticoat Junction* and *The Honeymooners* — which had no similarities to our own existence on Grace St., but which I misunderstood as that larger American reality, from which I was excluded only because of my parentage, not by geographic boundaries. And certainly not because these were phony, idealized domestic situations that only existed within a television tube.

7   This, I thought — flipping between *Leave It to Beaver* and *I Love Lucy* — is how people *really* live, except on my street: The privileged people, not the interlopers (like us), the imposters (like us); the ones who have proprietary first dibs on the country, the ones who drink milk at the dinner table, who have cereal for breakfast, who make sandwiches from pre-sliced white bread, who wear high heels in the house.

8   There was no Canadian flag, remember, as the most visible national icon. At Clinton Public School, they flew the Union Jack, but I thought that was just a weird variation on the Stars and Stripes. There was a photograph of the Queen at the head of the class, and this got me to thinking

about the relationship between the Queen and the president, who was also familiar to me from American TV news. We sang "God Save the Queen" in school, but at night, when the TV stations signed off, it was the American national anthem that accompanied the fade to black. There was no "O Canada."

Perhaps my main problem is that I never watched the CBC.   9

It dawned on me, somewhere around Grade 1, that I was not American   10 at all, although this growing suspicion was something I kept to myself for awhile. It's not the kind of thing you ask an adult about, lest you appear colossally stupid, and I was not in the habit of asking my parents anything. They were probably more alien to me than the Ricardos.

When I was forced to accept this reality, it was with a sense of loss.   11 Here I had been trying to visualize myself growing up and fitting into this bustling American lifestyle, this energetic and self-confident and purposeful country. But I was stuck with dreary old/young Canada. Second-rate by ancestry, third-rate by an accident of birth.

This dismay wore off, of course. Certainly, it was shed abruptly when   12 I met my bosom friend Barbara Zloty, in Grade 5. She really was an American but had moved to Toronto with her mother to stay with relatives because her father was fighting in Vietnam. I could not imagine having a father fighting a war in a distant country, maybe getting killed, maimed. Eventually, Barbara's father was wounded, and they returned to El Paso.

Barbara made me my first grilled-cheese sandwich, which seemed ter-   13 ribly decadent and decidedly *Inglese.* My mother, who did not believe that we should ever enter the homes of anyone outside the extended family — and rarely were any of us invited — had forbidden me to have lunch at Barbara's. I went anyway. When I got home from school that afternoon, my mother met me halfway up the street and hit me with her shoe.

This is supposed to be a narrative about My Canada, yet I'm not sure   14 what that means. I can tell you only small stories about growing up in a small piece of the country, as insular as any tumbleweed-tossed Prairie town or desolate Maritime hamlet.

I grew up not in a country but on a street. My territory stretched from   15 Bloor to Harbord, with traffic lights at either end, Christie Pits to the north, Bickford Park directly across from the house, Montrose Park to the south. Bickford Park, where I climbed every tree, had no amenities: no playground, no pool, no soccer pitch. Just a weary little softball diamond, one drinking fountain, and a huge sewer grate that was cool against your face when you lay across it on hot summer days.

16   And yet the park fascinated us, we over-protected young children who were never allowed to roam beyond the busy thoroughfares at either end of Grace. Once I saw a man running through the park with his mangled left arm hanging by just a few strands of sinew. Once I found a gold signature pin that said: Rosalba. That is my real name, abbreviated and Anglicized once I started school, in a desperate attempt to be less Italian, more English. It fills me with wonder, still, that I should have found such a pin, with that odd name, in the grass at Bickford Park.

17   There were many Italians on that street, some relatives, some merely *paisans*, some with no ancestral connection but part of the cultural fraternity that kept Us separate from Them. There were several Jewish families, too, and I remember feeling a kinship with them, because they were also aliens. (Later on, in my teens, we would move to a predominantly Jewish neighbourhood in Downsview. This resulted in one curious anomaly: My mother now speaks English with a Yiddish accent and is as likely to make a brisket for dinner as lasagna.)

18   I was mortified, in those days, by our Italian-ness. I begged my mother to shave her legs, to which she finally acquiesced, although she never did understand the fuss. I hated the tomatoes and tangle of vegetables in our backyard and longed for the banality of a grass carpet. I hated the pepper and onions that my mother would string like braids on the front porch.

19   In late spring, my father—a farmer and shepherd before emigrating— would dump a load of manure on the front lawn because this is the world's best fertilizer. On those occasions, returning from school, I would walk right past my house lest any classmates realize that I lived in such a Munsters-like place.

20   My father—and I respect him for this only in retrospect—never attempted to ingratiate himself with the *Inglese* by being less Italian or by altering the rhythms of his life, although he was impeccably hospitable and generous.

21   He hunted, not for sport, but for food, and I can see him now, skinning jackrabbits over the cellar sink. In the fall, he would slaughter a pig; at Easter, a lamb.

22   My parents made sausages and strung them to dry inside a makeshift smokehouse. Prosciutto would be salted and hung for a year in the wine cellar. My mother would spend weeks slicing fresh tomatoes and bottling them for sauce, sterilizing the bottles in a steel drum of boiling water in the backyard, stoking the fire underneath. She'd pickle cucumbers and artichokes, cauliflower and olives.

23   I loved all these foods, so common now in Italian restaurants and grocery stores, but I was ashamed of them then. I would throw away my lunch

at school and starve rather than expose these peculiar items to my *Inglese* friends. I pined for peanut-butter sandwiches.

Sometimes, I would go grocery shopping with my mother just so I could persuade her to buy all this ostensibly tasty English stuff that I saw advertised on TV: jelly rolls, Cap'n Crunch cereal, Pop Tarts, Wonderbread, SpaghettiOs, Campbell's soup, Kraft macaroni and cheese, marshmallows. It all tasted foul, it made me gag. But if this is what it took to be *Inglese*, I would suffer for my pride. 24

In autumn, after weeks of consultation and innumerable taste-testing expeditions, the crates of grapes would be delivered to the house: hundreds of them, stacked on the lawn. California grapes for homemade wine. Families would help each other out in the complicated wine-making process, churning and pressing and sifting and decanting. It was, I suppose, a different version of the barn-building efforts in other cultures, a community event. 25

Invariably, I would step on a nail. 26

Menstruating women were not allowed near the mulch, lest they spoil the wine. I, still a child, was humiliated on behalf of these women, who would be sent upstairs to make themselves otherwise useful. I only realized later that they considered it a blessing to be so ostracized from such back-breaking work, and the constant curses of the men. 27

I rebelled against all of it. The religious processions that were the high-light of the calendar year; refusing to parade along the street in my bride-like Communion gown; refusing to attend the Catholic school in which I had been enrolled (hiding out in the sewer pipes at Christie Pits) until my mother threw up her hands in defeat; refusing to kiss the aunts and the uncles (all of whom had chin whiskers); refusing to eat anything that had a hint of tomato in it; refusing to speak Italian. 28

Education was not valued highly in our family, which possibly made us, our sub-group of Italian immigrants, different from other ethnic groups washing ashore in Canada. Education was feared by these Italians — a fear nurtured and encouraged by the Catholic church. Education would take children away from their parents, the priests said, would make them ques-tion authority, would draw them into the outside world, which was a for-bidden place. 29

Yet every week, from the time I was very small, my mother would take me, in a clandestine venture, to the St. George main library, a good 20-block hike from our house. She could barely read Italian but she wanted me to learn something from the ridiculed pleasure of books. 30

An education, particularly a post-secondary education, was considered a waste on a girl. If I were to have any profession at all, it was decided on 31 my behalf, I would become a teacher: a feminine profession, respectable, akin to mothering. I played along and planned my escape.

32   So there came a time when the street, and the neighbourhood, became too small and too cramped an existence for me. Symbolically, it was enough for my parents. They finally felt safe and entrenched. They knew nothing about the rest of the country and did not care. They didn't know the difference between a city and a province.

33   They were clueless about the vastness of Canada, although they had come to Toronto from Halifax by train. They never ventured outside the city, rarely strayed from the neighbourhood. The most ambitious foray I can recall is one winter when we took the streetcar to the College St. Eaton's store — the most WASPish of establishments — to buy me a type-writer. I'd never seen an escalator before.

34   My parents never took a vacation — in 45 years, my father has yet to return to Italy for a visit — never mingled with another ethnic group (save for an Indian friend who was my dad's hunting companion, and the Jewish family in whose coin laundry my mother had once worked), never had any curiosity about politics or social issues or even the most innocent of *Inglese* pleasures. My father has never been to a movie, never gone to a hockey game, never attended a parent night at school.

35   When I'm being generous, I convince myself that he was merely shy, that he felt ignorant in this English culture. But I'm more inclined to believe that he lived completely within himself, and even his family was an intrusion.

36   Perhaps I have inherited his discomfort, his diffidence, because I don't feel particularly connected to this country, either, although I have a genuine fondness for it.

37   Too long an outsider, faking it, beseeching entry. Relentlessly *Inglese* in attitude and tastes, irredeemably Italian in my genes. But not hyphen-ated, never hyphenated. A clumsy hybrid, maybe.

38   I used to fret so much, in my younger days, about how I could ever reconcile these two cultures, how I could be Rosalba and Rosie and still stay intact. The struggle doesn't seem very important any more.

39   But I am constantly astonished by third-generation Italian Canadians who seem more proud of their ancestral homeland than the country of their birth, who chatter in Italian on St. Clair Ave., who seem more Italian to me now than my parents did 30 years ago. Cultural pride is one thing, but so much of this overt Italian sensibility seems to me to be a betrayal — of Canada, and to those of us who broke all the rules so that we didn't have to stay insularly Italian, imprisoned by culture, in this country.

I don't wave flags and I find the notion of Canada Day contrived, if   40
sweet. But I have felt moments of intense patriotism. Little moments, like
spotting a Maple Leaf on a teenager's backpack in Europe. Grand moments,
like when a Canadian wins a gold medal at the Olympics. Aching moments,
like when I visit the Canadian war cemetery in Cassino, just down the mountain from my parents' village. (As children, they survived the battle of Monte
Cassino.) And historical moments, like covering the referendum in Montreal
in 1995, and feeling a sudden swell of anxiety, as if we were letting something very precious slip away, through carelessness and self-absorption.

As an adult, when I visit my ancestral village in Italy — which lost half   41
its population to Toronto after the war — they always ask about life in
America. I have given up trying to make the distinction. It just doesn't
seem significant, from the perspective of a mountain top south of Naples.

It's funny, though. From the first time I set foot on Italian soil, I felt as if I   42
belonged. I looked like everyone else, my name didn't sound foreign. I felt a
thousand years of history rushing through my blood. But I couldn't live there.

And every time I come through Canada Customs, travel back across   43
the border, I breathe a sigh of relief. Home.

My parents are Canadian citizens now. Grace St. is long ago and far away.   44
They are living the good, Canadian life: a suburban home, a cottage, two cars,
a truck, money in the bank. They take occasional trips, mostly church-
organized, and are finally seeing a little more of the country. They vote. And
they try very hard to pretend that we are not a fractured, dysfunctional family.

They do not read English. They will not read this story. They have   45
never read a word I have written.

1997

NOTES

Rosie DiManno is a columnist and sports writer for *The Toronto Star.*

America Many immigrant groups refer to both Canada and the United
States as America. The Chinese, for example, use the term *gum san*, which
translates as "golden mountain," to refer to Canada and the United States.

Union Jack The British flag. The three crosses of England, Scotland, and
Ireland combine to make this symbol of the United Kingdom. These
crosses respectively belong to St. George, St. Andrew, and St. Patrick.

Stars and Stripes The flag of the United States of America. Originally, it
had only thirteen stars and stripes (one for each of the thirteen colonies at

the time of the American Revolution). Now the flag has fifty stars, one for each state in the union.

Ricardo The family name in the popular American TV series *I Love Lucy*. It was one of the first ethnically mixed marriages on TV.

Paisans Fellow countrymen and -women.

The Munsters A popular TV comedy series of the mid-1960s, featuring a family of monsters (a Frankenstein monster, vampire, witch, and were-wolf) trying to fit into the typical American society.

Prosciutto An Italian variation of ham.

Christie Pits A park in Metro Toronto.

WASP An acronym for "White Anglo-Saxon Protestant."

COMPREHENSION AND DISCUSSION

1. Why did the young Rosie DiManno believe she was American instead of Canadian?
2. What are some general criticisms DiManno has about Canada and Canadians?
3. How do the DiMannos preserve their old country ways?
4. Why did the author want to become part of the establishment and reject her Italian heritage?
5. Describe or explain DiManno's mixed feelings when she travelled to Italy.
6. How does DiManno define her identity now?
7. Explain what DiManno means in her conclusion. Can you see this in a larger context about the immigrant experience?

LITERARY TECHNIQUES

Memoirs Thoughts, reflections, and feelings recounted in written form. Often they are synonymous with autobiography or biography, diaries, and letters.

Autobiography The story of a person's life written by that person.

"Write what you know" is the standard advice for writers. Many authors write about their childhood. The topic is familiar and easily researched. All the writer needs to do is draw from memory — most of the time.

ASSIGNMENTS

1. Write a narrative about a childhood experience. What particular incident do you remember vividly and wish to put into words for your readers?
2. What did you want to be when you were a child growing up, and what changed for you?
3. If you are an immigrant or if your parents are immigrants, what are some of the hardest things to change and to accept?
4. Read the short story "Chickens for Christmas" (p. 61). Compare the non-fictional and fictional portrayals of immigrant life. What are the distinguishing characteristics?
5. What makes you Canadian?
6. Some people argue that there is no distinctive Canadian culture. Do you agree? What is Canadian culture?
7. What aspects of your ethnic heritage do you want to keep for yourself and your children? Why? What parts of your ethnic background do you want to drop? Why?

The Patterns of Eating
Peter Farb and George Armelagos

1   Among the important societal rules that represent one component of cuisine are table manners. As a socially instilled form of conduct, they reveal the attitudes typical of a society. Changes in table manners through time, as they have been documented for western Europe, likewise reflect fundamental changes in human relationships. Medieval courtiers saw their table manners as distinguishing them from crude peasants; but by modern standards, the manners were not exactly refined. Feudal lords used their unwashed hands to scoop food from a common bowl and they passed around a single goblet from which all drank. A finger or two would be extended while eating, so as to be kept free of grease and thus available for the next course, or for dipping into spices and condiments—possibly accounting for today's "polite" custom of extending the finger while holding a spoon or small fork. Soups and sauces were commonly drunk by lifting the bowl to the mouth; several diners frequently ate from the same bread trencher. Even lords and nobles would toss knawed bones back into the common dish, wolf down their food, spit onto the table (preferred conduct called for spitting under it), and blew their noses into the tablecloth.

2   By about the beginning of the sixteenth century, table manners began to move in the direction of today's standards. The importance attached to them is indicated by the phenomenal success of a treatise, *On Civility in Children*, by the philosopher Erasmus, which appeared in 1530; reprinted more than thirty times in the next six years, it also appeared in numerous translations. Erasmus' idea of good table manners was far from modern, but it did represent an advance. He believed, for example, that an upper-class diner was distinguished by putting only three fingers of one hand into the bowl, instead of the entire hand in the manner of the lower class. Wait a few moments after being seated before you dip into it, he advises. Do not poke around in your dish, but take the first piece you touch. Do not put chewed food from your mouth back on your place; instead, throw it under the table or behind your chair.

3   By the time of Erasmus, the changing table manners reveal a fundamental shift in society. People no longer ate from the same dish or drank from the same goblet, but were divided from one another by a new wall of constraint. Once the spontaneous, direct, and informal manners of the Middle Ages had been repressed, people began to feel shame. Defecation and urination were now regarded as private activities; handkerchiefs came

into use for blowing the nose; nightclothes were now worn, and bedrooms were set apart as private areas. Before the sixteenth century, even nobles ate in their vast kitchens; only then did a special room designated for eating come into use away from the bloody sides of meat, the animals about to be slaughtered, and the bustling servants. These new inhibitions became the essence of "civilized" behaviour, distinguishing adults from children, the upper classes from the lower, and Europeans from the "savages" then being discovered around the world. Restraint in eating habits became more marked in the centuries that followed. By about 1800, napkins were in common use, and before long they were placed on the thighs rather than wrapped around the neck; coffee and tea were no longer slurped out of the saucer; bread was genteelly broken into small pieces with the fingers rather than cut into large chunks with a knife.

Numerous paintings that depict meals — with subjects such as the Last   4
Supper, the wedding at Cana, or Herod's feast — show what dining tables looked like before the seventeenth century. Forks were not depicted until about 1600 (when Jacopo Bassano painted one in a Last Supper), and very few spoons were shown. At least one knife is always depicted — an especially large one when it is the only one available for all the guests — but small individual knives were often at each place. Tin disks or oval pieces of wood had already replaced the bread trenchers. This change in eating utensils typified the new table manners in Europe. (In many other parts of the world, no utensils at all were used. In the Near East, for example, it was traditional to bring food to the mouth with the fingers of the right hand, the left being unacceptable because it was reserved for wiping the buttocks.) Utensils were employed in part because of a change in the attitude toward meat. During the Middle Ages, whole sides of meat, or even an entire dead animal, had been brought to the table and then carved in view of the diners. Beginning in the seventeenth century, at first in France but later elsewhere, the practice began to go out of fashion. One reason was that the family was ceasing to be a production unit that did its own slaughtering; as that function was transferred to specialists outside the home, the family became essentially a consumption unit. In addition, the size of the family was decreasing, and consequently whole animals, or even large parts of them, were uneconomical. The cuisines of Europe reflected these social and economic changes. The animal origin of meat dishes was concealed by the arts of preparation. Meat itself became distasteful to look upon, and carving was moved out of sight to the kitchen. Comparable changes had already taken place in Chinese cuisine, with meat being cut up beforehand, unobserved by

the diners. England was an exception to the change in Europe, and in its former colonies — the United States, Canada, Australia, and South Africa — the custom has persisted of bringing a joint of meat to the table to be carved.

5   Once carving was no longer considered a necessary skill among the well-bred, changes inevitably took place in the use of the knife, unquestionably the earliest utensil used for manipulating food. (In fact, the earliest English cookbooks were not so much guides to recipes as guides to carving meat.) The attitude of diners toward the knife, going back to the Middle Ages and the Renaissance, had always been ambivalent. The knife served as a utensil, but it offered a potential threat because it was also a weapon. Thus taboos were increasingly placed upon its use: It was to be held by the point with the blunt handle presented; it was not to be placed anywhere near the face; and most important, the uses to which it was put were sharply restricted. It was not to be used for cutting soft foods such as boiled eggs or fish, or round ones such as potatoes, or to be lifted from the table for courses that did not need it. In short, good table manners in Europe gradually removed the threatening aspect of the knife from social occasions. A similar change had taken place much earlier in China when the warrior was supplanted by the scholar as a cultural model. The knife was banished completely from the table in favour of chopsticks, which is why the Chinese came to regard Europeans as barbarians at their table who "eat with swords."

6   The fork in particular enabled Europeans to separate themselves from the eating process, even avoiding manual contact with their food. When the fork first appeared in Europe, toward the end of the Middle Ages, it was used solely as an instrument for lifting chunks from the common bowl. Beginning in the sixteenth century, the fork was increasingly used by members of the upper classes — first in Italy, then in France, and finally in Germany and England. By then, social relations in western Europe had so changed that a utensil was needed to spare diners from the "uncivilized" and distasteful necessity of picking up food and putting it into the mouth with fingers. The addition of the fork to the table was once said to be for reasons of hygiene, but this cannot be true. By the sixteenth century people were no longer eating from a common bowl but from their own plates, and since they also washed their hands before meals, their fingers were now every bit as hygienic as a fork would have been. Nor can the reason for the adoption of the fork be connected with the wish not to soil the long ruff that was worn on the sleeve at the time, since the fork was also adopted in various countries where ruffs were not then in fashion.

Along with the appearance of the fork, all table utensils began to   7
change and proliferate from the sixteenth century onward. Soup was no
longer eaten directly from the dish, but each diner used an individual spoon
for that purpose. When a diner wanted a second helping from the serving
dish, a ladle or a fresh spoon was used. More and more special utensils
were developed for each kind of food: soup spoons, oyster forks, salad
forks, two-tined fondue forks, blunt butter knives, special utensils for various desserts and kinds of fruit, each one differently shaped, or a different
size, with differently numbered prongs and with blunt or serrated edges.
The present European pattern eventually emerged, in which each person is
provided with a table setting of as many as a dozen utensils at a full-course
meal. With that, the separation of the human body from the taking of food
became virtually complete. Good table manners dictated that even the cobs
of maize were to be held by prongs inserted in each end, and the bones of
lamb chops covered by ruffled paper pantalettes. Only under special conditions — as when Western people consciously imitate an earlier stage in
culture at a picnic, fish fry, cookout, or campfire — do they still tear food
apart with their fingers and their teeth, in a nostalgic reenactment of eating
behaviours long vanished.

Today's neighbourhood barbecue recreates a world of sharing and hos-   8
pitality that becomes rarer each year. We regard as a curiosity the behaviour of hunters in exotic regions. But every year millions of North
Americans take to the woods and lakes to kill a wide variety of animals —
with a difference, of course: What hunters do for survival we do for sport
(and also for proof of masculinity, for male bonding, and for various psychological rewards). Like hunters, too, we stuff ourselves almost whenever
food is available. Nibbling on a roasted ear of maize gives us, in addition
to nutrients, the satisfaction of participating in culturally simpler ways. A
festive meal, however, is still thought of in Victorian terms, with the dominant male officiating over the roast, the dominant female apportioning
vegetables, the extended family gathered around the table, with everything
in its proper place — a revered picture, as indeed it was so painted by
Norman Rockwell, yet one that becomes less accurate with each year that
passes.

1980

NOTES

Peter Farb and George Armelagos are anthropologists who have written extensively on food-related topics.

This reading is an excerpt from the book *Consuming Passions: The Anthropology of Eating*.

Erasmus (1469–1536) A Dutch humanist philosopher of the Renaissance and Reformation. His most famous work is *In Praise of Folly*.

Last Supper, the wedding at Cana, and Herod's feast Three paintings depicting episodes found in the New Testament in the Bible.

Norman Rockwell (1894–1978) An American painter who depicted a nostalgic past. He was best known for the covers he created for *The Saturday Evening Post* magazine.

COMPREHENSION AND DISCUSSION

1. What is the thesis of this article?
2. Why do we need table manners?
3. How is moving from the kitchen to a dining room a major step in social change?
4. Explain: "Once the spontaneous, direct, and informal manners of the Middle Ages had been repressed, people began to feel shame" (paragraph 3).
5. Explain the evolving nature of the fork and the knife at the dinner table.
6. How is the barbecue a throwback to the Middle Ages in terms of cuisine?

LITERARY TECHNIQUES

Extended paragraph The length of a paragraph varies, depending on the function and style of the article. However, in academic writing, a developed paragraph runs about 150 to 200 words. The extended paragraph is longer and has more details. It is not a common style in modern writing and requires rhetorical skill to sustain its length properly. Individual sentences also tend to be longer in this style.

Cause and effect This technique explains progression. Cause is usually what starts something to happen; effect is the consequence of the action. In other words, cause is the reason for an action; effect is the result of it.

Process analysis This method shows how things happen. Like cause and effect, it explains the logical sequence of events with as much detail as needed.

Diction Word choice. To set the tone of a piece, a writer must select the appropriate words. Note the formal use of language in this article. However, the words are not so technical as to force the reader to a dictionary.

ASSIGNMENTS

1. Consider buffets (as presented in Ursula Hegi's "Stolen Chocolates," p. 94). Describe the etiquette for serving yourself from a buffet.
2. Besides good table manners, what other things can you think of that would define a society as civilized or refined?
3. How is this article similar to David Bodanis's "Toothpaste" (p. 241)?
4. Farb and Armelagos show how our attitudes toward meat have changed. Some people have gone even further and embraced vegetarianism. Write an essay for or against the principles of vegetarianism.
5. While some cultures use the knife and fork at mealtimes, the use of chopsticks or fingers is the preferred method of eating in some cultures. Compare these methods, explaining the advantages and disadvantages.
6. Read Rita Sirignano's "Are Goody Bags a Good Thing?" (p. 334). With reference to "The Patterns of Eating," discuss whether goody bags are an evolution of older consuming patterns, such as the doggy bag from restaurants.

A Cell of Our Own Making

Moira Farr

1 I am not the first person to rail against cellphones, and I am sure I won't be the last. But recent television commercials have jolted me to a new level of alarm at what we are doing to ourselves with this rapidly metastasizing technology.

2 A certain purveyor of these devices is luring potential customers with this happy scenario: Imagine *never being alone*. Yes, everywhere you are, *they* are — whoever, in your case, they are. They scuttle behind you as you shop, this cling-on clan of yours. They wedge themselves into bed with you (perhaps installing that meter Leonard Cohen sang about in his darkly prophetic *Everybody Knows*). They hover over your shoulder at your computer and breathe down your neck as you root around in the fridge.

3 Ah, togetherness. With your cellphone connecting you at every waking moment to everyone you know, you've got it. And why stop at voice and text? Why not send pictures of yourself every chance you get to that special loved one from whose hip yours has been temporarily severed? After all, it's been hours, possibly even days (let's not cause mass hyperventilation by mentioning the prospect of weeks or months spent apart), since you witnessed each other in the flesh.

4 I'm only now getting up to speed on how widely this epidemic of attachment disorders has spread. Maybe I shouldn't be surprised. The inability of large portions of the population to get by without constant telephonic communication has been getting chronic for some time now. I used to enjoy the four-hour Ottawa–Toronto train journey, as uninterrupted reading and thinking time. That is difficult now, because for much of the trip, you will involuntarily listen in on teens and twentysomethings giggling with their cell-pals, and business guys (I'm sorry, but it is usually men) sharing their Earth-shatteringly urgent dealings with all of us.

5 The world now seems divided between those who understand that the human voice carries more loudly when on a phone than in live conversation, and those who blithely imagine that public space is just a convenient extension of private space — theirs.

6 I teach a course at Carleton University. It is now standard to ask students to turn off their cellphones before class. They ring, anyway. One student actually argued for permission to leave the phone on. "But I'm waiting for a really *important* call!" she wailed. I never thought I would have to explain: For centuries, scholars have sat in classrooms for hours at

a time, unavailable to the outside world, without undue damage to their private lives. Unless you are awaiting an organ transplant, or someone else will die if you personally do not administer CPR immediately, it is not important enough to interrupt my class.

I admit, cellphones are great in an emergency and, theoretically, they 7 can be used without disturbing others. But something's happening here to the way we perceive ourselves, the space we occupy, and the time we spend together and apart. I am not sure we fully appreciate what a revolutionary change it is.

Throughout centuries past, people had to get by with long spells away 8 from each other, even permanent physical separations. They left beloved homelands, forever to be apart from the people dear to them. On either side of that human experience, memories sustained love and hope. Absence made the heart grow fonder.

Months or years might go by before news, good or bad, got through. 9 Letters went astray, purloined, burned to ashes before their intended readers saw them. Ballads and folktales are full of these dramas of fate altered, usually cruelly, by thwarted communication. Human anguish stands, in the collective imagination, on a lonely windswept shore, clutching a letter that spells doom — or mourning one that never came.

Yes, tragedies there have been, in past cellphoneless ages, and I sup- 10 pose it's real fear that drives us to suckle so hungrily on this particular techno-teat. The problem is, we are only creating different, no less defeating, dilemmas for ourselves.

Our troubles now are those of overexposure, of too much communica- 11 tion of too much that is unimportant, and too little of what truly is. Comedian Dan Redican, once of The Frantics, now of *Puppets Who Kill* on the Comedy Network, once sang a pithy song whose title perfectly captures the problem: *I Miss You When You're Here*.

I pine for the days when people cultivated solitude, and could cope 12 with a bit of loneliness, should it sometimes descend. Not only cope with, but enjoy it.

More than any cellphone or Internet communication device, there is 13 something we can all turn to, as our best hope for getting through this life with a semblance of dignity and grace. It's invisible to the outside world, marvellously protean and portable. It provides hours upon hours of silent entertainment and, so far, is free of monthly charges.

It's called an inner life. Don't leave home without it. I put it in the "use 14 it or lose it" category.

15   And a society that loses it, en masse, is the most frightening thought of all.

2003

NOTES

Moira Farr teaches magazine writing at Carleton University, has written several essays and reviews, and is the author of *After Daniel: A Suicide Survivor's Tale*.

"Everybody Knows" A 1988 song by Leonard Cohen and Sharon Robinson that contains the lines "But there's gonna be a meter on your bed / That will disclose / What everybody knows."

COMPREHENSION AND DISCUSSION

1. How does Farr show that she thinks the advertiser's idea of "never being alone" is scary?
2. How does the use of a cellphone intrude on public space?
3. What does Farr think of cellphones in the classroom?
4. Paraphrase (put in your own words): "Ballads and folktales are full of these dramas of fate altered, usually cruelly, by thwarted communication" (paragraph 9).
5. What advantages are there to not being in constant communication with loved ones?
6. What does Farr mean by an "inner life"?
7. Most of us have very little quiet and solitude in our lives compared to what our ancestors had. Do people need this kind of time? Why or why not?
8. Can there be too much togetherness, or does absence make the heart grow fonder?
9. Consider the title of Farr's article. Does it have a double meaning? What ideas are conveyed in it?
10. Do you think cellphone use in public is a problem? What are the problems caused by cellphone users?
11. Do people really need to be constantly available by telephone?

LITERARY TECHNIQUES

Hyperbole One method of emphasizing a point is to draw it beyond its normal limits. Hyperbole, or exaggeration, makes something larger, something stretched out of proportion, something distorted. For example, Farr uses exaggeration to mock cellphone owners with such phrases as "mass hyperventilation" and "their Earth-shatteringly urgent dealings."

Use of "you" Although the use of the pronoun "you" to mean people in general should be avoided in academic writing, in informal essays such as this one by Farr, "you" is used to make a more direct connection between writer and reader.

ASSIGNMENTS

1. Write an instructional essay explaining the proper etiquette for using cellphones. Include some of the features such as built-in cameras.
2. Write an essay explaining the advantages or the disadvantages of having just a cellphone rather than a land line. Do not focus just on the advantages of cellphones in general.
3. Read the lyrics of Leonard Cohen's song "Everybody Knows" (available on the Internet). How valid are these lyrics to today's society and in particular to what Farr is writing about?
4. "Don't leave home without it" used to be a slogan for the American Express credit card. It has now made it to everyday expression that people use and recognize. Choose one advertising slogan that has become part of everyday language and explain why is it effective as a business tool and why it became popular.
5. Do personal music players, such as Walkmans, also intrude on public space and cut listeners off from the people around them?
6. Some cellphone companies offer a variety of services to help users lie about their location and get out of difficult situations. For instance, taped background noises and business-like backdrops for cellphone cameras can be used to mislead people about where someone is. Pre-arranged calls help people extricate themselves from a situation like a bad blind date. Write a report on some of these features and their use.

Don't You Think It's Time to Start Thinking?

Northrop Frye

1   A student often leaves high school today without any sense of language as a structure.

2   He may also have the idea that reading and writing are elementary skills that he mastered in childhood, never having grasped the fact that there are differences in levels of reading and writing as there are in mathematics between short division and integral calculus.

3   Yet, in spite of his limited verbal skills, he firmly believes that he can think, that he has ideas, and that if he is just given the opportunity to express them he will be all right. Of course, when you look at what he's written you find it doesn't make any sense. When you tell him this he is devastated.

4   Part of his confusion here stems from the fact that we use the word "think" in so many bad, punning ways. Remember James Thurber's Walter Mitty who was always dreaming great dreams of glory. When his wife asked him what he was doing he would say, "Has it ever occurred to you that I might be thinking?"

5   But, of course, he wasn't thinking at all. Because we use it for everything our minds do, worrying, remembering, daydreaming, we imagine that thinking is something that can be achieved without any training. But again it's a matter of practice. How well we can think depends on how much of it we have already done. Most students need to be taught, very carefully and patiently, that there is no such thing as an inarticulate idea waiting to have the right words wrapped around it.

6   They have to learn that ideas do not exist until they have been incorporated into words. Until that point you don't know whether you are pregnant or just have gas on the stomach.

7   The operation of thinking is the practice of articulating ideas until they are in the right words. And we can't think at random either. We can only add one more idea to the body of something we have already thought about. Most of us spend very little time doing this, and that is why there are so few people whom we regard as having any power to articulate at all. When such a person appears in public life, like Mr. Trudeau, we tend to regard him as possessing a gigantic intellect.

A society like ours doesn't have very much interest in literacy. It is com-   8
pulsory to read and write because society must have docile and obedient citizens. We are taught to read so that we can obey the traffic signs and to
cipher so that we can make out our income tax, but development of verbal
competency is very much left to the individual.

And when we look at our day-to-day existence we can see that there are   9
strong currents at work against the development of powers of articulateness.
Young adolescents today often betray a curious sense of shame about
speaking articulately, of framing a sentence with a period at the end of it.

Part of the reason for this is the powerful anti-intellectual drive which   10
is constantly present in our society. Articulate speech marks you out as an
individual, and in some settings this can be rather dangerous because
people are often suspicious and frightened of articulateness. So if you say
as little as possible and use only stereotyped, ready-made phrases you can
hide yourself in the mass.

Then there are various epidemics sweeping over society which use   11
unintelligibility as a weapon to preserve the present power structure. By
making things as unintelligible as possible, to as many people as possible,
you can hold the present power structure together. Understanding and articulateness lead to its destruction. This is the kind of thing that George
Orwell was talking about, not just in *Nineteen Eighty-Four*, but in all his
work on language. The kernel of everything reactionary and tyrannical in
society is the impoverishment of the means of verbal communication.

The vast majority of things that we hear today are prejudices and   12
clichés, simply verbal formulas that have no thought behind them but are
put up as pretence of thinking. It is not until we realize these things con-
ceal meaning, rather than reveal it, that we can begin to develop our own
powers of articulateness.

The teaching of humanities is, therefore, a militant job. Teachers are   13
faced not simply with a mass of misconceptions and unexamined assumptions. They must engage in a fight to help the student confront and reject
the verbal formulas and stock responses, to convert passive acceptance into
active, constructive power. It is a fight against illiteracy and for the matu-
ration of the mental process, for the development of skills which once
acquired will never become obsolete.

1986

NOTES

Northrop Frye (1912 – 1991) is considered one of the foremost academics of the 20th century. His writings reflect astute scholarship and original thinking, and his lectures at the University of Toronto were erudite and dynamic. This article appeared in *The Toronto Star*, so it was written for the general reader but with students in mind.

James Thurber (1894 – 1961) An American satirist and humourist in the earlier half of the 20th century. His most famous short story is "The Secret Life of Walter Mitty."

Walter Mitty The main character in Thurber's story. He is a middle-aged, hen-pecked daydreamer. We still allude to Walter Mitty to describe people with similar traits.

Pierre Elliott Trudeau (1919 – 2000) A prime minister of Canada from 1968 to 1979 and 1980 to 1984.

George Orwell (1903 – 1950) The pseudonym of Eric Blair, a British writer and satirist. His often reprinted writings are *1984*, *Animal Farm*, "Shooting an Elephant" (p. 305), and "Politics and the English Language."

Humanities A group of subjects in education, including culture, language, literature, religion, philosophy, the arts, and history.

COMPREHENSION AND DISCUSSION

1. According to Frye, what does the average student "see" as "thinking"?
2. What is daydreaming? Define.
3. Explain Frye's phrase "powers of articulateness."
4. Paraphrase this statement: "Most students need to be taught, very carefully and patiently, that there is no such thing as an inarticulate idea waiting to have the right words wrapped around it" (paragraph 5).
5. Why is thinking important to the individual and to society?
6. Frye criticizes our society by saying it is anti-intellectual and not really interested in literacy. Do you agree or disagree? Give examples to support your point of view.
7. Do you think Frye's criticism of students is justified?

LITERARY TECHNIQUES

This is an argument paper for a general audience. The tone is casual as evidenced by the vocabulary and by colloquial speech patterns such as shifts in pronoun with "you" and "we." Frye's choice of examples are everyday, and he uses familiar allusions, such as Walter Mitty and George Orwell's *1984.*

Frye begins with the specific and moves to the general. He captures the reader's interest by focusing on a typical student and then widening his point to include society. By doing so, he reinforces his point about the necessity of teaching the humanities to help the process of thinking.

Because this article is written for a newspaper (in fact, *The Toronto Star*), Frye uses shorter paragraphs than those used in more formal writing. He does so primarily because short paragraphs are easier to read and they fit better in narrow columns. Note that the first two paragraphs have only one sentence each. In addition, if you gather the first five paragraphs together into one, you will find a well-written developed introduction to his topic on thinking.

In short, the medium is as important as the message. In other words, how things are written is as significant as the content or ideas. In our textbook, we advocate the essay, a formal and structured way of writing for college and university students. However, the essay is not the only form of writing. As you can see here, an academic such as Frye can shift into another style effortlessly.

ASSIGNMENTS

1. Write a counterargument to Frye's assertion that we need to read more and think more clearly.
2. Some people think that computer technology improves students' ability to think. In an essay, agree or disagree with this point of view.
3. Explain how reading is a mental exercise.
4. Frye says intellectuals are not valued in our society. What does our society value?
5. In Alice Munro's "An Ounce of Cure" (p. 156), the protagonist does not think logically. Would she have benefited from reading Frye's article?

6. Read James Thurber's short story "The Secret Life of Walter Mitty" (or see the 1947 film by the same name, starring Danny Kaye). Does daydreaming fulfill a useful purpose?
7. Frye speaks of government and political propaganda brainwashing the populace. What about commercials, advertisements, and infomercials? Will being media-savvy help to counter this kind of brainwashing?

No Offence
Curtis Gillespie

If you're an Oilers fan like me, and were lucky enough to watch the team 1
in the 1980s, you'll remember that they were addicted to speed, a mon-
strously exciting, swarming band of goal-happy fools. In their four-
Stanley-Cup heyday, between 1984 and 1990, they averaged 378 goals a
year, compared to the league's highest-scoring team in 2003, the Detroit
Red Wings, who scored a mere 269. Okay, the Oilers were something of an
anomaly, a freakish gathering of talent that included Gretzky, Kurri,
Messier, Coffey, Lowe, Anderson, and Fuhr. But still, the game they played
was always about more than just winning; it was about scoring in bucket-
fuls and doing it with style.

And then came the Trap. 2

The Trap, that suffocating defensive system dreamed up by the Swedes 3
in the early 1980s to counteract the speed and skill of the Russians, has
been the NHL's strategy of choice for the last seven or eight years now. It
reached its perfect embodiment during this year's nearly unwatchable
Stanley Cup final between the Anaheim Mighty Ducks and the New Jersey
Devils. The games were tough, strategic . . . and dull, proving that the
Trap is to hockey what impotence must be to marriage: Sure, you can still
make it work, but where's the fun?

It was, by many accounts, Marc Crawford, former Team Canada and 4
Colorado Avalanche coach, and now behind the bench of the
Canuckleheads, who brought the Trap into the NHL in 1995. Shame on
him, to be sure; but the real blame might best fall on coach Jacques
Lemaire, the apotheosis of the Mad Trapper. He used the system to stultifying success with the Devils in the late nineties, and again this spring,
taking a ragtag band of castoffs (a.k.a. the Minnesota Wild) all the way to
the semifinals. The simple fact that Lemaire could take a team with so little
talent so far is proof that the Trap, damn it, works.

But what is the Trap, anyway? On a trapping team, all five skaters gen- 5
erally camp out in the neutral zone between the blue lines, where they
create a wedge formation. Then they just wait for the other team to try and
carry the puck through the clogged passing and skating lanes. The goal of
the V-shaped Trap is to take away the middle of the ice, to channel all the
action to the outside, where there is less room and less chance for direct
scoring opportunities. The only option left to the team in possession is to
dump the puck in, and try to chase after it. Then the Trap starts all over

again going the other direction. It's a simple and effective system — wait and block, wait and block — that requires rigid discipline but no exceptional individual talent, which is why coaches love it.

6   But here's the real problem: The Trap has killed the game's creativity. Until the mid-nineties, goals were regularly scored on the fly, by skaters, and shooters, and through the result of superb passing. Today, a tic-tac-toe passing goal is so rare that it makes Highlight of the Month on TSN. The NBA once made the zone defence illegal, precisely to avoid the situation in which hockey now finds itself. Scoring is exciting, and beautiful scoring is more exciting than the flukes, caroms, puck-cycling and net-crashing that account for most of today's goals.

7   This move away from beauty toward safety (meaning league parity) is attitudinal and corporate, not evolutionary, and it's reflective of what's going on outside the rink, too. More than ever before, we are managed in the various aspects of our lives, in the ways we play, work, consume, and meet one another. Credit information, media conglomerates, television schedules, even the way supermarkets arrange product lanes — all these steer us toward patterns of behaviour that business can predict and therefore profit from. Why should hockey — which is now run by lawyers and entrepreneurs — be any different?

8   The Trap is neatly symbolic of this shift from the creative to the controllable, from what can't be anticipated to what can be predicted. After all, even today's weakest teams successfully use the Trap to stay respectable. But so what? The Oilers of the eighties wanted nets filled to the brim with pucks, even if it sometimes meant their own. Every game was an event because you simply never knew what was going to happen. With the Oilers' goals for and against during that heady seven-year span, you knew that every night, nine pucks on average would find the back of the nets out of dozens of chances created by wingers in full flight, by rushing defencemen, by up-the-middle breakout passes, by four passes in quick succession along the length and width of the rink. Beautiful goals. Original
9   creations.

Think about that. When was the last time you could tune into a game, knowing that there would be dozens and dozens of scoring chances forged out of pure athletic skill and imagination, the kind of skill and imagination that many of today's players undoubtedly possess? I rest my case. The Trap, in all its forms, has to go. Maybe then we'll have something to cheer about.

2003

NOTES

Curtis Gillespie is an Edmonton writer whose work appears regularly in *Toro* magazine and other periodicals.

The Edmonton Oilers of the 1980s included Wayne Gretzky, Yari Kurri, Mark Messier, Paul Coffey, Kevin Lowe, Glenn Anderson, and Grant Fuhr.

Canuckleheads A derogatory nickname for the Canucks, combining their name with the insult "knucklehead."

Apotheosis The ideal of some concept, the glorification of someone or something.

Mad Trapper Usually refers to Albert Johnson, the Mad Trapper of Rat River, who was the subject of an incredible manhunt by the Mounties in the Northwest Territories in 1932. Because the term is established, Gillespie calls Jacques Lemaire a Mad Trapper even though the reference does not apply here.

COMPREHENSION AND DISCUSSION

1. What is the Trap and why is Gillespie against it?
2. How can the Trap be countered? Should it be made illegal in hockey?
3. How else could NHL-style hockey be improved?
4. How important is scoring to a game? Compare different sports. Soccer has been criticized for low scoring. Basketball has a lot of scoring. Baseball can be a pitcher's duel, with few runs scored; or hitters can tee off on the pitchers, resulting in a lot of runs scored.
5. Paraphrase (explain in your own words): "This move away from beauty toward safety (meaning league parity) is attitudinal and corporate, not evolutionary, and it's reflective of what's going on outside the rink, too" (paragraph 7).
6. Gillespie says that the Trap is "symbolic of this shift from the creative to the controllable" (paragraph 8). Where else do we see a tendency to control human behaviour and stifle creativity? Explain.
7. What is the appeal of spectator sports? What does the audience want to see? If the outcome is predetermined (as when a very strong team faces a much weaker one) or known in advance, is the game still exciting to watch?

LITERARY TECHNIQUES

Introduction Gillespie uses a three-paragraph introduction. His first paragraph gives an example of a specific team and is meant to get hockey fans excited thinking about the game. His second paragraph is extremely short—just a sentence fragment. This creates dramatic effect. It's like a drumbeat signalling the end of the fun. The third paragraph gives Gillespie's thesis and sets up his argument.

Sentence variety Gillespie uses both long, complex sentences and short sentences or fragments to great effect in this essay. The fragments serve to punctuate the piece. Short sentences emphasize, while long sentences explain. Good writers vary their sentence structure because too many long sentences give the reader no breather, and too many short sentences make the writing choppy, with no flow between ideas.

ASSIGNMENTS

1. Many suggestions have been made for improving NHL hockey, such as eliminating the red line, curbing violence, and increasing the size of the rink. Use the Internet and periodical databases to find articles on these topics. For example, "Saving the Game" by Ken Dryden (in *The Globe and Mail*, March 27, 2004, p. A21) is a cogent essay on why NHL hockey must be changed. Write a research essay on improving the game of hockey.
2. Research the growing use of protective equipment (masks, helmets, goalie pads, visors) and how this trend relates to the action on the ice. Drawing on your research, write an essay in which you give your opinion on the trend.
3. Write an essay arguing for improvements in another sport or activity.
4. Write a short report about the life of Albert Johnson, the Mad Trapper.

No Idol Industry Here

Charlotte Gray

Canada doesn't do heroes well. Look at our paper money for evidence of 1 the scarcity of national symbols. The current series of bills features prime ministers and birds in their natural terrain—emblematic of the only two brands of psychological glue that bind Canada together: political culture and love of landscape.

Of course, there is the Queen, too, with her Mona Lisa smile gleaming 2 out from the hallmarked paper. But the monarchy has always been included on Canadian money—a remnant of our colonial past. If she weren't part of the family furniture, Elizabeth II would have been dropped years ago.

Others countries have liberators, scientists, authors, saints, war 3 heroes—outstanding figures from the past who are supposed to represent the nation's greatness. We have the loon on our $20 bill and William Lyon Mackenzie King on our $50 bill. King, prime minister for 22 years, may have been one of our better leaders (number one out of 20 on a recent ranking), but he is hardly the figure to make Canadian bosoms swell with national pride.

Why are we so hero-poor? At one level, the answers to this question 4 are embedded in the nature of Canada itself. We live in a country that has a weak national culture and strong regional identities. As historian Daniel Francis pointed out in *National Dreams: Myth, Memory and Canadian History*: "In Canada, heroic figures have tended to emerge from the regions or from minority struggles against the status quo. By and large, they are sticks used by one part of the community to beat on another."

Louis Riel is a hero to Métis and francophones, and a mad trouble- 5 maker to anglophones. Even national figures are enmeshed in regional rivalries: Pierre Trudeau is the darling of Toronto's Liberal elite and a menace to Quebec nationalists and Alberta oilmen.

The majority of Canadians have only been in the country for two or 6 three generations. Most of the first European arrivals carry far too much baggage. How can we glorify explorers like Jacques Cartier when they treated the First Nations as savages? Or military heroes like Generals Wolfe and Montcalm when they fought each other? Finding common ground for homegrown heroes is a challenge. Countries with homogenous populations and histories stretching back beyond the printed word can pickle their heroes in the sweet vinegar of centuries.

7   Easy for the Brits to accept Boadicea as a heroine, or for the French to revere the memory of Jeanne d'Arc: The mists of history have obscured Boadicea's murderous reputation and Jeanne d'Arc's psychiatric problems. Any women in Canadian history must stand much more brutal scrutiny, and measure up to 1990s values. So Susanna Moodie, whose *Roughing It in the Bush* is a vivid and gripping record of 19th-century pioneer life, fails as a hero because she expressed the snooty disdain of her class towards Irish immigrants. And Nellie McClung, the Western novelist who in the early years of this century fought for female suffrage, factory safety legislation and women's rights, doesn't cut it for contemporary feminists because she glorified the traditional family.

8   Most countries choose individuals with larger-than-life qualities to mythologize: extraordinary imagination, against-the-odds bravery, brilliant creativity. There are colourful characters in our collective past who embody such qualities — think of Sir Sandford Fleming, inventor of standard time; Dr. Frederick Banting, co-discoverer of insulin; the fighter pilot Billy Bishop. Why aren't they on our money, instead of stuffy old Mackenzie King?

9   Fleming has never found an enthusiastic biographer, and Banting and Bishop are too damn controversial for Canada. Neither displayed the humility that is the first requisite of Canadian heroism. Prime Minister King, on the other hand, is respected (by those who respect him) for qualities that are seen as quintessentially Canadian — his skill at compromise, his success in keeping the country unified. "He was an unheroic leader," suggests historian Norman Hillmer, "who understood the contradictions of an unheroic country."

10   So we do heroes badly. Moreover, we do hero worship really badly. The United States has an idol industry for most of the founding fathers, plus a whole military-industrial complex for the Kennedys. British academics and writers churn out books on Churchill (and there is a blossoming Thatcher industry). France has myth-creation factories for both Napoleon Bonaparte and Charles de Gaulle. Each of these national heroes has sparked several million feet of film and a gazillion written pages (over 15,000 books on Napoleon and still counting).

11   It is not only national leaders who are celebrated in these countries: University library shelves groan with mega-bios and unpublished theses on Rockefeller, the American robber baron; Florence Nightingale, the autocratic Englishwoman who revolutionized nursing; or the French intellectual, Jean-Paul Sartre. Each of these characters incarnates a trait of which their country is proud: American industry, British guts, French brains.

But anti-heroes, such as Mackenzie King, don't spark such exuberant   12
hero worship. Most Canadians are more interested in King's weird side —
his interest in spiritualism and his penchant for table-tapping — than in his
determination to strengthen Canadian independence or his intuitive grasp
of how to make Canadians feel comfortable. In a fragmented country such
as Canada, successful leaders embody modest virtues. But biographers
looking for titans aren't interested in modest virtues. Cultural consumers
only embrace these virtues when they are accompanied by extraordinary
athletic prowess (come in, number 99) or teeth-gritting tragedy (Terry
Fox).

There have been attempts to establish a pantheon of heroes — iconic   13
reflections of our past and our psyche. In the early years of this century,
when we were still suffused with the Victorian assumption that bearded
patriarchs made the best heroes, the Toronto publisher George Morang
commissioned a series of volumes under the title *Makers of Canada*. The
"Makers" in this 20-volume collection, published between 1908 and 1911,
were all men, all either French- or English-speaking, and almost all
involved in public life, as governors, politicians and premiers. There were
three fur traders, but no entrepreneurs until the late addition of Sir William
Van Horne, president of the Canadian Pacific Railway. There was not a
single scholar, writer, artist, scientist or athlete.

Mr. Morang's reverential volumes never caught the public imagina-   14
tion. They were out of step with the emerging Canadian sensibility. Their
view of history was too restricted, and their style too prissy, for a young
country hurtling towards a multicultural future.

The qualities that are celebrated in our national life today are collec-   15
tive virtues — the bravery of our peacekeepers, the compassion of all
Canadians for Manitoba's flood victims. Our best-known artists are the
Group of Seven. When writers want to pump some adrenaline into our past
or present, they capture groups rather than individuals. Pierre Berton wrote
about the whole ruling class of Sir John A.'s day when he penned *The Last
Spike*. Peter Newman has described the raw ambition and acquisitive urges
of the business establishment as the 20th century has unfolded. The heroes
of other nations are usually fiercely individualistic — but individualism has
never been celebrated in Canada. It is not a useful quality for a loose fed-
eration perched on a magnificent and inhospitable landscape — a nation
that sees survival as a collective enterprise.

2000

NOTES

Charlotte Gray is an Ottawa-based writer. She has written about Canadian history in such books as *Flint and Feather* and *Sisters in the Wilderness.*

COMPREHENSION AND DISCUSSION

1. Is Gray's opening statement effective?
2. What is a hero? What qualities should a hero have? Who is your hero?
3. Discuss the statement "If she weren't part of the family furniture, Elizabeth II would have been dropped years ago." Do you agree with Gray? Is the monarchy important to Canada? What is its value?
4. Why doesn't Gray think William Lyon Mackenzie King qualifies as a hero?
5. Is Canada an "unheroic country"?
6. What do Canadians value?
7. Why is individualism not valued in Canada?
8. How are Canadians different from Americans?
9. Who do you think would qualify as a Canadian hero?
10. Reflect on the use of the word "idol." What does it mean to you? Is it appropriate for the TV show *Canadian Idol*? How does it compare to the meaning of "hero"?

LITERARY TECHNIQUES

Identifying references Gray mentions many famous people in her essay. Although her audience should be familiar with most of these people, she adds phrases to help identify them. Often these phrases are set off by commas: "And Nellie McClung, the Western novelist who in the early years of this century fought for female suffrage, factory safety legislation..." (paragraph 7). Another technique is to use an adjective phrase: "the fighter pilot Billy Bishop" (paragraph 8). Writers must consider their audience and what that audience is likely to know, and then give their readers enough information, but not too much.

The developed paragraph Academic or formal writing, unlike newspaper and magazine articles, prefers the developed paragraph. Because the medium is the page, and not the-two-inch-wide column found in most newspapers and magazines, the paragraph in a book can give some breadth to the discussion of one main topic. For the most part, Charlotte Gray's paragraphs begin with a definite topic sentence, which sets out the idea. Then she expands on that idea with examples, details, and other specific information.

ASSIGNMENTS

1. Gray laments the fact that Sir Sandford Fleming "has never found an enthusiastic biographer." Since she wrote these words, an acclaimed biography of Fleming has been published — *Time Lord: Sir Sandford Fleming and the Creation of Standard Time*, by Clark Blaise (Random House, 2000). Take a look at the book and its reviews, and write an essay on whether or not Blaise qualifies as "an enthusiastic biographer."
2. Research the life of one of the famous Canadians Gray refers to, or another famous Canadian. Write an essay on whether the person qualifies as a hero or not.
3. Canadian currency has been recently redesigned and is no longer the bird series Gray refers to. Research the new designs of bills and explain their significance.
4. What are the important qualities of heroes? Why are heroes necessary to society?

Once Upon a Time, A Story Meant Survival

Jay Ingram

1   Is storytelling more than an ancient and widely practised art? At least one scholar has argued that everything points to storytelling as an almost certain part of our evolutionary heritage, having arisen as a response to the daily needs of survival in our hunter-gatherer ancestors.

2   There are no direct clues that storytelling served our survival needs in the past. But look at the circumstantial evidence. Every culture on Earth tells stories, even those so isolated from others that there would have been little opportunity for borrowing. It is not just that every culture tells stories, but that every individual in a culture seems to be a natural-born spinner of yarns.

3   So all of us are good storytellers, yet we're the only species that does it. Only humans have the language capacity to tell stories or write them down. Storytelling in turn demands high-powered brains capable of understanding cause and effect and possessing something called theory of mind, the ability to put oneself into someone else's shoes.

4   Storytelling is likely an ancient skill as well. Modern hunter-gatherer peoples have well-established oral traditions and it is assumed that ancient people would have had them, too. Surely the people who created the Ice Age cave paintings of France and Spain 30,000 years ago were capable of telling a story. By their time, language had been established for tens of thousands of years; there had to have been stories told around the campfire.

5   But if stories are supposed to have an evolutionary benefit, what is it? What survival advantages accrue either to the storyteller or the audience? It's certainly good for the teller; if you can persuade an audience to share your beliefs by means of some dramatic narrative, you could recruit them to your side or even achieve the ultimate evolutionary benefit by persuading them to have children with you.

6   For storytelling to persist there must also be something in it for the audience. Michelle Scalise Sugiyama, an English professor at the University of Oregon, has argued that listening to stories provides an audience with a virtual-reality experience, allowing them to gather information about their environment without the risks involved in actually doing it themselves.

Hunting and gathering in ancient times were heavily dependent on   7
gathering reliable information: How does a mammoth behave when confronted with human hunters? Where along a tundra riverbank are edible
berries likely to be found and at what time of year?

But straightforward information about food gathering and predator   8
avoidance, as critical as it is, may not even be the most important intelligence for hunter-gatherers to possess. In the ruthless political/social world
of humans, who's doing what to whom and what one is allowed to do to
(or with) someone else is priceless information that contributes directly to
survival and reproductive success.

Stories are beautifully evolved ways of transmitting either of these cru-   9
cial pieces of information. As Sugiyama notes, getting this information
second-hand avoids the risk of gathering it in the first place. When anthropologists asked the African Kung hunter-gatherers whether a lion cub's
eyes were open at birth, the answer was, "If you go over there and look,
won't you be dead?"

Stories are time-saving as well. The Tehuelche, an aboriginal group   10
living in Patagonia, had a story about a fox and an armadillo, each of whom
ropes a mare to see who's the strongest. The armadillo wins by dragging
the mare into his labyrinthine cave, where she gets tangled in the rope and
dies. Having read this, you'll likely never forget that armadillo burrows are
full of twists and turns.

Why go to the trouble of inventing a story? Memory researchers   11
showed decades ago that a series of words is remembered much better if it
is presented as prose rather than a list. Repetition enhances that memory
effect: familiar stories like *Little Red Riding Hood* or *The Three Bears* contain much more detail than would be easily remembered from only one or
two hearings.

That's the argument. We tell stories for the same reason we invented   12
stone tools: survival. No wonder we're all attracted by a good story. We
can't help it.

2001

NOTES

A noted science writer and broadcaster, Jay Ingram hosts *Daily Planet* on
the Discovery Channel.

COMPREHENSION AND DISCUSSION

1. What is the thesis (main idea) of this essay? How does Ingram support his thesis?
2. Why does storytelling require a certain intelligence?
3. Why do people remember facts better when exposed to them in stories, rather than in non-fiction?
4. According to Ingram, what distinguishes human beings from animals? Do you think his opinion is valid? What criteria do you have to differentiate man from beast?
5. What makes a good story? What makes a poorly told story?
6. Summarize the points that Ingram makes about storytelling.
7. Do you agree with Ingram's theory about storytelling? Explain why or why not.
8. Today, our storytelling takes the form of short stories, novels, and movies. Why do we need such fiction in our lives?

LITERARY TECHNIQUES

Essay structure Magazine and newspaper articles, such as Ingram's piece, are written with very short paragraphs, only one or two sentences, because the narrow columns make longer, more developed paragraphs harder to read. Yet many essays do follow the basic structure of presenting a thesis and making points and supporting them. Ingram's first paragraph is his introduction, and his last is the conclusion. The paragraphs in between each make a point to support his argument.

ASSIGNMENTS

1. Read "The Cowherd" (p. 71). Is the folktale more memorable in its lesson than the admonishment, "Be kind to a mother who has uncomplainingly cared for you"? Use Ingram's arguments to support your viewpoint in your essay.
2. Many children's stories are labelled as cautionary tales, that is, stories that warn children about certain dangers. Read "The Three Little Pigs," "Little Red Riding Hood," or "Rapunzel." What else can you learn from these fairy tales? Why are they effective storytelling?
3. Which story tradition do you prefer: the oral tradition in which a story is told aloud, or the written one in which you read it yourself? Why?

4. Compare scripted television (sitcoms and dramas) with reality shows (such as *Survivor* and *The Amazing Race*) as examples of effective storytelling.

5. Read Northrop Frye's "Don't You Think It's Time to Start Thinking?" (p. 264) How relevant is it to Ingram's article? What do both writers say about language and knowledge?

Of Weirdos and Eccentrics

Pico Iyer

1   Charles Waterton was just another typical eccentric. In his 80s the eminent country squire was to be seen clambering around the upper branches of an oak tree with what was aptly described as the agility of an "adolescent gorilla." The beloved 27th lord of Walton Hall also devoted his distinguished old age to scratching the back part of his head with his right big toe. Such displays of animal high spirits were not, however, confined to the gentleman's later years. When young, Waterton made four separate trips to South America, where he sought the wourali poison (a cure, he was convinced, for hydrophobia), and once spent months on end with one foot dangling from his hammock in the quixotic hope of having his toe sucked by a vampire bat.

2   James Warren Jones, by contrast, was something of a weirdo. As a boy in the casket-making town of Lynn, Indiana, he used to conduct elaborate funeral services for dead pets. Later, as a struggling preacher, he went from door to door, in bow tie and tweed jacket, selling imported monkeys. After briefly fleeing to South America (a shelter, he believed, from an imminent nuclear holocaust), the man who regarded himself as a reincarnation of Lenin settled in Northern California and opened some convalescent homes. Then, one humid day in the jungles of Guyana, he ordered his followers to drink a Kool-Aid-like punch soured with cyanide. By the time the world arrived at Jonestown, 911 people were dead.

3   The difference between the eccentric and the weirdo is, in its way, the difference between a man with a teddy bear in his hand and a man with a gun. We are also, of course, besieged by other kinds of deviants — crackpots, oddballs, fanatics, quacks, and cranks. But the weirdo and the eccentric define between them that invisible line at which strangeness acquires an edge and oddness becomes menace.

4   The difference between the two starts with the words themselves: eccentric, after all, carries a distinguished Latin pedigree that refers, quite reasonably, to anything that departs from the centre; weird, by comparison, has its mongrel origins in the Old English *wyrd*, meaning fate or destiny; and the larger, darker forces conjured up by the term — *Macbeth*'s weird sisters and the like — are given an extra twist with the slangy, bastard suffix -o. Beneath the linguistic roots, however, we feel the differences in our pulses. The eccentric we generally regard as something of a donny, dotty, harmless type, like the British peer who threw over his Cambridge fellowship in order

to live in a bath. The weirdo is an altogether more shadowy figure — Charles Manson acting out his messianic visions. The eccentric is a distinctive presence; the weirdo something of an absence, who casts no reflection in society's mirror. The eccentric raises a smile; the weirdo leaves a chill.

All too often, though, the two terms are not so easily distinguished. Many a criminal trial, after all, revolves around precisely that grey area where the two begin to blur. Was Bernhard Goetz just a volatile Everyman, ourselves pushed to the limit, and then beyond? Or was he in fact an aberration? Often, besides, eccentrics may simply be weirdos in possession of a VIP pass, people rich enough or powerful enough to live above convention, amoral as Greek gods. Elvis Presley could afford to pump bullets into silhouettes of humans and never count the cost. Lesser mortals, however, must find another kind of victim.

To some extent too, we tend to think of eccentricity as the prerogative, even the hallmark, of genius. And genius is its own vindication. Who cared that Glenn Gould sang along with the piano while playing Bach, so long as he played so beautifully? Even the Herculean debauches of Babe Ruth did not undermine so much as confirm his status as a legend.

Indeed, the unorthodox inflections of the exceptional can lead to all kinds of dangerous assumptions. If geniuses are out of the ordinary and psychopaths are out of the ordinary, then geniuses are psychopaths and vice versa, or so at least runs the reasoning of many dramatists who set their plays in loony bins. If the successful are often strange, then being strange is a way of becoming successful, or so believe all those would-be artists who work on eccentric poses. And if celebrity is its own defence, then many a demagogue or criminal assures himself that he will ultimately be redeemed by the celebrity he covets.

All these distortions, however, ignore the most fundamental distinction of all: the eccentric is strange because he cares too little about society, the weirdo because he cares too much. The eccentric generally wants nothing more than his own attic-like space in which he can live by his own peculiar lights. The weirdo, however, resents his outcast status and constantly seeks to get back into society, or at least get back at it. His is the rage not of the bachelor but the divorcé.

Thus the eccentric hardly cares if he is seen to be strange; that in a sense is what makes him strange. The weirdo, however, wants desperately to be taken as normal and struggles to keep his strangeness to himself. "He was always such a nice man," the neighbours ritually tell reporters after a sniper's rampage. "He always seemed so normal."

10   And because the two mark such different tangents to the norm, their incidence can, in its way, be an index of a society's health. The height of British eccentricity, for example, coincided with the height of British power, if only, perhaps, because Britain in its imperial heyday presented so strong a centre from which to depart. Nowadays, with the empire gone and the centre vanishing, Britain is more often associated with the maladjusted weirdo — the orange-haired misfit or the soccer hooligan.

11   At the other extreme, the relentless and ritualized normalcy of a society like Japan's — there are only four psychiatrists in all of Tokyo — can, to Western eyes, itself seem almost abnormal. Too few eccentrics can be as dangerous as too many weirdos. For in the end, eccentricity is a mark of confidence, accommodated best by a confident society, whereas weirdness inspires fear because it is a symptom of fear and uncertainty and rage. A society needs the eccentric as much as it needs a decorated frame for the portrait it fashions of itself; it needs the weirdo as much as it needs a hole punched through the middle of the canvas.

1988

NOTES

Pico Iyer is a global citizen, born in England to Indian parents, raised in the United States, and now living in Japan. He is a travel writer and a novelist.

Theophrastus (370 – 285 B.C.), a Greek philosopher, began a form of writing called character sketches. He took stereotypical traits of people from every walk of life and described them. He used physiognomy, the art of revealing personality from bodily features, usually the face. This concept caught the fancy of later writers and became quite popular in the 18th century. It is still used in literature.

James Warren Jones (1931 – 1978) More commonly known as Jim Jones. His cult was called the People's Temple. The deaths in Jonestown, Guyana, occurred in 1978.

Charles Manson The charismatic leader of a group called "the family" that in 1969 killed several people, including actress Sharon Tate, wife of famed director Roman Polanski.

Bernhard Goetz The New York "subway vigilante." In 1984, he shot five black teenagers because he thought they were going to rob him on a subway train. He was found not guilty of attempted murder.

Glenn Gould (1932–1982) A great Canadian pianist, known for odd behaviour such as wearing many layers of clothing, even in the summertime.

Babe Ruth (1895–1948) Nickname for George Herman Ruth Jr., an American baseball pitcher and hitter, one of the best players ever.

COMPREHENSION AND DISCUSSION

1. Explain Iyer's distinction between weirdo and eccentric.
2. Explain: "[E]ccentrics may simply be weirdos in possession of a VIP pass, people rich enough or powerful enough to live above convention."
3. Is perceiving someone as a weirdo or eccentric a personal opinion or a societal one?
4. Why would Britain have more eccentrics than Japan?
5. Describe an example of eccentric or weird behaviour that you have witnessed.

LITERARY TECHNIQUES

Compare and contrast To compare is to look for similarities in two or more items; to contrast is to look for differences. This technique is helpful in drawing together or in separating one thing from another. In this case, Iyer shows the differences between weirdos and eccentrics.

Definition Making the meaning of a term or idea clear and distinct so the reader can understand it. The method can be formal or informal in structure, brief or extended, technical or common. Defining requires the inclusion of other writing techniques such as classification, example and illustration, comparison, and exposition.

Examples Note how the writer opens with an extended example to catch the reader's attention. An example is defined as a specific piece of information used to support a general statement.

Etymology How a word comes into use. Often in definition the writer explains the history of the word and its origins. Note Iyer's etymological explanation of "weird" in paragraph 4. The root or source of a word can shed light on its current usage.

ASSIGNMENTS

1. Consider some of the people mentioned in Charlotte Gray's "No Idol Industry Here" (p. 273). Would they be regarded as weirdos or eccentrics?

2. See the readings about Grey Owl (pp. 232, 236, and 327). Was Grey Owl a weirdo or an eccentric?

3. Write an essay defining two different kinds of people: tourist/traveller, cook/chef, amateur/professional athlete, gourmet/gourmand, doctor/nurse, secretary/assistant, children/adults.

4. Is it fair to categorize people by physical appearance, behaviour, or personality types? Why or why not?

5. How much eccentricity can our society accept? What boundaries are necessary?

6. Research a famous person who exhibits or exhibited eccentric behaviour. Explain the eccentricity. Should that person be vilified or accepted? How does the person's celebrity status affect the eccentricity? Some examples: Michael Jackson, Elvis Presley, Doug Henning, Howard Hughes, Glenn Gould, William Lyon Mackenzie King, Amor De Cosmos, Ludwig van Beethoven, Dennis Rodman.

Mess Up Your Kid's Education in 10 Easy Steps
Donna Kerrigan

It's now possible for busy parents to accomplish something once consid- 1
ered almost impossible. They can totally obstruct their kids' education.

There was a time when people thought a child just went to school in 2
kindergarten and emerged educated in about 13 years. It was thought the
process was natural and virtually unchangeable. Now we know that, with
the right kind of involvement in the home, an education can be snafued
right from the start. Here's how:

1. *Encourage your kid to practise negotiating skills.* 3
   Start early. A 3-year-old is not too young to determine when bedtime 4
   should be or whether vegetables will be acceptable for dinner. When
   your son or daughter reaches adolescence, you can graduate to passionate discussions about alcohol, sleep-overs and curfews.

   Negotiating skills are invaluable in the schoolroom, where a student 5
   who has received proper encouragement from home will entertain the
   class by arguing about every mark, every deadline, every word that
   comes from the teacher.

   Incidentally, such skills will also have a great impact on a kid's per- 6
   sonal relationships. "No" will never mean "no"—just "Push a little
   harder" or "Keep arguing. It wears down the opposition."

2. *Jump on the technology bandwagon with enthusiasm.* 7
   First, do not waste money on books or newspapers. Everything your 8
   kid needs to know about life can be seen on Jerry Springer's show and
   a choice vocabulary can be copied from Bart Simpson.

   Second, be sure you get the best computer money can buy, with 9
   plenty of games. This is sensible because, just as a new microwave
   makes you a Madame Benoit, a computer can make your kid an
   Einstein. Also, subscribe to an Internet service and give your kid free
   rein to surf.

   When your Grade 3 student downloads a 20-page research paper on 10
   the solar system, complete with colour graphics and a detailed explanation of orbit irregularities, be generous with your praise. When
   something looks good, it *is* good.

11   3. *Believe every word your child says.*

12   Your child is not a bully. If he or she says nothing could possibly justify the teacher's decision to issue a detention, that's the absolute truth.

13   Your child is not a cheater, either. You know for a fact the poor kid spent an hour downloading that assignment on the solar system. Threaten to fight an accusation of plagiarism to the fullest extent of the law.

14   4. *Never miss an opportunity to criticize your child's teacher.*

15   This is not as difficult as it sounds. Plenty of people, including the premier, actually seem to enjoy teacher-bashing. Teachers are overpaid and underworked, a fact recognized when you consider how easy their job is.

16   Think how successfully you yourself have taught your son or daughter important skills, such as cleaning the garage or tidying up the bathroom. Teaching something simple like reading to 35 kids would be laughably easy! A few pupils might be on medication to control their attention deficit disorders, others might be inattentive due to family stress, and still others might be struggling to learn the language. But teachers have it too soft — just look at the vacation they get.

17   So feel free to criticize the teacher, preferably in the child's presence. In no time at all, the kid will develop remarkable independence, rejecting any authority figure, anywhere.

18   5. *Apply the wisdom of the marketplace to your child's education.*

19   When you buy an object or pay for a service, you want satisfaction, not a hassle. As a taxpayer you're paying for a service — an education — and you want your money's worth. You shouldn't have to supervise homework, make a zillion trips to the library or consult with the teacher about progress reports.

20   For the money you pay, you want choice in the type of school your child attends. You want a computer on every desk in that classroom. You want bus service. You want sports teams, cheerleading squads, marching bands. You also want a tax cut.

21   6. *Demand instant gratification.*

22   Children should never be required to practise things such as spelling, arithmetic or the scale of C major. These are boring and repetitive, and your kids wants fun, fun, fun. He or she will tell you the teacher is mean, stupid and unfair.

7. *Be marks-sharp.*   23

You know the value of a dollar and you know the value of 100 per cent.   24
If your kid scores 88 per cent in math, encourage greater effort by suggesting 90 per cent would be better. And if your child received only 65
per cent for that project on the solar system, raise hell. It's worth 80 per
cent, considering the time spent downloading it.

If more kids and parents would make the effort to force teachers into   25
increasing the marks, half the high school grads would be convinced
they were geniuses.

8. *Promote your child's active social life.*   26

Your child wants to be popular and, face it, you feel a lot more suc-   27
cessful as a parent if your son or daughter is surrounded by a bevy of
friends. Give your kid plenty of time to socialize, even if it means sacrificing time that would be spent on homework.

And teen magazines are right: Your teenager's happiness and social   28
success depend on having a steady boyfriend or girlfriend. Only losers
spend time at home curled up with a book.

9. *Emphasize the importance of appearances.*   29

If clothes make the man, they can make or break a student, so indulge   30
your kid in all those "way cool" fashions. He or she will develop dis-
criminating tastes, deciding whom to befriend on the basis of sneakers,
earrings or tattoos.

But what if you, as a parent, are horrified when you see the styles   31
displayed in the school yard? In that case, go nuts. Nag about your
kid's clothing, accessories, hygiene. Expect rebellion. It goes with the
territory.

10. *Demand that your adolescent shoulder the major portion of the cost of*   32
his or her upbringing and education.

Children must learn the value of a dollar, the sooner the better. You   33
should not have to sacrifice to accommodate a kid's needs.

Besides, he or she can practise basic math at an after-school job: 34
How many burgers can a customer buy for $10?

Starting in early childhood and continuing right into adulthood,   35
these steps form a smooth process guaranteed to totally screw up your
kid's education. You can be sure that he or she will graduate and be
thoroughly fit for any endeavour, except one requiring diligence or co-
operation with others.

36   Parents who follow all these steps have the added benefit of their son's or daughter's company, snug in the family home, well after their friends' kids have flown from the nest. And although it may not seem likely now, your kid will know whom to thank.

1999

NOTES

Donna Kerrigan is an English professor at Niagara College in Welland, Ontario.

Teacher-bashing "Plenty of people, including the premier, actually seem to enjoy teacher-bashing." Kerrigan is referring to Mike Harris, Premier of Ontario from 1995 to 2002. Harris was very critical of teachers, implying that they were lazy and incompetent.

COMPREHENSION AND DISCUSSION

1. What is Kerrigan's purpose in writing this article?
2. How do we know that Kerrigan is being sarcastic?
3. What are Kerrigan's implied criticisms of technology? What do you think of technology in education? Is it used well?
4. Should parents believe their children and champion their cause unquestionably?
5. What is teacher-bashing? Why was it so politically successful? What are some of the misconceptions people have of teachers' work? Why do people criticize teachers? How is this criticism harmful to a child's education?
6. Is there a problem with viewing education from a consumer viewpoint? Explain your answer.
7. What point is Kerrigan making when she ends Step 5 with the statement "You also want a tax cut"?
8. Are students today less willing to work hard? Do they lack discipline? If you agree, explain why this is so.
9. Why are marks important to a student? Are marking systems fair?
10. How does a student's social life interfere with education?
11. What does Kerrigan mean when she says clothes "can make or break a student"? Do you agree?

12. What is the problem with parents nagging their children about clothes and hygiene?
13. Discuss Kerrigan's "guidelines." Are there any you disagree with? Are there any you would add?
14. What is Kerrigan implying about the practice of working part-time as a student?

LITERARY TECHNIQUES

Enumerating Making a list is a good method of organizing ideas for both the writer and the reader. The writer can neatly put ideas in a nutshell first before elaborating on them; the reader can find the information quickly. The ten-point plan is a popular and pragmatic way of ordering ideas. The reader can't miss "1," "2," "3," and so on. Note how after each step, Kerrigan explains the basic point before moving on to the next step.

Instruction Instruction is telling a person how to do something in a logical, sequential order. It can be as ordinary as giving directions to a tourist, or as complicated as explaining complex procedures in a technical manual. In any case, instructions must be clear and well ordered. They generally begin with command verbs such as "encourage" and "jump." Furthermore, the writer can provide explanations as to why something should be done.

Satire Satire is ridiculing someone or some institution or some idea, not only to show up its flaws but also to effect possible change. If readers are not aware of the mockery and take the meaning at face value, then the satirist has failed. Therefore, the writer has to make readers understand that he or she means the exact opposite of what is said. For example, Kerrigan writes: "A 3-year-old is not too young to determine when bedtime should be or whether vegetables will be acceptable for dinner." It would be hard for readers to accept this statement at face value; obviously, the opposite meaning is intended.

ASSIGNMENTS

1. Take one of the steps in this article and write an essay explaining the problem that Kerrigan is talking about. Take a stand on the issue.
2. Write an essay on how to foster children's education, the opposite of what Kerrigan says.

3. Read "The Story of Grey Owl" by Colin Ross (p. 327), and write a comparison essay showing the similarities and differences between Kerrigan's and Ross's satiric essays. Focus on technique rather than content.

4. In some cultures, teachers are highly respected. However, the conservative movement to reduce public spending in the late 20th century had a major effect on teachers, as one of the most visible groups of public servants. Research teacher-bashing of the period. Explore the reasons or the results.

5. Write a counterargument to Kerrigan's ten easy steps. For a long paper, try to argue point by point all ten steps. In a short paper, focus on fewer counterpoints.

6. Some people reading this satirical article will find nothing wrong with each of Kerrigan's steps. What are the problems of writing sarcastically?

Toxic Culture Syndrome

Kalle Lasn

If you reduced all of history's best advice on living well in two fridge-   1
magnet-worthy goals, they probably would be: 1) pursue excellence; or
2) pursue balance.

In other words, drill down—work with obsessive focus in one area,   2
try to create something new and valuable and lasting; or, go wide—bird-
watch or mediate, read good books, tend a garden, raise a kid or two, try to
be neighbourly. You know, all the stuff that makes life worth the price if
your job itself isn't all that fulfilling.

TV-watching doesn't exactly top either list.   3

When you sit down in front of the box—not occasionally, but on a   4
regular basis, as a lifestyle choice (and North Americans watch four hours
a day, on average, making TV-watching the lifestyle choice of choice)—
you're basically choosing neither path. You're neither rounding yourself
out in any appreciable way, nor sharpening some art or skill or craft. You're
just dropping out. Chronic TV-watching is like wearing sweatpants in
public. It's a public declaration: "I give up."

Write this off as a scold if you like, it won't hurt. We TV-turnoff pro-   5
ponents are forever being chided by hip critics as joyless, clueless prudes.
But have you ever noticed how these same critics often sound more earnest
in their support of television than anyone on the turnoff side does questioning it?

There are the predictable hymns to *The Simpsons* and *The Sopranos* (a   6
show that you might not get without an expensive extension to your
already expensive cable package), and the oh-but-the-cream-of-TV-is-
high-art shtick. It might be true. But "the cream" is an ever-diminishing
portion of the grand, bland banquet of commercial programming. And
anyway, the cream isn't what most people watch.

There are so many great reasons to go on a TV-fast for a week that the   7
case can be won without resorting to the merely good reasons. Jerry
Mander (*Four Arguments for the Elimination of Television*) pretty much
covered it 30 years ago. Besides, it doesn't make sense to talk about TV in
isolation these days.

The media environment is one big, complicated mass of connected   8
componentry, of which TV is but one element. You can't really pull out one
part and hold it to the light. You have to step back far enough to get a

picture of how the whole thing works. And when you do that, something interesting and a little bit scary happens. You start to discover things you might have been better off not knowing.

9   Recently, some credible researchers have taken that wide view, and published some powerful studies. Their work suggests that there's something wrong with our hypermediated way of life — that something psychologically corrosive is happening. The strong implication is that not just television and the Internet, but our whole commercial culture is toxic.

10   Social epidemiologist Myrna Weissman of Columbia University published two such studies in 1992 and 1996 in the *Journal of the American Medical Association*. She found a depression explosion in the United States. Not only are more Americans becoming depressed each year, they're becoming depressed at a younger age, and the severity and frequency of their depression are rising. Each of the last four generations has suffered more depression than its predecessor. Since the Second World War, the overall rate of depression has more than doubled.

11   A more recent study, published in the *Archives of General Psychiatry* in 2000, showed more than a doubling of depression in women from 1970 to 1992. Martin Seligman, a University of Pennsylvania psychology professor and head of the American Psychological Association, flatly claims the United States is in the throes of an "epidemic" of clinical depression.

12   What's going on? No one really knows. Probably a complex set of related causes is involved. Could some little-understood virus be making us genetically vulnerable? Or, might it be something in the environment — microwaves, electro-magnetism or a chemical in our food or water?

13   The accelerating pace of life is forcing breakneck adjustments; perhaps that's stressing us out. Or, maybe it's corporate identity branding? Or growing isolation, the "bowling alone" syndrome? Depression is "significantly more common" among people who live alone, reports the National Institute for Healthcare Research (NIHR) — and nightly sessions with Regis don't seem to fill the void.

14   It's been difficult convincing some people that culture itself is one of the prime culprits in our malaise — but the task has been much easier since William Vega's 1998 study published in the *Archives of General Psychiatry*.

15   A public-health researcher at Rutgers University in New Jersey, Vega followed recent immigrants from Mexico as they tried to integrate into American society. When they first arrived, they were much better adjusted than the Americans they settled among (they had half the incidence of psychological dysfunction). But as they Americanized, they got sicker and

sicker. After 13 years Stateside, their rates of depression, anxiety and drug problems had almost doubled (to 32 per cent from 18 per cent), to the point where they were now on par with the average American.

Mexican-Americans born in the United States got the full brunt of American toxic culture from the get-to, and their still-higher rates of psychological affliction show it: Just about half suffered a disorder, as defined by the standard tests.   16

Mexican-American men born in the United States were five times as likely as recent immigrants to experience a "major depressive episode."   17

Other studies have both replicated Vega's findings and extended them to other ethnic groups. Vega's conclusion: "Socialization into American culture and society [will] increase susceptibility to psychiatric disorders." That's a damning indictment — and hard to refute.   18

Except that it doesn't tell us which part of the culture is toxic: Is it the lack of community and family life? The junk food? The thousands of commercial messages the mass media pumps into our brains every day? The gradual blunting of emotions that comes from growing up in a violent and erotically charged media environment?   19

It could be any or all of these, but a 1992 study published in the *Journal of the American Medical Association* laid some of the blame on the atomizing effect of television and mass communications, which the study's authors suggested "have turned us into a single competitive group while destroying our intimate social networks."   20

Watching TV is the very opposite of a communal exercise — we finish up isolating ourselves, watching nature shows instead of going hiking with a friend, laughing at TV jokes instead of joking around ourselves, drooling over video sex and porn Web sites instead of having sex ourselves.   21

The authors of a Stanford University study released last year found that the Internet also steals time normally spent with other human beings. "If I go home at 6:30 in the evening and spend the whole night sending e-mail and wake up the next morning, I still haven't talked to my wife or kids or friends," the study's principal investigator, Norman Nie, told *The New York Times*. "When you spend your time on the Internet, you don't hear a human voice and you never get a hug." An on-line "community" can't possibly be a substitute for a real community, because the essential things — notably sensual interaction with other people — that make a community a community are absent.   22

David Korten, author of *When Corporations Rule the World*, points the finger at the whole capitalist rat race. He argues that we are all caught to some degree in "a downward spiral of deepening alienation." Our incessant   23 quest for money widens the gulf between ourselves and our family/ community. This separation creates an inner sense of social and spiritual emptiness.

24   Advertisers then get into the act by assuring us that their products can make us happy and whole again. So we go out and buy their stuff, which of course puts us right back at the beginning of the vicious cycle: Our incessant quest for money.

25   Have any studies isolated the toxicity of TV specifically? Actually, yes. In 1999, a team of Harvard researchers looked at chronic TV watching and found it correlated positively with low public engagement, lack of sociability and just general loutishness. It "even correlates positively with 'giving the finger to people,'" said David Campbell, a member of the research team. (The question remains, of course, whether chronic TV watching creates louts, or whether louts tend to watch a lot of TV.)

26   But we all know that quoting from studies is a mug's game. It's like marshalling statistics: You can selectively use them to tell just about any story you want. These studies tend to contradict the prevailing narrative that ever-more electronic stimulation is a good thing, and that mediated living is our inevitable future. Maybe that's why these studies haven't got much play outside scientific journals.

27   But for me and my culture-jamming friends, these statistics mean and explain something — they are fascinating, alarming, revolutionary.

28   Think about the average mental state of the average millennial serf steeped in electronic media: Always, always on the go, with never a quiet time to reflect, persistent low-level anxiety, rapid emotional swings from euphoria to boredom, daily bouts of frustration that threaten to tip into despair.

29   And all the while we have this unshakable conviction that happiness is right around the corner, as soon as the next raise comes or the Hawaiian vacation happens.

30   This is dire stuff. Put enough people who feel this way together, get them sharing the intimate details of their dis-ease, and what you have is a recipe for revolution.

31   Once people start making the connection between advertising/TV/ culture and their own mental health, we'll see a politicization of the mental environment and the birth of a movement every bit as potent and far reaching as the physical environmental movement.

32   As this "environmental movement of the mind" gathers momentum, it will alter the way information flows, the way meaning is produced.

Every bit of our mediated lives will be up for grabs. Parents will teach   33
their kids new rhymes like: "A bit less TV a day keeps the blues at bay."

Activists will challenge a TV system that delivers 15 minutes per hour   34
of station hype and ads, and, in the name of democracy and a free marketplace of ideas, they will demand that the six media corporations that now
control more than half of all the news and entertainment flows around the
planet be broken up into smaller parts.

And then, just about everybody will suddenly get into the act,   35
demanding all the media start paring back their usual celebrity gossip and
consumer hype and start providing some, well . . . balance.

These would be most excellent pursuits.   36

2001

NOTES

Kalle Lasn is the editor of *Adbusters* magazine, which is known for its
spoof ads.

Hypermediated When you cannot find words like this one in the dictionary, take it apart and look for obvious root words. The prefix *hyper-*
means over and beyond, as in *hypersensitive*. The verb *mediate* implies that
something is between people and reality.

Mug's game A foolish or worthless activity.

Culture-jamming Culture jammers are waging a war against corporate
culture by interrupting (jamming) messages such as advertising. For
example, they can distribute spoof ads or redirect web links.

Dis-ease Notice that with a hyphen this word means not being at ease,
rather than disease, although both meanings are appropriate.

COMPREHENSION AND DISCUSSION

1. Lasn begins his essay by talking about the purpose of life. Is this an
   effective opening?
2. Do you think life boils down to a choice between pursuing excellence
   or pursuing balance?
3. Lasn compares chronic TV-watching to wearing sweatpants in public.
   Is this a good comparison? Why or why not?

4. Lasn says that watching TV is making a choice to drop out of real life. Explain whether you agree or disagree.
5. What arguments does Lasn make about good-quality shows?
6. What is significant about the rates of depression in the United States? What happened to the Mexican Americans as they integrated into American society?
7. What does the author say about statistics? Explain his viewpoint.
8. Why is human interaction so important in people's lives?
9. What does the title mean? Is it effective? Why or why not?
10. Could we eliminate television? What advantages or disadvantages would that bring?
11. What is the thesis of this essay? Is Lasn's argument convincing? Why or why not?
12. On August 14, 2003, much of Ontario and the eastern United States experienced a massive blackout. That evening people came out of their homes and socialized with neighbours they hardly knew. How does that event support Lasn's argument?

LITERARY TECHNIQUES

Parenthesis Commonly identified by its round brackets, parenthesis has several uses in writing. It can be used to insert extra information in a sentence. For example, Lasn clarifies the psychological status of the Mexican immigrants by saying "they were much better adjusted than the Americans they settled among (they had half the incidence of psychological dysfunction)" (paragraph 15). Parenthesis is also used to give alternative names, such as acronyms; for example, "the National Institute for Healthcare Research (NIHR)." Furthermore, writers use parenthesis to add an aside: "There are the predictable hymns to *The Simpsons* and *The Sopranos* (a show that you might not get without an expensive extension to your already expensive cable package)" (paragraph 6).

Emphasis A speaker can stress a word (in other words, say it louder, longer, and higher) in a sentence to emphasize it. Writers, however, rely on a variety of other techniques. One is the single-sentence paragraph (such as paragraph 3 in Lasn's article), which stands out because of its brevity, just as a short sentence is more emphatic when placed after longer sentences. Another method is the parenthetical dash to set off some words. For instance, Lasn states: "That's a damning indictment — and hard to refute" (paragraph 18). This would be a grammatical sentence without the dash, but the emphasis would be lost.

Phrases as adjectives Lasn uses a phrase as an adjective twice in this article: "fridge-magnet-worthy goals" (paragraph 1) and "oh-but-the-cream-of-TV-is-high-art shtick" (paragraph 6). Notice that for these types of structures, the adjectives are connected by hyphens. Writers do this to coin new phrases and to get the reader's attention. Sometimes, however, a phrasal adjective can get too unwieldy. For instance, Lasn's first example is more successful than the second.

ASSIGNMENTS

1. Write an essay refuting Lasn's argument.
2. Read "Where Do the Children Play?" by Deborah Banks (p. 228). Where do Lasn's and Banks's arguments overlap? Write a comparison paragraph on the two authors' viewpoints.
3. Take a look at the *Adbusters* website. Do you support this type of ad spoofing? Is it effective? Important? Why?
4. Look up "culture jamming" on the Internet and write a report on what the activity entails.
5. Choose two TV programs, one that would be considered "the cream" and one that would be considered junk television. Write a review comparing the two programs, highlighting what makes one "good" while the other is not.
6. Explain the title of Lasn's article and show how it is apt in relation to the content.

Techno Dummies Need Not Suffer in Silence

Philip Marchand

1   You know how this happens. You're filling out a questionnaire and when you get to the last line you discover that you should have started by writing above the first line, or below the first line, as the case may be, and you did the opposite, so you've screwed the whole thing up. What an idiot you are.

2   Kim Vicente is here to tell you that you are not an idiot. You are also not an idiot because you never figured out how to stop the flashing clock on your VCR, or how to open a wine bottle with that new-fangled corkscrew that was supposed to make it easy.

3   "First people feel relieved because they realize, 'It's not just me,'" Vicente says of audiences he's spoken to. "The second thing they want to tell you all about is all the things they have at home that frustrate them. It's like a therapy session."

4   Dr. Vicente understands. He's not a shrink exactly, but something equally if not more helpful to the bruised of soul, a "human factors engineer." He teaches his brand of engineering at the University of Toronto, and he's just published a book entitled *The Human Factor: Revolutionizing the Way People Live with Technology*, an argument for making technology work for human beings instead of driving them crazy. The basic premise is that if you have been defeated by technology, it's not your fault. A questionnaire is a piece of technology just as much as a light bulb or a steam engine. If you couldn't figure out which line to write on, it's because the questionnaire was badly designed.

5   This does not mean there was an obvious flaw in the layout of the questionnaire, any more than there was an obvious flaw in the butterfly ballot that confused voters in Florida in the last U.S. presidential election. Vicente is not talking about technology that simply does not work or is obviously irrational. He's talking about technology that works on its own terms but is overly complicated for the user, or counterintuitive, or uncomfortable.

6   The problem is, there are two categories of people in this world: One consists of people who regard owners' manuals the way they used to regard trigonometry exams in high school. The other category, much smaller, consists of people who *like* to read owners' manuals. In this latter category are those who design our gadgets, and can't understand why the rest of us don't enjoy solving mechanical puzzles. They design things because they can, regardless of any need or use for them.

That's the reason we have, on one end of the scale, things like nuclear   7
power, and, on the other, electric toothbrushes. This is also why we have
things that are useful, but annoying in practice, like those paper-towel dis-
pensers in washrooms. They work fine if a part of the towel is hanging
below the opening, but if it's stuck you have to jam your fingers into that
narrow opening and try to pull out the towel. It makes you feel you have
all the dexterity of a gorilla trying to gift-wrap a Christmas parcel.

Vicente's book is full of examples of technology gone wrong. There's   8
the dashboard console of the BMW 7 Series, "iDrive," which offered
something like 700 or 800 features.

"Granted, a great deal of scientific and engineering knowledge was   9
required to pull it off," Vicente writes. "But the BMW 7 Series is a car,
not a spaceship." He quotes an article in *Car and Driver* magazine that
stated, "One of our senior editors needed 10 minutes just to figure out how
to start it."

Computers, of course, offer a rich field of exasperating technology.   10
May I vent about my own computer? Quite frequently, for no reason at
all — do you understand, reader? FOR NO REASON AT ALL — a square
will pop up on my screen with this message: "This program has performed
an illegal operation and will be shut down." It does this so often I'm beginning to wonder when the RCMP is going to surround my house: "Make it
easy for yourself, Phil. Drop that keyboard and walk out slowly with your
hands up."

"Oh yeah, come and get me, coppers!"   11

If this square has to keep popping up, I don't see why the computer   12
people can't at least remove that offensive and guilt-inducing message and
say something like: "Oops. Something's gone wrong. Perhaps you inadvertently touched the wrong command. Or perhaps it's our fault. Perhaps
Old Mrs. Motherboard is feeling cranky today. Whatever. Let's take a
second to chill, and try again, shall we?"

What do these people care about our feelings? They just want to sell us   13
gadgets, and more gadgets. How else to explain the existence of Palm
handheld computers? Actually, Vicente thinks the Palm is well designed
and relatively simple in its operation, and no doubt it is. I still can't figure
out what huge advantage it has over the appointment book, however, and
I'm happy to learn it's showing every sign of becoming a diminishing fad,
like instant messaging on computers. Remember that breakthrough in
human communication? It's clear now the feature is used only by bored
and restless teenagers, chatting with their friends on the next block.

14   Bored and restless teenagers also help to keep the cellphone companies profitable, which leads me to another rant. I used to be merely annoyed at cellphone users. Someone once remarked that talking on cellphones is like picking your nose — okay if you do it in private. Unfortunately, the truth of that remark has escaped a huge section of the populace, so that every time you're in a public space — a store, a streetcar, a sidewalk, a park — you're in danger of hearing somebody else's loud conversation. It gives you a feeling of being in the company of weird quasi-humans — their bodies are sharing the same space as you, but their minds are aggressively elsewhere, forging invisible links with other quasi-humans.

15   I can just see Dr. Vicente telling me to relax, breathe deeply, it's not that bad, we have to be a bit broad-minded in our acceptance of technology as well as critical. And I agree. But before I leave the subject, let me mention one more downside of cellphone technology, which I think Vicente would acknowledge as well. In many parts of the United States it is now virtually impossible to make a long-distance call without using a cellphone. I've spent a lot of time in phone booths desperately pleading with operators, offering to use calling cards and credit cards of every description in order to get a call through to Toronto. No dice.

16   That might not be so bad — I can use a cellphone if necessary — except cellphone companies often tack on "roaming charges" for long distance calls that are pure extortion. This is highly annoying. It is also a reminder that every new technology ends up costing its users time and money. (Computers, for example, require people to work harder and longer.) This is something worth remembering when the next big thing comes rolling along.

2003

NOTES

Philip Marchand is a columnist for *The Toronto Star*.

COMPREHENSION AND DISCUSSION

1. What is the thesis of Kim Vicente's book?
2. Marchand distinguishes between two types of people by referring to whether or not they read owners' manuals. Is this a valid way to make the distinction? What are other ways to describe these two types of people?

3. What's the problem caused by having these two types of people in the world?
4. Make a list of the complaints Marchand makes about different kinds of technology.
5. Explain some of the problems that can arise when technology design is poor. Use your own examples, not those in the article.
6. Marchand describes instant messaging on cellphones as a "diminishing fad." Is he right? Explain the popularity or lack of popularity of this feature.
7. Marchand says that computers "require people to work harder and longer." Do you agree? Give examples of computers both creating more work and reducing work.
8. Distinguish which parts of the article are Marchand's opinions and which are from Vicente's book.
9. Some people think that technology is the saviour of humankind. Explain why this is or is not so.

LITERARY TECHNIQUES

Using other writers' work for inspiration In this column, Marchand uses another author's work as inspiration, crediting that author's ideas and research and talking about his own similar experiences with technology. It's important for writers to identify what came from another writer. Notice how in paragraph 13, Marchand says, "Vicente thinks the Palm is well designed" and then introduces his own point with "I still can't figure out what huge advantage it has over the appointment book."

Humour Marchand injects humour into his point about computers' "illegal" operations with two techniques. First, he exaggerates: "It does this so often I'm beginning to wonder when the RCMP is going to surround my house." Second, he takes the well-known cops-and-robbers scenario from TV and movies when he imagines the ensuing confrontation.

Opening with the "you" example An anecdotal opener can capture a reader's interest quickly, and using the conversational "you" draws the reader into the scenario. Moreover, in that same sentence, the writer piques the reader's curiosity by offering a brief guessing game: "You know how this happens." No, the reader doesn't know how this (whatever it is) happens, but now he or she wants to know. The second sentence fulfills a certain expectation; the reader not only knows what the subject is about but also has perhaps shared the unfortunate experience of filling in a questionnaire improperly. Finally, the closing statement of the first paragraph reminds the reader of feeling foolish, incompetent, and frustrated because of an inability to succeed in a simple, everyday task. This prepares the writer to introduce the subject matter of his article or essay.

ASSIGNMENTS

1. Look up reviews of Vicente's book in a periodical database or on the Internet. Compare a review to what Marchand has written.
2. Choose a product that you are familiar with and write a critique of the design and how it could be improved.
3. If many of our everyday appliances are poorly designed and frustrate us daily, why do we not complain more to the manufacturers? Debate the pros and cons of complaining. What can it achieve, or not achieve? Do manufacturers really listen, or care? Why should the consumer care enough to write a complaint letter? And what should be in a complaint letter?
4. Both Marchand and Moira Farr ("A Cell of Our Own Making," p. 260) complain about cellphone users. Compare the points they make and how they make them.
5. Do consumers really need all the add-ons — Internet capabilities, text messaging, video recording, games, hundreds of ringing tones, and the like — to their cellphones? Write an essay on the advantages or disadvantages of such accessories.

Shooting an Elephant

George Orwell

In Moulmein, in Lower Burma, I was hated by large numbers of people — 1
the only time in my life that I have been important enough for this to
happen to me. I was sub-divisional police officer of the town, and in an
aimless, petty kind of way anti-European feeling was very bitter. No one
had the guts to raise a riot, but if a European woman went through the
bazaars alone somebody would probably spit betel juice over her dress. As
a police officer I was an obvious target and was baited whenever it seemed
safe to do so. When a nimble Burman tripped me up on the football field
and the referee (another Burman) looked the other way, the crowd yelled
with hideous laughter. This happened more than once. In the end the
sneering yellow faces of young men that met me everywhere, the insults
hooted after me when I was at a safe distance, got badly on my nerves. The
young Buddhist priests were the worst of all. There were several thousands
of them in the town and none of them seemed to have anything to do except
stand on street corners and jeer at Europeans.

All this was perplexing and upsetting. For at that time I had already 2
made up my mind that imperialism was an evil thing and the sooner I
chucked up my job and got out of it the better. Theoretically — and
secretly, of course — I was all for the Burmese and all against their oppres-
sors, the British. As for the job I was doing, I hated it more bitterly than I
can perhaps make clear. In a job like that you see the dirty work of Empire
at close quarters. The wretched prisoners huddling in the stinking cages of
the lock-ups, the grey, cowed faces of the long-term convicts, the scarred
buttocks of the men who had been flogged with bamboos — all these
oppressed me with an intolerable sense of guilt. But I could get nothing
into perspective. I was young and ill-educated and I had had to think out
my problems in the utter silence that is imposed on every Englishman in
the East. I did not even know that the British Empire is dying, still less did
I know that it is a great deal better than the younger empires that are going
to supplant it. All I know was that I was stuck between my hatred of the
empire I served and my rage against the evil-spirited little beasts who tried
to make my job impossible. With one part of my mind I thought of the
British Raj as an unbreakable tyranny, as something clamped down, *in
saecula saeculorum*, upon the will of prostrate peoples; with another part I
thought that the greatest joy in the world would be to drive a bayonet into
a Buddhist priest's guts. Feelings like these are the normal by-products of
imperialism; ask any Anglo-Indian official, if you can catch him off duty.

3   One day something happened which in a roundabout way was enlightening. It was a tiny incident in itself, but it gave me a better glimpse than I had had before of the real nature of imperialism — the real motives for which despotic governments act. Early one morning the sub-inspector at a police station the other end of the town rang me up on the phone and said that an elephant was ravaging the bazaar. Would I please come and do something about it? I did not know what I could do, but I wanted to see what was happening and I got on to a pony and started out. I took my rifle, an old .44 Winchester and much too small to kill an elephant, but I thought the noise might be useful *in terrorem*. Various Burmans stopped me on the way and told me about the elephant's doings. It was not, of course, a wild elephant, but a tame one which had gone "must." It had been chained up as tame elephants always are when their attack of "must" is due, but on the previous night it had broken its chain and escaped. Its mahout, the only person who could manage it when it was in that state, had set out in pursuit, but he had taken the wrong direction and was now twelve hours' journey away, and in the morning the elephant had suddenly reappeared in the town. The Burmese population had no weapons and were quite helpless against it. It had already destroyed somebody's bamboo hut, killed a cow, and raided some fruit-stalls and devoured the stock; also it had met the municipal rubbish van, and when the driver jumped out and took to his heels, had turned the van over and inflicted violence upon it.

4   The Burmese sub-inspector and some Indian constables were waiting for me in the quarter where the elephant had been seen. It was a very poor quarter, a labyrinth of squalid bamboo huts, thatched with palm-leaf, winding all over a steep hillside. I remember that it was a cloudy stuffy morning at the beginning of the rains. We began questioning the people as to where the elephant had gone, and, as usual, failed to get to any definite information. That is invariably the case in the East; a story always sounds clear enough at a distance, but the nearer you get to the scene of events the vaguer it becomes. Some of the people said that the elephant had gone in one direction, some said that he had gone in another, some professed not even to have heard of any elephant. I had almost made up my mind that the whole story was a pack of lies, when we heard yells a little distance away. There was a loud, scandalized cry of "Go away, child! Go away this instant!" and an old woman with a switch in her hand came round the corner of a hut, violently shooing away a crowd of naked children. Some more women followed, clicking their tongues and exclaiming; evidently there was something there that the children ought not to have seen. I rounded the hut and saw a man's dead body sprawling in the mud. He was

an Indian, a black Dravidian coolie, almost naked, and he could not have been dead many minutes. The people said that the elephant had come suddenly upon him round the corner of the hut, caught him with its trunk, put its foot on his back, and ground him into the earth. This was the rainy season and the ground was soft, and his face had scored a trench a foot deep and a couple of yards long. He was lying on his belly with arms crucified and head sharply twisted to one side. His face was coated with mud, the eyes wide open, the teeth bared, and grinning with an expression of unendurable agony. (Never tell me, by the way, that the dead look peaceful. Most of the corpses I have seen looked devilish.) The friction of the great beast's foot had stripped the skin from his back as neatly as one skins a rabbit. As soon as I saw the dead man I sent an orderly to a friend's house nearby to borrow an elephant rifle. I had already sent back the pony, not wanting it to go mad with fright and throw me if it smelled the elephant.

The orderly came back in a few minutes with a rifle and five cartridges,   5
and meanwhile some Burmans had arrived and told us that the elephant was in the paddy fields below, only a few hundred yards away. As I started forward practically the whole population of the quarter flocked out of their houses and followed me. They had seen the rifle and were all shouting excitedly that I was going to shoot the elephant. They had not shown much interest in the elephant when he was merely ravaging their homes, but it was different now that he was going to be shot. It was a bit of fun to them, as it would be to an English crowd; besides, they wanted the meat. It made me vaguely uneasy. I had no intention of shooting the elephant — I had merely sent for the rifle to defend myself if necessary — and it is always unnerving to have a crowd following you. I marched down the hill, looking and feeling a fool, with the rifle over my shoulder and an ever-growing army of people jostling at my heels. At the bottom when you got away from the huts there was a metalled road and beyond that a miry waste of paddy fields a thousand yards across, not yet ploughed but soggy from the first rains and dotted with coarse grass. The elephant was standing eighty yards from the road, his left side towards us. He took not the slightest notice of the crowd's approach. He was tearing up bunches of grass, beating them against his knees to clean them, and stuffing them into his mouth.

I had halted on the road. As soon as I saw the elephant I knew with perfect certainty that I ought not to shoot him. It is a serious matter to shoot a   6
working elephant — it is comparable to destroying a huge and costly piece of machinery — and obviously one ought not to do it if it can possibly be avoided. And at that distance, peacefully eating, the elephant looked no more dangerous than a cow. I thought then and I think now that his attack

of "must" was already passing off; in which case he would merely wander harmlessly about until the mahout came back and caught him. Moreover, I did not in the least want to shoot him. I decided that I would watch him for a little while to make sure that he did not turn savage again, and then go home.

7   But at that moment I glanced round at the crowd that had followed me. It was an immense crowd, two thousand at the least and growing every minute. It blocked the road for a long distance on either side. I looked at the sea of yellow faces above the garish clothes — faces all happy and excited over this bit of fun, all certain that the elephant was going to be shot. They were watching me as they would watch a conjurer about to perform a trick. They did not like me, but with the magical rifle in my hands I was momentarily worth watching. And suddenly I realized that I should have to shoot the elephant after all. The people expected it of me and I had got to do it; I could feel their two thousand wills pressing me forward, irresistibly. And it was at this moment, as I stood there with the rifle in my hands, that I first grasped the hollowness, the futility of the white man's dominion in the East. Here was I, the white man with his gun, standing in front of the unarmed native crowd — seemingly the leading actor of the piece; but in reality I was only an absurd puppet pushed to and fro by the will of those yellow faces behind. I perceived in this moment that when the white man turns tyrant it is his own freedom that he destroys. He becomes a sort of hollow, posing dummy, the conventionalized figure of a sahib. For it is the condition of his rule that he shall spend his life in trying to impress the "natives" and so in every crisis he has got to do what the "natives" expect of him. He wears a mask, and his face grows to fit it. I had got to shoot the elephant. I had committed myself to doing it when I sent for the rifle. A sahib has got to act like a sahib; he has got to appear resolute, to know his own mind and do definite things. To come all that way, rifle in hand, with two thousand people marching at my heels, and then to trail feebly away, having done nothing — no, that was impossible. The crowd would laugh at me. And my whole life, every white man's life in the East, was one long struggle not to be laughed at.

8   But I did not want to shoot the elephant. I watched him beating his bunch of grass against his knees, with the preoccupied grandmotherly air that elephants have. It seemed to me that it would be murder to shoot him. At that age I was not squeamish about killing animals, but I had never shot an elephant and never wanted to. (Somehow it always seems worse to kill a *large* animal.) Besides, there was the beast's owner to be considered. Alive, the elephant was worth at least a hundred pounds; dead, he would

only be worth the value of his tusks — five pounds, possibly. But I had got to act quickly. I turned to some experienced-looking Burmans who had been there when we arrived, and asked them how the elephant had been behaving. They all said the same thing: he took no notice of you if you left him alone, but he might charge if you went too close to him.

It was perfectly clear to me what I ought to do. I ought to walk up to   9 within, say, twenty-five yards of the elephant and test his behaviour. If he charged I could shoot, if he took no notice of me it would be safe to leave him until the mahout came back. But also I knew that I was going to do no such thing. I was a poor shot with a rifle and the ground was soft mud into which one would sink at every step. If the elephant charged and I missed him, I should have about as much chance as a toad under a steam-roller. But even then I was not thinking particularly of my own skin, only the watchful yellow faces behind. For at that moment, with the crowd watching me, I was not afraid in the ordinary sense, as I would have been if I had been alone. A white man mustn't be frightened in front of "natives"; and so, in general, he isn't frightened. The sole thought in my mind was that if anything went wrong those two thousand Burmans would see me pursued, caught, trampled on, and reduced to a grinning corpse like that Indian up the hill. And if that happened it was quite probable that some of them would laugh. That would never do. There was only one alternative. I shoved the cartridges into the magazine and lay down on the road to get a better aim.

The crowd grew very still, and a deep, low, happy sigh, as of people   10 who see the theatre curtain go up at last, breathed from innumerable throats. They were going to have their bit of fun after all. The rifle was a beautiful German thing with cross-hair sights. I did not know that in shooting an elephant one should shoot to cut an imaginary bar running from ear-hole to ear-hole. I ought, therefore, as the elephant was sideways on, to have aimed straight at his ear-hole; actually I aimed several inches in front of this, thinking the brain would be further forward.

When I pulled the trigger I did not hear the bang or feel the kick — one   11 never does when a shot goes home — but I heard the devilish roar of glee that went up from the crowd. In that instant, in too short a time, one would have thought, even for the bullet to get there, a mysterious, terrible change had come over the elephant. He neither stirred nor fell, but every line of his body altered. He looked suddenly stricken, shrunken, immensely old, as though the frightful impact of the bullet had paralyzed him without knocking him down. At last, after what seemed a long time — it might have been five seconds, I dare say — he sagged flabbily to his knees. His mouth slobbered. An enormous senility seemed to have settled upon him. One could have imagined him thousands of years old. I fired again into the same spot. At the second shot he did not collapse but climbed with desperate slowness to his feet and stood weakly upright, with legs sagging and head drooping. I fired a third time. That was the shot that did for him. You could see the agony of it jolt his whole body and knock the last remnant of strength from his legs. But in falling he seemed for a moment to rise, for as his hind legs collapsed beneath him he seemed to tower upwards like a huge rock toppling, his trunk reaching skyward like a tree. He trumpeted, for the first and only time. And then down he came, his belly towards me, with a crash that seemed to shake the ground even where I lay.

12   I got up. The Burmans were already racing past me across the mud. It was obvious the elephant would never rise again, but he was not dead. He was breathing very rhythmically with long rattling gasps, his great mound of a side painfully rising and falling. His mouth was open wide—I could see far down into caverns of pale pink throat. I waited a long time for him to die, but his breathing did not weaken. Finally I fired my two remaining shots into the spot where I thought his heart must be. The thick blood welled out of him like red velvet, but still he did not die. His body did not even jerk when the shots hit him, the tortured breathing continued without a pause. He was dying, very slowly and in great agony, but in some world remote from me where not even a bullet could damage him further. I felt that I had got to put an end to that dreadful noise. It seemed dreadful to see the great beast lying there, powerless to move and yet powerless to die, and not even to be able to finish him. I sent back for my small fire and poured shot after shot into his head and down his throat. They seemed to make no impression. The tortured gasps continued as steadily as the ticking of a clock.

13   In the end I could not stand it any longer and went away. I heard later that it took him half an hour to die. The Burmans were arriving with dahs and baskets even before I left, and I was told they had stripped his body almost to the bones by the afternoon.

14   Afterwards, of course, there were endless discussions about the shooting of the elephant. The owner was furious, but he was only an Indian and could do nothing. Besides, legally I had done the right thing, for a mad elephant has be to killed, like a mad dog, if its owner fails to control it. Among the Europeans opinion was divided. The older men said I was right, the younger men said it was a damn shame to shoot an elephant for killing a coolie, because an elephant was worth more than any damn Coringhee coolie. And afterwards I was very glad that the coolie had been killed; it

put me legally in the right and it gave me sufficient pretext for shooting the elephant. I often wondered whether any of the others grasped that I had done it solely to avoid looking a fool.

1936

NOTES

George Orwell (1903 – 1950) is a British author best known for the books *Animal Farm* and *1984* and for the essays "Politics and the English Language" and "A Hanging." This essay came out of his experiences in Burma, where he served in the 1920s.

Betel juice A very staining red juice.

In saecula saeculorum Generation of generations, or since time immemorial (Latin).

In terrorem To scare away, to frighten off (Latin).

Must In animals, a frenzied condition caused by sexual arousal.

Mahout Elephant keeper and driver (Hindi).

Sahib Hindi term for white, European master.

Dahs Knives about the size of machetes.

COMPREHENSION AND DISCUSSION

1. Why was Orwell in Burma? Why was he so hated by the local people?
2. Summarize the events that led up to Orwell's confronting the elephant.
3. Was the elephant a menace to human life when Orwell decided to shoot it? Why did he not want to kill this animal?
4. What justifications does he give for shooting the elephant? What was his real reason?
5. Why did the Burmese want him to slaughter the elephant?
6. What if Orwell had decided not to shoot? Speculate on the aftermath.
7. When is it justified to hunt animals such as black bears, deer, moose, and wolves?
8. Should sports hunting of all types be banned entirely? Why or why not?

LITERARY TECHNIQUES

Narration Telling a story. Storytelling requires not only the chronological ordering of events but also the explanatory information that the reader may not know. For example, Orwell informs the reader why he is hated by the Burmese, and this piece of information later plays an important role in his shooting the elephant. Moreover, the writer tells the reader about elephants, about their behaviour in calm and in must, and about this rogue elephant's rampage.

Orwell is not simply telling a story. He has two points to make. First, although he is in charge of the situation with the elephant, he is also being manipulated. Second, he tells of the underlying unease between Europeans and the Burmese, caused by British imperialism.

Latin phrases The scattering of Latin phrases was a common practice in learned and formal writing. The phrases speak to a time when Latin was widely taught in the British educational system and readers were likely to understand them.

ASSIGNMENTS

1. Write a narrative of an experience you have had.
2. Consider the way pets are pampered, as described in Judith Timson's "Pet-o-philia" (p. 338). Would either Orwell or the natives in this essay understand this treatment?
3. Have you ever been coerced by others into doing something you didn't want to do? Describe the situation.
4. Read Tim O'Brien's "The Man I Killed" (p. 174). Compare the reactions of the shooter in that story with Orwell's.
5. Rewrite this narrative from a Burmese point of view. Focus mainly on the episode involving the elephant.
6. Write an essay on the mercy killing of animals. What factors determine when it should be performed?

"Never Give In, Never"
Richard Pound

The flood of recent doping cases in sport offers hard evidence that the fight against doping has not been won. In the past week, we've learned of Canadian sprinter Venolyn Clarke's positive test for the steroid stanozolol at the world athletics championships in Edmonton, and the positive test of a Russian, Olga Yegorova, for the banned endurance-boosting hormone EPO. [1]

Many wonder if ground is not being lost. Some suggest that sports authorities should just give up and allow athletes to take whatever they want. At least that way, they reason, there will no longer be any cheating and the playing field will have been levelled—assuming, of course, that all athletes will be able to afford the same drugs. [2]

It probably comes as no great surprise to learn that I am unequivocally opposed to such a "solution" to the drug problem in sport. Some will conclude that as the president of the World Anti-Doping Agency (WADA), this conviction should be part of my job description. That much is true, but the order is reversed. I only agreed to take on this responsibility because I believe doping is antithetical to the very foundations of ethical sport. Any medal won, any result achieved by doping is anathema to everything for which sport should stand. [3]

Doping tarnishes the achievement. It destroys the accomplishment. It generates shame and the need for clandestine behaviour, the need to hide from those who have competed fairly. It generates the rot that attaches to the drug-assisted result. What begins as an honourable quest—to see how far one's talents and skills can be developed in accordance with freely agreed-upon rules of play—dissolves into conduct that must be hidden, that brings public shame if exposed, and a lifetime of private guilt even if it is not exposed. [4]

What should be a matter of pride becomes akin to Oscar Wilde's *The Picture of Dorian Gray*, where the reality of the individual, who purports to be pure, must be concealed from public view. [5]

But there is another reason for rules against doping, namely a justifiable concern for the health of the athletes who do it voluntarily or who are subjected to it (stanozolol, for example, has been linked to liver damage, hypertension and heart disease). Almost every prohibited substance is actually or potentially damaging to the health of the athletes involved. Whether or not this may sound paternalistic, the athletes need protection from themselves or their entourages. [6]

7   And what should we think of those who counsel athletes to use doping? Or who condone the use of drugs? Or who help make the drugs available to athletes in the full knowledge of the use to which they will be put? Of medical practitioners who ignore the ethical dictates of a learned profession that has a particular social responsibility? What kind of people are they who would expose young people to the risks of health and moral turpitude that come from such usage?

8   Where are their personal and professional responsibilities? How can parents and society allow them to have such formative influence on the youth of their communities?

9   I put it to you that there is no coach or team doctor or trainer worthy of the description who cannot be unaware of doping by an athlete under his or her charge. I put it to you as well that there should be a special onus on these professionals to stop such conduct and that any doping infraction affecting an athlete under their charge should be equally ascribed to them. Unfortunately, all too often, it is the athlete (who may bear only part of the responsibility) who bears the full penalty, while those more responsible escape all sanction.

10   But the fight against doping cannot be won by the sports world alone. There are many issues, such as the harmonization of legal penalties against doping and the trafficking of these drugs, that can only be resolved by the co-operative intervention of the world's governments.

11   This is why the World Anti-Doping Agency was created, to bring together the governments and the sporting world — including athletes — at the same time, at the same table, with the same objectives.

12   We understand the fight against doping in sport will not be won simply by developing better methods for detecting drugs and imposing sanctions. In the long run, it will be a matter of education, creating a common understanding that doping is not only ethically wrong, but also dangerous to the health of athletes.

13   It took a long time for people to accept the use of seat belts or to accept the folly of drinking and driving. Ultimately, it was not the legal penalties imposed for infractions, but the realization that the whole attitudinal approach to those issues had to be changed. The same will be true for doping in sport.

14   But more needs to be done. More work has to go into identifying the alleged links between poorly-labelled nutritional products that contain prohibited substances, such as the strength-building steroid nandrolone. The reasons the world's best athletes consume such large quantities of prescription medication during competition must be studied, as well as the

reasons why athletes are prepared to risk health, penalties and disgrace to use drugs in sport.

Unless we understand the genesis of the conduct, it will be difficult to 15 find the cure. We need to fund research to develop reliable detection methods for human growth factors such as HgH, oxygen-carrying agents similar to EPO, and techniques, such as genetic manipulation, which sound like science fiction today but tomorrow may be a frightening reality. (This September WADA is organizing a conference of international genetics experts to study the implications of this new field on sport.)

This is a battle that we simply have to win. As Winston Churchill said, 16 "Never give in, never give in, never, never, never — in nothing, great or small, large or petty — never give in except to convictions of honour and good sense."

2001

NOTES

Richard Pound competed in the 1960 Olympics for Canada in swimming. He is president of the World Anti-Doping Agency, is chancellor of McGill University, and was an executive board member and vice-president of the International Olympic Committee.

Oscar Wilde's famous novel *The Picture of Dorian Gray* (1891) tells the story of a man who lives a riotous life but remains young-looking. Instead, his portrait changes and the man in the picture looks old and debauched.

Winston Churchill was Prime Minister of England in the mid-20th century. His stirring speeches during World War II were especially famous. The "never give in" quotation comes from a speech he made to the students of Harrow School in 1941.

COMPREHENSION AND DISCUSSION

1. What is the thesis of this essay? In other words, what is Pound's main argument?
2. What is the relationship between Pound's stance on doping and his current job?
3. What arguments does Pound mention for stopping the fight against doping in sports? How can you tell that he does not support those arguments?

4. What arguments does Pound give for continuing the fight against drugs in sports?
5. Explain the point Pound is making with his reference to the story of Dorian Gray.
6. When athletes use drugs, who is mostly to blame — the athlete, the coach, the government, the system?
7. Why is it necessary to have an international anti-doping agency?
8. What social changes does Pound compare to the fight against doping? Is it a valid comparison?
9. Why does Pound end with Churchill's words?
10. What does the quotation from Churchill mean to you?

LITERARY TECHNIQUES

Quotation One attention-getting technique in writing is to use a recognizable quotation from a famous personality, celebrity, or expert. For example, Pound quotes Winston Churchill's words in the title of the article and in the conclusion. This technique has several advantages. The writer draws a relationship between Churchill's determination that England would never surrender to the Nazis and Pound's argument that the war on drugs in sports must not falter. Moreover, he creates interest and appeals to the reader's intellect with an emotive, heartfelt quotation. His cause is just and right. Finally, the words "never give in, never" not only draw attention but also reinforce his argument. Pound then extends the Churchill passage to round out his conclusion.

Literary allusion Having literary references in a non-fiction article is another writing strategy to gain reader interest. Certainly the reference must be apt, as Pound's reference to Oscar Wilde's character Dorian Gray parallels the drug abuse by athletes. All literature draws on what has been written before to make comparisons and allusions.

ASSIGNMENTS

1. Read a different viewpoint in Ian Ritchie's "Drugs in Sports: Why the Fuss?" (p. 322). Write a comparison of the two articles. Or, write an essay on your point of view with reference to what Ritchie and Pound have to say.

2. Research and summarize a well-known doping scandal: East German athletes, Pan American Games of 1983 (first widespread testing), Ben Johnson, U.S. track and field athletes of the 1990s, Steve Vezina, Silken Laumann, Ross Rebagliati, Michelle Smith, Chinese swimming teams of the 1990s, 1998 Tour de France, Mark McGwire, Beckie Scott's competition in the Salt Lake City 2002 Olympics, or others.
3. Look up some other famous quotations by Winston Churchill. Choose one and write a paragraph explaining it in context.
4. Debate the pros and cons of the concept of "win at any cost." You may widen the field to include business, government, school, and personal situations.

Have Wheels, Will Go A-Wooing

Kurt Preinsperg

1   On a Saturday morning the woman from my dance class called to suggest meeting for coffee. I had given her my business card a few days earlier and was delighted she called.

2   "We have to meet in my area," she said. "I don't have a car to get to your part of town."

3   "Great," I replied. "I don't have a car either, but I'm happy to take the bus to your part of town."

4   "What?" she said. "You don't have a car?"

5   "Actually, I don't like driving," I said, sensing another potential romance fizzle as I offered reasons for being ideologically opposed to cars. I sounded defensive, eccentric, and pathetic even to my own ears.

6   Being a non-driver is readily equated, in our society, with being too poor to afford a car. And evidence that a man is poor is not too charitably received during the early stages of courtship.

7   The woman's diminished enthusiasm was palpable when we met at the Art Gallery café. Her attitude was one of suspicion. (What's wrong with him? A man in his forties, and he doesn't own a car?)

8   Later, a colleague said: "Yep, a man gotta have his own wheels. Otherwise women think you're either cheap or kooky."

9   So here I was, middle-aged, single, employed, trying to explain to my date why I hadn't owned a car in years. Pretty soon I found myself slipping into a lecture about the adverse effects of cars.

10   First, the stress. I had several small accidents and near-accidents as a roving college instructor when, for seven years, I drove hundreds of kilometres each week as far from Vancouver as Chilliwack. Navigating through heavy traffic is so absorbing that one often isn't even aware of one's wasted nervous energy. My stress level went way down without a car.

11   Second, the cost. These days, a college instructor's salary is high enough to support a car, but low enough to make this a sizable expense. No wonder the middle class is emotionally invested in car ownership: We always value most what we make sacrifices for.

12   Third, the worries. A car accident can be crippling or even deadly to oneself or others, especially pedestrians. Cars usually involve repeat visits to such uninspiring places as repair shops, gas stations, Air Care centres, insurance offices, parking garages, and the impound lots of towing companies. Not having to worry about breakdowns, parking, car security, speeding tickets, and so forth can take real clutter off one's mind.

Fourth, the environmental damage. Billions of people around the world live in a poison cloud of exhaust fumes in areas of urban sprawl, which is both caused by cars and makes cars ever more necessary. 13

Fifth, the missed romance of bus travel. To be sure, there are indignities associated with bus travel: waiting in the rain while smoke-belching cars roar past, or spending an hour on a trip that would take ten minutes by car. But public transport not only frees time for reading, it often leads to meeting people. The bus, like the dance floor, is one of the few places where people can invade each other's space without affront. And bus travel frequently offers the delight of glimpsing a stranger whose looks resonate with some deep esthetic reflex inside one's psyche. 14

Impressed by the down side of car ownership, I vowed to live without a car—and to choose a partner partly on the basis of whether she could accept that. 15

Well, the evidence is in. The pickings have been slim. The lesson I learned is that a car is almost a necessity for a single man, both as a symbol of respectable masculinity and as a practical courtship tool. 16

A woman doesn't want to shiver at a bus stop on the way to and from a movie. A car is a cozy enclosure against the elements where two people can talk and negotiate the next step. Asking a woman "Do you want a ride home?" is a powerful code for saying "I'm interested in you." Without a car, a man deprives himself of one of our culture's most effective courtship manoeuvres. 17

In what follows, I want to generalize about men and women as statistical aggregates only, stressing that many exceptional men and women do not fit. Over the years I've come to believe in a kind of "sexual Marxism," heavily tinged with the influence of Freud, Foucault, and evolutionary psychology. Marx was partly wrong. It is not one's place in the system of economic production that fundamentally controls the shaping of a person's identity, but one's rank in the hierarchy of desirability to the opposite sex. 18

Members of both sexes compete for what are perceived to be desirable partners. It is no accident that most men's sexual interest is easily ignited by almost any healthy fertile-looking woman, whereas most women's more selective sexuality responds in part to a man's promise as a protector and provider. 19

Both men and women are strongly motivated to satisfy each other's mating preferences, but male sexual demand invariably faces a scarcity of female supply. This gender dynamic is the single most important driving force underlying all social life. 20

21   I'm sometimes tempted to think the human world is a veiled gynocracy and only superficially a patriarchy. Women's sexual power is the basic power; other kinds of power are largely derivative. A great deal of women's behaviour can be understood from the perspective of the possession or diminution of sexual power, and a great deal of men's behaviour can be understood from the perspective of the quest for a woman's sexual favours.

22   The economic and political spheres are just part of the superstructure of the sexual sphere; and the political and economic dominance of men is best explained, in large part, as a reaction to the sexual power of women. A very small proportion of men have any significant economic or political power; a much larger proportion of women have significant sexual power.

23   That is why most young men, propelled by a deep yearning to make themselves more acceptable to young women, are desperate to have a car. The humiliations of being outside the car-owning mainstream send all but the most stubborn idealists off to a car dealership as soon as they have enough funds or credit.

24   A few weeks ago, on a Sunday, it so happened that I felt shamed, belittled, rejected by three different women for not owning a car. That triggered an internal dialogue. Subconsciously, did I perhaps resist buying a car to punish myself? By not buying a car, was I really caught up in a perverse self-sabotage? In any case, I was clearly forgoing the satisfaction of basic emotional needs for the sake of utterly futile idealism.

25   The following Monday, I went to a place called Healthy Wheels and bought a used Toyota.

26   And judging from a recent turn of events, lonely times will soon be past. The carbon monoxide and other pollutants I add to Vancouver's air suddenly seem like a small price for my enhanced masculinity.

1997

NOTES

Kurt Preinsperg teaches philosophy and critical thinking in Vancouver.

A-wooing An old form, in which the *a-* prefix shows that someone is engaged in an activity. You won't see it very often, so don't worry about it too much. It shows up in old folksongs like "Frog went a-courtin'."

COMPREHENSION AND DISCUSSION

1. What is Preinsperg's thesis—his main point?
2. What are the five reasons why the author does not want a car? Are his reasons valid?
3. What is good about travelling by bus?
4. Why is a car essential to dating?
5. Put this statement in your own words: "It is not one's place in the system of economic production that fundamentally controls the shaping of a person's identity, but one's rank in the hierarchy of desirability to the opposite sex" (paragraph 18). What does Preinsperg mean?
6. As well as being a writer, Preinsperg teaches philosophy. What clues in the essay point to his profession?
7. Do you think the author made the right decision when he bought a car?
8. What else is important to make someone attractive to the opposite sex? What do you value in a prospective date?
9. Why are cars so important in Canadian society?
10. How can we deal with the problems of traffic gridlock and pollution caused by cars? What are the economic costs of these problems?

LITERARY TECHNIQUES

Anecdotal opening To catch your attention, Preinsperg gives a personal experience relevant to the topic of his article.

ASSIGNMENTS

1. Read T. Coraghessan Boyle's "Greasy Lake" (p. 33) and compare it with this article on the topic of cars and their uses.
2. What price in terms of health and sanity are you willing to pay to own a car? What does a car really mean to you?
3. North American society is too dependent on cars. Suggest ways to change this.
4. Is Preinsperg putting too much effort into dating, considering Robert Arnason's theory of relationships in "The Mathematics of Relationships" (p. 224)?

Drugs in Sports: Why the Fuss?

Ian Ritchie

1   Every Olympic year, we vicariously enjoy the efforts of Canadian athletes. At the Sydney Games, we felt Simon Whitfield's competitive spirit, intense nationalism, and passion for the sport of triathlon as he ran to his gold-medal finish. But every Olympic year, that sort of positive experience is tempered by stories of banned-substance abuse. Unfortunately, sport is inundated with the spectre of drug-related controversy, and tales such as equestrian rider Eric Lamaze's are now as much a feature of the Olympic landscape as Simon Whitfield's.

2   The drug stories are always punctuated with the same themes. They either dramatize the "masking-detection" race between athletes, coaches or physicians and International Olympic Committee-sanctioned laboratories, or lament the sorry state of affairs of elite sport, in which athletes use any means possible—including cheating—to win the elusive gold medal. Overriding these stories is general agreement that banned-substance use is wrong, that athletes who take drugs are cheaters, and that drugs threaten both the health of athletes and the integrity of sport.

3   Maybe there's another way of thinking about the issue. The problem of drug use in sport seems upsetting because it runs contrary to the ideals and values of sport. But perhaps we need to consider the idea that drug use is upsetting precisely because it conforms so well to sport's dominant ideals and values. In other words, using drugs to enhance performance might just make sense.

4   Many of the central ethical arguments are misunderstood. The "ethics" of drug use in sport is rarely discussed, the term commonly misunderstood to mean "efficacy" of drug testing, or determining which methods are the most appropriate and efficient ones for catching cheating athletes. But if the real ethical question—whether athletes ought to take drugs in the first place—is considered carefully, the issue becomes incredibly murky.

5   Take, for example, the main justification against the use of banned substances. Three central arguments are typically made, all of which are taken for granted in public discourse and cited officially in the preamble to the list of banned substances in the Olympic Charter. Banned substances are considered unethical because they are dangerous to the health of the athletes; they create an unfair "playing field"; and they're incompatible with the ideals and integrity of sport.

The health argument seems to make sound intuitive sense, for certainly   6
one of the most enduring images of high-performance athletes is that they
are healthy and have "clean" bodies. But if we take a close look at the real
world of elite sport, we see a strange mix of healthy bodies alongside physical risk and injury endured by athletes in competition and training.

Not only are the risks often very high — think of sports such as football   7
or downhill skiing — they are encountered in the normal course of athletic
training and competition. Even in what appear to be relatively risk-free
sports such as running, we find constant injury. Pick up any copy of *Runner's
World*, and you'll find articles on overcoming everything from cramps and
"runner's nipple" to iliotibial band syndrome and stress fractures.

During the Tour de France in 1998, American professional cyclist   8
Robert Millar described in graphic detail the physical (and often
unhealthy) hardships endured by elite cyclists in the normal course of
training and competition. Drug use, Mr. Millar implied, is a normal and
necessary part of cyclists' lives. But the issue becomes controversial
largely because of the public's unrealistic expectation that elite athletes be
squeaky clean when their lives are full of risk and injury.

Mr. Millar's comments imply that, if sports organizations such as the   9
IOC really hold the health of athletes to heart, they should ban many sports
in the Olympic program, discourage excessive training regimens, or both.
The contradiction in the health argument is that we willingly accept the so-
called "normal" or "natural" physical risks of high-performance training
and competition but hold up the risks involved with banned substances for
unusual scrutiny. The entire landscape of elite sport will have to look very
different from the current one if we really want it to be healthy and risk-free.

Like health, the fair playing-field argument seems to make intuitive   10
sense, but it does so largely because this "common sense" argument is
rarely discussed. As the argument goes, pop the magic pill and you're automatically propelled a few metres ahead of the competition — hardly a fair
situation. This scenario oversimplifies and misrepresents elite athletic
training and competition.

Elite sport involves a dizzying array of performance-enhancing   11
devices. Various training techniques, diet regimens, the sciences of
coaching, biomechanics, and physiology, the use of advanced technology
and equipment, state and private funding, and so forth represent the reality
of the high-performance athlete package. Banned substances are occasionally one of many such devices used. But it seems to me that athletes' popping the magic pill to gain advantage isn't significantly different from
putting on a new swimsuit to do the same.

12   The interesting question is why drugs are considered to be so unlike these other means of performance enhancement. The new technologically advanced swimsuits used by some Canadian athletes in Sydney (they minimize water resistance) seem as good an example of advantage or "magic pill" as many of the substances and methods on the IOC's banned list.

13   As for the ideals and integrity of sport, this argument is one of the least understood precisely because it is so vague. It is not clear which or whose ideals make up the "integrity" of sport, and a high-performance athlete's ideals might be very different from our own. Certainly sportsmanship and fair play are vital to the integrity of sport, but so, too, is striving to be the very best and pushing the limits of the human body to get there. After all, the Olympic motto is *citius, altius, fortius:* faster, higher, stronger. Doesn't drug use quite naturally support this ideal?

14   I do not condone the use of performance-enhancing substances. As head coach of the women's varsity rowing team at Queen's University, I never encourage athletes to consider such an option. My point, instead, is to suggest that dealing with the issue might require us to think much more rigorously about it. Taking drugs to enhance athletic performance might be wrong, but unfortunately it might be appropriate for the type and level of competition now pursued in international competition. If we want a more humane sporting world—something the modern Olympics founder, Pierre de Coubertin, certainly sought—we might have to move beyond our attempts to catch "cheaters" in sport to the more difficult job of imagining radical new ways in which sport can be practised.

2000

NOTES

Ian Ritchie is an assistant professor in the Department of Physical Education and Kinesiology at Brock University in St. Catharines, Ontario. He teaches and writes about sports history and Olympic drug policies.

Eric Lamaze An equestrian who was banned from competing at the Olympics because of cocaine use.

Iliotibial band syndrome A knee injury.

COMPREHENSION AND DISCUSSION

1. What is Ritchie's thesis? What aspect of drug use in sport is he questioning?
2. What are the three arguments used against the use of drugs in sports? How does Ritchie deal with each argument?
3. What other ways do athletes have of enhancing performance? Are these fair, according to Ritchie?
4. Is Ritchie arguing that athletes should use performance-enhancing drugs?
5. How do we decide what is fair in competition? Where do we draw the line? How do we decide whether taking vitamins is acceptable but taking steroids is not?
6. Eric Lamaze was banned from competition for using cocaine, not for using a performance-enhancing drug. Was that ban justified? Similarly, Ross Rebagliati was initially stripped of his gold medal in snowboarding at the Nagano Olympics because of a positive drug test for marijuana, but he appealed and won back his medal. What should the rules be for illegal drug use by athletes?

LITERARY TECHNIQUES

Essay structure This article follows the essay format: introduction with a clear thesis statement, support and discussion in the body, and a forceful conclusion. Because of the length (approximately 1500 words), the writer could afford a three-paragraph opening in which he sets forth his topic: drugs in sports. As he gives his readers some background on the controversy, he brings the discussion to his thesis: "In other words, using drugs to enhance performance might just make sense" (paragraph 3). Hereafter, in the body of the article, Ritchie reviews and deflates the common arguments as he asserts his reasons. Finally, in his one-paragraph conclusion, he recaps his thesis: "If we want a more humane sporting world . . . we might have to move beyond our attempts to catch 'cheaters' in sport to the more difficult job of imagining radical new ways in which sport can be practised" (paragraph 14).

Formal tone Often the writing situation dictates the tone and style of expressing ideas. Usually in government, business, and academic settings, letters, reports, and essays are in more formal language. That is, the choice of words and the expression of thought are more precise, more objective, and more proper than, say, those found in e-mail or popular magazine articles. Often the second-person "you" is sparingly used; even the first-person singular "I" is inserted with care to state an opinion contrary to that of the populace, or to emphasize a point. For example, near the end of the essay, Ritchie emphasizes, "I do not condone the use of performance-enhancing substances" (paragraph 14). In addition, the diction (or word choice) elevates the expression; for example, "The drug stories are always punctuated with the same themes" (paragraph 2).

Use of qualifiers Note how Ritchie uses the word "might" to qualify his statements. He wants us to consider the issues, but he is not arguing that drug use in sports is good. Modal verbs such as "might," "could," and "may" show possibility and probability, toning down a statement from absolute fact.

ASSIGNMENTS

1. Read a different viewpoint on drugs in sports in Richard Pound's "'Never Give In, Never'" (p. 313). Evaluate the arguments that both authors make. Who has the stronger arguments? Which essay is more effective? Write a paragraph supporting your opinion.
2. Research one of the methods used for enhancing athletic performance (such as steroids or blood doping), and write a report on its use and testing history.
3. Find out more about Eric Lamaze and Ross Rebagliati, and write an essay on whether or not drugs such as marijuana and cocaine should be considered in the same league as drugs such as steroids for athletes.
4. Write an essay that expresses your opinion on a controversial issue concerning drugs. For instance, should testing of athletes be abandoned since it is not always successful? How far should mandatory drug testing of employees be extended? Should marijuana be decriminalized?

The Story of Grey Owl
Colin Ross

Once upon a time there was a pervert called Grey Owl, who lived in the 1
Canadian woods. He is famous because he came to Canada and learned
how to imitate the Indians—he wore a disguise and grew his hair long.
The white people in Canada know so little about Indians, and about their
own woods, that Grey Owl fooled them all for a long time. But even after
they found out that the famous Indian was really only Archie Belaney from
England, even then they still respected him. Canadians have so few heroes
that they decided to have Archie Belaney for a hero—they said to themselves, "Old Archie sure fooled us, didn't he? What a great man he was, to
be able to fool us all, and live like an Indian."

Archie was only like an Indian on the outside though. That's why the 2
Canadians liked him, and made him a hero. They wanted to have a hero who
played little boy's games in the woods, and made friends with animals just
like in a story book. Canadians don't like Indians, on the outside or on the
inside. That's why they like Archie so well, and still do—they know that
he's just a pleasant Englishman on the inside, just like them. When they
know that, then they can love his Indian clothes and his Indian canoe, and
even think that maybe his Indian life is very beautiful. When it's only harmless old Archie Belaney inside that Indian costume, then the Canadian ladies
have nothing to be afraid of. Why *there's* an Indian who would just *love* to
talk to them, and tell them about his friendly animal pets in the woods.

The Canadian ladies may live in Canada, but they don't like Canada— 3
they don't like the cold, they don't like the bears, they don't like the lonely
prairies, they don't like the forest. They're afraid of all those things
and places. They don't have to be afraid of Archie Belaney—he writes
nice books for them, that sound just like Henry Williamson, and other nice
Englishmen who love nature. Archie Belaney had a very big heart, not like
Indians—if the Canadian ladies ever tried to talk to an Indian, that Indian's
heart wouldn't like them. They wouldn't like the Indian either.

All the Canadians are very grateful to Archie Belaney. His books are 4
such a relief for them. When they read his books then they're not afraid of
nature anymore—Archie makes them feel that nature is tame and friendly
and safe. The only difference between Archie's life in the woods and Mrs.
Smith's life in the city is that Archie has beavers for pets. Mrs. Smith, and
her neighbour Mrs. MacKenzie, both keep budgies. The Canadian ladies
are *very* grateful to Archie for keeping beavers for pets. Beavers seem like

the best symbol Canada could have, when you think of Archie Belaney's friendly pets. All those Indians care about is killing the poor beavers, and selling their skins.

5   "Yes sir, those Indians are awful," says Mrs. MacKenzie. "Why if they came to our city they'd probably eat my budgies. Those poor friendly beavers and rabbits that live in our beautiful forests, the Indians hunt and kill them. And Indians never write lovely books like Grey Owl does. Isn't it a shame that they never learned how to write!"

6   "Quite a shame," says one of the ladies.

7   "Yes," says Mrs. Smith. "You know, we should form a club to help those poor Indians. They have no books and no shoes, and all they ever eat is rabbits and wild things. We should help them. It's a shame. They're people too you know, just like us. Let's gather up some money and give it to the Indians to buy food and clothes. It would be *such* a good thing to do."

8   "Very good," says another one of the ladies.

9   The bridge party was at Mrs. MacKenzie's house that day. Mr. MacKenzie wasn't feeling well so he was at home. Mr. MacKenzie is a fireman. Mr. MacKenzie was serving the ladies tea and cakes—he had gotten up too early to bake them.

10   Mr. MacKenzie is very proud of being a Canadian man. He's very tough. He fights fires in the city, and in the fall he takes his holidays and goes hunting just like an Indian. Just like Grey Owl. Mr. MacKenzie spoke up and said, "The Indians were good people. They only killed the friendly animals in the woods because they needed them for food and clothes. They couldn't let their children go hungry. The Indians were good people, and very good hunters. They just weren't very smart, that's all—they weren't quite as high up as we are in the family tree of man." Mr. MacKenzie was talking to his wife, explaining about Indians to her. All the other ladies were listening.

11   "As a matter of fact," continued Mr. MacKenzie, "we're at the top. Yes, ladies, it's true. Now if the Indians had been able to build cars and houses like us, then I'm sure they wouldn't have killed so many of the poor animals in nature. They would have loved them just like you love your budgies."

12   The ladies knew Mr. MacKenzie was a very good fireman, and they listened to what he said with a great deal of respect. Mrs. MacKenzie knew her husband went hunting in the fall though. She didn't like the poor dead wild animals he brought back, and she wondered how he could ever bring himself to pull the trigger. But Mr. Mackenzie is so tough and strong that he still has hunting instincts just like a real Indian. Just like Grey Owl. You

can't expect him to stop hunting just because of the Canadian ladies. After all Mr. MacKenzie loves nature in his own way, and who is Mrs. MacKenzie to say his way is wrong?

The Canadian ladies are *very* grateful to Archie Belaney. They had   13
some bad feelings about nature, and about Indians, but after they read his books they felt all right. The bad feelings went away. After the Canadian ladies read Archie's books they felt that the woods and the Indians were safe and friendly after all. And Archie Belaney was so concerned about his animal friends he went *all* the way to England, just to talk about them. Wasn't that a great thing for Canada!

Mr. MacKenzie doesn't have much time for books. But his wife and   14
the other ladies have said such nice things about Grey Owl that *he* admires Grey Owl too. Mr. MacKenzie would never call Grey Owl just old Archie Belaney. If he did that then his wife's bad feelings about Indians might come back. That wouldn't be nice.

Mr. MacKenzie and his friends were so grateful to Archie for making   15
the bad feelings go away that they got together. They made Archie into a hero, and promised never to call him anything but Grey Owl. If they called him just old Archie Belaney, then he might seem like just another Englishman.

Yes, it was a good day for Canada when Archie Belaney came over   16
here and started pretending to be an Indian. There was quite a mystery to his life you know, not like the Indians, who just sneak around in the woods in a bad mood killing things. Let me show you what a nice guy Archie was — here's some of his writing. This is from his wonderful book which he called *Tales from an Empty Cabin:*

> There was a wood-chuck, a special chum of mine, who year after year made her home under the upper cabin, where she had every Spring a brood of wood-chucklets, or whatever they are called. She was an amiable old lady, who used often to watch me at my work and allowed me a number of privileges, including the rare one of handling her young ones. But if a stranger came, she would spread herself out so as to quite fill the entrance to her domicile, to keep the youngsters in, and when the stranger left she would emit a shrill whistling sound at his retreating back, very sure that she had frightened him away. She too has gone, her time fulfilled, and another has taken over her old home; a well-built, very trim young matron who stands up straight and very soldierly before her doorway and tries to look in windows.

17   Old Archie sure was a tame Indian wasn't he. *Isn't* Mrs. Smith grateful for that? When Archie Belaney left his three aunts in England and came over to Canada Mrs. Smith really felt good. She loved nature then. "Good!" she thought to herself. Mr. Smith and Mr. MacKenzie were so grateful they gave Archie a place to live in a special park, and paid him for the rest of his life to keep on playing games with animals. They never paid any real Indians.

18   When Archie writes a book, he writes just like an Englishman. That's the nicest way. He makes the woodchucks sound just like the ladies who read his books. Archie Belaney dressed up like an Indian and pretended to be one himself. The Canadian ladies loved him for that. But inside Archie was all the time an Englishman who called the woodchucks his chums. Archie had lots of friends. Some had feathers. Some had fur. Some wore hats to church. They were all one big happy family, Archie and Mr. Smith, and Mrs. Smith, and Mr. MacKenzie, and his wife, and Mrs. Woodchuck, and her woodchucklets. Archie sure had a nice time in nature. Wouldn't it be beautiful to live like an Indian too?

19   Indians are really very lovable people. If Mr. MacKenzie was an Indian he would be able to say wonderful things about nature too. Just like Archie and Geronimo. Archie Belaney was brought up by his three aunts in England. This was bad for little Archie — there were too many ladies around all the time. So when Archie got the chance he decided he'd *really* show his aunts he didn't need them. He'd go over to Canada and be a wild Indian, and no aunties would tell *him* what to do. Archie Belaney was one guy who sure was tough. He didn't need a bunch of aunties to take care of *him*. He was a wild Indian who lived by himself in nature and showed everybody. After he showed them real good, he came back to England.

20   Yes, Archie came back to England as an Indian, and gave speeches and went to dinners. He even went to dinner with that white man the King, and he sure didn't show him any respect. How could you expect a wild Indian to stand up when the King walked in the room? Boy, Archie really showed his aunts that time, when he went back to England.

21   Even when Archie was a little boy in England he used to play at being an Indian. But he couldn't play Indians in England and still live with his aunts when he was thirty or forty. Everyone would laugh at him. Archie was smart. He went over to Canada and played at being an Indian over there. No one laughed at him in Canada; in fact he fooled them all and played the game for the rest of his life. Trouble was, he wasn't really an Indian on the inside. Inside Archie Belaney was an Englishman who got lonely for his aunts. What do you think he did? Well, he made friends with

all the animals, then he never got lonely again, not for the rest of his life. When he wrote about his animal friends, in his books, he used words like "domicile," "chum," "youngsters," "matron," and maybe even "auntie."

The Canadian ladies are *very* grateful. They were worried about living in this country. But Archie helped them. He wrote books, and in his books he showed the Canadian ladies that all the wild animals are really just as warm and friendly as an aunt or a grandma. Wasn't that wonderful! Mr. MacKenzie and Mrs. Smith were grateful too. All the Canadian people loved Archie Belaney for doing this great thing, and promised *never* to call him anything but Grey Owl. And that's just what they did.

22

1979

NOTES

Indians A term referring to the Native peoples of North America. In Canada, we usually use the terms "Native," "First Nations peoples" or "Aboriginal Canadians."

Geronimo (1829 – 1909) A legendary Apache who fought against the U.S. cavalry.

COMPREHENSION AND DISCUSSION

1. How does the word "pervert" in the opening sentence set the tone of the article?
2. Why does Ross address Archie Belaney as "Archie" rather than the formal family name "Belaney" throughout?
3. How does Ross denigrate Grey Owl's achievements?
4. Show how, according to Ross, Archie Belaney won over the white middle-class Canadians of the 1930s.
5. How much of the mockery is directed at Canadians rather than at Archie Belaney/Grey Owl?
6. How does Ross, in the dialogues, reflect white Canadians' underlying prejudice toward Native peoples?
7. How does Ross show the tone of condescension (patronizing, superior attitude) of Mr. and Mrs. MacKenzie and Mrs. Smith?
8. Why doesn't Ross admire Archie Belaney/Grey Owl?
9. What do you think Ross's ethnic background is? Why do you think so?

LITERARY TECHNIQUES

Satire A biting commentary or analysis that ridicules or mocks a person, institution, idea, or thing. Satirists use exaggeration, innuendo, sarcasm, invective, and inversion to draw attention to the subject's flaws. Often satire attempts to bring about change or conformity through wit and humour.

"Just like" Note the mocking tone in this comparison: "[Mr. MacKenzie] fights fires in the city, and in the fall he takes his holidays and goes hunting just like an Indian. Just like Grey Owl" (paragraph 10).

Fairy-tale opening, "once upon a time" Ross wants to accomplish a number of things here. The fairy-tale opening creates a sense of unreality (which is undercut and contradicted by the real-life Archie Belaney). It permits Ross to use simplistic language and a sarcastic tone at the same time. It also lets Ross blend fact and fiction.

Composite characters Ross creates fictitious persons such as the Mac-Kenzies and Smiths in order to give a concrete basis to a general statement; that is, these people represent a major portion of white Canadians of the time. This technique is legitimate for this article because the writer focuses on exposing attitudes more than real people (other than Archie Belaney).

ASSIGNMENTS

1. Read the other two articles about Grey Owl: John Barber's "Grey Owl's Magnificent Masquerade" (p. 232) and Brian Bethune's "Truth and Consequences" (p. 236). Which essay is the most effective of the three? Which did you enjoy the most? Explain.
2. All three articles mention the writing style of Grey Owl's books. Ross gives you a sample. Explain how the writing style betrays the writer, showing that he could not possibly be who he says he is. Search out more samples of his writing.
3. Explain the techniques Ross uses to ridicule Grey Owl and the people who believed in him.
4. Ross mocks the attitudes of 1930s white Canadians. Have attitudes changed since then?
5. Using Pico Iyer's definitions in "Of Weirdos and Eccentrics" (p. 282), to which category would Archie Belaney belong according to Ross?
6. Read Stephen Leacock's "How We Kept Mother's Day" (p. 142). How is the mockery similar to or different from Ross's?

7. Appropriation of voice is a controversial issue in literature. For example, some people say that a white author should not write about the experience of non-whites. A famous recent example is the novel *Memoirs of a Geisha*, which is told in the first person by the author, Arthur Golden, who is neither female nor Japanese. Discuss the issue in an essay.

Are Goody Bags a Good Thing?
Rita Sirignano

1 First they get a star just for going No. 2 in the toilet.

2 Then there's the goody bag thing. Forgive me if I sound like your cranky grandmother for a moment but, in my day, you went to a birthday party, handed the birthday boy or girl their gift, ate a piece of cake usually made from a box mix, played a round of Pin the Tail on the Donkey, and went on your merry way, lucky if the kid's mother handed you a limp balloon on your way out the door. (Which you then happily tied on your wrist and refused to take off, even in the bathtub, until it met its end when your evil little brother snuck up and popped it with a thumbtack.)

3 Well, those days have gone the way of the rotary telephone.

4 In today's world, along with the birthday cake purchased at the Belgian *patisserie*, the hired magicians and clowns, pool parties catered by McDonald's, and Bonkers and Chuck E. Cheese franchises — which if Dante were alive today he'd surely have included in an inner ring of hell — the little party guests have to get something, too. And I'm not talkin' a candy necklace and a few sticks of gum in a brown paper lunch sack decorated with glitter. (I learned my lesson with that one. "That's all?" one sniffing child actually had the gall to inquire, after I handed him a bag miserably deficient in loot.)

5 There's actually an industry devoted to the bags themselves, (Pokémon, Digimon, Hello Kitty, Sailor Moon, *Jurassic Park*, *101 Dalmations*, etc.), not to mention what goes inside them: stickers, tattoos, Silly Putty, Bubbles, gel pens, superballs, lollipops with batteries in the stick to make them spin, disposable cameras. It's not difficult to drop a $20 per guest; my kids have received goody bags the contents of which were worth more than the price of the gift they brought. One friend's son went to a party where every kid got a remote-controlled car from Radio Shack. Another told me of a party her daughter attended where the girls all got gift certificates for makeovers at Merle Norman. I'm waiting for the day they hand out passes to Disneyworld.

6 Whatever happened to the concept of the birthday being a special day — special being the operative word — for the person who was *born on that day*? People came to the party to fete you. You, in turn, feted them on their birthday. No, now everything is *me too, me too*. God forbid someone feel left out, dejected that another is getting slightly more attention than they are; that a six-year-old might have to learn an iota of self-control: *"It's not your turn, Brittany."*

This same concept is behind the idea that one should get a trophy at the 7
end of six weeks of soccer just for showing up at least once for practice. I
have two boys, and 3,000 trophies in our basement. And my kids are both
still in grade school. Someday I will rent a small U-haul, back it up to the
basement door, load it up, and drive said trophies to the outskirts of town,
where they will join the 400 billion others at the trophy landfill, sharing
space with *Most Improved Three Year Old* and *Best Left-Handed First
Baseman Born in February.*

These children then grow up, and demand recognition just for getting 8
up in the morning—forget about making the bed.

What started my wool-gathering on this topic was the relentless media 9
coverage of the annual award season we are currently in the midst of.
Emmys, Tonys, Oscars, Genies, Obies, Grammys, Junos, Golden Globes,
SAGS, GLADS, the People's Choice Awards, the TV Guide Awards, blah,
blah, blah. The entertainment industry gave out 3,182 awards last year,
according to *Los Angeles Magazine.* My favourite hands-down was the
Teen Choice Award's *Best Hissy Fit in a Movie*—for which the winner
received a surfboard. Wasn't getting paid to throw a tantrum—something
that couldn't have required a great stretch of thespian ability, given that the
actor, and I use the term loosely, surely had lots of practice throwing fits
throughout childhood, especially when they didn't like the goody bag they
got—enough? Where will it end?

But, more importantly, which child psychologist is responsible for the 10
theory that prizes for all promotes good self-esteem? Isn't self-esteem
acquired when you actually *earn* something? I imagine the young psychologist, still in graduate school, reading in a biography of Hitler the conjecture that the germ of the Fuhrer's hatred of the Jews was planted when
the painting he entered in an art contest didn't win a prize. (The judge was
Jewish.) Light bulb goes off in young psychologist's head: "Give 'em all a
prize or we might create a monster!" Young psychologist writes bestseller,
Everybody Wins! Developing and Protecting Your Child's Fragile Ego, and
is now a consultant to the entertainment industry.

I want that psychologist's head on a platter. Or, alternatively, I want 11
him sentenced to 24 hours' community service at Bonkers, to be served
consecutively, with only two potty breaks and no Advil.

2001

NOTES

Rita Sirignano is a Calgary-based visual artist and writer.

Dante Alighieri (1265–1321) Italian poet famous for his work the *Divina Commedia*, composed in three parts: Paradiso, Purgatorio, and Inferno. This Christian allegory has had great influence on Western literature since its publication. Dante's Inferno is the most common reference; his "inner ring of hell" was reserved for the worst criminals.

COMPREHENSION AND DISCUSSION

1. Explain Sirignano's criticism of children's birthday parties.
2. What is the purpose of a birthday party? Compare it to other social events. Is there justification for the goody bag?
3. Sirignano uses the point about birthday parties to support her thesis of what is a wider problem in society. What is her general criticism of society?
4. How do trophies and award shows contribute to this problem?
5. Why is it hard to stop such a custom as giving elaborate goody bags at birthday parties?
6. Explain in your own words: "I imagine the young psychologist, still in graduate school, reading in a biography of Hitler the conjecture that the germ of the Fuhrer's hatred of the Jews was planted when the painting he entered in an art contest didn't win a prize" (paragraph 10).
7. Does our society offer too many rewards? Defend your opinion.
8. Is the proverb "'Tis better to give than to receive" valid in today's culture?
9. Do today's parents spoil their children?
10. What kind of "goody bags" and bonuses do adults receive today? For instance, celebrity presenters at award shows get gift baskets containing thousands of dollars' worth of gifts. Are these necessary and warranted?

LITERARY TECHNIQUES

Rant A rant can be either spoken or written. It is a personal venting of outrage or indignation at a particular subject. Like satire, a rant mocks and ridicules; unlike satire, the rant argues in a logical pattern. Note how Sirignano is fed up with "goody bags" and her tone is sarcastic.

ASSIGNMENTS

1. In the 1980s, it was felt that teachers needed to improve children's self-esteem. There was a big push in schools for such actions as offering smiley-face stickers for effort. This has led to such phenomena as students demanding high marks despite their poor achievement. Debate the pros and cons of self-esteem programs.

2. Some psychologists argue that North American society has gone too far with the emphasis on self-esteem. Excessive self-esteem leads to narcissism, a belief that one is the centre of the universe, and an over-estimation of one's abilities. We can see this in auditions for talent shows such as *Canadian Idol*, in which supremely untalented contestants cannot accept the verdict of the judges. Write a research essay exploring the causes and/or effects of excessive self-esteem.

3. Consider Sirignano's argument along with Margaret Wente's "If We're So Rich, Why Aren't We Happy?" (p. 342), Judith Timson's "Pet-o-philia" (p. 338), and Donna Kerrigan's "Mess Up Your Kid's Education in 10 Easy Steps" (p. 287). What criticism of modern society do they all echo?

4. Research the northwest Aboriginal custom of potlatch. In an essay, summarize the custom and explain how relevant it is to goody bags given out at children's birthday parties.

5. Write a point-by-point counterargument to Sirignano's essay.

6. Implicit in Sirignano's rant is a complaint that big business has a hand in promoting consumerism in children through the goody bag. For instance, spending on Halloween has multiplied in the last twenty years. What other holidays and events have been tainted by consumerism? Choose a holiday or event and write an essay examining the good and bad effects of such spending.

Pet-o-philia

Judith Timson

1   One day after my husband took our dog out for a walk, I received a phone call from a strange woman. "Hi, I just ran into your husband with your dog. I'm calling to find out who the breeder is." "Of my husband or the dog?" I inquired tartly.

2   That's the kind of neighbourhood we live in — dog crazy — and the kind of dog we have — adorable. Lucy, our oftentimes shaggy black cock-apoo (a cross between a cocker spaniel and a poodle), is almost eight now; but because of a tail that never stops wagging, an irrepressible spring in her step and the fact that she proudly carries in her mouth a big yellow Frisbee almost the size of her head, she easily passes as a puppy.

3   Lucy is everything good a dog could possibly be to our family — companion, cuddler, personal trainer (without her we wouldn't walk around the park) and instant mood elevator. It is hard to maintain either a teenage sulk or an adult funk with Lucy on your case.

4   I always thought we loved our dog. But lately, I've wondered if we don't love our pet with quite the same intensity as other people love theirs.

5   Today, pets are no longer just wonderful additions to people's lives. They *are* their lives. People refer to their dogs as their "kids" and are often introduced as "Bismarck's dad" or "Brandy's mom." In many neighbourhoods there are long-simmering conflicts between dog people who want to let their pets roam free and people people. The strangest incident I read about concerned a child terrified by a big dog bearing down, a frantic parent and a dog owner who actually shouted, "Don't yell! It upsets the dog."

6   Socially, otherwise sophisticated people turn up for dinners at golf clubs with their dogs in tow; not only will they not let them languish alone for an evening, they won't even vacation without them.

7   In a billion-dollar pet industry, besotted owners fork over millions for everything from designer dog dishes to Irish knit sweaters to gourmet foods. There is even a "doggy delight" cooking course that invites you to "treat your four-legged companion like the special person he is" by concocting such culinary delights as "pupsicles."

8   There are pets who undergo cosmetic surgery or acupuncture and pet owners who spend thousands to save the lives of seriously ill dogs and cats — up to $15,000 in one case to operate on a blind cat with terminal kidney disease. It's not only the wealthy, it's also the financially stretched who decide to do everything to keep their pets alive, regardless of the

animals' quality of life. Yet, I wonder whose quality of life is really being maintained. Some of this fervour seems way beyond the bounds of mere animal love. I'd even call it pet-o-philia—excessive love of one's pets. It is a troubling narcissistic trend: the me generation has now become the me-and-my-dog generation.

We live in a society in which child poverty is growing, but dogs get 9
gourmet biscuits, a world where urban dwellers keep huge farm-size dogs in tiny city houses and then pay other people to walk them because they are too busy, where deluxe resorts advertise "pet cabanas." (Maybe I could go as someone's pet—a cabana sounds fabulous to me.) Humane societies refuse to put down even the most difficult dangerous dogs. Is this animal activism or animal supremacy?

I wonder what this says about us emotionally. Divorce is rampant these 10
days (and by the way, doggy custody battles are growing,) loneliness is epidemic, and for many people, pets have become the emotional partner of choice. According to research, most North Americans tell their pets frequently—out loud—that they love them (and yes, I have been known to murmur endearments at both Lucy and our far more autocratic cat, Jesse).

But however much I may whisper sweet blandishments in a furry ear, 11
however much my heart aches for people dealing with the loss of their beloved pets, however much I dread facing that time myself, my priority remains people over pets.

Animals are not humans; your pets are not your children. They 12
shouldn't, to my mind, have the same civil liberties, designer sweaters or medical intervention as humans. Turning our pets into objects of lifestyle pampering and enmeshed affection robs them of something far more valuable than it gives them. My dog has more dignity as a dog than she ever will as a quasi-human. If that conviction puts me at the back of the pack, so be it.

2004

NOTES

Judith Timson writes for *Chatelaine* magazine.

The title is a made-up word based on a Greek word for love. English words ending in "-philia" or "-phile" mean "a love for" or "a lover of," respectively. For example, an anglophile loves all things English, while an audiophile loves sound and music and therefore has an elaborate sound system.

This suffix can also refer to an excessive or improper love, as in the word "pedophile," which is used for a child molester. Timson has used the model of these other words to coin a word meaning excessive love for pets.

COMPREHENSION AND DISCUSSION

1. What is Timson's thesis (main argument)?
2. What else could a cross between a cocker spaniel and a poodle be called? Do you think "cockapoo" is a good name?
3. Why do some people treat their animals as if they were their children? Is there anything wrong with this attitude?
4. Timson calls the trend to excessive animal love "narcissistic" (paragraph 8). What do you think Timson means? Is this a good word to describe it?
5. Paraphrase and explain this sentence: "Turning our pets into objects of lifestyle pampering and enmeshed affection robs them of something far more valuable than it gives them" (paragraph 12).
6. Do North Americans pamper their pets too much? Why or why not?
7. What do you think is reasonable spending for a pet? Where would you draw the line?
8. Many people choose to keep an animal despite allergies in the family. Is human health more important than keeping a pet? Explain your opinion.
9. When should an animal be put down? Should dogs who have attacked humans be rehabilitated and released from the humane society? Should people spend thousands of dollars on surgery to prolong their pet's life? Should an aging or ill pet be put to sleep?

LITERARY TECHNIQUES

Coining terminology Writers often make up new words. The word "pet-o-philia" is Timson's creation. New words cannot be any combination of letters — they work on patterns familiar to the reader. In this case, the word builds on the Greek suffix "-philia." The use of hyphens makes the root word "pet" clear to the reader and emphasizes that the word is made up.

Parallelism Parallel structure is balance. It can be done in a sentence in which a series of items or grammatically similar phrases are given equal weight. It can be done in consecutive sentences or paragraphs. It can be quite effective as an organizing principle in writing. For example, Timson writes: "But however much I may whisper sweet blandishments in a furry ear, however much my heart aches for people dealing with the loss of their beloved pets, however much I dread facing that time myself, my priority remains people over pets" (paragraph 11). The repetition of "however much" creates a serial effect, and given that each "however much" clause is incomplete until the principal clause is stated in the end, the writer achieves not only parallel structure but also a climactic ordering of ideas.

ASSIGNMENTS

1. Compare this article with Margaret Wente's "If We're So Rich, Why Aren't We Happy?" (p. 342). How are the two writers' arguments similar?

2. Compare the treatment of working animals, such as the elephant in George Orwell's "Shooting an Elephant" (p. 305) with pampered pets as described in Timson's article.

3. Using your dictionary and the Internet, make a list of other English words that contain the Greek root "phil" and write down the definitions. Here's a list of words to look up to get you started: bibliophile, cinephile, Philadelphia, philanthropist, philosophy, Sinophile.

4. Look up more information about the cockapoo (or other common breeds of dogs) and write a report on the dog's suitability as a pet.

5. Pets have been used for therapy in seniors' homes and prisons. Research this subject and write a report, or give a report as an oral presentation.

6. Write an essay, give a report, or have a debate on one of the many animal rights and pet issues. For instance, should animals be used for medical research? What leash and cleanup laws should there be and how should they be enforced?

7. How do cultures other than North America treat pets and domestic animals? Do some research on this topic. Write an essay supporting the philosophy you prefer.

If We're So Rich, Why Aren't We Happy?

Margaret Wente

1   If John Roth had wanted a better forecast of Nortel's business prospects, he could have just called me. I am what economists call one of your leading indicators. Eight or 10 months in advance of each recession, it's my habit to take a plunge on real estate—a house, a reno, a better house, etc. Several months ago, with a certain Shakespearean inevitability, my spouse and I made the ultimate useless acquisition—a piece of country property.

2   Who needs 50 acres of buckthorn with a view? Nobody. But that didn't stop us. Financial freedom could have been ours. Instead, like good modern consumers, we have chosen to live on the knife-edge of anxiety and desire.

3   Once upon a time, I used to think how pleasant life would be after I had acquired all of its necessities. Once upon a time, I thought that once I had the house, the car, the stereo and maybe just one simple pair of Manolos, I would stop spending money and be content. And if I had any money left over, I would give it to poor people.

4   That day has never come.

5   I've learned that Abraham Maslow got it wrong. The eminent psychologist thought that once we satisfied our basic need for food, clothing and shelter, we would seek a higher happiness through art, human fellowship and the life of the mind. Spiritual transcendence would be the ultimate payoff of prosperity. But it hasn't worked out that way. Instead, everyone would rather go shopping.

6   When my husband was a newborn (not so long ago), his parents took him home to their tiny one-room flat and put him in a dresser drawer to sleep. They had no car and no TV and no vacations in Florida, never mind a foreign nanny or a padded stroller or funny little outfits from Baby Gap. But they didn't mind. Neither did anyone else. They never even knew they were poor. Today, their neighbours would accuse them of child neglect.

7   Our unending lust for stuff is also known as the "upscaling of lifestyle norms." It means that your desires increase in lockstep with the earnings curve. Upscaling is why you need a digital camera and a high-speed Internet line, granite countertops, an SUV with leather seats, cellphones for the kids, and lots of other essential items that hadn't been invented 10 years ago. Acquiring and servicing these things is stressful. Therefore, you will also

require various stress-relieving activities (winter cruise, massage therapy) as an antidote to the stressed-out, busy life you lead. If your neighbours have these things and you don't, you will feel even more stressed out.

People on the left say the consumption spiral is a vice. It shows that we are merely slaves to materialistic capitalism and the empty lifestyle promises of Coke and Nike.   8

People on the right say the consumption spiral is a virtue. It demonstrates the glorious triumph of the market system, which now offers consumers an infinite array of choice. The hearts of economists soar when we are confident, and sink when we are not. So long as we keep consuming, there will be no crash, and Nortel will recover, and the factories will stay open, and we'll keep our jobs. According to them, consumption is not just a personal pleasure but a national, even global, necessity.   9

But what about the people in the middle, the ones with the maxed-out credit cards? Does all this stuff really make us happier?   10

I'm sorry to say the answer is no. The happiness experts (yes, such people exist) claim that probably you're no happier than your grandparents were. Just the opposite. The postwar prosperity boom has delivered an epidemic of depression in all the Western nations. Are you blue? You've got lots of company. Canadians go to the doctor for depression more than for any ailment except high blood pressure. The pharmaceutical industry is making billions inventing new psychotropic drugs and SSRI uptake inhibitors to cheer us up. Sometimes, shopping cheers us up, too, but not for long.   11

There's another explanation for why we keep consuming. It's hardwired into us. We have evolved as highly hierarchical, status-seeking animals. Consumption and display are the surest sign of status and class, and social status is essential to our sense of self. The more we have, the more we have to get to keep up with everybody else. Like low-status monkeys, low-status humans suffer terribly.   12

Which brings me back to our completely useless piece of country acreage. It's ours now, and so it needs a house. A simple house. The house needs a kitchen and the kitchen needs a sink. The sink it needs is an authentic reproduction old-time country sink from Ginger's. It costs $645. It comes with authentic reproduction country taps (a few hundred more). It is a fine sink. Only weeks ago, I had no idea that such a sink existed, and now I have to have one.   13

Is this desire a virtue, or a vice? Is it an empty way to assuage the anomie of modern life? Is it a confirmation of my taste and style, or just a   14 signal of my social standing, like the rump display of the mandrills and baboons?

15   I have no idea.

16   Will it make me happy?

17   Of course it will. Until I see a better one.

2001

NOTES

Margaret Wente is a columnist for *The Globe and Mail*. She was born in the United States and tells the story of her move to Canada in her book *An Accidental Canadian* (2004).

John Roth Former CEO of Nortel, a once-successful Canadian technology company that experienced a dramatic reversal of fortune in 2001.

Manolos Expensive stiletto shoes by designer Manolo Blahnik.

Abraham Maslow (1908–1970) A psychologist famous for his hierarchy of needs (physiological, safety, social, ego, and self-fulfillment). Wente summarizes Maslow's theory.

COMPREHENSION AND DISCUSSION

1. What point is Wente making in her opening paragraph? Is it effective?
2. Why does Wente think that Maslow's theory about human needs is wrong?
3. How were people two or three generations ago different from people today?
4. Explain the irony in Wente's statements: "They never even knew they were poor" (paragraph 6) and "lots of other essential items that hadn't been invented 10 years ago" (paragraph 7).
5. What does Wente mean when she says that "desires increase in lockstep with the earnings curve" (paragraph 7)?
6. Explain the difference between the two political views (left vs. right) on consumption.
7. What is the connection between consumption and status?
8. Are North Americans too materialistic? Explain your views.
9. What do people need to be happy? Is happiness a commodity that can be bought?

10. What do you need to be happy?

LITERARY TECHNIQUES

Presenting both sides of an argument Controversial issues often have two basic sides even though people do not neatly fall into one camp or another. One of the basic divisions is left wing (socialist) versus right wing (conservative). Wente achieves balance by presenting both views on the economic issue of consumption. Note that essay writers use phrases such as "people say" to present viewpoints other than their own and to distance themselves from that argument.

"Once upon a time" Writers may use "once upon a time"—the traditional phrase that begins a fairy tale—to evoke a simpler, happier past and contrast it with the harsh, complicated reality of present-day life. Wente uses the phrase twice (paragraph 3) to show how naïve her earlier thoughts were.

ASSIGNMENTS

1. In "Pet-o-philia," Judith Timson (p. 338) talks about excessive spending on pets. How does what Timson says overlap with what Wente says? Compare the two articles.
2. Wente states that having and needing more material goods do not make people happy. Does having only the basics or very little material wealth make people happy? What are the basic needs of humans in our society? Write an essay explaining your response.
3. Write a personal essay about what would make you happy and what you are doing to achieve that happiness.
4. "Potlatch" is an old Haida custom whereby a host of a party gave away as much material wealth as possible to his guests. Members of the tribe often had competitions to see who could give away the most. That person then gained social status and the respect of the community. Speculate about what kind of society we would have if we adopted such a tradition.

Rediscovering Christmas
Almas Zakiuddin

1 It was my first winter in Toronto and so cold it froze the frown on my face. I frowned a lot in those days, before I rediscovered Christmas. Of course, I always knew about Christmas. I had read about it, even seen people celebrate Christmas. I was a typical convent-school-English-educated South Asian, brought up in a family that combined Muslim postcolonial nationalism with heady tales of the good old British Raj. Which meant that we used knives and forks at the table, but said our *isha* prayers before sitting down to dinner. I was (and still am) a Muslim.

2 Before I came to Canada, I was under the impression that I was not supposed to celebrate Christmas; it was not the done thing. I told no one, certainly not my parents, but once in a while I used to wonder: What if I had been born in a family that celebrated Christmas? Like the family of (let's call her) Jennifer McDonald.

3 I was 15 years old, a plump, pimply day student at a convent school for girls in Karachi, Pakistan. Jennifer McDonald was that kind of person known as an "anglo," of mixed South Asian–British ancestry. She had golden-tan skin, light brown curly hair and hazel eyes. She wore lipstick (my mother said only "fast" girls wore lipstick), a skin-tight beige skirt, and an even tighter white blouse to school. I was made to wear a loose beige tunic, with baggy trousers called a *shalwar* and a white scarf.

4 Jennifer McDonald appeared at our end-of-term charity bazaar in the school gym in this incredible, short, fluffy, pink dress with frills that swished when she moved. She flounced to the centre of the room, tossed her curls, crossed her legs. "So what're yoa'll doin' fer Christmas, men?" she asked. ("Men" was a favourite term of endearment among anglos.) "I'm gonna have a bloody good time!" she laughed. ("Bloody" was another favourite anglo term.)

5 It was almost four decades later that I thought again about Jennifer McDonald. I was in a different country, almost a different civilization.

6 "And what are you doing for Christmas then?" asked the young woman at the corner store near my subway stop in Toronto. If I looked up in surprise it was because the young woman had not said a word to me in the six weeks I had been patronizing her store. "Oh, Christmas...? I don't know really. I'm...uh..." I mumbled, unsure of my plans. Someone wanted a jar of honey from the top shelf and the young woman disap-

peared. I wasn't sure why she had asked about my Christmas plans: It might have been because she wanted to be friendly.

It occurred to me, then, that people in Canada change during   7 Christmas, becoming almost friendly. I mean, they talk to strangers, even smile at them, occasionally. All this in spite of the cold, the wind-chill factor (minus 24 that evening), and the reality that I was yet another addition to the swelling ranks of hyphenated, multicultural Canada.

In the next week or so, I found myself experiencing a different kind of   8 Canada. There were new sounds, new sights, new smells, and new flavours, and they all connected, somehow, with Christmas. There were lights everywhere, there was mistletoe, decorations, tiny marzipan angels, tinsel. There were stockings waiting to be filled and red bows for doorways, and a bright costume for the old man, Father Christmas, Santa Claus. There was an air of fun that had not existed before. Neighbours appeared where none had been noticeable before, inviting me into their homes, showing me their lights, their decorations, their preparations. I went and got my own lights and spent a weekend doing up my front window — my tiny apartment looked quite festive when they were on.

As the holiday season progressed, I watched the people around me, of   9 all ages and backgrounds, people at the parties to which I was invited, people shopping, going to the cinema, ice skating, people at work. Everyone walked and talked with a little spring in their step. I turned on the radio, and the carols were beautiful, full of hope and joy. I quietly gave a few extra coins to an old man on the street, more conscious of the need to share the good things of life. Not a gloomy sign did I see, anywhere in these otherwise dark and bitterly cold days in Canada. I stopped frowning all the time. There was something happening here, something that I had not seen before. People were participating in a festival that was universal — or could be, if we allowed ourselves to make it so.

And this is when I rediscovered Christmas. During my first winter in   10 Canada, I realized that you don't have to be a Christian to celebrate Christmas. After all, Christmas hardly belongs exclusively to Christianity. By all accounts, the feast is originally pagan Roman, the tree of German innovation, the sleigh and reindeer Scandinavian. Santa himself is a mythical Nordic invention, the trimmings are now probably shipped from Bangladesh, and the carols recorded in Taiwan on digital equipment made in Hong Kong!

Christmas might trace some of its roots to an Anglo-Saxon heritage,   11 but so do the days of the week, the English language, the pizza, and the ballpoint pen — all of which are pretty essential to my personal survival.

It is as ludicrous to expect me to forgo any benefit from these things simply because their inventors were not of my race or religion as it is to expect the western world to stop counting because the modern world's numerals originally "belonged" to the Arabs.

12   Indeed, Christmas does not "belong" to anyone. At an office party later that week, I heard the many different languages, dialects, and accents. We were as multicultural a bunch of human beings as could exist on God's earth. There were Christians of various denominations—Greek Orthodox to Catholic—and the Jewish, Muslim, Hindu, and Parsi faiths, as well as people from virtually every continent.

13   This is when she came to mind, my classmate from a previous life, Jennifer McDonald, she of the pink, frilly, swishing dress who first made me want to celebrate Christmas—who first made me want to be different. I realized we were all, in one way or another, like Jennifer. Each of us has taken something—a ritual or a tradition or a tool, an item of food—from someone other than our "pure laine" ancestors.

14   I realized that it was okay to be a little "anglo." Here in Canada, you can be a Muslim, as I am. You can be a Canadian, as I am. This is the only country in the world where you can be everything you are and want to be.

15   And I realized that here, in Canada, you can celebrate Christmas, if you want to. Or not, if you don't want to.

1999

NOTES

Almas Zakiuddin, a Bangladesh-born broadaster and journalist, has worked for CNN and CBC Newsworld.

Raj Short for "raja," an Indian term for ruler or prince. During British rule in Asia, European men of position or rank were called a "raj" or "raja."

Fast A colloquial or slang term for someone with loose morals.

Anglos A colloquial term for white people or for people who speak English.

Bloody A British expression, considered swearing. In the past, "bloody" had a stronger emphasis than today.

Pure laine Literally, meaning "100 percent wool" (French). It has become a term used in Quebec to mean those Québécois who are descended from the early French settlers. It excludes recent immigrants of different nationalities and races and anglophone Quebeckers.

COMPREHENSION AND DISCUSSION

1. How old (approximately) is the writer at the time of this article?
2. Who is Jennifer McDonald? Why do you think the writer picked this name?
3. According to the author, what makes the sales clerk suddenly become friendly?
4. How does the author discount the notion that Christmas belongs only to the Christians? Note the origins of the various Christmas traditions.
5. Is Christmas truly universal? Do you celebrate Christmas as a secular or a religious holiday? Or not at all? Explain.
6. Why is the Muslim point of view in this article important? Would the article be the same if it had been written by a Christian?

LITERARY TECHNIQUES

Flashback Notice how the writer takes you back to her school days before returning to the present. The flashback is necessary so that the reader comprehends the context of the article.

ASSIGNMENTS

1. Read the short story "Chickens for Christmas" (p. 61) and the article "Growing Up on Grace" (p. 246). Write an essay on immigrant adaptation of a new culture. Discuss what type of adjustments immigrants must make.
2. Write about a holiday. Discuss what it means to you or how the holiday has been adapted for life in Canada.
3. Zakiuddin states: "This [Canada] is the only country in the world where you can be everything you are and want to be" (paragraph 14). Is this true of Canada's history? Research the history of immigration and multiculturalism in Canada.

4. Note the number of holidays in Canada. How many of them have a religious context? Is Sunday a religious holiday? Do you consider Thanksgiving to be a religious holiday or just a long weekend? Research the background of these holidays and show why Canadians celebrate them.

5. Should Canadians add legal holidays from other religious faiths?

part three | writing essays

Chapter 1

THE WRITING PROCESS

Writing begins with an idea or a thought. You have an opinion you want to express. You have a thought you wish to share. In short, writing starts when you have something to say and you want to say it.

Articulating what you feel and what you know requires deep thinking on the subject. After all, you are communicating a thought, an idea, or a piece of information to someone else. You must understand what your readers want and need to know. You must understand how much background information is necessary. On the other hand, you don't want to bore your readers by including too much unnecessary detail.

Writing is expressing ideas clearly, concisely, and coherently. Clarity in thought and expression is essential. It saves readers effort in trying to decipher your thoughts on the subject. Concise writing saves the readers time. Nothing is more exasperating than having to wade through long, windy prose. Coherence is the logically organized sequence of information or arguments. Your readers must be able to see the relationship between one idea and the next.

Writing is based on reading, the act of accumulating and synthesizing knowledge. Personal experience and contemplation can go only so far. Generating ideas requires background information. The wider your general knowledge, the better you will be in drawing ideas together, coming up with your own opinions, and expressing them. You can read more about the nature of thinking in "Don't You Think It's Time to Start Thinking?" (p. 264).

In addition, reading other people's writing will help you appreciate different styles of expression. Why do some writers prefer long, complex sentences? Why do some writers prefer a folksy way of addressing the reader? Why do some break the rules of grammar in their prose? Your analysis of the way others write will further your own style.

Reading also shows you how written English is different from spoken English. Spoken language tends to be less formal and less precise. Speakers rely on visual cues and other feedback from their audience. Listeners can ask questions or show by their facial expression that they do not understand, and the speaker can adjust by adding more information. Speakers also use gestures and tone of voice to help get their meaning across.

The spoken form of any language differs from the written form. Sometimes they are practically two different languages. However, the differences are on a continuum; a formal speech can be similar in structure and vocabulary to a written report, and a letter to a friend can be conversational in style. But, generally, written language is more formal and standardized than conversational speech. Two speakers of English, such as an Australian and an American, can sound very different when they talk, but their writing will be standard English with few differences.

Standard written English has a wider vocabulary than spoken English. For example, you can get by in everyday life with fewer than 1000 words of English, but you probably use about twice that, and the average educated speaker of English knows about 20,000 words. However, the *Oxford English Dictionary* has entries for more than 500,000 words, and it is estimated that there are another half million technical words not in the dictionary. Written language needs that large vocabulary to be clear and precise. A speaker can get away with using gestures and calling something a "thingamajig," but imagine a technical manual with the instruction "attach the thingamajig to that other thing over there."

Sentence structure is more complex in writing. Readers can follow longer sentences better than listeners can. Complex sentence structure allows writers to express more complicated ideas. For example, a subordinate clause (starting with "although" or "while") adds a less important (or subordinate) idea to a sentence. For example, in the sentence "Although SUVs are thought to be safer than regular cars, they are prone to rollovers," the main point of the sentence is that SUVs are prone to rollovers; the subordinate clause (starting with "although") adds extra information but is not necessary to make the main point.

Students who read little are at a disadvantage when they write. They are not as familiar with the forms and conventions of standard written English. As a result, their essays sound too much like conversational English. They are not as comfortable with the vocabulary and sentence structure common to composition.

Writers have a more difficult job than speakers. They need to anticipate what their readers will think. In addition, they have to address what questions their readers might have and what they want to know. Sometimes they have to make sure that their humorous comments come across as humour. They must prevent misunderstanding by using the correct words. However, writers also have the luxury of reflecting on their words and revising them, whereas speakers have less time to think and consider what they say. The written word is also subject to more analysis than the spoken word.

Finally, writing is hard work. You begin with a thought and a blank page. Now you must fill the pages with ideas. You must do it all with words, sentences, and paragraphs.

STEPS IN THE PROCESS

People handle the writing process differently. Some plan their work meticulously with detailed outlines. Others just slap some words together and keep on adding, deleting, and changing until they shape their writing into a coherent structure. If you are getting satisfactory results with your writing methods, feel free to carry on. However, if your essays receive poor marks, then you should consider changing the way you work.

Essentially, writing can be broken down into three stages. In the prewriting stage, you think through your ideas, decide what you want to say, and organize your points. Second comes the actual writing of a draft where you flesh your ideas into sentences and paragraphs. The third stage is revising and editing.

Writers who write directly on a computer often find these writing stages less distinct. They may start with a few guideline words, type in a few points, flesh out a couple of sentences, and then gradually add more while constantly revising. They may not make an outline as a separate document; instead, their outline gets absorbed into their draft.

BRAINSTORMING

The first step in the planning phase is coming up with ideas for your writing; this is sometimes called brainstorming. The more ideas you generate for a subject, the better your essay will be. Brainstorming can help you avoid writer's block — the state where you just stare at the page and can't think of what to put on it. You don't have to use every point you come up with, but having more to work with allows you to zero in on the best points. Thinking about the opposing side of an argument allows you to make your own argument stronger. For example, if you are writing an essay on the drawbacks of living in residence, it is wise to compare them with the drawbacks of living in an apartment, even if you do not put points of comparison in your essay.

Writers have different ways of dealing with the thinking stage. Some draw bubble diagrams, some create charts, some just list point-form ideas, and some do freewriting. If you've found a way that works for you, keep working with it. Otherwise, try different ways to brainstorm. Your teachers have probably shown you the various techniques. If not, ask your instructor for help.

Suppose you are asked the question "Who should bear most of the costs of postsecondary education—the government or the student?" Here's what you might come up with when you brainstorm on the topic:

The government

- the government already pays for most education (elementary and secondary)
- the government cannot afford the cost of education—schools suffering
- society requires more education: postsecondary education is now a requirement for good jobs
- the country benefits from an educated citizenry (greater productivity, lower health costs, more participation in civic life)
- more highly educated people get better-paying jobs, thus paying higher taxes
- education is a good investment for the government
- all people benefit from an educated citizenry (not just the graduates themselves)

The students

- students receive the most benefit from their education
- students are legal adults, not children who have to be taken care of
- students can get loans, jobs
- other taxpayers should not pay for students' benefit
- but some students cannot afford to pay, therefore higher education will be only for the upper classes
- students cannot handle the demands of schoolwork and working at the same time
- students cannot make enough money to pay for tuition in their summer jobs
- students should not be saddled with large debts just as they're starting their careers

ORGANIZING IDEAS AND OUTLINING

An outline is a map for you to follow. It keeps you on track. It can be as simple as deciding you want to explain what causes a problem before you discuss the various solutions. The longer your piece of writing, the more you will find an outline helpful.

An outline is a list of the ideas that you want to develop, organized in paragraphs. You want to have one main idea expressed in each paragraph. If you are writing a five-paragraph essay, you have to organize your ideas so that you can cover a lot in the three body paragraphs without repeating yourself.

Your instructor may ask you to show or submit an essay outline before you submit your final draft. An outline can be in point form or in full sentences. Here is an example:

Thesis: It is the responsibility of the government to bear most of the cost of postsecondary education.

A) cost is prohibitive for most students
   • they can't do well at their studies if they work part-time
   • working all summer does not earn enough for tuition
   • high costs limit education to the rich

B) education is a financial investment for government
   • higher-educated people get better jobs, paying more tax
   • fewer unemployed on welfare
   • employers need educated workforce
   • education employs people
   • educated people contribute to GNP

C) the country needs educated citizens
   • educated people become workers, producing goods and services for the country
   • educated people tend to be healthier, thus reducing health care costs
   • government provides basic education (elementary and secondary), but today a postsecondary education can be considered basic

WRITING A DRAFT

Once you have an idea of what you want to say, you can write your first draft. Don't worry about getting your wording perfect. You don't even have to worry about your spelling and grammar being correct at this stage — as long as you correct the mistakes before you hand in your work. An example of a first draft follows:

The costs of tuition has been steadily rising in Ontario. Whereas students used to pay about just a fraction of the cost of their postsecondary education, now they pay almost half. Schools need more money. There is overcrowding in classrooms. Buildings have not been properly maintained.

And new computer and lab equipment is desperately needed. But who should bear the responsibility of most of the cost? The government.

First, it's too expensive. In the old days, students could work during the summer and earn enough to pay for most of their university year. No longer. Minimum-wage jobs won't even bring in enough to pay the tuition alone never mind residence and books. Some students work long hours at part-time jobs while they are in school, thus not being able to spend as much time on their studies as they should be in order to get good grades and graduate with a degree. And they are poor and live on Kraft dinner which isn't very nutritious and doesn't help students who are starving and need good food to have the energy to work hard and succeed at their schoolwork. The parents can't afford to pay all the university costs. Some have more than one child in university or college. Even loans don't help. Some students are graduating with $20,000 and $30,000 debts. This cripples them financially for many years to come—the very years they want to get set up in life when they are not making much money but need to pay for housing, a car, and a work wardrobe. Many students decide college or university is financially out of reach. Only the rich can afford it.

The government, on the other hand, needs to realize that funding post-secondary education is a good investment. Highly educated people get good jobs and pay lots of taxes. They contribute to the GNP. A well-educated workforce means fewer people on welfare. When someone from a poor family goes to university, they can help their whole family when they get a good job. Employers need an educated workforce, so businesses are attracted to the country. Finally, the education industry also needs employees, and that makes more of a country's citizens gainfully employed and contributing to the economy.

The best investment is in its people. The government needs educated people. Educated people make better choices. Their jobs are better. Educated people tend to be healthier, thus reducing health-care costs. The government acknowledges its need to pay for basic education (elementary and secondary school), but today people need a postsecondary as a minimum.

The government should bear most of the cost of postsecondary education leaving students to pay less. It is what we need government to do.

Revising this essay would entail balancing out the paragraph length and changing conversational style to a more academic style.

REVISING AND EDITING

Revising and editing is a crucial stage. It doesn't mean simply correcting some of the grammar and spelling. It means taking a careful look at what you have written. Revision, after all, means "seeing again." Professional writers often spend more time on this phase than on any other.

It is always better to let your writing sit for a day or two before you revise it. This way you will be seeing it with fresh eyes and you are more likely to find weak areas.

Make sure your writing is concise. Get rid of needless repetition. Edit out unnecessary words. Be ruthless: no matter how beautifully written your sentence is, if it doesn't fit the paragraph, delete it.

On the other hand, make sure that you have said enough to make your points clear. Back up your general statements with explanation or specific examples.

Compare this revised essay with the first draft above:

> The cost of tuition has been steadily rising in Ontario. Whereas students used to pay less than a quarter of the cost of their postsecondary education, now they pay more than a third, and in some cases close to a half. However, higher tuition has not met the financial needs of schools, which are suffering from overcrowding, inadequate and poorly maintained facilities, lack of staff, and outdated equipment. Cash-strapped institutions need more money. It is up to the government to step up and fund institutions properly and reduce tuition fees for students.
>
> University tuition fees are too high for students to handle. Before fees were raised so precipitously, students could work during the summer and earn enough to pay for most of their university year. Minimum-wage summer jobs won't even earn students enough to make a dent in tuition. Some work long hours at part-time jobs while they are in school, decreasing the amount of time they can spend on their studies. Loans are not helping. Some students are graduating crippled financially with $20,000 and $30,000 debts. Therefore, many students decide college or university is financially out of reach. Only the rich can afford it.
>
> The government, on the other hand, needs to realize that funding postsecondary education is a good investment. Highly educated people get better jobs, paying more income tax in the end. They contribute to the GNP. A well-educated workforce means fewer people on welfare. In poor families especially, having someone graduate from university can benefit the whole family. Furthermore, employers need an educated workforce so businesses are attracted to the country. Finally, the education industry also

needs employees, so a thriving industry means that teachers and support staff are also gainfully employed and contributing to the economy.

The best investment a government can make is in its people. The government needs an educated citizenry. Educated people participate more in society. They are more informed about social and political issues. Their jobs are better. Educated people tend to be healthier, thus reducing health-care costs. Even areas that are not generally seen as practical, such as a liberal arts education, are valued by employers because this type of education produces creative thinkers. Strong universities participate in research and development, fuelling more advances in science and technology. The government acknowledges its responsibility to pay for basic education (elementary and secondary school), but today postsecondary education can be considered basic because it is hard to get a decent job without a college or university degree.

The government should bear most of the cost of postsecondary education, leaving students to pay no more than 20 percent. Money spent on education benefits the whole society and is a worthwhile investment. This benefit is so obvious that it should be made clear even to those who grumble about high taxes and the childless who protest against paying for the schooling of "other people's children."

CHECKING THE ESSAY

After your revisions are done, it is time to check and double-check for the little things. Look at your assignment sheet again and make sure you have done everything the instructor asked of you. For instance, check that your cover page has the title of your essay, your name, the course code, the date, and the instructor's name. If you are supposed to hand in an outline, make sure that it is attached.

Know your weaknesses. Write them down on a checklist. If you have trouble with run-on sentences, for example, screen your essay carefully for run-ons. If your particular weakness is spelling, check any word that you are unsure of. Don't rely on your software's grammar and spell-check functions, which can be helpful but can also introduce errors. Don't count on them to find all your mistakes. Proofread your work carefully.

You can get someone to read over your work. This person should not do the corrections for you, but should point out problem areas. A second reader can be particularly helpful for spotting lack of clarity. A tutor at your school's writing centre can help you polish your work.

To check your essay, use the principles of good writing explained in Chapter 2.

Chapter 2

THE PRINCIPLES OF GOOD WRITING

Writing has different purposes and is designed for different audiences. You write to explain, inform, reflect, entertain, and persuade. Whether you are writing an e-mail message or an essay, the same principles of good writing apply. You have to express your ideas in a way that makes communication successful. In other words, your message must be clear to your readers. Good writing is also succinct and to the point.

This chapter presents necessary elements that you have to keep in mind while you write. You have to consider your audience and purpose, you must strive for clarity and conciseness, and you have to be aware of your use of language.

AUDIENCE AND PURPOSE

Writing is communication. In order to communicate well, you must consider why you are writing something and who will read it. Your audience and purpose determine the content, organization of ideas, vocabulary, and writing style (formal or conversational). For instance, you would write a letter to a friend in a much more conversational style than you would to your supervisor. Moreover, a reader who is knowledgeable in the subject area will need less background information than a layperson. The expert can understand technical vocabulary, whereas the layperson cannot. For example, doctors would understand "cardiac infarction," whereas laypeople would prefer the term "heart attack."

The audience for your essay is your instructor, but academic writing is not like other forms of writing. Instead of writing to communicate new information, you are writing to show your instructor how you think, how well you have learned the material, and how well you communicate. Although in most pieces of writing, you try to avoid telling your readers too much of what they already know, in academic writing you are not giving the instructor new information. Instead, you are telling your instructor what you have learned.

The purpose encompasses the thesis, since the thesis is the main idea you want to communicate to your audience. For instance, if you are writing an essay arguing that all students should study history, your purpose is to make a sound argument for that idea.

For any piece of writing, success is determined by whether it fulfills the writer's purpose and suits the intended audience.

CLARITY

Writing must communicate your message, and therefore it must be clear. When you talk to people, you can check whether they understand you by just looking at them or asking them, but you can't follow your writing around to make sure all readers understand it. Therefore, clarity in writing is vital. What seems clear to you may not be clear to your readers, so it is wise to get a second opinion on what you say. Perhaps you can get a friend or tutor to read your work.

You achieve clarity in writing by knowing exactly what you want to say. Define your purpose. Organize your points so that you deal with them one by one. Skipping around from idea to idea simply confuses readers. Each paragraph should have one main idea. General statements have to be supported by specific ones, giving details, explanations, or examples. Sufficient explanation and examples are vital to clarity. Transition signals, such as "for example," "first," and "therefore," are essential to show the relationship between ideas.

Proper vocabulary is essential. If you use jargon or technical language, you should be sure your audience will understand it. If you are unsure whether you are using a word correctly, check a dictionary. Use precise words, not vague ones. Writing must be more precise than speaking. For example, you can't get away with writing such phrases as "that thing over there."

Gauging your readers' knowledge is difficult but necessary. In order to be clear, you have to know how much background knowledge is necessary. For example, in an essay about the Internet, you can assume that your audience knows what it is, but you may wish to give some historical background to show its development.

CONCISENESS

Good writing is short and to the point. Conciseness is hard to achieve, but essential. No reader wants to waste time ploughing through extraneous words and ideas to find the point of a document. Eliminate unnecessary repetition. You have to give enough information to make the ideas clear, but avoid padding your article just to reach the prescribed word limit.

You can achieve conciseness by reducing the number of non-essential words in your sentences. For instance, "now" is more concise than "at this point in time." Consider each word and phrase as you do your revision. The question you should ask is "Can I reduce this without changing the meaning?" Then cut to the bone.

Keep your purpose in mind. If an idea does not relate directly to your thesis, then it is irrelevant and can be cut.

COHERENCE

Coherence refers to sticking together. Your sentences should follow logically and should relate to each other. For instance, if you make a general statement, you could follow it with a specific example, introducing that sentence with transitions such as "for instance."

Your writing must be drawn together in some pattern. Often this requires organizing ideas for the reader. If your ideas are too scattered, they tend to confuse the reader. Some of the basic patterns are as follows:

- chronological (time sequence)
- climactic (from least to most important)
- logical (appropriate sequence or grouping of ideas)
- listing or anticlimactic (from most to least important)
- spatial (in one direction such as top to bottom, left to right, or clockwise)

Using transition markers is vital. Phrases such as "in addition" and "however" help your readers follow the relationship between ideas. You can find a list of such markers on page 441.

GRAMMAR

Good writing is grammatically correct. While some grammatical errors do not really hinder understanding, mistakes make your work look less professional. In addition, errors may distract the reader from the purpose of your piece. Then your reader may lose confidence in your argument. Serious grammatical errors include the misuse of clauses and incorrect verb tenses. ESL students have trouble with prepositions and articles, but these mistakes can generally be considered minor because they do not cause as many comprehension problems. Keep in mind, however, that writing at the college or university level is supposed to be free of grammatical mistakes.

If you use a usage guide to improve your command of grammar, you may have to learn some terminology in order to understand the advice. For example, you should know the basic terms for parts of speech: noun, verb, adjective, adverb, conjunction, preposition. You should know what "present tense" and "subordinate clause" mean. These terms are defined in dictionaries and grammar books. Learn the terms you need, but don't worry about mastering all the terminology. If you rarely make grammatical errors, then you don't need to become a grammar expert.

Grammar checkers are packaged with most word-processing software, but they are difficult to use effectively. Because computers cannot understand language, the program often makes mistakes in parsing the sentence (dividing the sentence into grammatical units). Grammar checkers can be useful for catching slips, but if your knowledge of grammar and sentence structure is not sound, the software may be more harmful than helpful. If you find your computer's grammar checker to be helpful, use it. However, be alert to the fact that the advice it gives may be just plain wrong.

Our advice on grammar is that if you are making mistakes and don't understand them, learn the formal grammar rules so that you can correct them. If your essays come back relatively unscathed by your instructor's marking pencil, then don't worry about stocking up on grammar books. Native speakers of English, especially those who read a lot, can develop a good sense of grammar without formal study. For instance, someone who does not know what "subjunctive" means may be able to write a grammatical sentence using it. Conversely, it is possible to find ESL students who can rhyme off the most subtle of grammar rules but who cannot apply them to their own writing.

Specific grammar problems are discussed in Chapter 8.

SENTENCE STRUCTURE

It's not enough to write grammatical sentences; you need to use appropriate sentence structure. Too many short, simple sentences, for example, can make your writing sound choppy or even juvenile. Complex sentences are especially important because they can express more complex ideas. For instance, you can put the less important information in a sentence by using a subordinate clause. To keep a reader's interest, you should use a variety of sentence structures. It's tiring to read a succession of long, involved sentences. Conversely, too many short sentences mean that your writing does not flow well.

SPELLING

Writing that is riddled with spelling errors creates a bad impression, even if the reader can figure out what you mean. It is up to you to improve your spelling. Use tools such as dictionaries and computer spell checkers. If your work contains spelling mistakes, make a list of these misspelled words. Write the correct form of those words dozens of times so that you will remember the proper spelling. Most English spelling is regular. Learn the rules, such as "*i* before *e* except after *c*." Spelling mistakes are relatively easy to fix, so not fixing them shows carelessness.

Use dictionaries and your computer's spell checker to help you correct your spelling. It is easier to find the correct word if you have spelled the beginning of the word correctly. English spelling is not phonetic; it does not follow pronunciation as does spelling in languages such as Italian and Polish. However, you can learn the different ways common sounds are spelled. For instance, an "s" sound could be spelled with an *s*, *c*, or *sc*.

Remember that a spell checker is a flawed tool. It cannot do your work for you. It will not pick up on spelling mistakes if you have just used the wrong word, for example, if you have typed "there" instead of "their." However, it is important to run your document through the spell checker because it can find those hard-to-see typographical errors. Just remember not to blindly accept the software's suggestions. Check the meaning of the alternatives in the dictionary if you are not sure. Be sure to proofread the document yourself to catch errors the computer missed.

Your spell checker may use a British or an American word list. However, Canadian spelling is different. In some cases, it uses the British style, preferring "centre" over "center," for example. In other cases, Canadian spelling uses American style, such as "organize" instead of "organise." You will also see variations within Canadian spelling. Different publishers may follow different style guides. In many cases, the two spellings are both accepted. Use a Canadian dictionary, and try to remain consistent. For instance, if you use *-our* endings, make sure you spell both "neighbour" and "colour" with the same ending.

VOCABULARY

English offers the writer a huge number of words from which to choose. The English language has absorbed words from many different languages. The Norman invasion of 1066 brought Norman French to England, and as a result Old English words acquired synonyms (words that have the same meaning) from French. For instance, you can describe something as "big" using an Old English word, or "large" using a word from French. Technical words, such as "television" and "psychosomatic," are from Latin and Greek. Many of the inconsistencies in the spelling and pronunciation system of English can be traced to imported words. For instance, the *ph* spelling of an "f" sound (as in "telephone") is from the Greek, which uses the letter phi.

It is important to use a variety of words in your writing and to use them appropriately. The larger your vocabulary, the more easily you will find the proper word. The best way to improve your vocabulary is to read a lot. Written language uses a wider range of words and expressions than does spoken language. Avid readers usually have a good vocabulary. Knowledge of Greek and Latin roots can help you build your vocabulary. For example, "autobiographical" is a simple word if you know that *auto-* means "self," *bio-* means "life," *graph* refers to writing, and *-ical* is an adjective ending. These same roots are found in such words as "autograph," "biology," "graphology," and "telegraph." You can look up the meaning of such common roots in the dictionary.

A dictionary is an essential tool, but don't reach for one every time you come across an unfamiliar word in your reading. You don't want to interrupt the flow of ideas. Moreover, constant use of a dictionary can become a chore. So try to guess the meaning of the word from the context. If you can't, and if the word seems important to what you are reading, then obviously you should look it up.

Another useful tool is a thesaurus, a book of synonyms (words with similar meanings) and antonyms (words with opposite meanings). A thesaurus can jog your memory about words with which you may be familiar but do not generally use. However, you should not use unfamiliar words from a thesaurus because you might use them incorrectly. Just because words are listed as synonyms does not mean they are always interchangeable.

In addition to knowing the denotation (meaning) of words, you must know the connotation (emotional value). For instance, "kill" and "murder" mean essentially the same thing, but "murder" is a much stronger word and has more of a negative connotation.

STYLE

Your writing should be in an appropriate style. Essays and business reports should be written in formal English, while personal letters can be written in a conversational style. Business communication today is much less formal than in the past, just like business dress is more casual, and there are different levels of formality. However, if you write in too conversational a style for academic and business writing, you risk giving the wrong impression. It's much like showing up in shorts and a T-shirt for a job interview — it's inappropriate.

In addition, written English is more formal and precise than spoken English. In speech, we rely on visual cues and context to understand what someone is saying. A piece of paper cannot carry those clues, nor can it carry gestures or tone of voice. You can simply point to something when you speak to someone; in writing you need the precise word to make sure your audience understands your meaning.

The more formal the writing, the less personal it is. Formality is always marked by distance. That does not mean you have to avoid using "I" completely, but you should realize that the "I" is often unnecessary. Your statements express your opinions (unless you say it is someone else's opinion), so you don't need phrases such as "I think" and "in my opinion." Using "you" in an essay also gives it a more conversational tone (see p. 447).

Writing that is too formal can also be a problem because it can be stilted and difficult to understand. However, this problem is more common among bureaucrats and academics than students. Students generally need to learn to write in a less personal, more formal style, suitable for school and work purposes. Examples of informal and formal style can be found on pages 437–438.

CHECKLIST

Unlike some disciplines where an answer is either right or wrong, English courses offer many challenges for evaluation. Instructors have many factors to consider when they assign marks. Some instructors break up the marks so that they give some for content, some for mechanics, and some for vocabulary. Others grade holistically, balancing good and bad points in their head, before assigning a mark. Instructors will consider the principles of good writing explained in this chapter.

Here are some questions you can ask yourself before you hand in your essay:

- Is the main idea (the thesis) of the essay clear? Is it a supportable idea, appropriate for a thesis?

- Does the assignment meet the set criteria? For example, do you answer the question posed? Is the essay too short or too long?
- Does the essay follow proper organization? Is there an adequate introduction and conclusion?
- Does each paragraph have one main idea, clearly expressed in the topic sentence?
- Are the points supported with specific explanations and examples?
- Are the arguments logical? Are they consistent (no contradiction)? Are they presented in a logical order, with clear transitions showing the relationship between ideas?
- Are your expressions clear? Is it easy to understand what you are trying to say? Are words misused? Is the vocabulary appropriate for college-level writing?
- Is the essay in an appropriate style — not too conversational?
- Is the essay free of grammatical errors?
- Is there variety in sentence structure? Are there enough complex sentences? Does the writing flow from sentence to sentence?
- Is spelling correct?
- Are punctuation and spacing correct?
- Did you follow formatting guidelines set out in the assignment? For example, is the print readable? Is the essay double-spaced? Are margins wide enough?
- Have you proofread your paper carefully?

Chapter 3

THE ESSAY

The essay is a means by which teachers can evaluate your skills in writing and communication and your ability to think through an idea. Derived from the French word *essayer* (meaning "to attempt"), the modern "essay" is an attempt to explain. The essay is an academic exercise in which you learn to express ideas and support your opinions. For reflections on the thinking process and how it relates to writing essays, read "Don't You Think It's Time to Start Thinking?" (p. 264).

Use of essays is not limited to school. You read essays in magazines and in the opinion and editorial pages of newspapers. These essays tend to be more loosely structured than academic ones. Many of the non-fiction selections in this book are such works.

Your instructor may lay out the structure you are to follow. The basic structure is a five-paragraph essay. Mastering this form allows you to move to more ambitious essays. As you practise essay writing, you learn how to organize a piece of writing, how to support ideas and explain them clearly, and how to introduce and conclude your work. These skills are transferable; whether you are writing a business report or a letter, essay-writing skills can help you.

The essay has three parts: beginning, middle, and end. The beginning is the introduction. It gets the reader's attention, gives the reader background information, and prepares the way for the meat of the essay. The middle paragraphs are also called the body of the essay. These paragraphs are developed paragraphs with a topic sentence introducing the main point and one to three minor points with supporting ideas. The last paragraph or section is the conclusion. In a long essay, the conclusion might contain a summary; in a short essay, the only summary is the restatement of the thesis. The introduction leads the reader into the essay; the conclusion leads the reader out.

PARAGRAPHS

The paragraph is a building block for essays. A paragraph expresses one main idea and is usually composed of several sentences. It has unity, coherence, and sufficient development. It is signalled by an indent. If block paragraphing is used, a blank line separates paragraphs. Whatever method is used, it is important for the reader to be able to clearly distinguish the beginning and end of each paragraph.

Paragraphs have shrunk. Nineteenth-century literature is full of examples of paragraphs that go on and on, sometimes for pages. Today, brief paragraphs reflect our shorter attention spans. Short paragraphs are essential in newspaper and magazine articles, where text is broken up into one or two sentences to make it more readable in column format. Modern fiction tends to have a lot of dialogue, requiring a new paragraph for each new speaker.

In academic writing, however, paragraphs tend to be longer. A one- or two-sentence paragraph will not suffice for an essay. Generally, paragraphs in essays are four to eight sentences long. You need to be able to fully explain an idea in each paragraph.

DEVELOPED PARAGRAPHS

Independent, developed paragraphs are, in a sense, mini-essays. They have a topic sentence, ideas supported and explained, and a concluding statement. Body paragraphs in an essay are developed paragraphs, while introductions and conclusions do not have the same structure.

In the following independent paragraph, you can see the structure and development:

> University tuition fees are currently too high. Before fees were raised so precipitously, students could work during the summer and earn enough to pay for most of their university year. Today, a student working a minimum-wage summer job will earn less than $5000. This may cover tuition, but won't stretch to cover books, residence, and incidental fees. Some students work long hours at part-time jobs while they are in school, decreasing the amount of time they can spend on their studies. They are thus defeating the purpose of their education if they are not learning all they should. Loans are not a solution. Some students are graduating with $20,000 and $30,000 debts, which cripple them financially just as they are starting on their careers. Therefore, many students decide college or university is financially out of reach.

You can see how this paragraph would work in an essay on pages 359–360.

Examine the structure in the following two examples. The first sentence, the topic sentence, gives the main idea of the paragraph. The second sentence is the elaboration of the topic sentence. The third sentence gives the first argument for the idea in the topic sentence. That argument is supported by example or explanation. Each paragraph has two more arguments, also supported. The last sentence is the concluding sentence.

> Canadians should pay more for their water supply. Because they get water so cheaply, they take it for granted. Raising the price would encourage conservation. For example, Canadians would think twice before washing cars or watering lawns on hot summer days when most of that water goes to waste. Secondly, the extra money could go to actual water treatment and inspection instead of having those costs come from general tax revenue. Canadians would realize that it does cost money to ensure a healthy water supply if those costs were directly related to what comes out of their taps. Finally, if water were seen as a valuable commodity, people would be less likely to poison it by dumping chemicals down drains. Canadians will not take care of their water supply and preserve it if they think so little of it, and the only way to have them value it is to make it more expensive. (154 words)

> Attendance is the key predictor of success in a college course. Just showing up for tests is not enough—students who don't come to class don't pass. Most importantly, classes are where the course material is presented and explained. Although some instructors just repeat what is in the textbook, most do elaborate, change, or add to the material. Their explanations are vital for comprehension because of the instructor's synthesis of ideas. If the textbook is long or difficult to understand, lectures can clarify points and reveal what is most important. Moreover, classroom time allows students to practise the skills being taught. For example, students may do grammar exercises or do group work for reading comprehension. Finally, students who attend class are better prepared for tests and exams. When tests are taken up in class, they learn what their instructor is looking for. Important points are stressed and summarized. The classes at the end of the course are the ones that many students skip, but instructors review material and prepare their students for the exam in those sessions. Students who decide not to attend class are not taking advantage of the most important resource in their education. (196 words)

TOPIC SENTENCES

Each developed paragraph should have a topic sentence to state your main idea. It should be specific enough for the reader to know what you are talking about, and it should begin your paragraph. You will note in the above examples that each paragraph begins with a clear topic sentence. A topic sentence can appear anywhere in the paragraph, or in some cases it may not appear at all. However, the most advantageous position is at the beginning. Thus, the topic sentence sets forth the idea in the form of a brief introductory statement.

Topic sentences are similar to thesis statements. While thesis statements express the controlling idea of the essay, topic sentences give the controlling idea of the paragraph. It is important that the topic sentence be a point that can be covered in the one paragraph. Each sentence in the paragraph should relate to the topic sentence. The paragraph must be unified, organized, and clear.

A good topic sentence sets up the whole paragraph, telling the reader the main idea. This works to the reader's advantage in academic writing because the reader can go quickly through a text reading just the first sentences of paragraphs to get the main ideas or to find information. A topic sentence should be general, but not vague. For example, "There are many things that make us believe Cecil would have murdered Moose Maddon" does not tell us as much as "Cecil could have planned and executed the murder of Moose Maddon because he had motive, means, and opportunity." A topic sentence should not just be a fact because it does not set a direction for the paragraph. For instance, "Moose Maddon bullies Cecil" says nothing about the argument; a better topic sentence would be "Moose Maddon bullies Cecil because of his own inadequacies."

In "The Patterns of Eating," you can also see topic sentences at work. Paragraph 5 begins with "Once carving was no longer considered a necessary skill among the well-bred, changes inevitably took place in the use of the knife, unquestionably the earliest utensil used for manipulating food" (p. 256). The first part of the sentence is a subordinate clause and thus is not the main idea; the reference to carving is a transition from the previous paragraph where carving was discussed. The main clause, "changes inevitably took place in the use of the knife," is the main idea. The whole paragraph talks about knives at the dinner table. Mention of the fork or spoon in this paragraph would be off topic. Paragraph 6 talks about the development of the fork, and it starts with this topic sentence: "The fork in particular enabled Europeans to separate themselves from the eating process, even avoiding manual contact with their food" (p. 256).

Take a look at the example paragraphs in the previous section and see how, in each paragraph, the topic sentence introduces the argument and is supported by the rest of the sentences in the paragraph.

THE SHORT ESSAY

In college or university, the length of a short essay ranges from 300 to 1000 words. You are expected to have something to say on the topic you have selected. In a literature paper, you can write about characters, plot twists, and themes, among other topics. In a response essay on an article or essay, you can argue the writer's stand on the particular subject.

One of the most common formats in essay writing in school is the five-paragraph essay. It has a one-paragraph introduction, three body paragraphs, and a one-paragraph conclusion. The essay in Chapter 1 (pp. 359–360) follows this format. This structure is a useful training ground—it teaches students writing skills. It is similar to learning computer programming with languages like Turing or Pascal, which are not used in "the real world" but which are good vehicles for learning the principles of programming. You probably won't have to write this kind of paper once you graduate from school, but you will learn useful skills, such as organizing ideas, supporting statements, and writing concisely. The five-paragraph essay structure is easily adapted to other pieces of writing. Business reports, for example, also have introductions, bodies, and conclusions.

THE THESIS STATEMENT

Like a topic sentence, the thesis statement gives the main idea. It tells your reader what you seek to prove in your essay.

A thesis statement that is too narrow, such as a fact that cannot be debated, is unworkable:

Microsoft is the largest software company in the world.

A statement that is too broad does not tell the reader exactly what your topic is:

Computers are very helpful.

A thesis should not be an announcement:

> In this essay, I will explain how people use computers.

A thesis statement is one sentence. Here is an example of an incorrect multi-sentence thesis:

> In "The Cask of Amontillado," Edgar Allan Poe uses four methods to sustain the horror for the reader. First, he creates suspense by having the villain vow unspeakable vengeance for a seemingly mild insult. Second, the author details Montresor's demoniacal progress in luring the victim to his downfall. Third, he plays on the reader's fear of being buried alive without hope of escape. Finally, he suggests that Montresor may get away with his crime on earth and in heaven.

The following example is an improvement. The thesis statement (underlined) is the last sentence of the introductory paragraph:

> In "The Cask of Amontillado," Edgar Allan Poe has written a classic story of terror and horror. To create the feelings of dread and repulsion in the reader, the author relies on proven methods. <u>The four elements of a successful horror story he uses are the insane villain, the unsuspecting victim, the primal fear of being buried alive, and the injustice felt by the reader at the ending.</u>

The introduction leads the reader to the thesis statement.

INTRODUCTION

The introduction is usually one paragraph in a short essay, but it can be more. An introductory paragraph is different from a developed paragraph because it does not start with a topic sentence. Instead, it leads the reader to the thesis statement (the main idea of the essay), which is usually at the end of the introduction. The introduction starts with a broad statement and gradually narrows down to the point of the thesis.

An introduction draws the readers' attention and prepares them for the essay. It gives them the necessary background information. It can be an anecdotal opening, telling a story from the writer's experience. It can start with a brief quotation from a well-known authority. Or, it can give historical information. For argument essays, it can explain popular opinions on the other side of the argument. The introduction should not, however, contain any points that support the thesis — those belong in the essay itself.

Here are some examples of introductions with different perspectives on the same topic:

Owning a private vehicle seems to be essential for getting to work. We do not always live close to work, especially with the demands of the modern workplace. We change jobs frequently, work short-term contracts, and have to visit different work sites, so we cannot change our home every time we change work locations. Moreover, we may not be travelling in the direction of most public transit—into the downtown core. The car solves the immediate problem of moving from home to work in the shortest time. However, the price of the commute is too high, encompassing financial cost, time, and stress.

What teenager has not dreamed about owning his own wheels at age 16, the moment he receives his driver's licence? The car, whatever size, shape, or age, is the ultimate status symbol—instant respect and admiration from friends, freedom to go anywhere and everywhere. The car has been romanticized by young people since the songs of the Beach Boys. However, teenagers must consider the cost, the responsibility, and the frustration of owning a car.

The family car has become a fixture in our society. In our grandparents' time, owning a vehicle seemed shameless excess. By our parents' generation, one car in the driveway was normal. For our generation, having two cars in a family is not keeping up with the Joneses anymore, but essential to daily routine; it is no longer a luxury but a necessity because of the demands of working parents, children's activities, and the modern lifestyle.

CONCLUSION

The conclusion finishes the essay and leads the readers back to your topic. It gives you a chance to explain the "so what?" of your topic and to suggest some future direction. Start with a restatement of the thesis statement and move on. Don't summarize in a short essay because it is too repetitive.

Too often essays peter out to an unsatisfactory conclusion. Students seem to run out of steam or ideas. It is important not to just repeat ideas at the end to fill up space. Additional points that support the thesis also do not belong in the conclusion.

Here are some examples of concluding paragraphs:

With all these disadvantages, it is clear that the daily commute is a high price to pay. It is not always possible to live near our work, especially when other family members have to be considered. The only solution is public transit. We must make clear to our governments the message that the development of commuter transportation is essential for all of us.

Owning a car, then, has inherent responsibilities and obligations. Teenagers should balance their dream of "wheels" with reality. If they don't, they may be in for a surprise — there is no such thing as a free ride.

Love or hate it, the car dominates all facets of our hectic lifestyles. Without the automobile, we are no longer mobile and autonomous, no longer free but captive by suburban distance, no longer living contented but disgruntled. That box of gears and gadgets has not made us independent but dependent on it.

Chapter 4

RESEARCH

In a research paper, you use information from other sources to support your ideas. Within your essay, you paraphrase and quote what you have read. However, the essay should still have your ideas and not just repeat what others say. It's not a cut-and-paste exercise.

Generally, research essays are longer than the five-paragraph essay common in writing classes, and you are given several weeks to complete the assignment. Don't leave the project until the last minute. Research essays require more time than other expository essays, especially for finding source materials. You don't want to run the risk of not being able to find material on your topic the night before the paper is due. The book you want could be checked out, your Internet service could be down, or you might have to make a trip to another library.

Be sure to keep all your notes and drafts at least until the course is finished and you have received your final mark. You may be called on to support the statements in your essay. Also keep a backup copy of your paper. Keep a copy on disk in addition to the one on your computer's hard drive or your school's server.

In your research, you need to distinguish between primary and secondary source materials. The primary source is the play, poem, short story, book, or article you are interpreting or analyzing. For example, on the topic of "Ritual sacrifice in Shirley Jackson's 'The Lottery,'" your primary source is, of course, the short story itself. The secondary source is anything that is written about the primary source. That is, any introduction to the story, editor's notes, literary analyses (other than yours), interpretations, lecture notes from your instructor, or anything written about the story is considered a secondary source. In other words, a secondary source is anything but the primary source.

All sources, whether primary or secondary, must be referenced and documented. You must give credit where credit is due. In short, if you use someone else's material, either exact words or an idea (not a fact), you need to acknowledge your indebtedness. The information must be complete and accurate so that your readers can go to the sources you used. Incorrect use of sources or incorrect documentation can lead to charges of plagiarism or cheating, a serious offence (see pp. 436–437).

BEFORE STARTING THE RESEARCH

Your instructor will probably give you a choice of topics. These might be very specific, or they might be broad topics that you have to narrow down to something manageable within the word limit. You may be able to suggest your own topic in consultation with your instructor. Make sure you understand the demands of the topic. Read the question carefully. Discuss the topic with your instructor. You may wish to check how much information is available on a topic before you choose.

Before you head off to the library or log onto the Internet, jot down your own ideas and questions about the topic. This brainstorming session will help you distinguish your own ideas from someone else's and recognize what is general knowledge. Then it will be easier to know what to reference.

Plan your research. Make a list of questions. Be prepared to return to some information sources if you find something that changes your view or even your search terms. Schedule your work so that you don't have to do it all in one day. You might have to take some time to track down a book, for example.

Read more than what is needed. You have to accumulate general information and background knowledge on your subject—even though you may not put all that information in the body of your essay.

FINDING, CHOOSING, AND EVALUATING INFORMATION

You should consult a variety of sources for your research. Don't limit your research to just books or just web pages. Even if you have a recent current events topic, you don't have to limit yourself to the Internet; you can get general background information from a book. You can start with an encyclopedia article for a general summary and move to magazine and journal articles. With a variety of sources, you can make sure your information is accurate.

You have to judge the reliability of your sources. What credentials does the author have? Is the publication reputable? What kind of evidence does the author present? Is the evidence well documented, with references you can check? Is the information up to date?

You should be aware of bias in your research materials. For example, if you use a company's website or promotional literature as your only source of information on that company, you are getting only one side of the picture—the positive spin.

Check the date of the sources you are using. Even Internet information can be out of date. Look for the publication date of books on the copyright page (the back of the title page) and check whether the book has been revised since then, or just reprinted.

If you are working on a specific Canadian topic, make sure you use Canadian reference materials such as *The Canadian Encyclopedia.* American books and reference sources dominate the market, but their coverage of Canadian topics is notoriously weak.

Be prepared to go back to sources again if you find out new information that would help your search. For example, let's say you are researching the koi fish. You don't find very much at first, but then you find an article that mentions that koi is a kind of carp; you would try the search again with the term "carp."

Get to know your school library and your public library, the central branch as well as the local one. Try out the catalogue to see what subject coverage there is. Find out what databases your library subscribes to and how they work. Talk to the librarians when you need help.

SEARCH TERMS

Library catalogues, CD-ROM encyclopedias, and Internet search engines generally use similar keyword searches. Become familiar with the way the particular search engine works.

Boolean operators—"and," "or," and "but"—are used to combine search terms. "Or" broadens the search because it takes into account both search terms. If the search engine does not recognize "or," you have to redo the search for each alternate term.

"And" limits a search because you are asking the program for documents that contain both terms. Most search engines assume you mean "and" when you put more than one word in. If you want the words to be treated as a unit, you can put quotation marks around them in some Internet search engines. For example, if you are looking for a person's name, putting quotation marks around the first and last names ensures that the search engine will look for the two names together and not as two separate words. This feature is particularly useful if you are looking for a phrase that has common words, such as the title of the Shakespeare play *As You Like It.*

The third Boolean operator, "not," is used to exclude items from your search. Some Internet search engines use the minus sign to show "not." For example, if you want to find out more about Kalle Lasn's work aside from *Adbusters*, you could input (leaving out the quotation marks) "Kalle Lasn – Adbusters".

It is important to use keywords properly to get accurate results. Use correct spelling. Don't use words that are too common. Try synonyms. Look for the help feature or the hints offered by the program.

REFERENCE WORKS

The reference section of the library has a wide variety of reference books, including dictionaries, encyclopedias, almanacs, directories, and year-books. Most of these have been replaced by online sources of information, but it is useful to get to know the traditional reference tools and how to use them. Encyclopedias, for instance, offer a brief overview of a subject, which is often a good starting point. A "Who's Who" directory gives biographies of well-known people. Students whose only experience is with search engines sometimes find it frustrating using print forms. For instance, they may not realize that they must look up a person by the last name. Despite the convenience of the electronic formats, you will need to use the old-fashioned methods sometimes. For example, for security reasons, your school may allow you to use print dictionaries for tests and exams but not the electronic variety.

BOOKS

Although proponents of electronic information sources have declared the book to be dead, it is too early to write an obituary. Books are important for a thorough treatment of a subject. You can check out a biography, a history book, a science text, or a how-to manual. Fiction is housed separately from non-fiction. Your library's online catalogue will help you locate the book you need.

Non-fiction works are generally catalogued by one of two systems. Elementary schools, secondary schools, and public libraries use the Dewey decimal system. This system uses a numerical base, dividing knowledge into sections from 001 to 999. For example, books on applied sciences are catalogued in the 600s. The other system is the Library of Congress (LC), which is used in college and university libraries. You can recognize these codes because they start with two letters of the alphabet. If you look at the copyright page (the other side of the title page) of this book, you can see the suggested cataloguing numbers; the Dewey decimal call number for this book is 808.0427, and the LC call number is PE1417.E53 2005.

Don't be discouraged from using books because of their length. You don't have to read the whole book. Skim and scan the contents to get the general idea. Use the table of contents and index to find specific information. If you are not doing in-depth research, you can also try the children's section for simple introductory books on various subjects.

PERIODICALS

Periodicals include newspapers, magazines, and academic journals. In other words, they are publications that come out periodically — daily, weekly, monthly, or a few times a year. Newspapers can be national dailies or sensationalist tabloids. Magazines range from news magazines such as *Maclean's* and *Time* to publications aimed at a specific audience such as snowboarders, home office workers, or computer technicians. Academic journals publish the latest research results.

Periodicals are valuable resources. They offer more up-to-date information than books and can focus on narrow, specific topics. In-depth news items often include sidebars of quick information, facts and statistics, and interviews with experts in the field. For example, in stories about an outbreak of *E. coli* at Walkerton, Ontario, newspaper articles carried information about strains of bacteria, the political controversy, sewage management, and legal implications.

Many periodicals have online versions, but these are often very limited. Newspapers might put main stories only online, and older editions or the full archives may be available only from a paid subscription service.

DATABASES

Databases help researchers access articles from newspapers, magazines, and journals. Print indexes were used in the past to help researchers find articles on their topics, but this was tedious as they had to look in several volumes. Today, electronic databases have taken the place of these indexes. These databases allow researchers to type in the subject, title, or author's name, and the search engine will bring up articles that fit the criteria. Some databases will just find the location of the article and perhaps include an abstract summarizing the content. The most useful are full-text databases because they will show the whole text of the article so that researchers do not have to hunt for it in the original periodical.

School libraries often subscribe to several database services, which allow access to publications not freely available on the Internet because of licensing agreements. Usually, students can use either school computers or their own machines to log onto their school's database services. The library website usually gives descriptions of each database and its coverage.

Make sure you choose a database with coverage suitable for your needs. For example, you may need a database of Canadian publications. Check the dates of coverage. Sometimes older issues have not been converted to online format but might be available on CD-ROM or microfiche. Become familiar with the way the different search engines work. Above all, do not hesitate to ask a reference librarian for help when you need it.

THE INTERNET

Unlike publishing houses, newspapers, and magazines, which have the reputation of their institution to uphold, the Internet is a publishing free-for-all. Anyone can put up a website and say anything at all—he or she doesn't have to be an expert in the field. There is no system of reviewers and editors approving the work. That makes the information unreliable. Therefore, you must approach Internet information cautiously.

One way to verify the information is to check it against other sources. If you find the information in more than one place, it is more likely to be correct. However, even this is not foolproof. Newspapers have been known to publish the urban legends that circulate on the Internet, and misinformation can be repeated in other sources.

When you use a website, check out the source of the information. If the site is hosted by a reputable organization, such as a university, it is more likely to have been verified. However, some organizations have misleading names. For instance, the Canadian Outdoor Heritage Alliance is not an environmental group, but an organization of trappers, anglers, and hunters. Be wary of pages that don't include names of authors and organizations and a way of contacting them.

The Internet has a reputation for offering the latest information, but every researcher has come across pages that should have been deleted from the system, such as those announcing events that are long past.

Another way to get information is from newsgroups and chat rooms. Again, you have to be careful. Many people spout off opinions in newsgroups without real knowledge of the topic. These postings have to be documented just as other references do.

Referencing Internet sites is also difficult. Many lack identifying information such as authors' names.

TAKING NOTES

The old methods of note-taking, such as using index cards and notebooks, seem to have fallen by the wayside. Now students are more likely to cut and paste articles from the Internet, or copy pages from books, and consider it note-taking. This is often done indiscriminately, however, and students are likely to end up with a pile of photocopies and printouts and no clear idea of how to proceed.

One of the most important principles of research is identifying clearly all the information you find. Internet printouts should include the URL and the date of access, articles from databases should have their bibliographic notation along with the database designation, and photocopies should be clearly marked with the source information. Each section you copy from an electronic source should be clearly marked. You can do this in short form if you keep a working bibliography. For instance, a quotation marked "(Asimov 58)" refers to page 58 of the Asimov book or article you are using. You should have the full reference in the bibliography. This is discussed in more detail in Chapter 5 ("Documentation") and shown in the sample research essay (pp. 421–426).

Clearly identifying all your reference material not only helps you keep track of your information, but also protects you from inadvertent plagiarism. If you use the words of another writer without fully showing that they are not your own words, you can be guilty of academic dishonesty (see pp. 436–437).

You can mark up your printouts and photocopies to help you find the choice passages. Use highlighters and write margin notes. Summarize the important points in your own words. Choose apt quotations for possible use in your essay. After you have read an article, jot down your thoughts about it: Why is this article important for your research? What is the main idea? What is the author's point of view and what is it based on? Keep track of articles that you dismiss for your research so that you don't look them up again by mistake.

Keep in mind that the Internet is unreliable. You may have trouble finding a site again, so bookmark it. Websites are frequently altered, so get printouts of very important sites.

Don't throw out the notes once you've finished the paper. You may be called on to support something in your paper, or, if disaster strikes and you lose the essay itself, you may have to redo it.

WRITING AND EDITING THE RESEARCH ESSAY

Once you have completed your research, sit back and think about your essay. What points do you want to make? What is your thesis? How do you want to organize your essay?

Write an outline. Go back through your notes and highlight information that you should use to support your points. Choose a few relevant quotations.

As you write the first draft, incorporate the information you found in your research. Use it to support your ideas. Don't just summarize everything you have read.

As you put your research information in the draft, be sure to include references for both quotations and paraphrases from other sources. Document everything except general knowledge (such as the fact that the War of 1812 was between the Americans and the British) and your own opinions. Refer to your brainstorming to help you see what you knew about the topic before you started your research.

Chapter 5 details how to cite references and prepare a bibliography. Refer to the research essay (pp. 421–426) to see an example.

After you have finished your first draft, put it aside for a day or two. You'll have a fresher view of it as you do the revisions. Look at your content first. Are there any other points you need to make? Is the essay well organized? Have you supported your ideas with examples and explanations? Have you used transition markers to show the relationship between ideas? Is everything clear? Once you are sure your essay says what you want it to say, look critically at the language. Are there unnecessary words and sentences that you can cut? Are your vocabulary choices the best you can make? Do any necessary revising and editing. (See the checklist on pp. 367–368.)

Make sure you have fulfilled the requirements of the assignment—from answering the question posed to submitting a cover page or outline as requested.

The final step is to proofread your paper thoroughly and carefully, perhaps several times. Remember that running a spelling and grammar checker is not enough. Look for errors you have made before. If your weakness is spelling, check every word. If you have a problem with sentence fragments, go through every sentence to make sure each is complete.

PARAPHRASING

As you incorporate the information from your research into your essay, you will be paraphrasing, putting an author's ideas into your own words. You still need to reference the information as it is not your own. You must also be accurate in relating the content. You must understand the subject matter well enough so that you can rephrase it for your reader. Do not twist the author's meaning to fit your argument.

Paraphrasing involves more than simply slotting in synonyms or changing the words around. Here is a quotation from Deborah Banks's "Where Do the Children Play?":

> "It behooves parents to be more vigilant, to ensure that their sons and daughters walk in the natural world and learn to feel the peace that can only come when one makes meaningful connections with the planet that sustains us" (229).

Here is a poor paraphrase, with few word changes:

> It requires parents to be more protective, to make sure that their children walk in nature and learn the peace that comes when they make real connections with the earth that nourishes us.

Here is another poor paraphrase:

> When we make meaningful connections with the planet that sustains us we can feel the peace, so we need to walk in the natural world. Parents should make sure their children do this.

Here is a good paraphrase:

> Parents should make sure that their children experience nature in order to understand their relationship with the earth.

Remember the rules of reported speech when you are paraphrasing. For example, quotation in the first person should be rendered in the third person, since the paraphraser is not the author.

Banks says, "I used to hold the fantasy that children were children no matter where you went."

Banks says that she used to believe children were the same everywhere.

In most cases, your paraphrase will also be a summary, as it will be shorter than the original text. For example, here is a paraphrase of the conclusion of "Grey Owl's Magnificent Masquerade":

John Barber insists that despite Grey Owl's deception, he is a true hero because he showed Canadians the value of their wilderness, something worth safeguarding by the environmental movement (p. 233).

Paraphrasing is also important in reading comprehension tests, since a good paraphrase shows true understanding of a text, while words can be copied from a passage with no real understanding at all.

CHOOSING QUOTATIONS

In your notes, you may choose to highlight sentences that could make useful quotations. Quotations should be short and relevant. Don't just quote statements of fact that can be easily paraphrased. Quote when the author's wording is particularly apt or expressive, as in these examples:

Gillespie calls the Trap a "suffocating defensive system" that was used to "stultifying success" (p. 269).

Mr. Truepenny is described as a man who "had a Don Quixote air about him, a sense that he was forever tilting at windmills" (de Lint 53).

Copy the passage accurately, word for word, punctuation marks and all. If there is a mistake in the passage, you are expected to copy it and put "[*sic*]" after it. "*Sic*" is the Latin for "thus"; it means that you have discovered a mistake and it is not yours, but the author's. If you leave out words, use ellipsis points (...) to show the omission.

Quotations should be neatly integrated into your essay. Don't say, "Here is a quotation from Winston Churchill to support this statement." Instead, say something like "The grammar rule about not ending a sentence with a preposition is a ridiculous restriction on the English language, as Winston Churchill showed when he said, 'This is the sort of English up with which I will not put.'"

You can see examples of quoting in the sample research essay on pages 421–426.

SUMMARIZING

Summarizing is an important skill to develop, for both academic and non-academic purposes. For example, summarizing a chapter of your textbook is an excellent way to learn the material and to make notes you can use for studying. If you just read the chapter, you wouldn't retain as much of the material as you would if you were to write a summary of it.

If you are writing about a story or article that you know your readers have not read, you might have to summarize the action of a story or recount the main points of an article.

For secondary sources, summarizing becomes much more important. Instead of merely outlining one source, you will be gathering information from many sources. Moreover, you will discover that all these sources have a common denominator. For example, in researching the Shirley Jackson story, you will come across several articles that focus on the use of stones and the symbolic nature of stoning. Instead of listing them all, you can assemble the common elements in these sources and make your statement:

> From the earliest critical review of "The Lottery" to the most recent, many literary scholars, folklorists, and anthropologists have drawn attention to stoning the victim. Accordingly, stoning is a ritual practised in many societies, and is done as a communal effort. It not only expresses the collective scorn of the villagers but also releases the blood lust repressed in every individual in that community. It is catharsis, a purging in the participants.

Immediately afterward, reference the main sources you found that drew you to the collective viewpoint.

WRITING A SUMMARY

In addition to summarizing for your own notes, you may be asked to write a summary of an article. Summaries tend to be about a tenth of the original length of the article. Thus, a 1000-word article can be summarized in a 100-word paragraph. The first sentence of the summary should identify the article (author, title, and, if necessary, the source information) and give a general idea of the article's content.

Sometimes you may be called on to write summary statements. These are one-sentence summaries that give the main idea of the article. If you are asked to do an annotated bibliography, your instructor may request a summary statement on each item. Here are two examples of summary statements:

Bodanis, David. "Toothpaste." *Fiction/Non-Fiction: A Reader and Rhetoric.* 2nd ed. Ed. Garry Engkent and Lucia Engkent. Toronto: Thomson Nelson, 2005, 241 – 43. Bodanis explains in detail the ingredients found in toothpaste.

Farr, Moira. "A Cell of Our Own Making." *Globe and Mail.* Dec. 8, 2003, A18. Farr criticizes cellphones for their intrusion on public space.

Here is an example of a summary paragraph:

Jay Ingram's "Once Upon a Time, A Story Meant Survival" explains the importance of storytelling in human evolution. The proof is in human beings' natural narrative skills, the existence of stories in every culture, and the evidence of oral traditions from prehistoric times. Storytelling is used to sway an audience and relay information about food supplies, predators, and dangers. Transmitting important, and perhaps even life-saving, information in a story reduces risk and saves time. Moreover, researchers have shown that people remember details better in a story than in a list. (91 words)

Conciseness is vital in a summary. Compare these two examples sentence by sentence to see how redundant and unnecessary words have been eliminated in the second version:

In the article "Have Wheels, Will Go A-Wooing," the author Kurt Preinsperg explains how he feels about having to own a car. Preinsperg says that he preferred using public transit rather than buying a vehicle. According to him, it was less stressful because he didn't have to worry about getting into accidents. Taking the bus cost him far less than maintaining a car. In addition to that, he didn't want to cause more pollution in the environment. However, he found that it was difficult to date the ladies without a vehicle. Women expected him to own a car so he could take them out on dates rather than wait for bus service. He was viewed as a poor potential provider when he explained that he didn't own a car. He explains that women have such sexual power over men that they are able to make men change their behaviour in order to be date material. Preinsperg finally decided that he needed to buy a car so he bought a car in order that he could go out on dates like every other male in the city. (186 words)

In "Have Wheels, Will Go A-Wooing," Kurt Preinsperg explains his views on car ownership. He preferred to travel by bus because it was less stressful, less expensive, and less polluting than operating a car. However, he found it difficult to date without a vehicle. Women expected him to own one, and his worth as a future provider plummeted when he explained his lack of a car. According to Preinsperg, women's sexual power over men allows them to dictate men's behaviour. Preinsperg finally gave in and bought a car to improve his love life. (93 words)

To write a summary of a story or article, follow these guidelines:

1. Read the article or story completely so that you understand the main ideas.
2. Write down the main ideas in your own words.
3. Follow the organization of the original piece.
4. Leave out illustrations, examples, explanations, and non-essential details. Avoid adding your own commentary.
5. Use your own words rather than copy phrases from the original. Be brief.
6. Compose a paragraph from your notes. Write complete sentences; join ideas with transition markers.
7. Identify the article and give the reader some idea of the topic.
8. Make sure that your reader will understand the summary without going to the original piece.
9. Revise your draft by checking for slips in grammar, spelling, and punctuation.
10. Proofread your final, clean copy carefully before submitting it.

Chapter 5

DOCUMENTATION

Once you have done your research, you must write your essay, incorporating the information you have found. In the body of your essay, you might quote from other works or you might just refer to them. In both cases, show the reader the author's name and a page reference if necessary. The full citation information is found in your bibliography at the end of the essay. This chapter goes over the basic rules of referencing; an example of a research essay with citations is found at the end of Chapter 6.

Currently, the preferred method of documentation is to incorporate references or acknowledgments briefly in parentheses right after the citation. Two of the most popular methods are the MLA style and the APA style. The Modern Languages Association (MLA) format is endorsed by writers in the arts and humanities; the American Psychology Association (APA) style is used by those in the sciences and social sciences. While they both reference research material after the quoted passage, they differ slightly in format. Our focus is on the MLA style because that is the one favoured in English courses in college and university.

Footnotes and endnotes are also used to document writing. Superscript numbers appear after a direct quotation, paraphrase, or acknowledgment of an idea, and then the source information for that number is given at the foot of the page (footnotes), or at the end of the document (endnotes). This method, mostly commonly based on *The Chicago Manual of Style*, is used in high-school writing and in some non-academic books. Even though references in parentheses are more common in academic articles and essays, you may find that some instructors still use the words "footnotes" and "footnoting" as generic terms for referencing in a research paper, even if the information does not appear at the bottom of a page in an actual footnote.

Your instructor or your school will tell you which style to use in your essays. Usually, handouts are available with details. Check at the library or on your school's website.

The different methods of citation have more similarities than differences, however. They all have some way of signalling the reference within the body of the text and a page at the end giving the full source information. For each citation, you must give the following information in the order shown:

- author(s) name(s)
- title of the book or article
- (name of journal or periodical)
- place of publication
- publisher
- date of publication

The essential information for citing websites is the same as for any source; you must cite the author, the title, and the location (the full URL, or address). Because websites can change frequently, give the date on which you accessed the site as well as the date the site was created. Some of this information may not appear on the website, but record as much as is available. Check the referring home page; sometimes you can find the author or host institution named there.

Referencing can be a finicky business, and we cannot cover all possible situations in this book. If you do not know how to reference a source, you can try the following:

- Look for a similar example in this text.
- Check the documentation handout from your college library or writing centre.
- Consult English handbooks and textbooks that deal with essay writing and referencing.
- Look on the Internet for more style guidelines.
- Consult the *MLA Handbook*, which should be in the reference section of the library (or the APA style guide if appropriate).
- Ask a librarian for help.
- Ask your instructor for help or clarification.

BIBLIOGRAPHY: "WORKS CITED" OR "WORKS CONSULTED"

The research essay should have a bibliography at the end, starting a new page. "Bibliography" is the generic and most familiar term for the list of resources even though the word itself refers only to books (by its etymology). MLA style uses the title "Works Cited" for the list of references that you actually referred to (or cited) in your essay and "Works Consulted" for a list of all the resources you used. Depending on your professor's instructions, attach either "Works Cited" or "Works Consulted" but not both. Essentially, these lists contain enough information so that a reader can locate the exact sources you used. The parenthetical references after a quotation or paraphrase are a short-form reference to the full citation in the bibliography. For example, after a quotation you may have something like "(Asimov 47)"; this tells the reader that the author of the cited piece is Asimov, that the quotation is from page 47, and that the full reference is in the bibliography under the name "Asimov."

Your list of sources should be in alphabetical order by author's family name. If there is no known author, then you should use the title of the article or story. Do not include "A," "An," or "The" in the alphabetization; instead, alphabetize by the next word.

A distinction is made between the titles of shorter works (stories, articles, poems) that appear in larger works (books, newspapers, magazines). Story and article titles appear between quotation marks, while the names of books and newspapers are underlined.

Italics and underlining are equivalent. Underlining was traditionally used in manuscripts because they were typed on typewriters, which did not have italic keys. The typesetters would replace the underlining with italics once the book was published. Now that computers are used, it is easy to use italics instead of underlining in your essays. However, MLA prefers underlining for book titles in essays because some typefaces have italic prints that are not sufficiently distinguishable from the regular print.

The Works Cited page is double-spaced, with run-on lines (those after the first line) indented five spaces. This is called a "hanging indent." Most word-processing software can handle this feature; check out the Help function if you do not know how to format this.

The examples below show what we expect to be the most common types of references used by college students. However, the situation can change. For instance, a few years ago CD-ROM reference materials such as encyclopedias were popular, but now most researchers can find the same entries online. Some newer libraries don't even have reference works in print, but since those are still basic sources of information, we have included them here. If you cannot find an example that shows the kind of referencing you need, check your library for its MLA guidelines.

BOOKS

[Author. Book title. Place of publication: Publisher, date of publication.]

Campbell, Joseph. The Hero with a Thousand Faces. New York: Meridian Books, 1949.

---. Myths to Live By. New York: Bantam Books, 1973.

Canada. Citizenship and Immigration Canada. A Look at Canada. Ottawa: Minister of Public Works and Government Services Canada, 2003.

Farb, Peter, and George Armelagos. Consuming Passions: The Anthropology of Eating. New York: Houghton Mifflin, 1980.

Ferguson, Will. Why I Hate Canadians. Vancouver: Douglas & McIntyre, 1997.

Findlay, Isobel, et al., eds. Introduction to Literature. 5th ed. Toronto: Thomson Nelson, 2004.

Griffiths, Rudyard, ed. Great Questions of Canada. Toronto: Stoddart, 2000.

In these examples, note that an author can be a government agency or other institution, such as a corporation. Also, anthologies (books that are collections of readings by other authors) are shown by the designation "ed." or "eds." after the editors' names. If there is more than one author for a work, only the first author's name is reversed with the family name first. If there are more than three authors (the Findlay book listed above has five authors), you can give just the first author's name and use *et al.* ("and others") for the rest. If there are two works by the same author, use three hyphens (---) instead of the name for the second and subsequent entries; list the publications in alphabetical order by title. Note that if the book is not the first edition, this information is also given.

WORK IN AN ANTHOLOGY

[Author. "Article title." Book title. Editor's name. Place of publication: Publisher, date of publication. Page numbers.]

Bissoondath, Neil. "Dreaming of Other Lands." Great Questions of Canada. Ed. Rudyard Griffiths. Toronto: Stoddart, 2000. 27-31.

Lau, Evelyn. "Marriage." Introduction to Literature. 5th ed. Ed. Isobel Findlay, et al. Toronto: Thomson Nelson, 2004. 588-92.

Scott, Barbara. "Lifeguard." Fiction/Non-Fiction: A Reader and Rhetoric. 2nd ed. Ed. Garry Engkent and Lucia Engkent. Toronto: Thomson Nelson, 2005. 190-99.

The original publication information, which is usually found in the publication credits or acknowledgments, can also be included.

If you use several articles from the same anthology, you can cross-reference instead of giving a full citation for each article:

Asimov, Isaac. "The Fun They Had." Engkent and Engkent 28-30.
Banks, Deborah. "Where Do the Children Play?" Engkent and Engkent 228-29.
Engkent, Garry, and Lucia Engkent, eds. Fiction/Non-Fiction: A Reader and Rhetoric. 2nd ed. Toronto: Thomson Nelson, 2005.
Lasn, Kalle. "Toxic Culture Syndrome." Engkent and Engkent 293-97.

ARTICLE IN A REFERENCE BOOK

[Author. "Article title." Name of Reference Book. Publication information if necessary. Page numbers if necessary.]

"Largest Box of Chocolates." Guinness World Records 2004. 110.
"Poltergeist." Harper's Encyclopedia of Mystical and Paranormal Experience. Rosemary Ellen Guiley. Edison, N.J.: Castle Books, 1991.
"Sasquatch." The New Encyclopedia Britannica: Micropedia. 15th ed. 1994.
Smith, Donald B. "Belaney, Archibald Stansfeld." The Canadian Encyclopedia. 2nd ed. 1988.
"Society." The Canadian Oxford Dictionary. 1998.

Include the author's name for an encyclopedia article if it is given; the author's name or initials (identified elsewhere in the work) would appear at the end of the entry. Unsigned articles appear with the title first. If the work is a well-known regularly published reference book such as a major encyclopedia, you need include only the year of the edition. If the entries appear alphabetically in the reference book, you don't need the volume information and page number. Note that these are the rules for print sources only.

ARTICLE IN A PERIODICAL (PRINT VERSION)

[Author. "Article title." Name of periodical Date: pages.]

Farquharson, Vanessa. "Lies, Cheats, Scams, and Deception: You Can Have It All for Just One Low Monthly Fee." National Post 3 Aug. 2004: AL1+.
"Job Laws Lagging behind New Reality." Editorial. Toronto Star 3 Aug. 2004, Metro ed.: A14.
Macklem, Katherine. "The Myth of Rich." Maclean's 2 Aug. 2004: 24-30.
Taylor-Mendes, Cosette. "Our Names." TESL Canada Journal 21.1 (2003): 97-101.

For magazine and newspaper articles not printed on consecutive pages, write only the first page number with a plus sign. For academic journals, include the volume number.

ARTICLE FROM AN ELECTRONIC SOURCE

Citing electronic sources can be tricky, but keep in mind the fundamental principle: your reference information should allow the reader to find the exact same source that you used.

You should distinguish between periodicals that are on the World Wide Web and those that are in a subscription service database. This can be confusing since both have URLs, both may be accessed from your home computer, and both may have limited access by subscription. One way to tell is that you enter subscription databases through the library's website and log in with your student I.D. and password. However, your library may include links to outside websites along with its links to databases. Look at what shows on your screen carefully. That information, the URL, and the headings should tell you whether you are in a database or not. For database articles, include the name of the database, the subscription service, and the subscriber (usually your school library). For website articles, give the URL (the website address) unless it's a long search string address, in which case you can give the URL of the referring page. Note that articles are sometimes collected and "reprinted" on a website that is not maintained by the original publisher.

The author's name is sometimes not prominent, so make sure you do a thorough search for it. Check the page where there might be a copyright notice. Or go back to a referring home page.

When you're looking at a publication's website, keep in mind that it may keep only current issues on its website before archiving them in a database, so you may have to print out the article.

ARTICLE (DATABASE)

[Author. "Article title." Name of periodical Date: pages. Database name. Name of service. Name of organization subscribing to the service. Access date.]

> Lazarus, Eve. "Adbusters Out to Step on Nike's Toes." Marketing Magazine 8 Sept. 2003: 2. Canadian Reference Centre. EBSCOhost. Seneca Learning Commons. 3 Aug. 2004.

McMurdy, Deirdre. "Can't Work the VCR? Here's Who to Blame." <u>Calgary Herald</u> 2 May 2004, final ed.: E7. <u>Canadian Newsstand</u>. ProQuest. Seneca Learning Commons. 25 July 2004.

"Vicente Wins Business Award." <u>Examiner</u> [Barrie, Ont.] 23 April 2004, final ed.: C2. <u>Canadian Newsstand</u>. ProQuest. Seneca Learning Commons. 25 July 2004.

ARTICLE (WITH URL)

[Author. "Article title." Name of periodical Date. Access date <URL>.]

Bower, Bruce. "Buyer Beware: Some Psychologists See Danger in Excessive Materialism." <u>Science News</u> 6 Sept. 2003. LookSmart. 27 July 2004 <http://www.findarticles.com/p/articles/mi_m1200/is_10_164/ai_108149513>.

King, Thomas. "Not Enough Horses." <u>Walrus</u> July/Aug. 2004. 3 Aug. 2004 <http://www.walrusmagazine.com>.

Starr, Linda. "Sticks and Stones and Names Can Hurt You: De-myth-tifying the Classroom Bully!" <u>Education World</u> 11 July 2000. 3 Aug. 2004 <http://www.education-world.com/a_issues/issues102.shtml>.

If the URL of the site is long and complicated, showing the search string information, you can give the URL of the site's search page instead. If you must print it on two lines, break it after a slash and don't add any hyphens or other marks.

WEBSITES

[Author. "Title of web page." <u>Title of the site</u>. Date of latest update of website. Access date. <URL>.]

"Advice to Parents." <u>Bullying Online</u>. 2003. 24 July 2004 <http://www.bullying.co.uk/ parents/parentsl_advice.htm>.

"Doping-Free Sport: Substances and Methods: Banned." <u>Canadian Centre for Ethics in Sports</u>. 2004. 6 June 2004 <http://www.cces.ca/forms/index.cfm?dsp=template&act=view3&template_id=69&lang=e>.

Katz, Leslie. "Families Feel Pressure to Have Bigger, Better Party Bags." <u>Bay Home Site</u>. 24 July 2004. 25 August 2004 <http://www.insidebayarea.com/bayarealiving/ci_2380898>.

"King, William Lyon Mackenzie" <u>The Prime Ministers of Canada</u>. 28 June
2004. Library of Parliament. 24 Sept. 2004.
<http://www.parl.gc.ca/information/about/people/key/
pm_hist/pm_hist.asp?lang=E&Source=pm&PM=10>.

If you get to a website through a search engine and it does not have enough
information for your reference, try to find the site's home page. Look for
links that say "Home" or "About Us." You can also try going up levels in
the web map by deleting what comes after the last slash in the URL.

FILMS

[<u>Title of the film</u>. Name of director. Names of performers. Film company
name, copyright date.]

<u>Shakespeare in Love</u>. Dir. John Madden. Perf. Gwyneth Paltrow, Joseph
Fiennes, Geoffrey Rush, and Colin Firth. Miramax, 1998.
<u>Star Wars</u>. Dir. George Lucas. Perf. Mark Hamill, Harrison Ford, and Carrie
Fisher. Twentieth Century Fox, 1977.

PARENTHETICAL REFERENCES FOR QUOTATIONS AND PARAPHRASES

Whenever you use the words or ideas of another writer in your research
paper, you must note this with a citation. In MLA style, a parenthetical reference (i.e., in round brackets) contains the author's name or the title of the
work and the location (usually a page number) of the borrowed information. (This format replaces the footnote used in other styles.) This reference
leads the reader to the full bibliographic citation in the Works Cited or
Works Consulted list. Unless otherwise noted, these references are from
this textbook.

Television viewing does not encourage interaction with the real world:
"Watching TV is the very opposite of a communal exercise — we finish up
isolating ourselves . . ." (Lasn 295).

Note that there is no comma between the author's name and the page
number. Ellipsis points (. . .) show that words have been left out of the
quotation, such as the end of the sentence.

If you mention the author's name just before the quotation, you do not need to include it in the brackets. Note that this example has the quotation after a colon:

> A level of civility or good manners begins at the dinner table. According to Peter Farb and George Armelagos, the humanist Erasmus offered this piece of advice for good etiquette: "Do not poke around in your dish, but take the first piece you touch. Do not put chewed food from the mouth back on your place; instead, throw it under the table or behind your chair" (254). Today, we do not play with our food, and we no longer spit out gristle with abandon. Rather, we swallow it or wrap it discreetly in a napkin.

Integrate your quotations smoothly into the text; don't just drop them in haphazardly or introduce them with unnecessary phrases such as "the following quotation illustrates." In this example, a shorter quotation fits right into a sentence:

> Accordingly, the hero may not always be able to accomplish his task by himself, and often an older or more experienced person "provides the adventurer with amulets against the dragon forces he is about to pass" (Campbell 69).

Here is the full citation for this quotation:

> Campbell, Joseph. <u>The Hero with a Thousand Faces</u>. New York: Meridian Books, 1949.

If you are quoting a longer passage (more than three lines), don't use quotation marks. Instead, set the passage off from the main text of your essay. The passage is indented as in the following example:

> The dinner knife has an interesting evolution. The sharp, pointed cutting blade changed to the dull, rounded utensil:

>> The knife served as a utensil, but it offered a potential threat because it was also a weapon. Thus taboos were increasingly placed upon its use: It was to be held by the point with the blunt handle presented; it was not to be placed anywhere near the face; and most important, the uses to which it was put were sharply restricted. It was not to be used for cutting soft foods such as boiled eggs or fish, or round ones such as potatoes, or to be lifted from the table for courses that did not need it. In short, good table manners in Europe gradually removed the threatening aspect of the knife from social occasions. (Farb and Armelagos 256)

> The dinner table knife today is no more than a butter knife, and its presence is at times decorative rather than practical. So, when we need to cut into a steak, we are given a different knife with a serrated blade.

Make sure you copy the passage accurately, even if there are errors in the original. You are expected to note the errors (using "[*sic*]" after the mistake), but not correct them. Note that the parenthetical reference in an indented quotation appears after the period.

Unless you can skilfully integrate your words with phrases from a source, you should avoid quoting snippets or short phrases and stringing them in your sentences. This creates a choppy sentence, as in this example:

> According to Farb and Armelagos, as "spontaneous, direct, and informal" meals gave way to propriety, the people of the Middle Ages "began to feel shame." No longer did people blow their noses with fingers but "handkerchiefs came into use" and "napkins were in common use" at the dinner table (254-55).

If you are quoting a quotation, you have to show that. Single quotation marks are used within double ones. The reference is the source where you found the quotation.

> Grey Owl's language reveals his British origins: "There was a wood-chuck, a special chum of mine, who year after year made her home under the upper cabin, where she had every Spring a brood of wood-chucklets, or whatever they are called. She was an amiable old lady . . ." (qtd. in Ross 329)

If you are quoting from a source that does not have an identified author, use the first few words of the title to identify the source, but include the word by which it is alphabetized:

> Special dinners were also a feast for the eye: "Royal Medieval feasts also included lavish 'solteties,' which were fanciful representations of saints, heroes and warriors, made from sugar and presented in a dramatic display" ("Brief History of Cooking").

The above parenthetical reference would point to this full citation in the Works Cited list:

> "A Brief History of Cooking and Dining." Eras of Elegance. 2002. 23 July 2004 <http://www.erasofelegance.com/entertaining2.html>.

Electronic sources usually do not include page numbers, so you cannot give that information in your parenthetical reference.

Remember that if you take an idea (not a well-known fact) from another writer and put it in your own words, you need to credit it. The same type of referencing is used for the paraphrase, but without quotation marks.

Accordingly, the hero may not always be able to accomplish his task by himself, and often an older or more experienced person gives the hero some magic token to ward off enemies and monsters (Campbell 69).

More examples of quotations and parenthetical references can be seen in the sample research essay (pp. 421–426).

Chapter 6

TYPES OF ESSAYS

This chapter expands on the information about essay writing by showing the different kinds of writing you may do. Most essays are essentially an argument because you are setting forth a point of view and supporting it. However, essays that focus on comparison differ slightly from essays that explain causes. Your purpose determines what kind of essay you are writing. For instance, if your goal is to explain how something is done, you are writing a process essay. In a longer essay or report, you may have more than one mode. For instance, you may include a paragraph of definition or description as background information. The different purposes are explained below and can also be seen in the reading selections.

NARRATION

Narration is essentially storytelling. Short stories and novels are narratives. In essay writing, you may use narration to tell of an experience you or someone else had to illustrate a point.

It is important that your storytelling is clear. Give as much detail as is necessary. Short-story writers give a lot of detail because their goal is to involve the reader in the action. In an essay, however, narration tends to be less detailed and includes less dialogue. To see this difference in action, compare the narration in the essay "Growing Up on Grace" (p. 246) and the short story "Chickens for Christmas" (p. 61).

Newspaper and magazine articles often start with an anecdote (narration) before going into the main argument. Essay writers also use narration as an effective technique. Notice how Kurt Preinsperg starts with a narrative (the story of a particular date he had), followed by a list of his anti-car arguments in "Have Wheels, Will Go A-Wooing" (p. 318).

In everyday life, you might have to use narration to explain how an accident happened or to describe the history of something. In your academic essays, you may use narration to explain your experience with something. Good storytelling requires that the information be presented clearly so that readers can follow the action. Generally, chronological order is preferred. How much detail you give depends on the situation, the audience, and the purpose.

DESCRIPTION

Description goes hand in hand with narration. It fleshes out the skeletal form of the telling by adding details. It shapes the reader's imagination. For example, in "Where Do the Children Play?" Deborah Banks describes time outdoors as "a lazy summer afternoon while bathing in a cacophony of insect melodies" (p. 229).

Description is not restricted to narrative. In business, job descriptions outline requirements and tasks to be done by the employees. In science, researchers describe the changes of states or conditions of chemicals, cells, or atoms. A photograph can reveal only the visual aspects of its subject, but a description can evoke other senses for the reader.

Describing is not a matter of tossing in adjectives, adverbs, or modifiers to fill out a sentence or a paragraph. Your description should be organized logically. For instance, if you are describing a scene, you might want to go from near to far, or from right to left. Your description should be selective; the details you give should be important. You must be sure of the words you are using.

In your essays, you might need to use description to give details to the reader, as in this example:

> While the trend toward more casual dress in the workplace can liberate employees, it can also go too far and be disrespectful. Last week, one of my co-workers showed up for Casual Friday in ragged blue jeans that looked as if they would not survive another wash. The seams were frayed and the material looked almost transparent in places. His T-shirt used to be white, but it had greyed with ineffective washing. The worst offence was the saying on the T-shirt, which hinted at sexual harassment. Even though this employee is not within public view, his appearance was an insult to his co-workers.

ILLUSTRATION

To make points clear, writers use illustration and give examples to add detailed information. Illustration is part of every essay, but some essays function as illustrative essays, simply explaining a situation to the reader without much argument. You might use definition, description, and comparison as part of your illustration.

In "Toothpaste," David Bodanis gives us a good example of illustration as he methodically explains one of the ingredients in toothpaste:

The individual chalk particles—the size of the smallest mud particles in your garden—have kept their toughness over the eons, and now on the toothbrush they'll need it. The enamel outer coating of the tooth they'll have to face is the hardest substance in the body—tougher than skull, or bone, or nail. Only the chalk particles in toothpaste can successfully grind into the teeth during brushing, ripping off the surface layers like an abrading wheel grinding down a boulder in a quarry. (p. 241)

When you give an example to illustrate something, you usually signal the reader that it is an example and not the whole situation. To do this, you use expressions such as "for example" and "for instance" to introduce sentences, "such as" for phrases, and verbs such as "include." Do not use "e.g." and "etc." in your essays; these Latin abbreviations are fine in your notes, but not in academic prose.

Here is an example of an illustration essay:

In "Have Wheels, Will Go A-Wooing," Kurt Preinsperg compromises his ideals when he decides to buy a car to salvage his social life. Television programs such as *Queer Eye for the Straight Guy* and *The Date Patrol* show people changing their appearance, their communication style, and their environment for the sake of the opposite sex. Obviously, people feel that it is worth changing themselves in the pursuit of what all humans value most—love and companionship. People often improve their appearance, their behaviour, and even their attitudes in order to please a potential boyfriend or girlfriend.

Appearance is often easy to improve. Clothes make up a big part of one's look. Dressing in clean, fashionable clothes makes people more attractive, while sloppy, dirty clothes send the message that they do not care. Women may go as far as dressing in revealing, skimpy clothes to enhance their sex appeal. In addition, they use makeup and perfume to up the ante in the attraction game. Men, too, have become more aware of the importance of grooming and are even going to spas for manicures and waxing. Some people go to the extreme of altering their looks with plastic surgery, but just taking some care with appearance can make a big difference.

People also change their behaviour to make themselves more attractive. Politeness goes a long way toward scoring points with others. Flirtatiousness can tell a potential love interest that the person is available and interested. Being attentive toward a love interest is also a behaviour modification people can easily make. For example, a boyfriend who lets his girlfriend choose the movie, even if it is a chick flick, shows consideration on his part. Some people carry behaviour modification so far as to become someone very different from their real selves.

Attitudes may be harder to change deliberately, but as people grow and develop as persons, their attitudes can improve. This improvement can come from both education and maturity. For example, people who have sexist or racist views may grow out of them by first making the step to be less overt about such opinions when they are chastised by others. Learning that others do not approve can lead people to change their own views. Falling in love can ultimately improve a person's mind.

Changing appearance, behaviour, and attitude is all part of the game in attracting the opposite sex. People always strive to better themselves. Moreover, making such changes does not end when people do form a relationship. Husbands and wives continue to compromise and change in the interests of getting along together.

ARGUMENT

In everyday speech, we generally use the word "argument" to refer to a fight, a quarrel, or a disagreement. However, an argument can simply be a reason for something. For example, the high cost of owning a vehicle is an argument for using public transit. An argument essay can also be persuasive: you try to make your reader accept your point of view. Argument can be like a formal debate, in which you take one point of view and support it. It does not have to be what you personally believe; indeed, you should be able to argue both sides of an issue as an intellectual exercise. In marking an argument essay, your instructor is not looking to see whether you agree with him or her, but whether you can present logical reasoning.

The sample essay in Chapter 1 is an argument essay (pp. 359–360). Two different opinions on the same issue can be found in "Drugs in Sports" (p. 322) and "Never Give In, Never" (p. 313). Kurt Preinsperg explains the reasons he does not drive in "Have Wheels, Will Go A-Wooing" (p. 318), and Kalle Lasn argues that television is dangerous in "Toxic Culture Syndrome" (p. 293).

In an argument or persuasive paper, it is important to have a clear position in your thesis statement. This stand must be firm, unequivocal, and clear. Don't sit on the fence. Depending on the topic, you may need to give some background so that the reader has some grounding. Then you proceed to argue your case. You present your evidence in the form of facts and statistics, testimony of experts, logic, and reasons. Your organization must be logical, giving an item-by-item account of your evidence.

Argument requires you to address the views of the opposition. Unlike a debate, an essay does not give you a chance to deliver a rebuttal. You must anticipate the objections your readers will have and deal with them. One way to do this is concession. Conceding a point is a way of saying "Yes, but," as in this example:

> Although the cost of postsecondary education represents a huge chunk of the government's budget, the money can be seen as a good investment, especially when the financial burden is shared among all citizens, all of whom benefit from an educated citizenry.

Weak arguments are referred to as "logical fallacies." Here are some common logical fallacies to avoid:

- Don't argue against the person. Argue against his or her opinions or ideas.
- Don't use hasty generalizations, such as drawing conclusions from little evidence.
- Don't use unfounded cause and effect, saying that because something occurred it caused something else to happen.
- Don't give circular reasoning, as in "He is a good person because he is good."
- Don't appeal to popular prejudices, as in "Only snobs listen to opera."

Here is an example of an argument essay:

> In "Don't You Think It's Time to Start Thinking?," Northrop Frye says that there is a "powerful anti-intellectual drive which is constantly present in our society" (p. 265). At first, this seems an odd statement. After all, Canadians seem to value education. In election polls, education along with health care is at the top of the list of voters' priorities. Colleges and universities are bursting at the seams. However, all this is just lip service paid to the importance of education. In truth, modern North American society discourages intellectualism.
>
> First, students are not encouraged to achieve academic greatness. In high school, "brainers" are ridiculed and are never the popular kids, unless an assignment partner is needed. Some gifted children even underperform in their schoolwork to avoid being labelled a brainer. Even though parents can take pride in their offspring's straight-A report cards, they get more

recognition if their children are sports stars. More dads dream of their sons winning a Stanley Cup rather than a Nobel Prize. They may even push their children toward achievement in sports at the cost of their schoolwork. In addition, book learning is not modelled in many homes. Parents tell their children to do their homework, but they spend more money on Disney videos than books.

Furthermore, intellectuals are not rewarded by money or fame. Our society idolizes athletes, models, actors, and musicians, and rewards them financially. While lawyers, doctors, and scientists may earn good salaries, they do not approach the millions that even mediocre professional athletes are given. Academic prizes and scholarships are relatively negligible. While Pierre Trudeau made no secret of the fact that he was an intellectual, many recent politicians go so far as to downplay their brains in their quest to get elected. Bill Clinton did not trumpet his achievement as a Rhodes scholar so as not to distance himself from the common person. Some politicians achieve success despite an apparent lack of intellectual prowess.

Finally, popular entertainment prizes the stupid over the intelligent. The movie industry tries to appeal to the teen demographic and puts out hundreds of movies like *Dumb and Dumber*—the title says it all. North American television has little that makes the audience think and learn. The latest fad of reality programming caters to the lowest common denominator. It titillates rather than educates with shows such as *The Simple Life* and *The Bachelor*. Programs that make people think earn the lowest Nielsen ratings. Even the news programs present sound bites rather than insightful analysis. It is easier to report traffic accidents or violent crimes than provoke a debate over their causes and consequences. No news programmer dares raise the intellectual stakes for the six o'clock news.

Although we still have some great minds to guide us, the majority of us would rather remain mentally lazy in a non-intellectual society. Thinking deeply is hard work. Moreover, we see no reward in developing our mental competence and prefer entertainment that does not tax our grey cells. Ironically, we take pride in our mental sloth and leave the thinking to someone else.

COMPARE AND CONTRAST

In a comparison paper, you draw similarities between two items. In a contrast essay, you show differences between two items. However, we use the term "comparison" to refer to essays in which either similarities or differences are discussed.

Your comparison has to be justified. You wouldn't write an essay comparing a horse and a desk because there is no reason to compare those two things. Generally, you would choose to show similarities between things that seem different or differences between things that seem similar. For instance, if you were writing about computer engineering and computer science programs at a university, it would be more logical to show how they are different rather than how they are similar. An essay could show how job hunting and fishing are similar activities.

In any comparison, you must have areas in common in order to compare or contrast. For example, to compare two schools, you might talk about location, courses offered, and staff. It is important that you do the work for the reader. It is not enough to describe one thing and then the other, and then conclude "As you can see, they are very different."

There are two main methods used for comparison essays. In point-by-point organization, you go back and forth, dealing with one point of comparison for each item you are comparing and then moving on to a second point. In the block method, you deal with one item fully before you go on to the next. The topic sentence of the paragraph should mention both.

Point-by-point organization:
    Point 1: Item A
               Item B
    Point 2: Item A
               Item B
    Point 3: Item A
               Item B

Block organization:
    Item A: Point 1
               Point 2
               Point 3
    Item B: Point 1
               Point 2
               Point 3

Here is an example of a point-by-point comparison paragraph:

> Isaac Asimov's vision of a mechanical teacher in his 1957 short story "The Fun They Had" is quite different from modern computers. Asimov's machine is very mechanical. The County Inspector fixes the machine with "a whole box of tools with dials and wires." A modern computer technician would be more inclined to use software to fix problems. If there were faulty components in the hardware, a technician would simply slot in a new component. The inspector says the machine is "geared a little too quick." This kind of problem would not happen in a modern computer because the software would be able to offer the appropriate level. Another difference is the interface. Margie has to do her work on punch cards and insert her homework in a slot for the machine to read. A modern student uses a keyboard and a mouse. What is typed appears directly on the computer screen. Asimov's short story shows us how computers have evolved over the last fifty years.

Here is the same comparison, presented in a block paragraph:

> Isaac Asimov's vision of a mechanical teacher in his 1957 short story "The Fun They Had" is quite different from modern computers. Asimov's machine is very mechanical. The County Inspector fixes the machine with "a whole box of tools with dials and wires" because the machine is "geared a little too quick." Margie has to do her work on punch cards and insert her homework in a slot for the machine to read. A modern computer technician would be more inclined to use software to fix problems. If there were faulty components in the hardware, a technician would simply slot in a new component. The problem of an appropriate level would be dealt with in the software. As for the interface, a modern student uses a keyboard and a mouse. What is typed appears directly on the computer screen. Asimov's short story shows us how computers have evolved over the last fifty years.

Take note of the structure of this comparison essay:

> In "Shooting an Elephant" and "The Man I Killed," George Orwell and Tim O'Brien present the subject of death in a realistic manner. Both writers draw from their personal experiences to show that killing or taking a life is a serious matter, the first in an essay and the second in a fictionalized story. Although Orwell recounts the execution of an animal and O'Brien describes the lifeless body of a human being after a firefight, both reflect on the circumstances and aftermath of the kill. They explain how the killing came about, why they killed, what happened to them psychologically, and what they learned from the traumatic experience.

For both Orwell and O'Brien, the killings were a direct result of their being in a foreign country: the former was a constable in Burma, and the latter a soldier in Vietnam. For Orwell, the situation was that an elephant in sexual heat went wild, escaped from its master, and created havoc. It destroyed property, trampled a Burmese to death, and caused terror in the village. For O'Brien, in the Vietnam War, his platoon on patrol was ambushed by the Vietcong. The American soldier repulsed the attack. Both the British policeman and the American GI were in a physically dangerous situation that could have become more dangerous if a solution had not been found and acted upon. Orwell shot the elephant, and Tim, the autobiographical character in O'Brien's story, killed a Vietcong soldier.

At the time of the killings, both the British constable and the American soldier were performing their respective duties. As a policeman whose job is to keep the peace, Orwell was responsible for the safety of the villagers and their property. He had been called in specifically to stop the elephant. "It had already destroyed somebody's bamboo hut, killed a cow, and raided some fruit-stalls and devoured the stock; also it had met the municipal rubbish van, and when the driver jumped out and took to his heels, had turned the van over and inflicted violence upon it" (306). In addition, the elephant caught a coolie "with its trunk, put its foot on his back, and ground him into the earth" (307). As a soldier, Tim was duty bound to vanquish the enemy of the United States and South Vietnam. Moreover, on a more personal level, it was not just a situation of kill or be killed; he did so to save his buddies. As Kiowa, Tim's friend, said much later, the Vietcong had a weapon.

Surprisingly, both Orwell and O'Brien share a common experience in the act of killing: they regretted their actions. Orwell felt sorry for the elephant as it tried to stay alive after the policeman poured several bullets into the mouth and heart of the beast: "a mysterious, terrible change had come over the elephant. He neither stirred nor fell, but every line of his body altered. He looked suddenly stricken, shrunken, immensely old" (309). Tim — frozen in his tracks, unable to move and unable to stop staring at the dead Vietcong — understood that the enemy was also a human being, a patriot. The Vietcong was only defending his own country: "He was a citizen and a soldier. In the village of My Khe . . . patriotic resistance had the force of tradition, which was partly the force of legend" (174). Both policeman and soldier may have done their respective duties but they didn't feel good about doing so.

Finally, the Englishman and the American both came to understand themselves better as a result of the kill. Orwell learned that he could be pressured and manipulated into committing an act that he knew was morally wrong. He saw himself as a man who did not want to be seen as foolish in front of other people. He had given in to personal weakness — "solely to avoid looking a fool" (311) — rather than doing what was right by not shooting the elephant. In a similar vein, Tim saw that the man he killed was really no different than he. The Vietcong was not a faceless enemy: like Tim, he was a human being and had a childhood, a family, a loved one, a dream. So, Tim the soldier offered this "almost dainty young man of about twenty" (178) immortality "in the stories of his village and people" (177).

In the two narratives, George Orwell and Tim O'Brien show that death is not just someone or something dead, lifeless. Although they acted properly and their reasons for the deed may be justifiable in the respective situations, the Englishman of the 1930s and the American of the 1970s are deeply moved by the experience. Both writers describe different incidents, but they reveal the lingering effects of the kill.

CAUSE AND EFFECT

Cause is the reason for an action. Effect is the result of the action. You can approach a cause-and-effect paper in three ways. First, you can show reasons why such an incident occurred. For example, you may want to explain why the North West Mounted Police were needed in the territories that now form the Prairie provinces. Second, you can explain the result of something that has happened or will happen. For example, due to the establishment of law and order by the North West Mounted Police, the Canadian government did not have to face the Indian wars that marked the American western expansion in the mid-1800s. Third, you can write about the reasons for and results of an incident. Sometimes you will describe a chain reaction, with one thing leading to another and then to another.

In "Shooting an Elephant" (p. 305), George Orwell demonstrates how the mechanism of cause and effect works. The cause of the rampage is a rogue elephant that is in an uncontrollable frenzy; the effect is that Orwell as a policeman must go investigate. Although Orwell is reluctant to shoot the elephant, he is goaded on by the native spectators (cause). He kills the elephant, in his words, "to avoid looking a fool" (effect). Another example is Kalle Lasn's essay (p. 293), which exposes the bad effects of television-watching.

This paragraph focuses on the effects of over-praising students:

> When Canadian educators were so focused on their students' self-esteem in the 1980s, they may have gone too far, creating monsters instead of well-adjusted members of society. Too much self-esteem can lead to narcissism. One effect is the students' belief that the world revolves around them. They think that their needs and wants are more important than others' and they are unlikely to sacrifice for the sake of other people. Second, unwarranted praise, like a smiley-face for effort, can lead people to have an inflated opinion of their own ability. They think they have skill and talent even if they do not. This can be seen in the audition shows of talent contests such as *Canadian Idol*, where contestants seem genuinely surprised to hear they are bad singers. Third, self-esteem makes people cynical and despondent when the bubble bursts and they must face reality. With their spirits shattered, they either take it out on their classmates, friends, and family, or withdraw from opportunities that life offers. Although not all children who are over-praised become narcissistic, the self-esteem trend in education is where the pendulum may have swung too far—from too much criticism of students to too much praise.

When you want to describe the causes or reasons for an event, keep in mind the questions "Why did this happen?" and "What led to this?" Effects are the results and your essay should explain "What happened then?"

DEFINITION AND CLASSIFICATION

Definition is essential to comprehension and clarity. Sometimes you will have to define a term in your essay. For instance, if you are writing about how to be successful, you may have to give your definition of success. You could, however, write a whole essay defining success. A dictionary can give a short definition of a word, but it may not be enough to explain the nuances of the term. You may need to describe current usage, explain where the word came from and how it changed over time, or compare the word with similar concepts.

Sometimes definition includes classification. Donna Kerrigan classifies and lists the types of mistakes parents make, albeit satirically (p. 287). Pico Iyer compares weirdos and eccentrics (p. 282).

Here is an example of a classification paragraph:

Television-watching is not the same kind of activity for everyone. One type of viewer is very focused, almost mesmerized by the activity on the screen. Such a person does not like to be interrupted by conversation or other extraneous stimuli. Often this person watches little TV but gives it his or her full attention. This viewer is very different from the type who uses the TV as background noise, much like a radio. This viewer can usually watch a program in bits, and wander off and do something else. He or she is a true multi-tasker, who can even read or do chores while watching TV. Another type of viewer is the couch potato, who has indiscriminate and voracious viewing habits. As a channel-hopper, this person has a short attention span and uses the remote to click to another channel frequently. Researchers who study the effects of watching television should take into consideration the different patterns of viewing behaviour.

Methods used in extended definitions include:

- explaining the history of the word or idea, or its root (etymology)
- comparing or contrasting the word with something else
- describing its features
- using illustrations, examples, or analogies
- showing how the word is used or showing its relationship to another thing
- negating what it is not (for example, unlike a quarrel, argument is a debate)
- isolating unique features that separate it from something else

PROCESS DESCRIPTION

Process description or analysis explains what happens and how something occurs. It is different from instruction, which is a set of steps you follow to accomplish something. For example, you may write a process description of an earthquake happening, but you cannot write a set of instructions to make an earthquake. Instructions are written in the second person ("you") and have command sentences ("do this"). They are often written in numbered lists. Recipes are an example of instructions. In technical writing courses, you may have to write instructions. In general English courses, you may be asked to write process description.

In "No Offence," Curtis Gillespie uses process description to explain a hockey strategy:

But what is the Trap, anyway? On a trapping team, all five skaters generally camp out in the neutral zone between the blue lines, where they create a wedge formation. Then they just wait for the other team to try and carry the puck through the clogged passing and skating lanes. The goal of the V-shaped Trap is to take away the middle of the ice, to channel all the action to the outside, where there is less room and less chance for direct scoring opportunities. The only option left to the team in possession is to dump the puck in, and try to chase after it. Then the Trap starts all over again going the other direction. It's a simple and effective system — wait and block, wait and block — that requires rigid discipline but no exceptional individual talent, which is why coaches love it. (269–270)

The use of the passive voice is common in process description. For example, in "Toothpaste," David Bodanis writes: "The tube of toothpaste is squeezed, its pinched metal seams are splayed, pressure waves are generated inside, and the paste begins to flow" (p. 241). The receiver of the action is more important than the doer, so the receiver becomes the subject of the sentence. In short, it is a matter of focus. While the active voice is generally preferred because it is easier to follow, the passive voice does have a place, especially in process writing.

Sometimes you find a mix of process and instruction in one piece of writing, especially with the move toward less-formal writing. Because "you" is used as a pronoun meaning both the reader and people in general, it may be difficult to tell the difference. Instruction, however, is generally written in a list of steps rather than in a prose paragraph.

In order to describe procedures, it is important to know your audience and purpose. For example, you should know if your readers are comfortable with technical jargon or if they are already familiar with similar processes. You should decide whether you are simply describing the process or whether you are giving instructions that will have to be followed. Both types of writing involve breaking down the action into a series of small steps, in proper order. Clarity is, of course, essential.

A SAMPLE RESEARCH ESSAY

In this section, we show some of the steps involved in writing a research essay, from the assignment topic to the finished product.

ASSIGNMENT TOPIC

Usually, you have a choice of essay topics. Choose one you understand on a topic or reading you like.

Here is a question that might be asked for a research paper: "Show how sacrifice is important in Shirley Jackson's 'The Lottery.' Research the concept of sacrifice."

BRAINSTORMING

After choosing the topic, think about the story and about the question posed. Read the story over several times. From the story itself, you draw out the related episodes and details. You might take notes such as the following:

- stones, piles made by school kids in the opening
- stoning Tessie Hutchinson
- drawing lots, use of black box and chits
- ceremony in town square
- Old Man Warner, 77 years, escaped being sacrificed
- related to farming, vegetation, fertility
- rhyme about June and corn soon

Before looking at secondary sources, you should establish a list of ideas to consider:

- define sacrifice, scapegoating (see dictionary)
- symbolism of stones and stoning (martyrs in Christian terms)
- Bible stories about sacrifice: Jesus, Abraham, and Isaac
- anthropology theories, fertility rituals, religion, superstition
- symbolic action: Freud? Jung? (see Joseph Campbell, James Frazer)
- what has been written on this topic, especially regarding Jackson's story?

Write down your own ideas before you do research so that you know which ideas belong to you alone and which you have researched.

WORKING BIBLIOGRAPHY

Keep a working bibliography to keep track of your references. If you have a full citation written down, you can use quick references to your bibliography in the notes themselves.

Works Consulted

Adler, Jerry. "The Gods Must Be Hungry: Religion Has a Bloody History That's Not All in the Past." <u>Newsweek</u> 6 Nov. 1995: 75. <u>CPIQ</u>. Gale. Seneca Learning Commons. 10 Aug. 2004.

Chetwynd, Tom. <u>A Dictionary of Symbols</u>. London: Paladin, 1982.

Frye, Northrop. <u>Anatomy of Criticism: Four Essays</u>. Princeton, N.J.: Princeton University Press, 1957.

"Human Sacrifice." <u>Britannica Concise Encyclopedia</u> 2004. Encyclopedia Britannica Premium Service. 6 Aug. 2004 <http:// www.britannica.com/ebc/article?eu=392848>.

"Human Sacrifice." <u>Wikipedia: The Free Encyclopedia</u> 21 Jul. 2004. 10 Aug. 2004 <http://en.wikipedia.org/wiki/Human_sacrifice>.

Jackson, Shirley. "The Lottery." <u>Fiction/Non-Fiction: A Reader and Rhetoric</u>. 2nd ed. Ed. Garry Engkent and Lucia Engkent. Toronto: Thomson Nelson, 2005. 107-14.

Parker-Pearson, Dr. Mike. "Bodies for the Gods: The Practice of Human Sacrifice." 1 Mar. 2002. 10 Aug. 2004 <http://www.bbc.co.uk/ history/ancient/prehistory/human_sacrifice_01.shtml>

Slochower, Harry. <u>Mythopoesis: Mythic Patterns in the Literary Classics</u>. Detroit: Wayne State University Press, 1970.

Walker, Barbara G. <u>The Woman's Dictionary of Symbols and Sacred Objects</u>. San Francisco: HarperCollins, 1988.

Weekley, Ernest. <u>An Etymological Dictionary of Modern English</u>. 2 vols. New York: Dover, 1967.

NOTE-TAKING

As you research your topic, write down relevant quotations and paraphrased notes. Make sure that you know where each piece of information originated, including the page number.

Slochower, p. 333
"Primitive man depended for his existence on the elements and the seasonal changes. He felt them to be divine powers that spelled drought or deluge, an arid or fertile soil — that is, death or life. They were not regarded as automatic events, but had to be adjured by elaborate ceremonies. The seasonal rituals were at once commemorations of what had happened and incantations that they happen again. The succession of the seasons represented a crisis and the entire community was engaged to meet this crisis by rituals of propitiation."

Chetwynd, p. 345
- conscious life sacrificed by one generation (the dead) in order to be bestowed on the next (the living)

Walker, p. 177
"the sacrifice most acceptable to the gods was man"; then, in later ages, "for the man a horse was substituted, then an ox, then a sheep, then a goat, until at length it was found that the gods were most pleased with offerings of rice and barley."

Frye, p. 106
- *pharmakos* or sacrificed victim, who has to be killed to strengthen the others

"Human Sacrifice," Britannica
- human sacrifice: the offering of the life of a human being to a deity
- sacrifices offered in return for victory in war
- sacrifice for earth's fertility explains why most adopted by agricultural (not hunting) peoples

OUTLINING

When you have completed the research, you should make a reasonably detailed outline. This outline becomes the skeleton of your paper, showing how your ideas will be organized. The example below lies somewhere between a scratch outline and a very developed outline. Your instructor may ask you to hand in an outline as partial fulfillment of the research project.

Concept of sacrifice in Jackson's "The Lottery"
Introduction
Working thesis: examine nature and history of sacrifice and how it changes in "The Lottery."

Topic 1: Use dictionary definition of word "sacrifice"
Bible episode: Abraham & Isaac
Change from human to animal or vegetable: use Walker's passage

Topic 2: What sacrifice entails
Concept in the past: why important
Use Slochower to show man's need to sacrifice

Topic 3: Sacrifice as ritual action
Fertility and vegetation
See quotes from Britannica and Chetwynd
Relate this idea to "The Lottery": Old Man Warner & Tessie

Topic 4: Degeneration of the concept of lottery/sacrifice
Civilization changes rituals
People impatient
Use Frye about sacrifice
Change purposes: violence and bloodlust in "The Lottery"

Conclusion
Ending in "The Lottery"
How nature of sacrifice changed in the story.

PREPARING A DRAFT

Use your outline to prepare your first draft. This version may be quite rough, lacking polished sentence structure. The main goal is to put the information down on paper.

At the end of "The Lottery," Shirley Jackson has the townsfolk all throw stones at one of their neighbours, Tessie Hutchinson. Even her own young child, Davey, cast a pebble at his mom. They all do this to kill her and by stoning her to death they make a sacrifice of her to get harvest in the fall. This sacrifice seems important for the welfare of the community. However, Shirley Jackson makes a difference between the ritual and what the ritual has become. So, in order to understand the story and the ideas therein, we must look at the nature of human sacrifice, history of sacrifice and the changes in sacrifice in "The Lottery."

Sacrifice is a religious act because from the dictionary the term comes from the Latin meaning holy and making, therefore holy action. In this case, human beings are killed for some purpose. We have the Bible story of Abraham and Isaac. In this story, God wanted to test Abraham's faith so God asked that Abraham sacrifice Isaac. But at the last minute, God told Abraham he could use an animal instead. What this story shows is that human beings were sacrificed and practised since Biblical times and longer ago. In *The Woman's Dictionary of Symbols and Sacred Objects*, B. Walker says: (see p. 177)

> Sacrifice is something that a community must give up, even though it can't afford it, but must in order to survive. Sacrifice is absolutely necessary. In primitive days, all members of the tribe are important and useful; to lose one may jeopardize the community. From child to elders, all have something to contribute. However, these primitives see that there are many powerful and unfriendly forces about and they need to be appeased or else.

Slochower says: (see p. 333) By offering up one of their own, the community is saying that they mean business, and the gods might look kindly on that group.

Sacrifice then is also related to vegetation and fertility. (Use Britannica quote). This concept is relevant in "The Lottery" in which Tessie Hutchinson is stoned to death. Old Man Warner repeats the saying about Lottery in June, corn be heavy soon. So Tessie must die in order that the others might live. (paraphrase from Chetwynd, 345). Without a sacrifice of blood and life, man's connection with nature and harvest is cut. Without food, every man, woman and child may die from starvation.

However, this concept of sacrifice gets lost as societies become more sophisticated and civilized. Shirley Jackson shows that the lottery ritual has transformed, even degenerated over the years until all the symbols of sacrifice — the box and the chits — lose significance. The long ceremony before the sacrifice is lost and becomes short. The townsfolk are impatient to end the ceremony so that they can start stoning the loser of the lottery, in this case, Tessie Hutchinson. According to Frye (148), the sacrificed victim has to be killed to strengthen the others, but Jackson says the only reinforcement in this situation is blood lust.

The people in "The Lottery" retain human sacrifice. But it is not to appease the gods of harvest and fertility. Sacrifice is not a serious business, at least not religious, anyway. They don't care about losing a valued member of society. They just want to have a chance to express their dark side — the desire to maim, hurt, and kill Tessie Hutchinson.

REVISING AND EDITING

After completing the first draft, you should leave it for a day or two so that you will have a fresh eye when you revise it. Rushing too quickly into a second draft may cause you to lose objectivity.

Consult the checklist in Chapter 2 (pp. 367 – 368). In some cases, be prepared to revise several times to get the research paper right. Be critical with your work. Check your references. Are quotations copied accurately? Do your citations follow the proper style? Proofread carefully.

FORMAT

When instructors give an assignment, they generally stipulate formatting guidelines for students to follow. Their preferences may depart from the prescribed MLA format. For example, although standard MLA style does not require a cover page, many instructors prefer students to include one. MLA guidelines allow for such variation. Follow whatever format requirements your instructor gives you for the assignment. Most instructors still prefer hard copies. If your instructor wants a paper submitted electronically, follow the guidelines given.

Instead of creating a cover page, MLA style recommends that you place your identification on the first page of your research paper. On the left-hand side, double-spaced, give your name, your professor's name, the course code, and the date. Then put the title of your essay centred on the page. Your essay starts immediately after this identifying information. Each page, including the first one, has the running head of your last name and the page number. Some instructors prefer that the first page is not paginated.

Here are some common formatting guidelines:

- Use a word processor for assignments.
- Use black ink and white paper (standard 8½ × 11). Make sure your printout is clear and dark enough to read.
- Use a regular typeface such as Times New Roman. Do not use typefaces that imitate printing or handwriting. The best size is 12 point for most fonts.
- Include a cover page with the title of your essay, your name and student number, the course code, the instructor's name, and the date submitted.
- Double-space the whole essay, including quotations and bibliography. (Double-spacing means a full blank line between each line of print.)
- Use left justification and a ragged right margin.
- Print on only one side of the page.
- Except for page numbers, leave margins at least one inch wide on all sides of the page.
- Indent paragraphs with five spaces or one tab (set at ½ inch). Do not use block-style paragraphing (in other words, there should be no extra space between paragraphs, and each starts with an indented line).

- Make sure all sentences start with a capital letter and end with a period.
- Use correct spacing around punctuation marks. There should be only one space after periods (pre-computer typing style called for two spaces). There should be no space between the last letter of the word and the comma, period, or other end punctuation.
- Make sure each page has a page number, if the assignment is longer than one page. Do not number the cover page. Use the header function of the word processor to create a running head with your last name and the page number. This heading should appear in the top right-hand corner.
- Staple pages together in the left-hand corner. Do not use folders or paper clips.

THE FINAL DRAFT

The final essay with documentation follows. It is 787 words long.

Sacrifice and Shirley Jackson's "The Lottery"
by
Joanna Lesage
#90008765

for Prof. Engkent
ENG 101 Sec. D
October 6, 2005

In Shirley Jackson's classic story, "The Lottery," the neighbours, friends, and family of Tessie Hutchinson hurl stones and kill her without a qualm and without hesitation. The moment she draws the lot that would condemn her to death, Tessie becomes a victim of an ancient ritual. She is the blood offering to appease the deities of the natural order and to bring about propitious harvest for the community. Like countless others before her, Tessie is the unwilling sacrifice. Jackson brings to the foreground the features of sacrifice, the nature of sacrifice, and its relevance to the short story.

"Sacrifice" comes from two Latin words: *sacer* ("holy") and *facere* ("to make") (Weekley). The act of sacrificing is a religious ceremony in which human beings are offered for some specific purpose. We find this in the Biblical story of "Abraham and Isaac" in which the patriarch is asked to give up his only male child on an altar as proof of his faith. Fortunately, this allegory ends happily: God changes his mind and is willing to accept an animal as burnt offering instead of Isaac. Nonetheless, what the story shows is that the slaughter of human life is acceptable and has been practised from the dawn of civilization. Barbara Walker makes this point: "the sacrifice most acceptable to the gods was man"; then, in later ages, "for the man a horse was substituted, then an ox, then a sheep, then a goat,

until at length it was found that the gods were most pleased with offerings

of rice and barley" (177).

Sacrifice involves the giving up of something that a person or the

community can ill afford to lose. In short, sacrifice hurts, costs, and is

necessarily given. In primitive society, every member of a village or tribe

has a meaningful role to play. For example, young children can forage the

surrounding areas for firewood or berries. Women can bear children so

the village can grow and propagate. Men protect the village from other

tribes and dangerous beasts, and hunt for food. And the old can dispense

wisdom and the history of the tribe. To lose one productive member

means reducing the chances of surviving the often harsh and capricious

seasons of nature. Yet there are dangerous, powerful, and unfriendly

forces surrounding primitive man that require appeasing. To him, they are

gods. Slochower explains:

Primitive man depended for his existence on the elements and

the seasonal changes. He felt them to be divine powers which

spelled drought or deluge, an arid or fertile soil—that is, death

Lesage 3

or life. They were not regarded as automatic events, but had to

be adjured by elaborate ceremonies. (333)

By giving the gods something of great value, man impresses upon them

his sincerity in the sacrifice. Then they just might let man survive another

cycle of the seasons.

As a ritual, sacrifice has strong ties to vegetation and fertility, espe-

cially among agricultural societies. Giving up a member of the tribe just

might ensure from the gods "the fertility of the soil" ("Human Sacrifice").

This explanation seems relevant in the light of Tessie Hutchinson's death

in "The Lottery." Old Man Warner repeats the ritualistic axiom: "Used to

be a saying about 'Lottery in June, corn be heavy soon'" (Jackson 111).

Accordingly, one person must be sacrificed so that the whole community

and the next generation may survive (Chetwynd 345). Without this sacri-

fice of life and blood, man's link with nature and thus with harvest is sev-

ered. And without a bountiful harvest, every man, woman, and child

would probably starve and die.

Unfortunately, as societies become more civilized and sophisticated,

the meaning of the sacrifice becomes blurred, even forgotten. In "The

Lottery," Jackson explains how the ritual has transformed, even degenerated over the years, when the concrete symbols — the black box and the

chits — lose proper significance. Instead of long ceremonies with solem-

nity and fanfare, the ritual of sacrifice becomes brief. The meaning of sac-

rifice gives way to blood sport, communal purging of primitive savagery.

This is evident from the innocent-looking piles of stones the youngsters

gathered together to the setting upon Tessie Hutchinson with stones for

the ritualistic kill. Accordingly, the sacrificed victim has to be killed to

strengthen the others (Frye 148). Jackson says, however, the only

strengthening here is bloodlust.

Unlike people in other places, the villagers in "The Lottery" never

abandoned human sacrifice. To them, sacrifice is no longer to appease

harsh gods for a better yield in the fields. To them, sacrifice is not a

sacred, solemn act; it is not about losing a valued member. They forget its

true purpose but retain its most basic impulse — the desire to hurt, maim,

and kill.

Works Cited

Chetwynd, Tom. A Dictionary of Symbols. London: Paladin, 1982.

Frye, Northrop. Anatomy of Criticism: Four Essays. Princeton, N.J.:

Princeton University Press, 1957.

"Human Sacrifice." Britannica Concise Encyclopedia 2004. Encyclopedia

Britannica Premium Service. 6 Aug. 2004 <http://www.britannica.com/

ebc/article?eu=392848>.

Jackson, Shirley. "The Lottery." Fiction/Non-Fiction: A Reader and

Rhetoric. 2nd ed. Ed. Garry Engkent and Lucia Engkent. Toronto:

Thomson Nelson, 2005. 107-14.

Slochower, Harry. Mythopoesis: Mythic Patterns in the Literary Classics.

Detroit: Wayne State University Press, 1970.

Walker, Barbara G. The Woman's Dictionary of Symbols and Sacred

Objects. San Francisco: HarperCollins, 1988.

Weekley, Ernest. An Etymological Dictionary of Modern English. 2 vols.

New York: Dover, 1967.

Chapter 7

TROUBLE SPOTS

This chapter reviews some common problems in essay writing and literature analysis. Some are minor (referring to the author by first name), and others are major (plagiarism). Students can refer to the topics that pose a problem for them.

CONFUSING NARRATOR AND AUTHOR

Do not assume that because the writer does not identify the narrator of the short story by a specific name, the narrator is the writer. For example, in "Greasy Lake" (p. 33), T. Coraghessan Boyle does not give a name to the "I" narrator, but Boyle is not talking about himself. He has created a character, speaking in the first-person point of view. You must distinguish between character/narrator and author.

In some stories, the dialogue will reveal the narrator's name. If not, you can call that character "the narrator," "the speaker," or "the unnamed character." Sometimes you can use other identifying characteristics. For example, you could refer to the narrator of "An Ounce of Cure" (p. 156) as "the girl" and the narrator of "How We Kept Mother's Day" (p. 142) as "the son."

In articles and non-fiction prose, you can usually assume that the author is writing in his or her own voice.

REFERRING TO THE AUTHOR BY FIRST NAME

In essay writing, the accepted practice is to refer to writers by their family names rather than their given names. Using an author's first name gives your writing undue familiarity because you imply that you know the writer personally.

The first time you mention the author, give the whole name, such as "Katherine Govier." Afterward, you can refer to her as "Govier" or use the pronoun "she." You can also refer to "the writer" or "the author," but don't use such terms too often because this usage can make your writing awkward.

Most of the time you can tell whether to use "he" or "she" by the author's first name. This is not foolproof, however, since some authors use initials, some first names can be either male or female (such as "Robin" or "Chris"), and some first names can be surprising. For instance, names such as "Evelyn," "Beverly," or "Ashley" used to be boys' names, but today they are generally given to girls. Moreover, if English is your second language, you may have trouble telling the gender implied by a name. If you are not sure of the author's gender, try to avoid using "he" or "she."

NOT ANSWERING THE QUESTION

An academic essay generally starts with a topic given or a question posed by the instructor. Students thus have some leeway. For instance, they can narrow down a topic from the broad one suggested. However, part of the testing aspect of essay writing is whether the students answer the question asked.

English courses are fundamentally communication courses, and the most basic of communication tasks is asking a question and getting an answer to that question. College students being prepared for the work world must realize the importance of following instructions. It's as simple as going to a restaurant, ordering a chicken dinner, and getting a steak dinner instead. It does not matter how superbly the steak dinner is cooked—it's not what was asked for. Similarly, it does not matter how wonderfully written an essay is if it's not on topic.

Which of the following two paragraphs answers the topic question better? Explain why.

Topic: Should college students rely just on a cellphone and not get a land line?

Cellphones are essential in modern life. They are useful in emergencies and give people the security of being able to call for help whenever they need it. People can be in contact wherever they go, and features such as voice mail and text messaging make it easy to stay in touch with friends. Students can find a phone plan that works for them, so that it is more economical to chat. Now with extra features they can surf the web, pick up their e-mail, and even take pictures. Phones are even a smart fashion accessory. All students should buy a cellphone.

Students moving into an apartment or house should consider using a cellphone only and not bothering to get a land line installed. First, cellphones offer portability, and between their academic work, their social life, and maybe even a part-time job, students are often not at home. Second, a cellphone belongs to the individual, so there is no worry about splitting the phone bill and figuring out each person's long-distance charges. Students do not have to depend on their roommates to pass on phone messages. In addition, they do not have to worry about paying installation costs and getting a new phone number every time they move. Monthly costs for both kinds of phone services are comparable. Despite the drawback of poorer reception than land lines, a cellphone can serve students' needs much better and there is no need to have both.

INADEQUATE DEVELOPMENT OF IDEAS

Writing essays involves making statements and supporting them. A general statement needs to be supported with explanation or specific examples. Always try to answer the implied question "Why?" or "How?"

The following example shows unexplained ideas:

It is hard to believe that Grey Owl's masquerade was so successful, given that his writing and his appearance revealed his British origins. However, at that time Canadians were duped because of their lack of knowledge and their willingness to be misled. Thus, the masquerade was effective and was not publicly revealed until after Belaney's death.

In the following revision, the points are supported by specific information and explanation:

It is hard to believe that Grey Owl's masquerade was so successful, given that his writing and his appearance revealed his British origins. However, at that time Canadians were duped because of their lack of knowledge and their willingness to be misled. First, even though Grey Owl did not look anything like an "Indian," the image most Canadians had of Native people was provided by Hollywood. They were used to non-Native actors portraying Indians and therefore accepted Grey Owl's appearance. Second, Canadians needed an international champion of nature and Aboriginals, and Grey Owl was their articulate "noble savage." After all, he made the lecture circuit and he journeyed all the way to England to meet the King. Therefore, the masquerade was effective and was not publicly revealed until after Belaney's death.

In essays, paragraphs should be fully developed. One-sentence paragraphs are inadequate as part of the body of the essay. For an average expository paper, each paragraph should have at least 100–150 words or four to ten sentences. Shorter paragraphs are sometimes used as transitions, but generally you should avoid writing one- or two-sentence paragraphs.

INADEQUATE INTRODUCTIONS AND CONCLUSIONS

Students often find the introduction and the conclusion paragraphs difficult to write. They have the body of the essay all laid out but don't know what to say at the beginning and the end. The introduction and conclusion should not contain points that belong in the body — statements that support the thesis. Introductions and conclusions are discussed in Chapter 3. If this area is still your weakness, here are some tips and examples.

If you are stuck on the introduction, write the body of the essay first, and come back to the introduction. Then you may have a better idea of what you need to include in or exclude from the opening paragraph.

Make sure you put your thesis statement at the end of your introduction. If you start with it, you will have nothing else to say in your introduction. However, your conclusion should start with your thesis statement — but expressed differently from its wording in the introduction.

Think of the introduction as a funnel, narrowing down from broad statements to your specific thesis. The conclusion is the opposite, starting with the narrow restatement of the thesis and leading to broader statements.

Here is an inadequate introduction, followed by an improved version:

> In both the article and short story, the two authors show that Christmas is a good idea even for non-Christians and that it is worth celebrating because it promotes goodwill and gets people together and makes them happy. Therefore, Christmas is good even if you are not Christian.

> Christmas has evolved from a religious holiday to a national one. Time off school and work is supplemented by parties and various festivities. While some Christians bemoan the secular nature of Christmas, non-Christians criticize so much effort put into a holiday that is not theirs. However, other non-Christian viewpoints are shown in "Rediscovering Christmas" and "Chickens for Christmas," where both Almas Zakiuddin and Garry Engkent focus on the positive aspects of Christmas.

Here is an inadequate conclusion, followed by an improved version:

> Orwell and O'Brien have explored the death theme in their respective works showing that death is serious.

> In the two narratives, George Orwell and Tim O'Brien show that death is not just someone or something lifeless. Although they acted properly and their reasons for the deed may be justifiable in the respective situations, the Englishman of the 1930s and the American of the 1970s are deeply moved by the experience. Both writers describe different incidents, but they reveal the lingering effects of the kill.

SUMMARIZING THE PLOT

Writing literary essays demands analysis of the story. Sometimes students just retell the story and think they are analyzing it. The action of the story can be recounted, but this information should be given as supporting information. In other words, you should make a point and then show that something in the story supports the point.

You can avoid the problem by opening your paragraph with a topic sentence that reflects an opinion and makes a point. Second, select only the items or episodes that support the topic sentence. Third, reorder these supporting items in a logical or climactic sequence rather than in the same order as they appear in the article or story.

Here are illustrations using T. Coraghessan Boyle's "Greasy Lake" (p. 33). The assignment topic is "Show how the boys are immature in 'Greasy Lake.' "

Plot summary, which does not answer the question:

> When the three boys got bored of cruising the streets, they got drunk and drove to Greasy Lake. There they spotted a car parked near the lake and assumed that a friend was in it making out with a girl. They disturbed the two people in the car, and one angry stranger then came out and started beating up on them. They thought they could handle one greasy guy. They were wrong. The narrator had to take a tire iron to the stranger's head, and he thought he had killed the guy. Anyway, the half-naked girl started screaming bloody murder, and the boys attempted to molest her. Suddenly, another car came by and the three boys scattered into the woods and the muddy lake. Luckily, the stranger came to, so the boys didn't kill anybody. Then the stranger and the others took out their anger on the car,

which was actually the narrator's mother's Bel Air. In the morning, the strangers left Greasy Lake. The three boys returned to the car, which was seriously damaged: smashed windows, grill, headlights, ripped seats and everything. However, it was still drivable. Now the boys had to drive home and explain why the car was so damaged.

Analysis, which does answer the question:

The three 19-year-olds — Digby, Jeff, and the narrator — show their immaturity or lack of good judgment in three ways. First, they get drunk and start to look for trouble at Greasy Lake. Second, they take on a tough guy in a brawl because they mistakenly believe that three against one is excellent odds. Third, when the narrator almost kills the tough guy with a tire iron to the head, he should have immediately sobered up and realized his action was serious and criminal. Instead, the three boys try to rape the unconscious man's half-naked girlfriend. At each step the three 19-year-olds could have stopped themselves, but because they let their drunken bravado loose, they got deeper into trouble.

In a literary essay, it is unnecessary to recap the story before you begin your analysis. You assume your reader — basically, your instructor — knows the plot or the particular episode. What that person does not know is your perspective, opinion, or interpretation of the story. Moreover, the instructor needs to know whether you have answered the assignment question. To this end, you explain how you "see" the narrative.

Now, this rule is not carved in stone. In some cases, if you are writing to a larger audience who may not have read the story, you may wish to give a plot summary. Other times, your instructor may ask you to recap the story to show your understanding of it. In general, though, summarizing the plot does not answer the question in an essay or test.

WEAK ESSAY STRUCTURE

One of the hardest things in essay writing is dividing up what you have to say about a topic so that it fits into separate paragraphs. The key to this is to make sure that each of your body paragraphs begins with a topic sentence that relates to and supports your thesis statement. For example, if your topic is "Discuss the reasons why people get tattoos," each paragraph should focus on a different reason or type of reason. An essay with three body paragraphs explaining why children get tattoos, why young people get tattoos, and why adults get tattoos is an example of dividing a topic up by situation rather than by argument—a structure that leads to repetition. A better structure would have been to give artistic reasons (decoration of the body) in one paragraph, social reasons (such as belonging to a group) in another, and personal statements (such as rebellion) in a third.

Your body paragraphs should be well balanced. Too often students have a strong first body paragraph and then the essay peters out in shorter and weaker body paragraphs as the students run out of ideas. Thorough brainstorming and careful outlining are the keys to avoiding this problem.

OVER-QUOTING

Including a lot of quotations in your essay does not make the paper better; it merely makes it longer. It shows your instructor that you do not yet have the skill to select relevant information. Like your own writing, quoting must be concise and appropriate. This is true for both primary and secondary sources (the story itself and the research materials). Generally, students over-quote because they believe that the author's wording is preferable to their own, because they are padding their essay, or because they do not know how to paraphrase or summarize someone else's words.

Keep the length and number of quotations from the story or article to a minimum. Be judicious and select only the appropriate statements needed to illustrate or support your point. For example, a statement of fact rarely has to be quoted.

Rosie DiManno describes her background: "My parents are Italian immigrants and I was born in Toronto, grew up on Grace St. downtown, but didn't learn English until I started school" (p. 246). These facts are easily paraphrased:

> As the daughter of Italian immigrants, Rosie DiManno grew up in Toronto and learned English in school.

An explanation of summary and paraphrase can be found in Chapter 4.

PADDING AND WORDINESS

Padding a paper generally occurs when you don't have enough content in your essay. To meet the suggested word count, you may repeat points or stretch out ideas. This problem is similar to over-quoting, in which the writer extends a point or a comment for no practical purpose other than to fill up space.

Some telltale signs of padding include wordiness, retelling the story, repeating ideas in different words, and going off topic entirely.

Here is an example of padding with unnecessary words:

> In the story "All the Years of Her Life," the character Alfred Higgins does not come to the realization that his mother, who has come to save him once again from juvenile mistakes of his own making, is a woman frightened for her own future and for her family's and that she is tired of it all and getting old until he sees her alone in the kitchen trying to steady herself with a cup of tea. (77 words)

To improve this, cut unnecessary words:

> In "All the Years of Her Life," Alfred Higgins does not realize that his mother is frightened, tired, and old until he sees her in the kitchen with an unsteady hand holding a cup of tea. (36 words)

The "there is/are" structure is unnecessarily wordy:

> There are many teenagers who have trouble reasoning out the consequences of their actions.

> Many teenagers have trouble reasoning out the consequences of their actions.

To fix the problem of going off topic, be critical of your writing. An outline can help you stay focused. Here is an example of what happens when a writer drifts into something else:

> It makes more sense to pay for social services with taxes than with user fees. Education, health care, welfare, and recreation are all vital to society and must be funded across the board. If the cost is shared by all, it is cheaper. It may take only a few dollars on the actual tax bill to pay for medical care that would cost individuals thousands of dollars. In addition, the cost is borne by those who can afford it, since taxes are generally tied to income. Moreover, all people should pay for social services because they benefit either directly or indirectly. For example, higher education levels mean better-trained workers for the whole society. Welfare for the less fortunate lessens the gap between the rich and the poor, an inequity that can lead to social problems such as crime. Crime is a real problem in our society because people are afraid of being victimized even though the actual crime rate itself is down. They won't go out after dark and they lock their houses up tight. They want to spend more money on policing even though this money would be better spent on prevention. For example,

youth programs to prevent dropping out of school are a good idea because then the kids will get a good education that will lead to a good job, which would lead to more taxes paid for social services to help other people. Young people also need more places to hang out so they won't get in trouble on the street. Furthermore, governments that invest in recreation services may save money on health care for people who are not fit. Indeed, taxes mean that money is saved in administrative costs since user fees require some sort of additional collection service. People may grumble about paying taxes, but they get a high return for their money.

This paragraph goes off topic when it starts talking about crime. The writer needs to focus on the topic sentence and make sure all the statements in the paragraph fit that topic.

Your instructor may give you guidelines concerning the length of your paper. You should try to meet the guidelines, but not at the expense of handing in a poorly written paper. A word count is an approximation. Quality is always better than quantity.

To make sure your essay is as lean as it should be, ask yourself these questions:

- Can I say the same thing in fewer words? What is irrelevant information?
- Am I merely retelling the plot and not explaining my point? What is my point?
- Am I on topic? Is this example or illustration appropriate for the topic?
- Am I going in circles, saying the same thing?

FAILING TO MAKE YOUR POSITION CLEAR

The essays you write in college or university are expository papers; that is, you are explaining or commenting on a given topic and making your ideas clear to your instructor. In most cases, you are presenting an argument — a point of view that you take. Sitting on the fence does not make for an effective paper. You need to take a stand. Even if you are presenting the advantages and disadvantages of something, you should take a position that one outweighs the other.

While creating interest is acceptable, dramatizing your essay is not. Don't confuse analytical with creative (imaginative) writing. An analytical paper is not like a mystery novel in which the detective reveals all at the end. Withholding essential information in the introduction until the conclusion is an improper strategy in an essay.

Here is an example of an improper thesis statement:

> Whether John Barber's "Grey Owl's Magnificent Masquerade" or Colin Ross's "The Story of Grey Owl" is closer to the truth about Archie Belaney (Grey Owl) is debatable. So I propose that we weigh both articles in the balance, and then I will tell you which side I am on.

In this introduction, the thesis is clear:

> Both John Barber in "Grey Owl's Magnificent Masquerade" and Colin Ross in "The Story of Grey Owl" explore the deception that Archie Belaney (Grey Owl) perpetrated on the Canadian people. Barber praises Belaney's efforts; Ross mocks the man. Ross makes a better case.

You must state your thesis, opinion, or idea at the beginning of your paper. In an expository paper, sitting on the fence on an issue is a bad strategy.

PLAGIARIZING AND CHEATING

Plagiarism is the act of deliberately using someone else's words or ideas in part or in total without proper acknowledgment and calling that work your own. The plagiarism could involve as little as one sentence copied from another writer or a whole essay downloaded from the Internet. Cheating is handing in someone else's work and claiming it to be your own. This includes getting a paper from another student or from an essay-writing service.

Sometimes students inadvertently cross the line between doing research and plagiarizing, between getting help and cheating. In some education systems, for example, students may copy authors' words as a model for their writing. Students who get help from tutors and friends may hand in work that has been so rewritten that it is no longer the student's own writing.

English instructors are knowledgeable about writing style and can identify work that has not been done by their students. One telltale sign of plagiarism is inconsistency in expression. Part of the essay may have numerous grammatical errors, while another part is not only error-free, but also sophisticated in sentence structure, vocabulary, and thought. Another clue is glaring discrepancy between work done in class and work done outside of class.

The penalties for cheating can vary from one institution to another. The policies are generally stated in the school calendar or handbook and in instructors' handouts. A first offence of plagiarism may result in a mark of zero on that assignment, a warning, and an official report filed in the student's record. On subsequent offences, the penalties increase to a failure in the course and even expulsion from the school.

It is important that your assignments be your own work, in your own words. In research papers, be sure to document and reference your sources properly. (See Chapters 4 and 5 for more information on using research.) When using the school's writing centre, be sure your tutor is not over-zealous in correcting your words.

USING CONVERSATIONAL STYLE

Although North American society has moved toward less formality in all spheres, it is important to be able to write in more formal styles when the occasion demands it. Just as you would not wear jeans to a job interview, you should not use overly conversational style in academic, business, and technical writing.

Students who do not read much have more difficulty writing formal prose. They are used to speech, which is generally less formal than writing, and are unaware of the conventions of prose. They may pepper their essays with expressions such as "Well, let's see" or use slang words such as "jerk" and "ten bucks."

Below are some examples of conversational style followed by more formal styles:

Slang, idioms, and informal expressions:

> The kids were blown away that it cost only 12 bucks.
> The children were surprised that it cost only 12 dollars.

Conversational expressions:

> Well, let's see, I think it's not gonna happen.
> It is unlikely to happen.

Personal pronouns "I" and "you":

> In my opinion, I think that school uniforms are good for high-school students.
> School uniforms are good for high-school students.

> When you read about all the stuff in toothpaste, you wonder why you ever put it in your mouth and grind it into your teeth.

Knowing all the ingredients in toothpaste, consumers may wonder why they ever brush with it.

Contractions:

He should've been paying more attention.
He should have been paying more attention.

Phrasal verbs:

He will check out the new proposal.
He will examine the new proposal.

Starting sentences with coordinate conjunctions ("and," "but," "for," "or," "so," "yet"):

And then she hired a new manager.
Then she hired a new manager.

But the initiative was underfunded.
However, the initiative was underfunded.

It is important to remember that informal expressions have a cumulative effect. Using idioms once or twice in your essay or starting a few sentences with coordinate conjunctions does not make it completely informal, but the more of these characteristics your essay has, the less formal your writing will tend to be.

On the other hand, it is also important not to make your writing so formal that it sounds stuffy and pedantic. Some writers delve into their thesaurus to find synonyms to pump up their writing. It is a mistake to look for a bigger word just to sound erudite and academic. For instance, don't say "eschew obfuscation" instead of "be clear." You can use multi-syllabic words if they convey precisely what you mean and if you are comfortable with the meaning and usage.

Remember that the most important quality of good writing is clarity. Write to communicate, not to impress, and use standard written English for your essays.

Chapter 8

COMMON GRAMMAR PROBLEMS

This chapter provides an overview of some grammatical mistakes common in student writing. The problems are explained briefly and illustrated by correct and incorrect sentences. Incorrect sentences are marked with an asterisk (*).

This chapter is not meant to be a comprehensive explanation of grammar. We offer brief explanations, grouping some points together. We have also tried to simplify our use of grammar terminology, but some terms are unavoidable. For example, to understand why "but" and "however" cannot be used in the same way, students must understand that "but" is a conjunction and "however" is an adverb. If you need a more detailed explanation of a particular grammar point, ask your teacher or consult a grammar book or usage guide.

MISUSE OF CONJUNCTIONS AND ADVERBS

A conjunction joins two sentences or parts of sentences. Adverbs modify a sentence or part of a sentence. In the following examples, conjunctions are in boldface and adverbs are underlined:

> **If** I pick up the report before the meeting, <u>then</u> I'll have the time I need.
> **Although** we hired more staff, we could not complete the project by the deadline.
> We hired more staff, **but** we could not complete the project by the deadline.
> <u>Unfortunately,</u> we had to re-enter the figures.
> I was summoned to his office <u>immediately,</u> **and** he read me the riot act.

Some adverbs are called conjunctive adverbs because they act almost like conjunctions:

> We hired more staff. <u>However,</u> we could not complete the project by the deadline.
> We needed to get clearance, **so** we contacted him at home.
> We needed to get clearance. <u>Therefore,</u> we contacted him at home.

One of the easiest ways to tell these two parts of speech apart is to recognize that while conjunctions can appear only between the clauses or phrases they join, conjunctive adverbs can appear in different spots in a sentence, as in the following:

<u>However,</u> the students could not raise the money for their trip.
The students, <u>however,</u> could not raise the money for their trip.
The students could not raise the money for their trip, <u>however.</u>

"But" is a conjunction with the same meaning as "however," yet it could not be substituted for "however" in the second and third sentences above.

*The students, **but**, could not raise the money for their trip.
*The students could not raise the money for their trip, **but**.

Coordinate conjunctions are used to join two sentences or parts of sentences:

and, but, for, nor, or, so, yet

Examples:

I talked to Anne yesterday, **and** she explained the situation in detail.
We had to work with inadequate data, **yet** we managed to make a scenario.
You have to be tough **but** compassionate.

In formal English, coordinate conjunctions are not supposed to begin sentences. However, this rule is relaxed in less formal styles. The following sentences would be considered unacceptable in academic writing:

So I asked him to return the file.
But he said he didn't have it.
And he directed me to the other department.

Subordinate conjunctions can also be used to join sentences, but the subordinate conjunction begins a subordinate clause that is less important than the main clause:

after, although, as, because, even though, if, since, when, whereas, while

Examples:

While we were discussing his inability to focus, his cellphone rang.
Because we had so many problems on this project, we made a new plan of action.
We will establish new criteria **after** we have finished our post-mortem.

Note that sentences can start with "because" in English. Some teachers warn against it to prevent their students from writing sentence fragments (see p. 442), but it is allowable as long as the sentence is finished with a main clause.

Conjunctive adverbs can be grouped according to their meaning:

Addition	also, finally, first, furthermore, in addition, moreover, next, second
Cause and effect	accordingly, as a result, consequently, therefore, thus
Comparison	likewise, similarly
Contrast	however, in contrast, instead, nevertheless, on the contrary, on the other hand, otherwise
Emphasis or clarity	in fact, indeed, in other words, of course, that is
Special features or examples	for example, for instance, in particular, mainly, specifically
Summary	in brief, in closing, in conclusion, in short, on the whole, to conclude, to summarize
Time relations	afterward, at that time, earlier, in the meantime, lately, later, meanwhile, now, then

Incorrect use of conjunctions and conjunctive adverbs can lead to sentence fragments and run-ons (see pp. 442–443).

SENTENCE FRAGMENTS

Sentence fragments are incomplete sentences or non-sentences. A sentence requires a subject and a complete verb. An -*ing* verb form, for instance, is not a complete verb. A sentence starting with a subordinate conjunction must have a main clause. Here are some examples of sentence fragments followed by corrections.

*Being a sore loser.
Being a sore loser, she objected to Khaled's interpretation of the rules.

*Because it is due at the printers tomorrow.
We must finish editing this report now because it is due at the printers tomorrow.

*Although they would rather take the train.
Although they would rather take the train, they agreed to fly.

*The managers at the proposal meeting.
The managers are at the proposal meeting.
The managers at the proposal meeting could not agree on the next step.

*The report commissioned last year.
The report was commissioned last year.
The report commissioned last year is still not complete.

*Reason being he hadn't prepared for the exam.
He did not pass because he hadn't prepared for the exam.

*For example, people who talk all the time in class, especially when something is being explained.
One example is people who talk all the time in class, especially when something is being explained.
For example, some people talk all the time in class, especially when something is being explained.

It should be noted that sentence fragments are often found in less formal kinds of writing, such as novels and magazine articles. However, you should avoid writing sentence fragments in essays.

RUN-ON SENTENCES

Run-on sentences are sentences that should be divided into more than one sentence, either for grammatical or stylistic reasons. Grammarians differentiate between run-on sentences and comma splices (two sentences incorrectly connected with a comma), but both are fundamentally the same error.

A grammatical sentence contains a subject and a verb in the main clause. If the sentence has more than one clause, a conjunction is necessary.

> *I had to translate the document they had trouble with the technical language.
> *I had to translate the document, they had trouble with the technical language.
> I had to translate the document. They had trouble with the technical language.
> I had to translate the document because they had trouble with the technical language.

> *The music teacher was a skilled musician she lacked people skills.
> *The music teacher was a skilled musician however she lacked people skills.
> The music teacher was a skilled musician; however, she lacked people skills.
> The music teacher was a skilled musician, but she lacked people skills.
> Although the music teacher was a skilled musician, she lacked people skills.

> *Archie Belaney was not a real Aboriginal he took on the name of Grey Owl.
> *Archie Belaney was not a real Aboriginal, he took on the name of Grey Owl.
> Archie Belaney was not a real Aboriginal; he took on the name of Grey Owl.
> Archie Belaney was not a real Aboriginal. He took on the name of Grey Owl.

To fix run-on sentences, make two separate sentences, use a semicolon, or add a conjunction.

VERB TENSES

Sometimes students get tangled up with verb tenses in their writing. While it is easy to say use the present for the present, the past for the past, and the future for the future, it is not always that simple. However, the following pointers can help.

Use the simple present tense to describe facts and general situations:

The earth is round. The sky is blue. I love you.
TV addicts do not interact enough with other people.
He walks to school every day.

Sometimes students use a continuous form or a simple future when a simple present tense would be more appropriate and concise:

The author is saying that we need technology to simplify our lives.
The author says that we need technology to simplify our lives. *(better)*

Students will often doze during lectures.
Students often doze during lectures.

Literature is discussed in the present tense, even though the writer may be long dead:

Shakespeare tells the story of mad ambition in *Macbeth.*

Use the past tenses to describe past events with a definite past time:

The author grew up in an Italian neighbourhood of Toronto.
I bought a coffee maker at a garage sale.

The present perfect is a tense that straddles the past and present. It is used to describe past situations and experiences that are still true.

I have lived in Montreal for five years. *(I still live in Montreal.)*
I lived in Montreal for five years. *(I no longer live in Montreal.)*
I have never been skydiving. *(In the past, and still true now.)*
He has recently taken up skydiving.

In essays, it is important to avoid switching tenses unnecessarily:

*Professors are careful to avoid situations that may be perceived as favouritism or harassment. For this reason, they suggested students see counsellors instead of telling their professors about personal problems. They are not wanting to get too close to students. Male professors will try to avoid seeing female students alone.

Professors are careful to avoid situations that may be perceived as favouritism or harassment. For this reason, they suggest students see counsellors instead of telling their professors about personal problems. They do not want to get too close to students. Male professors try to avoid seeing female students alone.

Students sometimes have trouble with verb forms and write incorrect forms such as "can being" or leave an auxiliary (helping) verb such as "should" without a verb to complete it. Auxiliary verbs such as "do" and "will" and the modal verbs (*can, could, may, might, should, would*) are completed with the base form of the verb (the infinitive without the "to"):

He **should go** now or he **will be** late.
You **may borrow** the DVD if you **can watch** it tonight.

When *have* is used as an auxiliary, the verb form after it must be the past participle, which is the *–ed* form of regular verbs:

I **have visited** Paris many times, but I **have** never **been** to Rome.
He **has** not **seen** the new proposal, but he says he has faith in us.

When the verb "to be" (*am, are, is, be, being, been*) is used as an auxiliary verb, the next verb will be an *-ing* verb if it is an active meaning and a past participle (*-ed* ending) if it is passive:

I **am going** to the office to see whether the grades **are posted**.

These rules for auxiliary verbs hold even when they are used with other auxiliaries:

I **should have been paying** attention when the teacher **was reviewing** that lesson.
I **could have been chosen** leader for that project.
He **has been waiting** for a response for three weeks now.

PRONOUNS

A pronoun refers to a noun. It must agree with the noun in person and number (singular, plural).

The author discusses common problems with technology. **He** says **they** are due to poor design. *("He" refers to the author, and "they" refers to problems.)*

When you are referring to a company or an institution, it is tempting to use the pronoun "they" to refer to the people in the company. While this usage is accepted in less formal writing, it is grammatically incorrect.

*Thomson Nelson publishes a variety of college textbooks. They are always looking for new writers and new ideas.

Thomson Nelson publishes a variety of college textbooks. It is always looking for new writers and new ideas.

SPECIFIC PRONOUNS

its/it's

"It's" is a contraction of "it is" or "it has." "Its" is the possessive pronoun, meaning "belonging to it." If you can replace "it's" with "it is" or "it has," then you need the form with an apostrophe. If a word such as "his" makes more sense as a replacement, you need the possessive form ("its"). You would not put an apostrophe in "his," so don't put one in "its."

It's time to take the dog for its shots.
It's been nice seeing you again.

whose/who's

"Who's" is a contraction of "who is" or "who has." "Whose" is the possessive pronoun, meaning "belonging to whom." This distinction is similar to "its/it's."

Whose coat is this?
Who's going to replace Hasim as vice-president?

their

"Their" is often misspelled or misused as "there" or "they're." "Their" is the possessive pronoun, showing that something belongs to "them."

Jane and Kyoko should pay attention to their own work.

Another error is using "their" for singular subjects. However, this grammatical error is commonly found and is somewhat controversial. Some writers accept this usage because it is widespread in speech, it can be found in the works of famous writers such as Jane Austen and Charles Dickens, and it solves the "he/she" problem in pronoun reference. In essay writing, however, you should try to avoid this usage.

*Each student must bring their own sleeping bag.
Each student must bring his own sleeping bag. *(Grammatically correct, but might be considered sexist.)*
Each student must bring his or her own sleeping bag. *(Works for a single use, but it can be tedious saying "his or her" repeatedly.)*
*Each student must bring his/her own sleeping bag. *(Slashed words are not acceptable in essays.)*

All students must bring their own sleeping bags. *(The use of the plural avoids the problem.)*

Some writers solve the problem by alternating between male and female pronouns in their prose, but this should not be done within a single paragraph.

you
The pronoun "you" has two meanings in English. It can refer to the audience (the reader, the listener) directly, or it can refer to people in general.

As you can see in Charlotte Gray's essay, few famous Canadians are idolized.

When you are young, you think you know everything about the world, and then as you mature you realize how little you know.

In essay writing, avoid using "you." It makes your essay too conversational. Use the third person.

As is evident in Charlotte Gray's essay, few famous Canadians are idolized.

When people are young, they think they know everything about the world, and then as they mature they realize how little they know.

MISPLACED MODIFIERS

One kind of misplaced modifier is the dangling participle, an adjective form of the verb that is modifying the wrong noun.

*Breathing heavily, the race was stopped finally.
Breathing heavily, we stopped running the race.

In the above example, the participle "breathing" is describing the race in the first sentence. It should, of course, describe the people. Relative clauses (beginning with "who," "which," "that") should be as close as possible to the noun they modify.

*He wanted to eliminate the identification test from the final grade, which the students found too difficult.
He wanted to eliminate the identification test, which the students found too difficult, from the final grade.

ACTIVE VS. PASSIVE VOICE

The active voice is the basic sentence pattern of SUBJECT + VERB + OBJECT (e.g., "Tom ate the pie"). In the passive voice, the object comes before the verb and the verb is in the BE + PAST PARTICIPLE form (e.g., "The pie was eaten by Tom").

The active voice is preferred because it is easier to understand and more concise. Here are some examples:

> This novel was read by Joe and this analysis was written by him. [13 words]
> Joe read the novel and wrote this analysis. [8 words]

> Cautionary tales were told to children by protective mothers so the children would not come to any harm. [18 words]
> Protective mothers told cautionary tales to children so they would not come to any harm. [15 words]

> In an emergency, the alarm must be activated. [8 words]
> In an emergency, activate the alarm. [6 words]

The passive voice is useful when the writer wants to de-emphasize the doer of the action.

> The city was founded in 1806.
> Joe was brought in as a replacement.
> The burglar was identified in the line-up.
> The monthly fees have not yet been paid. *(Less accusatory than "You have not yet paid the monthly fees.")*

A rule of thumb is that if you need a "by" phrase in the passive, the sentence would work better in the active.

PARALLEL STRUCTURE

When parts of the sentence are joined by "and," they should have the same grammatical structure.

> *Her goals were to head the task force, eliminate unnecessary steps in the process, and proving her worth to the company.
> Her goals were to head the task force, eliminate unnecessary steps in the process, and prove her worth to the company.

*Robin likes reading philosophy, attending art exhibitions, and chess.
Robin likes reading philosophy, attending art exhibitions, and playing chess.

*People get tattoos to make a statement, as decoration for their bodies, and because they belong to a group.
People get tattoos to make a statement, decorate their bodies, and show allegiance to a group.

PUNCTUATION

APOSTROPHES

Incorrect apostrophes are epidemic in written English. You can see incorrect usage in signage and publications. Apostrophes are used to indicate possession, contractions, and rare plural forms in which the -*s* alone would be difficult to read. They are not used for regular plurals or verb forms.

*The Johnson's are hosting a reception for the newcomer's.
The Johnsons are hosting a reception for the newcomers.
The Johnsons' party was meticulously planned.

*Rhianna try's too hard to please her mother.
Rhianna tries too hard to please her mother.

*Dions record collection of old 45's is being sold on eBay.
Dion's record collection of old 45s is being sold on eBay.

*How many As did you get in your first-year course's?
How many A's did you get in your first-year courses?

COMMAS

The comma has specific uses in writing: it separates items in a series, it sets off interjections and words in apposition, and in a periodic sentence it distinguishes the dependent clause from the independent.

The comma should never be used to separate subject and verb:

*George Orwell, was badgered into shooting the elephant by the crowd of spectators.
George Orwell was badgered into shooting the elephant by the crowd of spectators.

The comma should never be a breath stop:

*I think, I can go to, the store once I, catch my, breath.
I think I can go to the store once I catch my breath.

The comma should not be used to join two complete sentences:

*The students were asking for a public debate, the principal did not allow
it.
The students were asking for a public debate; the principal did not allow it.

Commas are used to separate clauses when the division is not marked by a conjunction:

If the plan fails, the test will be have to be rescheduled.
The test will have to be rescheduled if the plan fails.

Although SUVs are supposed to be safe vehicles, they are less stable and
are prone to rollovers.
SUVs are less stable and are prone to rollovers, although they are supposed to be safe vehicles.

I have to go to the bank, and James is going to wait for me at the diner.
I have to go to the bank and the diner.

Commas are used before items in a series (note that it is also correct to omit the comma before "and" and "or" in lists):

I need shrimp, sausage, ham, and green peppers for the jambalaya.
I already have the rice and chicken.
I can't decide if I should have the pizza, hamburger, or salad.

Commas are used to set off extra information in a sentence. This can make a difference in meaning for restrictive and non-restrictive relative clauses:

The B4 section students, who failed the exam, have to take the tutorial.
(The whole class failed.)
The B4 section students who failed the exam have to take the tutorial.
(Only the students who failed have to take the tutorial.)

Note the difference in meaning in these two sentences:

Students go to school to learn not to have fun.
Students go to school to learn, not to have fun.

SEMICOLONS AND COLONS

The semicolon acts like the coordinate conjunction "and" in most cases. It separates two complete sentences.

The students enjoyed the field trip; however, they did not learn much about mushrooms.

Do not confuse the semicolon with the colon. The colon sets up an example or a list.

Everything we have for the party is here: salads, cold cuts, rolls, butter, casserole, plastic forks, and paper plates.

These are the books you must read this semester: *Lord of the Rings, The Magic Mountain, Finnigan's Wake,* and *War and Peace.*

HYPHENS AND DASHES

The hyphen is used within a word. It is used for compound words (such as *Indo-Canadian, best-kept secret, co-author*) and to break a word into syllables if it does not fit on a line. The hyphen is a character on the standard keyboard.

The dash, a longer stroke than a hyphen, is not on the regular keyboard; however, it can be represented by two hyphens or with an em-dash, which is available as a special character in word-processing software. (Em-dashes are the width of a the letter *m*. The en-dash is the width of the letter *n* and is used with numbers, as in "1998 – 1999.") The em-dash is also referred to as a parenthetical dash. It is used to emphasize something or to allow the writer to go off topic for a moment before returning to the topic.

When we were kids, George and I—we know better now—used to put our ears to the railway tracks to listen for an approaching train.

SUBJECT – VERB AGREEMENT

Students sometimes make errors in verb forms when they do not pay attention to the grammatical subject of the sentence. In the following examples, the grammatical subject is in boldface and the verb is underlined:

*One of the students are missing.
One of the students <u>is</u> missing.

*The class that sold the most pizzas are going to get a bonus.
The **class** that sold the most pizzas <u>is going</u> to get a bonus.

In correlatives such as either/or, neither/nor, and not only/but also, the verb agrees with the closest noun.

*Neither Shawna nor her brothers sees the problem.
Neither Shawna nor **her brothers** <u>see</u> the problem.

*Not only the club members but also the honoured guest were given mementoes.
Not only the club members but also **the honoured guest** <u>was given</u> mementoes.

WRONG WORDS

Many errors in writing are the result of confusion between words that sound the same or are otherwise similar. Here is a list of some commonly confused words. If you are not sure of the difference, check your dictionary.

accept, except	plain, plane
advice, advise	quiet, quite
affect, effect	right, write, rite
a lot, allot	scene, seen
are, our, hour	stationary, stationery
assure, insure, ensure	than, then
choose, choice, chose	their, there, they're
complement, compliment	though, thought
cite, sight, site	to, too, two
does, dose	threw, through
hear, here	weak, week
hole, whole	wear, were, where, we're
its, it's	weather, whether
knew, new	which, witch
know, no, now	who's, whose
loose, lose	you're, your
passed, past	

Appendix: APA Style

The American Psychological Association (APA) style is used in the sciences and social sciences. It differs from the MLA style mainly in its use of dates, italics, and lowercase letters instead of capitals. In essays, double-spacing is used for both quotations and the reference list.

QUOTING

In referencing a quotation within the body of the essay, APA includes the year of publication. The first example shows the author mentioned in the text, while the second has the author's name in the parenthetical reference.

> A hero cannot always perform the task alone. Campbell (1949) says, "For those who have not refused the call, the first encounter of the hero journey is with a protective figure (often a little old crone or old man) who provides the adventurer with amulets against the dragon forces he is about to pass" (p. 69).

> A hero cannot always perform the task alone. "For those who have not refused the call, the first encounter of the hero journey is with a protective figure (often a little old crone or old man) who provides the adventurer with amulets against the dragon forces he is about to pass" (Campbell, 1949, p. 69).

If the author is not named, use the first few words of the title instead, along with the year and the page number.

REFERENCES

The bibliography in the APA style is called "References." The reference list starts on a new page at the end of the essay. Like the MLA, the APA requires double-spacing, hanging indent, and alphabetical order.

[Article by single author]

Bethune, B. (1999, October 4). Truth and consequences. *Maclean's*, 58-59.

[Book by single author]

Campbell, J. (1949). *The hero with a thousand faces.* New York: Meridian Books.

[Book by government agency]

Citizenship and Immigration Canada. (2003). *A look at Canada.* Ottawa: Minister of Public Works and Government Services Canada.

[Book by two authors]

Farb, P., & Armelagos, G. (1980). *Consuming passions: The anthology of eating.* New York: Houghton Mifflin.

[Internet article, no author]

Katherine Govier. (2004, August 27). Retrieved September 1, 2004, from http://www.wier.ca/kgovier.html

[Film or DVD]

Madden, J. (Director), Parfitt, D., Gigliotta, D., Weinstein, H., Zwick, E., & Norman, M. (Producers). (1999). *Shakespeare in Love* [DVD].

[Article by author, found in database]

McMurdy, D. (2004, May 2). Can't work the VCR? Here's who to blame. *Calgary Herald*, p. E7. Retrieved September 2, 2004, from *Canadian Newsstand.* ProQuest. Seneca Learning Commons.

[Article by author, found in Internet]

Starr, L. (2000, July 11). Sticks and stones and names can hurt you: De-myth-tifying the classroom bully!" *Education World.* Retrieved August 3, 2004, from http://www.education-world.com/a_issues/issues102.shtml

For more information and examples, consult the *Publication Manual of the American Psychological Association* or the official website at <http://www.apastyle.org/>. Follow the assignment guidelines given out by your college or your professor.

Credits

Author and Title Index

Subject Index